BLOODY SPRING

BLOODY SPRING

Forty Days That Sealed the Confederacy's Fate

JOSEPH WHEELAN

DA CAPO PRESS
A Member of the Perseus Books Group

Designed by Timm Bryson
Set in 11 point Adobe Garamond Pro by The Perseus Books Group
Library of Congress Cataloging-in-Publication Data

Wheelan, Joseph.
  Bloody spring : forty days that sealed the Confederacy's fate / Joseph
Wheelan.
    pages cm
  Includes bibliographical references and index.
  ISBN 978-0-306-82206-3 (hardcover) — ISBN 978-0-306-82207-0 (e-book)
  1. Overland Campaign, Va., 1864. I. Title.
  E476.52.W46 2014
  973.7'36—dc23

                              2013048710

Published by Da Capo Press
A Member of the Perseus Books Group
www.dacapopress.com

10 9 8 7 6 5 4 3 2 1

To the memory of my father,
John R. Wheelan, USMC (Ret.),
who knew firsthand what war is

CONTENTS

LIST OF MAPS

Illustrations following page 204

ACKNOWLEDGMENTS

Anyone embarking on a Civil War project encounters a dazzling body of work by scholars and military historians who have dedicated their careers to various aspects of the most divisive period in the nation's history.

In the first rank stand Douglas Southall Freeman, Shelby Foote, Bruce Catton, James McPherson, Alan Nevins, James Robertson Jr., and William McFeely. Besides these giants, there is a legion of other historians and writers, too, who provide the important service of describing the war's military operations, large and small.

I am indebted to them all, and to the libraries and librarians that led me to the primary sources that I needed.

Foremost among these is the University of North Carolina at Chapel Hill. The shelves at Davis Library hold a vast collection of Civil War memoirs, diaries, journals, and unit histories, as well as hundreds, if not thousands, of battle histories and biographies. The North Carolina Collection and Southern Historical Collection at UNC's Wilson Library contain first-person accounts that could not be found anywhere else.

The State Archives of North Carolina in Raleigh and the Library of Virginia and the Virginia Historical Society Library in Richmond also provided important information and insights.

Finally, this book is a testament to the support of my wife, Pat, scientist and student of history, and to our ongoing conversations about the past.

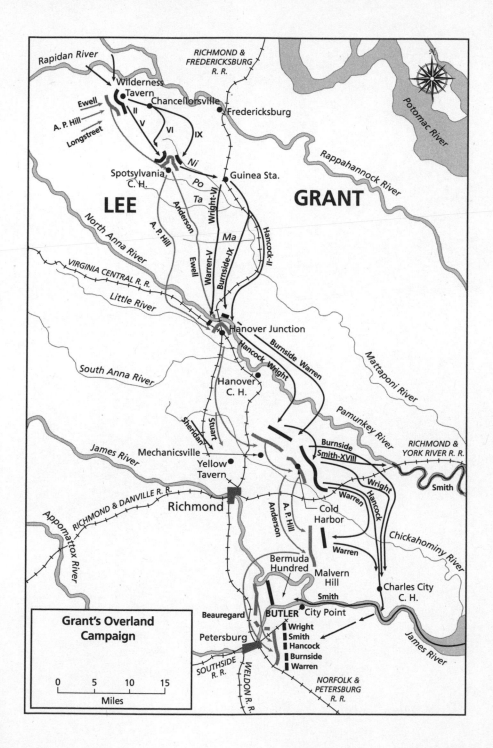

Grant's Overland Campaign

PROLOGUE

If I am obliged to retire from this line, either by a flank movement
of the enemy or the want of supplies, great injury will befall us.
—ROBERT E. LEE TO JEFFERSON DAVIS[1]

Monday, May 2, 1864
Clark's Mountain, Virginia

BELOW THE MOUNTAINTOP where Robert E. Lee and his eleven lieutenants were gathered, the Rapidan River flowed peacefully eastward toward its union with the Rappahannock. Across the water to the north, it was all activity in the sprawling Union army encampment. The camp extended several miles north to Culpeper, where General Ulysses Grant had made his headquarters, and which coincidentally also happened to be the birthplace of A. P. Hill, one of the generals on Clark's Mountain. Through his spyglass, Lee studied the vast city of canvas tents, wooden huts, smoky fires, horses and wagons, and men under arms. "I think those people over there are going to make a move soon," he told his generals.[2]

The warm, sunny weather had made their ride up the 1,100-foot dome-shaped mountain almost seem like a lark, but there was nothing lighthearted about the business at hand: the beginning of the war's fourth campaigning season. The men in the pewter-gray uniforms with the gold-starred collars knew there would be few occasions in the coming months for outings such as this, unspoiled by gunfire.

Early spring's bright-green foliage rioted among the undulating hills below. To the east, a tangled snarl of vegetation crowded the Rapidan's southern shore. Concealed by a dense canopy of second-growth trees, vines, and matted undergrowth, the forbidding region known as the Wilderness encompassed fifteen square miles of low ridges, hollows, sluggish streams, and swamps. Exactly a year ago, Lee had fought Joe Hooker's army there and had driven the Yankees back over the river, although at a terrible price—the loss of General Thomas J. "Stonewall" Jackson. Six months later, George Meade led the Army of the Potomac over the river again, but withdrew when Lee's army burrowed into impregnable defensive positions at Mine Run.

Lee directed his generals' attention to the opaque-green jungle, and to two river fords six miles apart, Ely's and Germanna. Through their field glasses, the officers studied the crossings. Lee told them that Grant would soon cross the Rapidan at one or both of those places.

Lee had a knack for placing himself in his adversaries' boots, but it was just one of the ways that he anticipated their moves. A lifelong student of warfare, Lee had spent weeks studying the terrain and the proclivities of his new opponent, Grant.

Since March, when Grant was named general-in-chief of all Union armies, Lee had known that he would ready the Army of the Potomac's three corps, nominally under Meade's command, for a major offensive. "Every train brings it [the Union army] recruits, and it is stated that every available regiment at the North is added to it," Lee had told Jefferson Davis, the Confederacy's president and de facto war secretary, on March 30. General Ambrose Burnside, Lee wrote, was at Annapolis with yet another Union corps. On April 9, he informed Davis that the fact "that additions have been made to General Meade's army is shown by an increase of tents," and a week later he urged Davis to quickly send rations, supplies, and forage, as well as more cavalry and artillery. "If I am obliged to retire from this line, either by a flank movement of the enemy or the want of supplies, great injury will befall us," Lee warned. On April 18, Lee sent the army's surplus baggage to the rear in anticipation of action.[3]

Two days before the expedition to Clark's Mountain, Lee's skill in seeing things through an adversary's eyes produced a remarkably accurate set of predictions that he shared with Davis. In addition to the Army of the Potomac's campaign, Lee told Davis, "there will no doubt be a strong demonstration made north and south of the James River, which [General Pierre G. T.]

Beauregard will be able successfully to resist. I judge also, from present indications, that [General William] Averell and [General Franz] Sigel will move against the Virginia and Tennessee Railroad or Staunton." For the James River campaign, Lee predicted that the Union would draw troops from the Southeastern coast.[4]

Here on the Rapidan, Lee and his generals agreed that the bustle in the enemy camps indicated that the long-anticipated offensive was nearly at hand. But would the blow strike the Rebel right, prefatory to a drive south to Richmond, or land on its left, the preamble to a march to the railroad junction at Gordonsville, followed by a descent on Richmond from the west? Lee and his generals didn't have the answer; they must wait for Grant to act.

But if Grant elected to march through the close confines of the Wilderness in order to maneuver around the Confederate right, the notoriously aggressive Lee intended to hit him quickly with everything that he had—and send the Yankees reeling back over the Rapidan.

In the meantime, it was understood that Hill's Third Corps would remain at Orange Court House; Richard Ewell's Second Corps, near Mine Run; and James Longstreet's First Corps, near Gordonsville, in case Grant tried to march around Lee's left flank. Lee was unwilling to presume that Grant would maneuver to the Confederate right when guessing wrong would be so disastrous for the Confederacy.

Lee asked Sergeant B. L. Wynn, who was in charge of the Clark's Mountain signal station, whether he was in the habit of posting a night guard. When Wynn replied that he was not, Lee told him, "Well, you must put one on." Lee ordered his lieutenants to distribute three days' rations to their troops and await developments.[5]

The Army of Northern Virginia's top generals swung into their saddles and began the ride down Clark's Mountain. Death, battle wounds, illness, and captivity would thin their numbers before May ended. None would return to Clark's Mountain during the war.

NEARLY 200,000 HEAVILY armed soldiers and miles of supply trains and artillery batteries were converging on northern Virginia's blighted countryside, where thousands of men had already fought and died.

But during this May and June, the carnage would surpass anything seen during the war's previous three years. Lee and Grant would match wits across the dense woods, swamps, and fields of northern Virginia during forty unprecedented days of nearly ceaseless combat operations. This would be something new in Western warfare: daily fighting and massive troop movements punctuated by spasms of extreme bloodletting.

Because the battles followed one another so closely, the battlegrounds—at the Wilderness, Spotsylvania Court House, and Cold Harbor—would not lodge as deeply in the collective memory as had Gettysburg, Vicksburg, Chancellorsville, Shiloh, Fredericksburg, Manassas, and Antietam. Soaked in blood, gore, and horror though they were, the battlefields of Grant's Overland Campaign would remain relatively unknown.

The Union campaign conflated daunting military and political stakes. Grant's destruction of Lee's army would assure the survival of Abraham Lincoln's administration and the defeat of the Confederacy; conversely, Lee's triumph would sink the Lincoln administration and all but guarantee the Confederacy's survival.

The war's length, its cost, and the rising number of deaths were sapping the support of Northern voters. Without important victories in 1864, Lincoln could not expect to be reelected in November. His successor would likely negotiate peace with the Confederacy, permitting it to coexist as a sovereign nation beside the Union—a situation that Lincoln, if reelected, could never tolerate.

Lee and Grant were their respective armies' best commanders, but they had never fought one another. Masters of both maneuver and head-on fighting, they were their nations' most naturally aggressive commanding generals. It was axiomatic in the Confederate army that Lee was its "most belligerent man," while Grant was once described as someone who appeared "determined to drive his head through a brick wall."[6]

The clash of these men and their armies would father two strategic innovations: the continuous offensive campaign of attrition, and the use of defensive fortifications as a force multiplier. These would become hard-and-fast strategic and tactical tenets during the Great War that would be fought fifty years hence.

Grant's army won no battles during the Forty Days, but it won the campaign—indeed, the war—by never turning back, and by using its overwhelming advantages in manpower and material to grind down the Rebel army, something that none of Grant's predecessors had attempted.

A year earlier in Mississippi, Grant and William T. Sherman had waged a remarkably similar campaign whose climax was the siege of Vicksburg and its capture. During three weeks in May 1863, Grant's army marched 180 miles and fought five battles, beginning with its May 1 victory at Port Gibson, the army's beachhead on the Mississippi River.

His and Sherman's operations in Mississippi became the template for their 1864 Virginia and Georgia campaigns. Grant's army would advance 100 miles southward before placing Petersburg under siege. At the same time in Georgia, Sherman's army would march 130 miles south from Chattanooga and, after a dozen battles, besiege Atlanta.

Indeed, in Mississippi—as in Virginia and Georgia a year later—Grant and Sherman forded rivers; fought a chain of battles lasting weeks; conducted flank maneuvers; methodically destroyed enemy farms, factories, and a large part of the city of Jackson; and cut loose from supply bases, living off the land.

In Mississippi, Grant was also cognizant of both the military and political stakes. He made a risky amphibious assault in enemy territory and campaigned aggressively, knowing that the Northern people were becoming discouraged and were beginning to favor the idea of a negotiated peace. The 1862 elections had clearly shown that war support was waning. Moreover, voluntary enlistments had fallen off, and draft resistance was growing. Grant knew that he must "move forward to a decisive victory, or our cause was lost. No progress was being made in any other field, and we had to go on."[7]

Grant might have said the same for the situation that he faced in Virginia in May 1864; indeed, his army's immense campaign preparations portended a bloody spring. Lee and the Army of Northern Virginia patiently waited for him to make his move.

CHAPTER I

Spring 1864

An ordinary, scrubby-looking man, with a slightly seedy look, as if he was out of office on half pay.

—DESCRIPTION OF ULYSSES S. GRANT
IN MARCH 1864[1]

You may rest assured he is not an ordinary man.

—GENERAL GEORGE MEADE ON GRANT[2]

1

THE WASHINGTON PRESS corps had never seen General Ulysses S. Grant, which complicated their job of reporting on his arrival at the Baltimore and Ohio Railroad depot. War correspondents Simon Hanscom and Lorenzo Crounse, who were among the bustling crowd at the train station, knew only that Grant had a beard, that he was of medium height, and that he usually forswore dress uniforms for the nondescript blue worn by privates, save for the general's stars sewn on the shoulders. In other words, Grant might have been any of the scores of officers who thronged the busy station.

Fearing that Grant might slip by them without their recognizing him, Hanscom and Crounse rushed to Matthew Brady's studio in the hope of finding a photograph of the general. But Brady's only picture of Grant was useless—a hat obscured his features. Brady, however, agreed to return to the station with the reporters.

When a hatless, uniformed man and a boy emerged from a car in a group of people, Brady grew excited; he remembered the lines around the man's mouth. It was Grant, he told the reporters.[3]

And then there was no mistaking that it was Grant. People suddenly pressed in upon him from all sides, and a company of the Invalid Corps formed ranks and presented arms. Grant, the boy, and a knot of staff officers passed through the depot to the street, and stepped into hacks that took them to Willard's Hotel, where he registered as simply, "U.S. Grant and son, Galena, Ill."[4]

A short time later, the general and thirteen-year-old Frederick Dent Grant entered Willard's dining room. A man recognized Grant and shook his hand, and the news that the new general-in-chief had arrived instantly spread through the dining room. The diners spontaneously got to their feet and cheered. They crowded around the table of the blushing general, known for reserve and not conviviality.[5]

One unimpressed observer described Grant as "an ordinary, scrubby-looking man, with a slightly seedy look, as if he was out of office on half pay." A journalist wrote that Grant might easily be mistaken for "a country

3

merchant or a village lawyer. He had no distinctive feature; there are thousands like him in personal appearance in the ranks." Indeed, there was little about Grant's appearance to suggest the unyielding warrior who consistently won battles.[6]

THIS BEING TUESDAY, it was levee night at the White House and, as usual, hundreds of people had come to see the president and first lady, some of them even hoping to get a private audience with Abraham Lincoln.

It was about 9:30 when Grant alighted from a hack outside the White House. In the Blue Room, where the Lincolns always greeted their guests, the president and Grant met for the first time. Until this moment, Lincoln had known Grant only by reputation and from telegrams, battle summaries, and the reports of men who had observed him in the field.

The crowd, which could become rowdy at these functions, uncharacteristically kept a respectful distance, evidently sensing the meeting's historical import. "There was no rude jostling, or pushing or pulling," wrote John Nicolay, Lincoln's private secretary.

Lincoln entrusted Grant to the care of Secretary of State William Seward, who introduced the bashful general to the other guests in the Blue Room and then led him into the East Room. When the people there caught sight of Grant, they launched into cheer after cheer and charged in to shake his hand.

"Laces were torn, crinoline mashed, and things were generally much mixed. People mounted sofas and tables to get out of harm's way or to take observations," wrote Noah Brooks, a correspondent for the Sacramento (California) *Daily Union*. Grant, too, climbed onto a sofa to avoid being mobbed by the "torrent" of people that now filled the East Room. After an hour of standing on the couch, vigorously shaking hands with all comers, Grant was "flushed, heated, and perspiring."[7]

Later that night, Grant met with Lincoln and his blunt, hard-driving secretary of war, Edwin Stanton, to discuss the next morning's ceremony, when Grant would be formally presented with his commission as lieutenant general.

It was of enormous importance to Lincoln that he and Grant strike just the right tone, wrote Nicolay, who was present. During three years of war, no general, Union or Confederate, had wielded the power that Grant would have. In fact, just one other American, George Washington, had ever permanently held lieutenant-general rank (though Winfield Scott had been a brevet, or temporary, three-star general).

On February 26, Lincoln had signed a law reviving the rank. Grant's friend and patron, Congressman Elihu Washburne of Illinois, who introduced the measure in December, had asserted what was the absolute truth: that Grant was the only candidate for the position. "He has fought more battles and won more victories than any man living; he has captured more prisoners and taken more guns than any general of modern times," Washburne said. No one disputed that, and when Lincoln sent Grant's name to the Senate, it had swiftly confirmed him.

Lincoln told Grant that at the next day's ceremony, he would give a short speech, to which Grant was to reply with a few words of his own. Lincoln handed Grant a copy of what he planned to say and suggested that Grant's remarks should attempt to dispel the lingering resentments of some generals. He urged him to say something positive about the Army of the Potomac.

In his speech the next day, Grant did neither. He pledged to try not "to disappoint your expectations. I feel the full weight of the responsibilities now devolving on me and know that if they are met it will be due to those armies, and above all to the favor of that Providence which leads both Nations and men."

Grant's brief address, good enough on paper, suffered in its delivery, according to Nicolay. Grant, he wrote, appeared "quite embarrassed" by the occasion and made "rather sorry and disjointed work of enunciating his reply," which was "almost illegibly written . . . on the half sheet of note paper, in lead pencil."[8]

IN A WAR that had wrung rivers of gore from battlefields large and small, North and South, it was ironic that Grant, who had now become the chosen instrument of even greater bloodletting, recoiled from it. "I cannot bear the sight of suffering," he confessed to an aide, Lieutenant Colonel Horace Porter. Grant later wrote that during a battle, "one can see his enemy mowed down by the thousand or the ten thousand, with great composure; but after the battle these scenes are distressing, and one is naturally disposed to do as much to alleviate the suffering of an enemy as a friend."

The apotheosis of Grant's blood aversion might have occurred in April 1862 at Shiloh. He had taken shelter from the driving rain in a log house where, to his horror, he witnessed surgeons busily amputating the arms and legs of wounded men and "blood flowing in streams." He had hastily withdrawn, electing to spend the soggy night under a tree.[9]

Grant's abhorrence of blood and suffering extended to hunting—"as a sportsman I was a failure"—and to the food that he ate. As beef was about the only meat that he liked (he abhorred fowl and game), it had to be cooked to a blackened crisp; the merest trace of red would kill his appetite.[10]

Squeamish though Grant was, no Union general had been as successful as he. In February 1862, he had briefly fanned hopes for a short war with his capture of Fort Henry and Fort Donelson in Tennessee—the latter a joint army-navy operation that had bagged 15,000 prisoners. At Shiloh, Grant's army had taken a beating the first day, but the next day it defeated the Rebels. Then came the siege and the momentous capture of Vicksburg on the Fourth of July of 1863. That victory had secured the Mississippi River for the Union, severing the Southwest from the Confederacy.

In the fall of 1863, after the Rebels smashed General William Rosecrans's army at Chickamauga, drove it into Chattanooga, and invested the city, Lincoln replaced Rosecrans with Grant. In November, his army broke the Confederate encirclement by capturing Lookout Mountain and Missionary Ridge.

For three years, Lincoln had watched with disappointment as his Eastern generals dithered, delayed, and twice failed to destroy Robert E. Lee's Army of Northern Virginia before it could retreat from Maryland into Virginia. It was time, the president believed, to try a general from the Western theater, one who could make things jump. By all accounts, Grant was just the man for the job.

Moreover, not only would Grant command the hard-luck Army of the Potomac, which Lee had bloodied every time that it had advanced toward Richmond, he would direct Union armies everywhere. No general during the war had ever been given such sweeping powers: Grant would command 533,000 men, organized into twenty-one army corps—one of the largest armies in history.[11]

Yet, Grant had never commanded troops in the East. He had never faced Lee, who had yet to lose a major battle in Virginia, and whom many of the Army of the Potomac's generals regarded with awe and fear.

Lincoln's patience with the Army of the Potomac had run out in December 1863, when its commander, General George Meade, had neither attacked Lee at Mine Run nor intercepted the Confederate First Army Corps when it marched from eastern Tennessee to rejoin Lee's army.

Meade's inaction had provoked an uncharacteristic outburst from Lincoln: "If this Army of the Potomac was good for anything—if the officers had anything in them—if the army had any legs, they could move thirty thousand men down to Lynchburg and catch Longstreet. Can anybody doubt if Grant were here in command that he would catch him?"[12]

BEFORE LINCOLN MADE Grant his general-in-chief, he had to first satisfy himself on the sensitive issue of whether Grant had presidential ambitions; there had been discussion of a Grant candidacy among Democrats and even a few Republicans, as well as in some large-circulation Eastern newspapers. Fully intending to seek reelection in November, Lincoln knew that his winning a second term depended on Union army victories in 1864— which was why he wished to elevate Grant, with his record of Western triumphs.

Another embarrassing defeat in Virginia might also reinvigorate the Peace Democrats and their extremist wing, the "Copperheads." Forced underground by fears of reprisals from prowar Republicans, the Copperheads had formed secret societies throughout the lower Midwest, which had been settled largely by Southerners. One such group, the Sons of Liberty, was reportedly arming itself for insurrection. On April 8, Representative Alexander Long, an Ohio Democrat, outraged the House by urging recognition of the South as a separate nation. The House censured Long, and nearly expelled him.[13]

Lincoln had been asking questions about Grant for nearly a year now, and he was now satisfied that Grant, if given the authority, had the moral fiber, tenacity, and leadership to end the war swiftly. But if Grant defeated Lee and marched into Richmond, would he then challenge Lincoln for the presidency? Lincoln had to be sure that by naming Grant he wasn't sowing the seeds of his own defeat.

The president quietly sounded out Grant's staunch ally from Illinois, Congressman Washburne, who directed Lincoln to J. Russell Jones, a friend of Grant and his investment counselor.[14]

Grant, too, had heard the presidential talk, and he didn't like it a bit. To squelch it, he had gone so far as to write letters to several people disavowing any interest. To Barnabas Burns, who had sought Grant's permission to enter his name into nomination at the War Democrats' convention in January, Grant wrote, "The question astonishes me. I do not know of anything I have ever done or said which would indicate that I would be a candidate for any office." In another such letter, he said, "This is the last thing I desire. I would regard such a consummation unfortunate for myself if not for the country."[15]

When Jones met with Lincoln to discuss Grant, he brought one of Grant's letters. After reading it, Lincoln breathed a sigh of relief. "You will never know how gratifying that is to me. No man knows, when that presidential grub gets to gnawing at him, just how deep it will get until he has tried it; and I didn't know that there was one gnawing at Grant."[16]

GRANT'S RISE HAD been so swift as to nearly defy belief. From the time he left the army in 1854 until his return at the beginning of the Civil War, his life had been a train wreck of miscalculations, bad luck, and failures, leavened by periods of disappointment.

Hiram Ulysses Grant was born on April 27, 1822. Hiram—"exalted one" in the Hebrew tradition, although the Grants were not Jewish—was a family name; Grant's mother, Hannah Simpson Grant, called him Ulysses.

The document of his appointment to the US Military Academy gave his name as "Ulysses Simpson Grant." Grant pointed out the error, but West Point refused to correct it; his name appeared on the cadet rolls as "U. S. Grant." His classmates playfully called him "United States" and "Uncle Sam" and, finally, just "Sam." He was an indifferent student, graduating twenty-first among the thirty-nine members of his Class of '43. However, everyone agreed that Grant was his class's best horseman.[17]

During the Mexican War, Lieutenant Grant served in General Zachary "Rough and Ready" Taylor's army at Palo Alto, Resaca de la Palma, and Monterrey—where Grant was remembered for his daredevil ride through the gunfire-swept streets with ammunition for the troops. When General Winfield "Old Fuss and Feathers" Scott expropriated Taylor's best soldiers for his amphibious assault on Vera Cruz and brilliant march to Mexico City, Grant went with Scott. At the San Cosme Gate into Mexico City, Lieutenant Grant and his men trundled a small cannon into a church belfry that commanded the approaches to the gate and scattered the Mexican defenders so that US troops could enter the city. From Taylor, Grant learned simplicity in dress and deportment, and calmness in crises; from Scott, strategy.[18]

Back in St. Louis in 1848, he married Julia Dent—her brother Frederick was Grant's best friend at West Point—but Julia and their children did not accompany him to his Pacific Coast assignments. There, naivety and poor business instincts cost Grant his savings, and at Fort Humboldt, a bleak coastal outpost, he hit rock bottom. Depressed and alienated, Grant drank heavily; gossipy fellow officers whispered that Grant was a drunkard.

Grant resigned his captain's commission in 1854 and returned to Missouri, where he farmed and worked as a rent collector. Alone, Grant built a house—solid and well-made—and gave it the fitting name "Hardscrabble." Despite his strenuous efforts, Grant struggled just to feed and clothe Julia and their four children. Desperation drove him to sell firewood on St. Louis street corners in his faded army overcoat. One day while he was hawking firewood, Grant encountered another struggling former West Pointer, William Tecumseh Sherman; they spoke briefly and parted.

In 1858 Captain E. B. Holloway was passing through St. Louis with two other army officers and looking for a fourth person to play "brag" when he happened to spot Grant on the street. Holloway, who had known Grant in the army, invited him to play. Another of the card players was Major James Longstreet, a close friend of Grant's at West Point who had been a guest at his wedding. They reminisced about their Mexican War days.

Grant, wrote Longstreet, impressed him as a man "looking for something to do." They met again the next day on the street, and Grant handed Longstreet a $5 gold piece to repay an old loan. Longstreet initially refused to take the money, certain that Grant needed it more than he, but "seeing the determination in the man's face," he accepted the coin and shook Grant's hand.[19]

Forced to admit his failure as a farmer, in 1860 Grant swallowed his pride and asked his father, Jesse Grant, for a job in the family leather business in Galena, Illinois. In 1861, then, he was a clerk at Grant and Perkins, working for his younger brothers, Simpson and Orvil, when Congressman Washburne and the family business's lawyer, John Rawlins, addressed a town meeting days after war broke out. Grant, the only professionally trained soldier in Galena, was chosen to lead a recruiting drive. It was the beginning of an enduring friendship among the three men.

In June 1861, with Washburne's help, Grant was appointed colonel of an Illinois regiment sent to fight in Missouri. By August, he was commanding a brigade and had been promoted to brigadier general.[20]

Adversity had made Grant self-reliant, self-contained, and determined to push on through failure and hardship. A woman who saw Grant several times around Washington after he became general-in-chief wrote that he carried himself with "a peculiar aloofness. . . . He walked through a crowd as though solitary."[21]

WHEN GRANT WAS besieging Vicksburg in 1863, War Secretary Stanton dispatched Charles Dana to Mississippi to observe the Western general who won battles. Stanton and Lincoln had doubts about Grant, fed by countless rumors and complaints about his performance at Shiloh—which Lincoln brushed off with the words, "I can't spare this man; he fights."

It would have been impossible to find a better man for the job than Dana. He had worked alongside Horace Greeley at the New York *Tribune* for fifteen years until the day in April 1862 that Greeley fired him, evidently because Dana was too prowar for Greeley. Within a week, Stanton offered Dana a job in the War Department; months later, he was promoted to assistant war secretary.

Dana's cover story was that he was investigating the army's payments system. But instead of auditing the books, Dana sent Stanton reports on Grant and his generals encoded in a War Department cipher. Initially, Dana was mightily impressed by Sherman's agile mind, but he had difficulty penetrating Grant's reserve. When he finally did, he gushed that Grant was "the most modest, the most disinterested, and the most honest man I ever knew, with a temper that nothing could disturb, and judgment that was judicial in its comprehensiveness and wisdom. Not a great man, except morally; not an original or brilliant man, but sincere, thoughtful, deep, and gifted with courage that never faltered."[22]

Because of his strict Methodist upbringing, Grant didn't swear or dance, but he sometimes drank whiskey. In his reports to Stanton, Dana never mentioned Grant's taking a drink, but rumors persisted in Washington. Largely apocryphal, they did, however, contain a kernel of truth.

Grant's friend and aide-de-camp, John Rawlins of Galena, had accompanied him to Missouri in 1861 and had since remained on Grant's staff. Rawlins strove to keep Grant sober. In March 1863, he had made Grant pledge to "drink no more during the war," but sometimes Grant slipped. During the Vicksburg siege, a Rawlins letter to Grant dated June 6, 1863, began, "Dear General: The great solicitude I feel for the safety of the army leads me to mention, what I had hoped never again to do, the subject of your drinking." Rawlins's letter went on to recount how Grant had that night drained a bottle of wine "in company with those who drink and urge you to do likewise." He reminded the general of the pledge he had made in March.[23]

Just before Vicksburg's capitulation, a self-appointed committee visited Lincoln at the White House and demanded Grant's removal. Puzzled, the president asked why. The men said that Grant drank too much whiskey.

"Ah!" replied Lincoln. "By the way, gentlemen, can either of you tell me where General Grant procures his whiskey? Because, if I can find out, I will send every general in the field a barrel of it!"[24]

2

Thursday, March 10, 1864
Brandy Station, Virginia

THE DAY AFTER being commissioned lieutenant general, Grant traveled by train to the Army of the Potomac headquarters at Brandy Station, Virginia, fifty miles south of Washington to meet with the army's commander, George Meade.

The train pulled into the station in a downpour. Meade and his large staff were waiting. Meade and Grant had last met in 1848 in Mexico as lieutenants, and they now were the two most powerful generals in the Union army.

At forty-nine, Meade was Grant's elder by seven years and had been his senior in rank until Grant's promotion to three-star general. Meade was intelligent and accomplished and possessed magisterial bearing: he was tall, lean, and dignified-looking with a long beard, spectacles perched on a large, curved nose, bulging eyes, and a high forehead. Meade was a Philadelphia aristocrat, son of a wealthy merchant, Richard Worsam Meade, who was ruined financially when he supported Spain while serving as a naval agent there during the Napoleonic wars. The family's financial straits were a major factor in George's decision to attend the US Military Academy, from which he graduated in 1835. He left the army the following year to practice engineering, but returned in 1842. With Zachary Taylor's army during the Mexican War, he, like Grant, saw action at Palo Alto, Resaca de la Palma, and Monterrey.

Because of his savage temper, Meade was nicknamed "The Old Snapping Turtle." His disposition was at times so foul that Morris Schaff, Meade's chief ordnance officer, wrote, "I have seen him so cross and ugly that no one dared to speak to him—in fact, at such times his staff and everybody kept as clear of him as possible." General Carl Schurz, a division commander in XI Corps at Gettysburg, wrote that while Meade did not inspire warmth, "this simple, cold, serious soldier with his business-like air did inspire confidence."

Grant later found that no one was more sensitive to Meade's explosive temper than Meade himself, and he judged him to be "an officer of great merit . . . brave and conscientious . . . [commanding] the respect of all who knew him."

When the Civil War began, Meade was appointed brigadier general in charge of a brigade of Pennsylvania volunteers that he led during McClellan's unsuccessful Peninsula campaign to capture Richmond; he was wounded at Glendale and during Second Manassas. At Antietam, he led the only division to lodge in the Rebel lines, and at Chancellorsville, he commanded V Corps.

On June 28, 1863, Meade replaced Joe Hooker as commander of the Army of the Potomac. Three days later, the Battle of Gettysburg began.

Afterward, Lee's defeated army began withdrawing to Virginia. Initially ecstatic that the Rebels' invasion had been turned back, Lincoln and Stanton were appalled when Meade let Lee escape to Virginia without trapping him at the Potomac.

"I do not believe you appreciate the magnitude of the misfortune involved in Lee's escape," Lincoln wrote in exasperation to Meade on July 14. "He was within your easy grasp, and to have closed upon him would, in connection with our other late successes, have ended the war. As it is, the war will be prolonged indefinitely."

Meade offered to step down, but Lincoln and Stanton refused to accept his resignation. Then, Meade further antagonized them in early December 1863 when, at the last minute, he called off a major attack on Lee at Mine Run in northern Virginia; so glacially had the Yankees maneuvered that Lee's men had had time to strongly fortify their positions, commanding a mile of open ground with massed artillery and infantry. Meade's decision was a relief to his officers and men, but it further turned opinion against him at the War Department and White House, which at that time was considering Grant for a lieutenant generalship.

"FOR GOD'S SAKE and your country's sake, come out of Washington," Grant's good friend, Major General William Sherman, had advised Grant when he learned of his promotion. Sherman had invited Grant to "come West" and oversee the Union army's operations from his headquarters; Sherman now commanded all of the Western armies. "[Major General Henry] Halleck is better qualified than you to stand the buffets of intrigue and policy."

"Old Brains" was now army chief of staff; he had resigned his titular position as general-in-chief—Lincoln appointed him to it in 1862 as a curb on General George McClellan—to make way for Grant. Halleck had proven during his hypercautious campaign against Corinth, Mississippi, in 1862 that he was a better administrator than field commander. As chief of staff, Halleck would interpret Grant's military dispatches for the president, and share Lincoln's strategic ideas with Grant.

Grant agreed with Sherman, but chose to direct the Union armies from Meade's headquarters at the Army of the Potomac rather than from

Sherman's Western army. He recognized that beating Lee would be his primary mission. With spring at hand, the Army of the Potomac would soon campaign against Lee's Army of Northern Virginia, unbowed and dangerous despite its defeat at Gettysburg the previous summer.[25]

With the campaigning season about to begin, the Army of the Potomac was still feeling the aftershocks of a massive reorganization. Two of its five corps had been eliminated; I Corps was merged into V Corps, and III Corps became part of II Corps. The ostensible rationale for reordering more than 30,000 men was the large number of depleted regiments. But another likely reason was to remove I Corps' commanding general, John Newton, a sybarite and backbiter; and III Corps' William French, rebuked for slowness at Mine Run.[26]

WHEN GRANT AND Meade sat down to talk, Meade urged Grant "to remove me at once, if it suits your plans." It was a magnanimous offer—and one that Grant wisely rejected. Had he accepted, Grant would have had to direct the Army of the Potomac's day-to-day operations while at the same time supervising the other Union armies scattered over thousands of miles from Virginia to Louisiana. It would never have worked.[27]

But from the beginning, the arrangement was flawed. In theory, Meade would continue to lead the Army of the Potomac, while from his nearby headquarters Grant would direct all of the Union field armies—Meade's included—leaving their commanders to work out the details. As the campaign unfolded, however, the temptation to assume tactical control of the Army of the Potomac would prove too much for Grant; fortunately, Meade had the capacity to be an excellent subordinate. "He had the first virtue of a soldier—that is, obedience to orders," wrote Assistant War Secretary Dana. Indeed, Meade would become Grant's perfect tool: one whose ideas could be safely ignored, but who would punctiliously carry out Grant's plans. Yet, Meade would fume when Grant, and not he, got credit for the army's successes.

After their meeting, Lieutenant Colonel Theodore Lyman of Meade's staff jotted down his impressions of Grant: "a very still, steady man, but evidently enjoys a pleasant joke. He also makes quiet, sarcastic remarks, without moving a line of his face." Meade told his wife, Margaretta, that

Grant was "not a striking man, is very reticent, has never mixed with the world, and has but little manner, indeed is somewhat ill at ease in the presence of strangers; hence a first impression is never favorable." Grant's West Point education was likely the full extent of his learning, wrote Meade, and since graduating, "I don't believe he has read or studied."

For all that, Meade believed that Grant had "natural qualities of a high order, and is a man, whom, the more you see and know him, the better you like him. He puts me in mind of old Taylor, and sometimes I fancy he models himself on old Zac." Meade's respect for Grant had risen further a week later, when he wrote to Margaretta, "You may rest assured he is not an ordinary man."[28]

When Grant returned to Washington on March 11, Lincoln told him that Mrs. Lincoln had arranged a dinner in his honor at the White House. While appreciating the First Lady's intended kindness, Grant, uncomfortable in formal social gatherings, declined the invitation; he had to leave that night for Tennessee, he told Lincoln. "Time is very precious just now and, really, Mr. President, I believe I have had enough of the *show* business." Twelve military officers attended Mrs. Lincoln's dinner, but not Grant.[29]

ONE OF LINCOLN's secretaries, William Stoddard, was home ill during Grant's appearances in Washington and, when he recovered, he asked the president what the new general-in-chief was like.

Lincoln, his lanky frame sprawled on a chair, laughed silently, and then said, "He's the quietest little fellow you ever saw. Why, he makes the least fuss of any man you ever saw. I believe two or three times he has been in this room a minute or so before I knew he was here. . . . The only evidence you have that he's in any place is that he makes things *git*. Wherever he is, things move!"

The president enthused that Grant was "the first general I've had!" The others would bring Lincoln a plan and ask him to decide whether or not to proceed with it, in effect making him responsible for the plan's success or failure. Grant didn't tell Lincoln his plans, and, unlike his predecessors, did not demand more resources—usually cavalry—that Lincoln could not provide. "He doesn't ask me to do impossibilities for him, and he's the first general I've had that didn't."[30]

GRANT WAS GOING to Nashville to consult with his friend Sherman. The angular, hyperkinetic redhead had been Grant's right hand at Shiloh, Vicksburg, and Missionary Ridge. When Grant was summoned to Washington to become lieutenant general, he had immediately shared the news with Sherman, along with his determination not to make Washington his headquarters. In the same letter, Grant expressed his warm feelings for Sherman and General James McPherson, "the men to whom, above all others, I feel indebted for whatever I have had of success. . . . I feel all the gratitude this letter would express, giving it the most flattering construction."[31]

Sherman was Grant's great admirer, too. His respect for his friend had steadily grown since the first day at Shiloh, when Grant's army had taken a terrible pounding and was clinging to the south bank of the Tennessee River. Sherman had had three horses shot out from under him and was wounded in the hand. As rain drenched the dying and wounded on the battlefield, Grant's generals were incredulous when at 5 p.m. Grant told them to prepare to attack at dawn. Several hours later, Sherman went looking for Grant to propose putting "the river between us and the enemy."

He found Grant outside a log house where surgeons were at work with their quick knives. He was standing alone under an oak tree with his collar up around his ears, rain sluicing off his hat. He held a lantern and had a cigar clenched between his teeth. For reasons never stated, Sherman spontaneously decided to not bring up the subject of retreat.

Instead, he said, "Well, Grant, we've had the devil's own day, haven't we?" The indefatigable Grant replied, "Yes, lick 'em tomorrow, though."

Grant's promotion had inspired Sherman, in a letter to Grant on March 10, to explain the reasons for his high regard for his friend. "I believe you are as brave, patriotic, and just, as the great phototype [sic] Washington— as unselfish, kindhearted and honest, as a man should be, but the chief characteristic in your nature is the simple faith in success you have always manifested, which I can liken to nothing else than the faith a Christian has in his Saviour. . . . I knew wherever I was that you thought of me, and if I got in a tight place you would come, if alive."[32]

FOR TWO DAYS in Nashville beginning March 17, Grant met with Sherman and his top Western generals—McPherson, John Logan, and Grenville

Dodge—all of them having just returned from a scorched-earth march from Vicksburg to the Rebel supply depot at Meridian, Mississippi. Along the way, Sherman's army had methodically destroyed crops, livestock, and barns; upon reaching Meridian on February 14, Sherman's men used fire and wrecking bars to demolish the city's supply facilities and a hundred miles of railroad tracks. The march foreshadowed a new policy of strategic destruction; henceforth, enemy logistics and food sources would become targets, in order to undermine the Confederacy's fighting capacity and civilian morale.

When Sherman and Grant first met in Nashville, wrote Lieutenant Colonel Adam Badeau, Grant's military secretary, the outspoken Sherman said, "I cannot congratulate you on your promotion; the responsibility is too great." Badeau noted Grant's reaction: "The other was silent and smoked his cigar." During the informal sessions, Grant sought the generals' opinions about conducting the spring campaign.

On March 19, Grant embarked for Washington, inviting Sherman to accompany him as far as Cincinnati. On the train Grant described the campaign that he envisioned, and that he had not yet committed to writing. The men pored over maps in their Cincinnati hotel rooms, and produced a rough draft of the campaign, with Sherman left to work out the details of his role. In his typical epigrammatic style, Sherman distilled Grant's strategy to its essence: "He was to go for Lee, and I was to go for Joe Johnston. That was the plan."[33]

THERE WAS MORE to it than that, of course. Grant planned to attack the Rebel armies everywhere at once to prevent the Confederate high command from shifting forces from its quiet sectors to those under attack. Previously, "the armies in the East and West acted independently and without concert, like a balky team," but no more. Grant planned to "hammer continuously against the armed force of the enemy and his resources, until by mere attrition, if no other way, there should be nothing left to him" except surrender. Latter-day historians would describe it as a strategy of "attrition" or "exhaustion," achieved by grinding down not only the enemy's manpower, but his logistical underpinnings—railroads, food, supplies, arms, clothing, and other necessities, as Sherman had done in Meridian—while preventing him from reinforcing his armies.

When Grant described his plan to Lincoln during the weekly meetings that began with Grant's return from the West, the president immediately grasped it. This was unsurprising, because in January 1862 Lincoln, frustrated by the Union army's inaction, had advocated just such a plan, to "threaten all their positions at the same time with superior force, and if they weakened one to strengthen another, seize and hold the one weakened." When discussing Grant's plan, however, Lincoln acted as though it were new to him. "Oh, yes!" he said to Grant. "I see that. As we say out West, if a man can't skin, he must hold a leg while somebody else does."

The strategic plan was staggering in scope and unprecedented during this war: large armies thousands of miles apart beginning operations on the same day, and their commanding general receiving telegraphed reports on their movements that very night.[34]

LINCOLN, HALLECK, AND Grant, however, had not always agreed that the campaign's primary target should be Lee's army in northern Virginia. Two months before Grant's promotion, Lincoln and Halleck had asked him to submit a plan for a Virginia spring offensive. He had startled them with something wholly different.

"I would respectfully suggest whether an abandonment of all previously attempted lines to Richmond is not advisable, and in lieu of these one be taken farther south," Grant wrote on January 19. The Union army had already tried six times to bludgeon its way toward Richmond, the last being the failed Mine Run campaign in late 1863; it was presumed that Grant would sketch a plan for a seventh attempt.

Instead, Grant proposed marching from Norfolk, Virginia, to Weldon, North Carolina, in order to seize the Confederate rail center there. With Weldon's capture, Union troops would destroy one of the Confederacy's two north-south railroads and threaten the second. Virginia's supply line from the Deep South would be severely strained, and hunger would spread through the Virginia armies and Richmond. Lee would be compelled to march south to recapture Weldon, leaving Richmond weakly defended. "It would draw the enemy from campaigns of their own choosing . . . to new lines of operations never expected to become necessary," Grant wrote, adding that the campaign could begin immediately because of the mild winters farther south.[35]

But Grant's plan revived the great fear that fitfully brooded over the Lincoln administration: the Northern capital left virtually defenseless, and Lee's army swooping in to capture it. In his reply to Grant on February 17, Halleck warned that his plan might open the door to Lee. "Would not Lee be able to make another invasion of Maryland and Pennsylvania? Uncover Washington and the Potomac, and all the forces which Lee can collect will be moved north, and the popular sentiment will compel the Government to bring back the army in North Carolina."

Halleck, also speaking for Lincoln, was unequivocal about what must be done. "Our main efforts in the next campaign should unquestionably be made against the armies of Lee and Johnston," he wrote. Breaking the Army of Northern Virginia, the Confederacy's best fighting force, was the great imperative. "If we cannot defeat him here with our combined force, we cannot hope to do so elsewhere with a divided army."[36]

Grant evidently failed Lincoln's and Halleck's test, but they promoted him anyway; after all, he had won battles in the West. More importantly, as Lincoln had observed a year earlier, "he fights." Not only did he fight, but fighting was Grant's habit of mind, and quitting was unthinkable. A week after Lincoln and Halleck rejected Grant's campaign plan, the Senate passed the bill making him general-in-chief.

Halleck's and Lincoln's recommendation became Grant's spring offensive plan: to attack Lee and Johnston, as Grant had proposed that he and Sherman do. The rest—the involvement of the other Union armies, and their coordinated attacks—was Grant's work, but the White House staff remembered Lincoln's earlier plan.

"The President has been powerfully reminded, by General Grant's present movement and plans of his (President's) old suggestion so constantly made and as constantly neglected by Buell & Halleck et al to move at once upon the enemy's whole line so as to bring into action to our advantage our great superiority in numbers," wrote John Hay, Lincoln's assistant secretary. "This idea of his own, the Prest. recognized with special pleasure when Grant said it was his intention to make all the line useful."[37]

ON MARCH 30, Grant asked Halleck to send him every soldier who could be spared from garrisons and recruiting depots in the North. That included

Washington, where some of the city's ten large artillery regiments, Grant believed, might be converted into fighting infantry regiments.

Grant's attempts to withdraw troops from the capital to reinforce the Army of the Potomac alarmed War Secretary Edwin Stanton, who believed it would leave the city dangerously vulnerable. Twenty-five thousand soldiers manned the fifty forts around Washington and guarded its 180,000 residents. But Grant believed that Washington would be safe from attack so long as his armies were on the offensive.

When Grant did not back down, Stanton took his grievance to Lincoln, who told him: "You and I, Mr. Stanton, have been trying to boss this job, and we have not succeeded very well with it. We have sent across the mountains for Mr. Grant, as Mrs. Grant calls him, to relieve us, and I think we had better leave him alone to do as he pleases."[38]

WHEN GRANT FULLY developed his master plan, it consisted of five offensives, all of them launched at the same time: in northern Virginia, up the James River to Richmond, in the Shenandoah Valley, in Georgia, and a joint army-navy operation against Mobile, Alabama. Meade's Army of the Potomac would cross the Rapidan River and march south toward Richmond, with the object of destroying Lee's Army of Northern Virginia. Sherman was to target Atlanta, drawing Johnston into a series of battles that would chew up his army.

Unfortunately for Grant, "political" generals, two without any prior military experience, would lead the other three operations. General Benjamin Butler, a former Massachusetts Democratic leader whose support was valued by Lincoln Republicans, would menace Richmond from the southeast with his Army of the James, denying Lee reinforcements from the capital, while destroying the railroads entering Petersburg from the south. General Franz Sigel, who had fought in Germany and was popular with St. Louis Germans, would march up the Shenandoah Valley with columns from West Virginia, wrecking Virginia's breadbasket and the Rebel army there. Finally, there was General Nathaniel Banks, former Massachusetts governor and former speaker of the US House of Representatives. He was currently traveling up Louisiana's Red River to neutralize the Rebels in the Southwest (Grant had opposed the operation, but Lincoln and Halleck overruled him), but was to conclude the campaign quickly and lead his army against the Rebel port of Mobile. After seizing Mobile, Banks would join Sherman in Georgia.

But Grant's plan was more involved than the five simultaneous offensives. In a letter to Sherman on April 4, Grant described his "design" as working "all the parts of the army together, and somewhat towards a common center." The center, Grant later wrote, was the Army of the Potomac; everything west of it was the right wing.

British military historian C. F. Atkinson described Grant's strategy as "an immense left wheel" by the right wing—marches by the Union's Western armies against Atlanta, Charleston, and North Carolina, and into Lee's rear. Sherman would conduct the "wheel," pivoting on Grant, who would "fix" Lee's army in place in Virginia.[39]

Grant urged his generals to not permit the enemy to rest or refit. "Lee's army will be your objective point," read his orders to Meade. "Wherever Lee goes there you will go also." Richmond was Butler's objective; menacing the Confederate capital would pin down troops that otherwise might be sent to Lee.

Butler's threat to Richmond and Meade's hounding of Lee were the chief elements of Grant's Virginia campaign. Two West Virginia columns would drive toward Lynchburg and Saltville, Virginia, cutting the Virginia and Tennessee Railroad's main lines to Richmond, while Sigel marched up the Shenandoah Valley. "I don't expect much from Sigel's movement," Grant confessed. "It is made principally for the purpose of preventing the enemy in his front from withdrawing troops to reinforce Lee's army." He told Halleck that Meade's army would attempt to turn Lee's flank, but should Lee fall back on Richmond's fortifications, Grant intended to "form a junction with Butler, and the two forces will draw supplies from the James River. My own notions about our line of march *are entirely made up* [emphasis added]."

To his friend Sherman, Grant wrote that after he destroyed Johnston's army, he was to "get into the interior of the enemy's country as far as you can, inflicting all the damage you can against their War resources." Sherman had efficiently waged this kind of destroying warfare in Mississippi. It constituted an escalation of hostilities against the Confederacy.[40]

To FURTHER PRESSURE the Confederate army, Grant suspended prisoner exchanges. The Confederacy held 26,000 Union prisoners; the Union had at least as many Rebel captives. A July 1862 agreement had permitted routine prisoner exchanges, but War Secretary Stanton suspended them in July 1863 when the Confederate government refused to exchange black prisoners and threatened to execute their white officers. Since then, prisoner trades had been sporadic.

But Grant wanted them stopped altogether. On April 1, Grant visited Butler at Fortress Monroe, where he gave "emphatic verbal directions" to stop all exchanges until further notice. "We got no men fit to go into our army, and every soldier we gave the Confederates went immediately into theirs," Grant told Butler. Exchanging all of the Rebel captives would give the Confederacy a corps "larger than any in Lee's army, of disciplined veterans . . . well-fed, -clothed, and -rested." With the spring campaign approaching, it was absolutely imperative, he said, that the Union army maintain numerical superiority and deny Lee reinforcements. After meeting with Butler, Grant wrote to Secretary of State William Seward, "We have got to fight until the military power of the South is exhausted, and if we release or exchange prisoners captured, it simply becomes a war of extermination."

Butler, however, thought Grant's reasoning too coldly calculating to play well with Northerners, infuriated as they were by the semi-starvation of Yankee prisoners in Southern prisons. Any policy prolonging their incarceration would raise a "clamor," Butler warned. He advised Grant to lay down insuperable conditions that must be met before exchanges could resume. When the Confederates rejected the conditions, they could be blamed for the suspension.

Grant took Butler's shrewd advice. On April 17, he stated that the exchanges could continue only if the Rebels met two provisos, both patently impossible. They must release more than 30,000 Union prisoners—more than they had, in fact—to compensate for having sent paroled Confederates captured at Vicksburg back to the ranks before they were formally exchanged. The rules expressly prohibited this. The Rebels also must make no distinction between black and white prisoners held by the Confederacy. The issue of black soldiers in the Union army ranks so enraged the slaveholding South that it recoiled from exchanging black war prisoners. The Confederacy met neither condition.[41]

3

April 1864
The North

IN THE NORTH, the war was costing $2 million a day, and one could see why when touring the railroad sidings at Brandy Station, where supplies, covered by tarpaulins, were stacked three stories high, upon seeing the Army of the Potomac's vast city of canvas-roofed log huts overspreading the country around Brandy Station and Culpeper.

Morale was excellent in the 100,000-man army. The soldiers dined on fresh beef, bread, salted pork, beans, rice, sugar, and coffee. They drilled every day, received their mail and their pay on time, and attended nightly prayer meetings in chapels built by the Christian Commission. "Probably no army on earth ever before was in better condition in every respect than was the Army of the Potomac," wrote the army's quartermaster general, Rufus Ingalls.[42]

In grim contrast to the snug Union camps was the surrounding Virginia countryside, desolated by years of war. "Outside the town [Culpeper], not a house nor a fence, not a tree was to be seen for miles, where once all had been cultivated farm-land, or richly wooded country," wrote Badeau, Grant's military secretary. "Here and there, a stack of chimneys or a broken cistern marked the site of a former homestead, but every other landmark had been destroyed. . . . This desert extended almost from Washington to the Rapidan."

The bleak setting was made worse by the understandable hostility of the remaining Virginians. "This was the beaten field of war," wrote Orson Curtis of the 24th Michigan. "Few inhabitants were left except the old and decrepit, women and children, who were often dependent upon our commissariat for food. They were all 'Secesh' and the 'Bonnie Blu [sic] Flag' [a popular song celebrating an early Confederate banner] was sung with spirit by the lassies who had a hatred of all Yankeedom."[43]

NORTH OF THE Potomac River, the economy had quickly rebounded from the 1861 financial panic that attended the severing of relations with the South and the departure of a half-million men for military service. Industrial production soared. Bountiful harvests produced surpluses of wheat, corn, pork, and wool. The Union government bought much of it, and kept textile mills running full tilt to meet the army's demand for uniforms. Thirty-eight arms factories produced 5,000 infantry rifles each day, while a day's work in the South yielded just 100 new rifles, each individually made. Before the war ended, the federal government would spend $1.8 billion, two-thirds of it on goods and services for the armies. The money for it all came from new taxes, including the first personal income tax. The Army Quartermaster Department grew larger than any private US business, with 100,000 civilian employees.

The federal government's role expanded exponentially, with the 1862 Legal Tender Act, which authorized printing federal paper "greenbacks" for the first time; the National Bank Act of 1863, establishing a national banking system; and the 1862 Homestead Act, which awarded 160-acre tracts of public land to settlers. The government authorized state land-grant colleges, and set aside 120 million acres of public lands for a transcontinental railroad.

Record amounts of coal, iron, copper, salt, gold, and silver were mined, and oil first appeared as an energy product. While the Union navy blockaded Southern ports, major Northern ports boomed, as did commercial railroad and canal traffic. Hundreds of thousands of European immigrants poured into the North. Thanks to the railroads, many went to the Midwest, where Chicago became the principal trade center, with 7,000 new structures built there in 1863 alone. The same year, fifty-seven new factories went up in Philadelphia. Financial houses flourished, and university endowments and construction soared. "It was distinctly a money-making age," wrote Emerson Fite of the North's Civil War economy.

At times, life went on as if it were peacetime; the North sometimes appeared to be waging war one-handed. College rowing and baseball teams continued to compete, and new schools were established: MIT, Cornell, Vassar, and Boston College. Prosperous Northern civilians purchased new jewelry and horse carriages, and thronged grand operas, theaters, horse races, and prize fights. In the thriving cities and in the Midwestern farm country, one could almost forget that two huge armies were engaged in a death struggle just miles away.[44]

GRANT PRESIDED OVER the massive preparations for the coming campaign from a brick house near the Culpeper train station. Meanwhile, the Army of the Potomac's officers and men observed their new commander's actions with a mixture of curiosity and skepticism. Enlisted men liked Grant's unpretentiousness and reserve, and approved of his transfer of rear-echelon troops to the front. Many officers, however, disliked Grant's slouching, unmilitary bearing, and were disturbed by his long silences. More seriously, though, they doubted his abilities, never tested in the East.

Grant's chief of staff and friend, General John Rawlins, was highly irritated by the whispering about Grant. In a letter to his wife, Rawlins wrote that the naysayers deprecated Grant's Western victories, saying: "'Well, you never met Bobby Lee and his boys; it would be quite different if you had.'"

During his weekly trips to Washington, Grant was often seen on the streets of the capital. Some observers disapproved of his demeanor. Richard Henry Dana Jr., a government attorney and popular author, judged the general-in-chief to be scruffy-looking and unimpressive. He "had no gait, no station, no manner," and possessed "rather the look of a man who did, or once did, take a little too much to drink." It offended Dana to see Grant in a crowd of men outside Willard's hotel, "talking and smoking . . . in that crowd . . . the general in chief of our armies on whom the destiny of the empire seems to hang!"

Returning to Culpeper after one of these trips, Grant noticed that a cloud of dust hung in the air; Lieutenant Colonel John Mosby's partisan rangers had just galloped through Culpeper minutes earlier, hot on the heels of Union cavalry. "Had he seen our train coming, no doubt he would have let his prisoners escape to capture the train," as well as the general-in-chief, Grant later wrote.

On Grant's forty-second birthday, April 27, he set the date for the campaign's opening—a week hence, on May 4. "The Army of the Potomac is in splendid condition and evidently feel [sic] like whipping some body," he wrote to General John Smith, who was with Sherman's army and had served under Grant at Vicksburg and Chattanooga. "I feel much better with this command that [sic] I did before seeing it. There seems to be the very best feeling existing." His good spirits were evident when he wrote to his wife Julia that same day, "This is my forty second birth day. Getting old am I not?" He divulged nothing about the upcoming campaign. "Would not tell you if I did know."[45]

ALTHOUGH THE ARMY of the Potomac might have appeared fit and battle-ready, manpower was a concern in the North. Three years of war had largely squelched the ardor that had inspired so many men to volunteer in 1861 for three-year enlistments.

Many of them were now rotting in shallow graves in Virginia, Maryland, and Pennsylvania. In the seemingly random violence of the battlefield, some regiments had been nearly wiped out, while others had suffered lightly. The unlucky ones included the 2nd Wisconsin, which had the highest casualty rate of any Union regiment, and the 5th New York, which lost 347 of its 490 men in just one battle, Second Manassas.[46]

The survivors were anxious to go home. When the three-year men began mustering out in the spring, few were expected to reenlist, despite the offer of $400 bonuses and thirty-day furloughs, and the War Department's promise to "veteranize" units with high retention rates, meaning that the reenlisted soldiers would remain in their original regiments and not be reassigned.[47]

In March, there was one of the largest draft calls of the war for 200,000 men to replace the departing three-year soldiers and the thousands more who would become casualties during the 1864 campaigns. Since the federal draft was enacted in March 1863, each state was given a quota to fulfill. With volunteers scarce, the names of eligible men between the ages of twenty and forty-five were entered into a draft lottery and selected randomly.

The draft was highly unpopular, and some states sued to have it declared illegal. During the riot-wracked summer of 1863, people died in mob violence in Danville, Illinois. Lawrence, Kansas, was sacked, and 200 people were killed. In New York City, an eruption of murders, looting, and arson got so out of hand that Union troops were summoned from the Gettysburg battlefield. In March 1864, five people died in Charleston, Illinois, when a mob attacked furloughed soldiers.

The draft fell heaviest on the poor, especially recent immigrants, who could not come up with $300 to pay substitutes to serve in their places. The sullen conscripts were sometimes unwisely assigned en masse to newly formed regiments, instead of being sent to seasoned units where they might have been taught their trade.

Another manpower-raising tactic, paying "bounties," ensured a yield of inferior recruits. To meet their quotas, many Northern counties and states dangled as bait hundreds of dollars in bounties—sometimes as much as $2,000, including contributions from corporations and wealthy men— unintentionally fostering a thriving money-making scheme for the criminal class: "bounty-jumping."[48]

Upon enlisting in the 11th New York Battery at the age of fifteen in late 1863, farm boy Frank Wilkeson was shocked when he was thrown in with a "shameless crew" of nearly 1,000 men who had enlisted for the express purpose of absconding with their bounty money at the first opportunity. Trusting none of them not to run away, the army locked them all up in the state penitentiary in Albany until it was time to take them to the front.

Wilkeson's companions, mostly thugs and petty criminals, immediately robbed him of everything of value. "There was not a man of them who was not eager to run away. Almost to a man they were bullies and cowards, and almost to a man they belonged to the criminal classes," wrote Wilkeson. The most admired of them all, he wrote, was a pickpocket who had jumped bounty in a half-dozen cities.

The men got their bounties and were marched into Albany, guarded by a double line of sentinels. Bystanders laughed at them, and boys threw mud balls. Three recruits tried to run for it—and were shot dead on State Street by their stone-faced armed guards, many of them invalided combat veterans.

The soldiers locked them in a ship's hold, whiskey was somehow smuggled in, and the vessel became "a floating hell," wrote Wilkeson, with everyone shouting and brawling. Even bounty men were robbed, and some were nearly beaten to death. "It was a scene to make a devil howl with delight." As the men were marched through New York City to the ship that would take them to Virginia, four recruits bolted and were shot down on the street. During the final stage of the trip to the Virginia front, five diehards leaped from a moving train, only to be riddled by the soldiers' gunfire; their bodies were retrieved and thrown into the last car.[49]

In April 1864, cracks were apparent in the Army of the Potomac that had not existed a year earlier. Larger and better equipped than ever before, the army, in its vast encampment at Brandy Station and Culpeper, appeared unstoppable, but hidden were the quiet changes wrought by waning enthusiasm for the war, and the draft and bounties. To make fighting men of the new breed of recruits, discipline necessarily grew harsher, and the camaraderie between officers and enlisted men that had marked the war's early years virtually disappeared.

The veteran volunteers eyed the newcomers with disdain; they were draftees, substitutes, bounty men, and "coffee boilers"—stragglers who could be found making coffee when real fighting happened. One veteran told Frank Wilkeson: "They are not Americans, they are not volunteers. They are the offscouring of Europe. They disgrace our uniform."[50]

IN WASHINGTON, THE widespread feeling that fighting would resume any day infused the capital's already lively nightlife with a frenzied gaiety. "Monster hops" were held at the National Hotel and Willard's Hotel; the popular dances were the polka and "the lancers," a new variation on the quadrille. Ford's and Grover's theaters drew large crowds, and people strolled along Pennsylvania Avenue, serenaded by brass bands. Soldiers thronged Washington's taverns and the streets surrounding them, where the city's nearly 5,000 prostitutes practiced their trade.[51]

The anticipation increased on April 25 when Major General Ambrose Burnside's IX Corps, with banners flying, marched down 14th Street on its way to the Virginia front. From a balcony at Willard's Hotel, President Lincoln, with Burnside and his staff, reviewed the more than 25,000 infantrymen, cavalrymen, and artillerymen as they passed by amid drum rolls and martial band music. Among them were eight regiments of black soldiers, the largest such formation in the army.

Bystanders applauded the black troops and shouted, "Remember Fort Pillow!" The North was still in an uproar over the slaughter of 231 of the

Mississippi River fort's 571 troops, most of them black, after its capture April 12. Union officers said the Rebels massacred the black troops after the garrison surrendered; the Rebels claimed the defenders died during the fighting. The Confederate commander, Nathan Bedford Forrest, boasted that "the river was dyed with the blood of the slaughter for two hundred yards," adding that "Negro soldiers cannot cope with Southerners." Lincoln was polling his cabinet on how the North should retaliate (it would not). When the black soldiers saw the president standing on Willard's balcony, they cheered him loudly. It began to rain, but Lincoln refused to go inside. "If they can stand it, I guess I can," he said.

The parade of IX Corps through the city and over the Potomac River into Alexandria, Virginia, wrote newspaper correspondent Noah Brooks, was "a memorable one for Washington, which seldom sees so large a force moving at one time through the city." Navy Secretary Gideon Welles, and practically everyone else, knew what it signified: "All the indications foreshadow a mighty conflict and battle in Virginia at an early day."[52]

BURNSIDE'S MARCH THROUGH Washington to join the rest of the army in Virginia revealed an organizational aberration: IX Corps was not part of the Army of the Potomac, whose three corps—II, V, and VI—had been in Virginia for months. This was because Burnside was Meade's senior in rank, and therefore, under the military protocol, he would not report to Meade; he would instead report directly to Grant. It was an awkward arrangement that invited delays and misunderstandings. But Grant was determined to use every available man in the East during the coming campaign—sub-optimally, if necessary.[53]

4

April 1864
The South

IN RICHMOND, THE people were starving by inches. "We are all good scavengers now, and there is no need of buzzards in the streets," wrote John Jones, a War Department clerk who had become so thin that he could count his ribs. "We see neither rats nor mice about the premises now. This is famine." Hunger caused a sharp rise in burglaries, and nighttime thefts of cows, pigs, bacon, and flour. Sometimes, even sitting hens vanished from barns and sheds.

The city with a prewar population of 38,000 was now home to 140,000 people. The newcomers included war refugees, soldiers, civilian and army bureaucrats, and those in the vast military hospital system. Richmond was looking rundown; most of the mechanics were in the army, leaving no one to fix the leaky roofs or broken gates and railings or to replace the rotting wood. Inflation was rampant: corn cost eighteen times more than in 1861; meat, twenty-three times its price three years earlier. "You take your money to market in the market basket and bring home what you buy in your pocketbook," the diarist Mary Chesnut observed.

The poor suffered most, but no one was immune. In April 1863 in Richmond, emaciated women had rampaged through the retail district, crying "bread!" and smashing windows and looting stores until a company of Confederate troops dispersed them. Even Richmond's well-to-do, who had previously attended parties where they feasted on delicacies and drank wine, now went to "starvation parties," where they danced but did not eat. On the last day of 1863, the Richmond *Examiner* dourly observed, "Today closes the gloomiest year of struggle. . . . We do not know what our resources are, and no one can tell us whether we shall have a pound of beef to eat at the end of 1864." By April 25, 1864, food shortages in Richmond persuaded President Jefferson Davis to transfer some government departments to South Carolina, where food was more plentiful.[54]

The crisis's causes were readily apparent. Before the war, the South had depended heavily on trade with the North and England, but the Union naval embargo had closed nearly every Southern port. Formerly, cotton was the South's trade currency, but with farmers urged to plant food crops instead, cotton had been marginalized. The fighting had taken hundreds of thousands of acres of good Virginia farmland out of production, and the loss of Vicksburg in July 1863 stopped shipments of meat and sugar from Louisiana and Texas.

The food that did reach Virginia came from the Deep South or the Shenandoah Valley, having to negotiate a rickety railway system that lacked even a uniform track gauge. On the overburdened rail lines, freight trains carrying food had to give way to troop trains and weapons and ammunition shipments. Sometimes the food rotted on sidings; when it did manage to complete the gantlet, the Rebel armies—100,000 troops within just a day's ride of Richmond—had first claim on it, followed by the civilians, who paid exorbitant prices. The dregs went to the Yankee prisoners locked up in the Richmond warehouses and on the cruelly misnamed Belle Isle in the James River, where they died by the dozens every day of starvation, exposure, and disease.[55]

In 1864, the Confederate government, feeling pinched in nearly every respect, was compelled to adopt unpopular measures in order to continue the war. To address the food shortage, government agents were sent into the countryside to appropriate food from farmers, paying market prices. In February, the Confederate Congress extended an 1863 tax that was universally loathed, and expanded the pool of draft-eligible men.

The new draft law lowered the minimum age by one year to seventeen, and raised the maximum age from forty-five to fifty, while ending most exemptions, abolishing substitutions, and extending enlistments until the war ended. Despite these urgent measures, during the first four months of 1864 the Confederacy raised just 15,820 conscripts to replace its losses during 1863, when it was at the zenith of its military strength. On April 30, the Confederate Bureau of Conscription reported that the South's pool of available fighting men was "nearly exhausted" and "necessity demands the invention of devices for keeping in the ranks the men now borne on the rolls."[56]

JEFFERSON DAVIS, THE Confederacy's stern, iron-willed president, was a man of principle, delicate health, and ascetic tastes. His greatest flaw was his absolute belief that no Confederate general, Robert E. Lee excepted, was as visionary a military strategist as he. Davis jealously guarded his prerogatives as commander-in-chief, refusing to cede his authority over all Rebel armies, even after Braxton Bragg's appointment as titular general-in-chief.

While Bragg attended to the army's logistical and manpower needs, and the defense of Richmond, Davis remained the Confederacy's principal strategist. He also tightly controlled the compartmentalized Confederate army, divided into a half-dozen "departments"—changing as needs arose and receded, and rarely acting in concert. Lee's Department of Northern Virginia was one of them. In actuality, Davis was Grant's strategic antagonist on the grand scale, while Lee was his strategic and tactical adversary in northern Virginia.

The foundation for Davis's military conceit consisted of a single command that he had held during the Mexican War, when his Mississippi regiment retrieved the day at Buena Vista in 1847, and four years as secretary of war during the Franklin Pierce administration. As commander-in-chief, Davis second-guessed his generals, and sometimes favored mediocre but loyal commanders—Bragg chief among them—over better ones, such as P. G. T. Beauregard and Joseph Johnston, whom he intensely disliked.

Davis micromanaged the Confederate government with the same obsessive attention to detail. Working day and night, he performed tasks that should have been left to subordinates in the belief that only he could do them properly. And with James Seddon in poor health, Davis had also become the Confederacy's de facto war secretary.

Never wildly popular, by 1864 Davis had sunk further in his countrymen's estimation. Casualties, food shortages, the tightening Federal blockade, and no hope of European intervention had turned a growing number of Southerners against Davis; they blamed him for everything that was going wrong and complained that he had assumed dictatorial powers. The states' governors bridled at his directives and sometimes ignored them. Although the thin-skinned president was stung by the criticism, he rarely admitted fault and did not change.

As Davis readied his armies for the enemy offensives expected that spring, he declared April 8 to be a national day of humiliation, fasting, and prayer. The South's hardships had become fuel for a great firestorm of religious devotion, especially in the army, where brigades gathered for daily prayer meetings and nightly sermons. Even in cold weather, before chapels were built at the Confederate encampments, "these soldiers would come in crowds, many of them barefooted to our outdoor meetings," wrote chaplain John Jones.

There were revivals in thirty-two of the Army of Northern Virginia's thirty-eight brigades; thousands of soldiers became eager converts. Another minister described the gatherings as having "all the primitive simplicity with which we are accustomed to think of John the Baptist, of Christ, and of the apostles, as standing in the midst of dense crowds and speaking to as many as could get near enough to hear anything. . . . I freely confess, that it far surpasses anything I ever expected to realize." David Holt, a soldier in the 16th Mississippi, wrote, "We had more church services that winter [1863–1864] than we had during the whole war put together."

Southerners believed that if they would only obey God's laws, the Confederacy would triumph, a sentiment that inspired Robert E. Lee's general order following the defeat at Gettysburg: "We have sinned against Almighty God. We have forgotten his signal mercies, and have cultivated a revengeful, haughty, and boastful spirit. We have not remembered that the defenders of a just cause should be pure in His eyes. . . . God is our only refuge and our strength. Let us humble ourselves before him."

In announcing the April 8 national fasting and prayer day to his army, Robert E. Lee again counseled humility, "asking through Christ the forgiveness of our sins, beseeching the aid of the God of our forefathers in the defence of our homes and our liberties, thanking Him for His past blessings, and imploring their continuance upon our cause and our people."

General John Gordon wrote that the Confederate soldiers committed themselves to God's protection and guidance, and "hopefully and calmly awaited the results of the coming battle." "Why should we doubt?" asked Ted Barclay, an officer in the Stonewall Brigade, if the Rebels believed their cause "to be a just one and our God is certainly a just God." Perhaps by declaring a day of religious observance, Davis hoped to bend God's will to the South's advantage.

Meanwhile, the newspapers exhorted the Southern people to fight on, to never give in. The Federals wish "to rob us of all we have on earth, and reduce our whole population to the condition of beggars and slaves," warned the Richmond *Dispatch*. The Charleston *Daily Courier* accused Union troops of burning homes, the murder of "gray-headed men and nurslings . . . and, in a word . . . every possible deed of baseness, cowardice and cruelty. . . . Who would not rather die than consent to live again under the shadow of their hateful flag?"[57]

THE PRAYERS AND fear-mongering were signs that the soaring optimism of 1863 was gone, dashed by the defeats at Vicksburg, Gettysburg, and Chattanooga, and Stonewall Jackson's death. Scarcely more uplifting was Jefferson Davis's Third Message to Congress of May 2, although understandably so:

only the day before, Davis had buried his five-year-old son, Joseph, as more than 1,000 children joined the procession from St. Paul's Episcopal Church to Hollywood Cemetery. The president's favorite child was climbing on a balcony railing at the Executive Mansion on April 30 when he lost his balance and fell twelve feet onto a strip of granite. A servant found the unconscious boy, blood pouring from his mouth and nose. All that night, Davis paced alone beside his son's body in his study, moaning, "Not mine, O Lord, but thine," while his wife Varina screamed away the hours of darkness.[58]

Davis's annual message to the Confederate Congress—it would be his last—was brief and cheerless. "It is enough for us to know that every avenue of negotiation is closed against us: that our enemy is making renewed and strenuous efforts for our destruction," wrote Davis. No help could be expected from Europe. Meanwhile, enemy armies resorted to "plunder and devastation of the property of non-combatants, destruction of private dwellings and even edifices devoted to the worship of God, expeditions organized for the sole purpose of sacking cities"—alluding to the punitive expeditions against Jackson and Meridian, Mississippi, in 1863. Davis attempted to mitigate the bad news by citing some recent battlefield successes, all minor, and reminding Congress that Confederate armies in north Georgia and northern Virginia still barred the Yankees' path. "And our generals, armies and people are animated by cheerful confidence."[59]

5

Friday, April 29, 1864
Near Gordonsville

LIEUTENANT GENERAL JAMES Longstreet's veterans carefully polished their newly issued Enfield rifles and cartridge belts, and greased and shined their shoes and boots and their brass buttons and belt buckles. A dress review, the first in nearly two years, was scheduled. General Lee, their revered leader, was coming to inspect them. A week earlier, the corps had returned to Virginia after a hard winter in Tennessee. It was now camped in a broad valley near Gordonsville.

The First Corps had been absent eight months from Lee's army—sent to north Georgia in September 1863 to reinforce Braxton Bragg's army. Together, Longstreet and Bragg had smashed the Union General William

Rosecrans's army at Chickamauga and besieged Chattanooga. When Grant broke the siege by capturing Missionary Ridge and Lookout Mountain, Longstreet and his corps were more than 100 miles away, attempting to dislodge Burnside from Knoxville. For the First Corps, Knoxville was the beginning of months of unproductive operations in east Tennessee.

While Lee was watching the enemy making obvious preparations for an offensive, he had lobbied Jefferson Davis for the return of his best fighting unit, led by the ruggedly built Dutchman whom Lee affectionately called his "War Horse" (a nickname Longstreet disliked). Davis had consented to send Longstreet back to Lee with two of his three divisions—George Pickett's remained detached for Richmond's defense—or about 10,000 men. Leaving Tennessee was agreeable to "Old Pete," as Longstreet's men sometimes called him. He had soured on Tennessee after months of tactical futility, and clashes with Generals Evander Law and Lafayette McLaws— whom he had arrested or court-martialed for questioning his orders.

Ten miles to the northeast, at Orange Court House, were the encampments of the Army of Northern Virginia's two other army corps: the late Stonewall Jackson's Second Corps, now led by Richard Ewell, and Ambrose Powell Hill's Third Corps. With Longstreet's return, Lee had 66,000 men, including cavalry and artillery. "We have more men here now than we ever had had before, and they are all in high spirits," wrote Francis Marion Whelchel of Cobb's Legion of the First Corps.

A few days earlier, Longstreet's men had received new rifles and uniforms and, for once, plentiful rations. The veteran soldiers were thrilled that Lee was coming from his headquarters at Orange Court House for what would be Lee's last troop review.

Lee rode Traveller to a knoll overlooking the broad valley of rich pastureland. A thirteen-gun salute boomed a welcome as "the general reins up his horse, & bares his good gray head, & looks at us & we shout & cry & wave our battleflags," wrote Longstreet's artillery commander, Brigadier General Edward Porter Alexander.

The men shrieked their Rebel yells and flung their hats into the air as their regimental bands played "Hail to the Chief." Lee rode along the lines, and then the regiments marched in review.

"There was no speaking, but the effect was that of a military sacrament, in which we pledged anew our lives," wrote Alexander.

Chaplain William E. Boggs of the 6th South Carolina asked Colonel Charles Venable of Lee's staff: "Does it not make the general proud to see how these men love him?"

Venable replied, "Not proud; it awes him."[60]

THE CONFEDERATE ARMY'S most impressive man, Lee was also one of its most aggressive. Lee was a bona fide Virginia aristocrat, but beneath the veneer of cavalier dignity—silver hair, granite integrity—beat the heart of a brawler. Lee longed to attack and destroy the enemy. Disappointed when Meade had withdrawn from Mine Run without a fight in early December, Lee had exclaimed to his generals, "I am too old to command this army; we should never have permitted these people to get away." Alexander wrote that Lee possessed "phenomenal audacity."

Lee's instinct for offensive warfare had exacted a high toll on the Army of Northern Virginia: by one modern estimate, 81,000 casualties between his promotion to field command in June 1862 through Mine Run, with especially heavy losses at Malvern Hill, Antietam, Chancellorsville, and Gettysburg. But no one in the South, much less the army, uttered a word of complaint, because at the outset of this fourth year of war, Lee was the South's great, last hope; no one in the South was more revered than Robert E. Lee.

His army had beaten McClellan, Pope, Burnside, and Hooker, and it had stopped Meade. His appearance on a battlefield inspired hardened combat veterans to reckless valor. "Lee stood before [Grant] with a record as military executioner unrivalled by that of any warrior of modern times," wrote General John Gordon.[61]

Superficially, Lee and Grant could not have been more dissimilar. The Lees were a First Family of Virginia. Robert's father, "Light Horse Harry" Lee, was a Revolutionary War hero; his father-in-law, George Washington Parke Custis, was George Washington's adopted son. Lee himself was an enigmatic man of stiff dignity—a devout Christian who strictly followed the rules. At West Point, he had graduated second in his class and without a single demerit, a rare achievement.

Grant was a tanner's son, and a rumpled, sometimes even shabby-looking man. His passage through West Point was littered with demerits, and he finished in the bottom half of his class. While raised as a Methodist, he was not devoutly religious like Lee, an Episcopalian.

Yet Lee and Grant were alike in important ways: both were highly intelligent, self-confident men who preferred attacking to defending, and who were gifted in using topography to their advantage. Lee was more excitable than the imperturbable Grant, but both thrived in emergencies, issuing orders rapidly.[62]

Lee's soldiers and officers did not really know what to think of Grant, but it seemed that everyone had an opinion about him. Among enlisted men, George Nichols of the 61st Georgia said Grant had a reputation as "a terrible 'bull-dog,' and that he never turned loose." Lee's officers were not as impressed. "He will find, I trust, that General Lee is a very different man to deal with," wrote Lieutenant Colonel Walter Taylor, Lee's adjutant. He predicted that Grant "will shortly come to grief if he attempts to repeat the tactics in Virginia which proved so successful in Mississippi." Longstreet's artillery commander, Alexander, was confident that no matter what Grant did, "we simply could never be driven off a battlefield."

But Longstreet, who knew Grant well, warned his fellow officers to not underestimate Grant or his army. "We must make up our minds to get into line of battle and to stay there; for that man will fight us every day and every hour till the end of the war."[63]

In February, Lee had wanted to bring back Longstreet from Tennessee and launch a preemptive attack on Meade. "I might succeed in forcing Genl Meade back to Washington & exciting apprehension, at least for their own position to weaken any movement against ours," he wrote to Jefferson Davis.

While aware that his army was in no shape for a sustained campaign in the North, Lee told Davis that his plan to surprise Meade, "can alarm & embarrass him to some extent & thus prevent him undertaking anything of magnitude against us." Lee's plan might have dislocated the Army of the Potomac's spring campaign, but it could not be carried out because of insufficient rations and Longstreet's unavailability. Lee had no choice but to wait for the enemy to act.[64]

Food had been Lee's chief concern all winter long. At one point, the shortage of rations became so acute that it threatened the army's very operational capability. "The great obstacle everywhere is scarcity of supplies," Lee wrote to Longstreet. Things might reach a pass, he said, where the

Confederate armies could only "concentrate wherever they are going to strike us," and become incapable of taking the offensive.

Private William Dame of the Richmond Howitzers called it "the hardship hardest to bear." The Rebels, he wrote, were hungry all the time. They were accustomed to the wet and cold, to hard work, to standing guard at night, and to fighting, but "you don't season to hunger. . . . We had more appetite than anything else, and never got enough to satisfy it—even for a time." The effect of their subpar diet, primarily corn meal and mashed potatoes, was evident in the soldiers' "sallow complexions" and poor physical condition, wrote Lieutenant McHenry Howard.

A private anonymously sent Lee a tiny slice of salt pork packed between two oak chips, along with a letter saying that this was his daily ration, which he supplemented by stealing. The communication caused Lee "great pain and anxiety," which he alleviated by writing strongly worded complaints to the Commissary Department.

Normally ascetic in his own habits, Lee denied himself even small indulgences when his men were hungry. He ate meat no more than twice weekly, according to a Mobile (Alabama) *Advertiser* article. "He believes indulgence in meat to be criminal in the present straightened [sic] condition of the country," the newspaper's Richmond correspondent wrote, adding that Lee's usual dinner fare consisted of "a head of cabbage, boiled in salt water, and a pone of corn bread."

Shortages of food and supplies compelled some brigades, when assigned to picket duty, to excuse hundreds of men because they lacked warm clothing. Unsurprisingly, there was "general rejoicing" when spring arrived, "although every man in that army knew that it meant the opening of another campaign and the coming of Grant's thoroughly equipped and stalwart corps."

When Lee's protests failed to persuade commissary officials to send more rations and clothing, Lee appealed directly to Davis, predicting disaster if nothing was done. The army might simply dissolve unless more food was sent, Lee warned. "I cannot see how we can operate with our present supplies," he told the Confederate president on April 12. "Any derangement of their arrival, or disaster to the R.R. would render it impossible for me to keep the army together and might force a retreat into North Carolina. . . . Every exertion should be made to supply the depots at Richmond and at other points."

Lee's blunt portent of calamity got results: the army quickly received more food and, at last, new clothing, blankets, shoes, and weapons.[65]

WHEN SCOUTS REPORTED trains full of troops arriving at the Union camps, Lee asked Davis to return to him six brigades detached from his army to North Carolina for the siege of New Bern. "Everything indicates a concentrated attack on this front," Lee told Davis on April 30, "which renders me the more anxious to get back the troops belonging to this army." While Lee acknowledged that "advantages" would result from New Bern's capture, they would not "compensate us for a disaster in Virginia or Georgia." The necessity of concentrating forces in northern Virginia and Georgia was "immediate and imperative."

But Davis declined to act on Lee's request, electing to wait until the Union armies began their campaigns. Lee's roughly 64,000 effectives would have to suffice against enemy forces nearly twice their number.[66]

Despite the supply and manpower problems—as well as a wave of desertions by men who could not bear to face another campaign—the Confederate army was ready to fight. Asbury Hall Jackson told his sister that the winter's hardships had tested the soldiers, but they "are not ready nor willing to give up, in short, not whipped." Alexander Haskell of South Carolina described the Rebels as quietly confident. "The indications of spirit are of a better kind than I have ever seen them," he observed. William Ruffin Cox, of the 2nd North Carolina, wrote, "The same spirit that controlled our actions in the beginning of this Struggle *still animates us* [original emphasis]." Isaac Bradwell of the 31st Georgia and his comrades "consoled ourselves with the reflection that we could die if necessary for our country and, that Divine Providence was on our side, while we had a leader in General Lee who, we felt, would be equal to the occasion."

But some Confederate soldiers detected a subtle change in the war's character. A friend of artillery Major Robert Stiles, whom he called "Billy," sensed it when he returned from a furlough in early May. His comrades, he observed, appeared to lack the buoyancy of previous years when they were poised to begin a spring campaign. In its place, Billy told Stiles, he felt "a sort of premonition of the definite, mathematical calculation, in whose hard, unyielding grasp it was intended our future should be held and crushed." Grant himself could not have better described his object.[67]

Two Bloody Roads

The Wilderness

The May-weed springs; and comes a Man
And mounts our Signal Hill;
A quiet Man, and plain in garb—
Briefly he looks his fill,
Then drops his gray eye on the ground,
Like a loaded mortar he is still:
Meekness and grimness meet in him—
The silent General.

—Herman Melville,
"The Armies of the Wilderness"[1]

A butchery pure and simple it was, unrelieved by any of the arts
of war.

—J. M. Waddell, historian for the
46th North Carolina, which lost
201 of its 340 soldiers in the Wilderness[2]

1

Wednesday, May 4, 1864
Along the Rapidan River

THE UNION CAVALRY went first. Breaking camp just after midnight, David Gregg's 2nd Cavalry Division and James Wilson's 3rd Division rode toward two Rapidan River crossings: for Wilson's men, Germanna Ford, nine miles east of the Rebels' right wing; and for Gregg, Ely's Ford, six miles downriver from Germanna. A year ago nearly to the day, the Army of the Potomac had gone over the Rapidan at these very crossings—and three days later had come thundering back across after Stonewall Jackson flanked the army and General Joe Hooker lost his nerve. The Army of the Potomac had returned to try again with a new general.

A guard was posted at every home along the army's marching routes to prevent the inhabitants, all ardent secessionists, from alerting the enemy. Upon reaching the river, the troopers were to seize the fords and scatter or capture any Rebel pickets. Engineers would throw down pontoon bridges for the three infantry corps that would begin crossing the river at dawn. General Alfred Torbert's 1st Cavalry Division remained on the north bank to guard the army's rear.

Marching behind Wilson's troopers were V and VI corps. II Corps followed Gregg, a lavishly bearded thirty-one-year-old veteran who had distinguished himself while leading the 2nd Division at Gettysburg.

No moon was visible, but the stars seemed to be etched in the clear sky. At Ely's Ford, the 1st New Jersey Cavalry halted when it spotted enemy pickets on the south shore. "The night was dark, and the air in the hollow near the river very cold and chilly," wrote the regiment's chaplain, Henry Pyne. Intending to capture the pickets, a company waded across the numbingly cold river, "the men carrying their arms and ammunition above their heads." The pickets fled when the rest of the division began splashing into the river.

Engineers laid down two pontoon bridges, 220 feet long and 50 feet apart, at each of the fords. A fifth bridge was added at Culpeper Mine Ford, between Germanna and Ely's; it would accommodate most of the Army of the Potomac's massive wagon train, which, if it had been placed in a single column, would have stretched from the Rapidan to Richmond, 60 miles away. By 5:30 a.m., about a half-hour after daybreak, the bridges were completed.[3]

POISED TO CROSS the Rapidan was the greatest host ever assembled on US soil: the 100,000 men of the Army of the Potomac's three infantry corps, its Cavalry Corps, and its artillery battalions. Behind this vast army were 20,000 more troops from Ambrose Burnside's IX Corps, a separate organization from Meade's army that would operate closely with it.

The Army of the Potomac's infantry corps had begun moving toward the Rapidan shortly after midnight, the men forbidden to make bonfires that might alert the enemy. In the first light of day, every road north of the Rapidan was jammed with blue-clad troops.

"From the summit of the swells of ground we could see the long, dark lines, which looked like fences dividing the country, but the glitter of many thousand musket-barrels showed them to be masses of men moving in columns," wrote Chaplain Alanson Haines of the 15th New Jersey, part of VI Corps and following V Corps to Germanna Ford, where 3,000 men began crossing the Rapidan every hour.

"As far as you could see in every direction, corps, divisions and brigades, trains, batteries, and squadrons, were moving on in a waving sea of blue; headquarters and regimental flags were fluttering, the morning sun kissing them all," wrote Lieutenant Morris Schaff, chief ordnance officer to General George Meade. "Every once in a while a cheer would break, and on would come floating the notes of a band. . . . The troops were very lighthearted, almost as joyous as schoolboys."

The soldiers' bearing and buoyant mood inspired Charles Page, a correspondent for the New York *Tribune,* to write, "I have never seen the army move with more exact order, with a less number of stragglers, and with so little apparent fatigue to the men. . . . The rank and file will fight this fight with more than the élan of the French, with more than the pluck of the British. They feel it in their bones. . . . "[4]

EACH OF THEM carried three days' rations and fifty cartridges in addition to their muskets and personal items. New soldiers tried to bring everything they had and strained beneath bulging knapsacks, but the veterans knew better; they brought just the barest necessities. They rolled up their food and gear inside a canvas half-shelter, wrapped the tent in a gum blanket, tied the ends with twine, and slung it over one shoulder. They carried new cartridge boxes, which they liked better than the old ones because they hung from the front rather than the side of the waist belt for better weight distribution. Wagons hauled the rest: an additional ten days' rations per man, and forage and extra ammunition. Each wagon was carefully labeled with a corps badge, a division color, and a brigade number, and was marked to denote its contents: ammunition, whether for artillery or infantry; forage, if grain or hay; and rations, labeled by type. Beside the wagon trains, drovers prodded along lowing cattle, to be butchered as needed.[5]

When the men broke up their winter camps, they left windrows of discarded stores. "Twenty families could have set themselves up in housekeeping from the remnants of one regiment alone. Crockery, clothes, furniture, bedding, ham (boiled and raw), potatoes, pork, bread, etc., were thrown away without thought," wrote Captain Robert Carter of the 22nd Massachusetts.

Many of the soldiers, perhaps anticipating the horrors before them, fondly remembered their last dress parades before breaking up their camps. Private Frank Wilkeson, a teenage gunner in the 11th New York Artillery, remembered the "soft spring air," the tattoo of drums, and the silence that descended when the review ended. Private Theodore Gerrish of the 20th Maine recalled bands "playing warlike music; the shrill, keen notes of the bugles . . . ringing out over the hillsides and down though the meadow . . . banners were waving; and soldiers cheering as the general officers rode along the lines. Our men were anxious for the campaign to open, hoping it would be the last one of the war." Captain Carter remembered a sudden windstorm that filled the air with dust and sent the men racing to their tents to prevent them from blowing away. If some portents are real, and not imagined, this was one.

As THE TEMPERATURE rose and the dusty miles passed, castoff blankets, overcoats, and dress coats—many of them never worn—accumulated in heaps alongside the roads. Before setting out on his first campaign,

Wilkeson had permitted a veteran gunner to rummage through his stuffed knapsack, discarding nonessentials. He now traveled light, with a single change of underwear, three pairs of socks, an extra pair of shoes, three plugs of navy tobacco, a rubber blanket, and a pair of woolen blankets. The gunner advised him to pick up nothing except food and tobacco, and to fill his canteen whenever he got the opportunity.[6]

ULYSSES GRANT, IN observance of the day's significance, startled his aides by emerging from his tent in his dress uniform. He had never worn it into battle before, his usual attire being a plain private's uniform with stars sewn onto the shoulders. But on this day, his pants were tucked into new boots. He wore an unbuttoned uniform frock coat over a blue vest, a black slouch hat with gold cord, his sword and sash, and "yellowish-brown thread gloves." As Grant rode out of Culpeper Courthouse on his big, fast bay, Cincinnati, and down the Germanna Road, "lusty shouts" erupted from the long columns of VI Corps troops bound for Germanna Ford.

Grant had slept little the previous night. Well into the early morning hours, he had met with his staff in a freewheeling session at which he had revealed the details of the Army of the Potomac's impending campaign. He also outlined his plans for Sherman, Butler, Sigel, and Banks. The latter's Red River campaign had already ended in disaster, and his army would neither be able to move against Mobile nor to aid Sherman. There were many questions, and he answered them all. The discussion failed to alleviate his aides' apprehensions. "The plan was so comprehensive, the result hung upon it so stupendous, the chances were so various, the obstacles so formidable, that no man's spirit was buoyant, though all were trustful; all believed in the chief who had so often been victorious," wrote Lieutenant Colonel Adam Badeau, Grant's military secretary.

Later that morning, Badeau rode with the general-in-chief and the rest of the staff. "The day was superb, the marching smooth and close, and the men were in fine spirits," he wrote. In Grant's entourage was a man dressed in "funereal-looking citizen's clothes," exciting speculation that he was the general's "private undertaker." But the stranger was Congressman Elihu Washburne of Illinois, Grant's loyal patron.[7]

FOUR DAYS EARLIER, Abraham Lincoln had bid Grant farewell in a letter that expressed his "entire satisfaction with what you have done up to this time, so far as I understand it." The president said that he did not wish to know "the particulars" of Grant's plans. "You are vigilant and self-reliant; and, pleased with this, I wish not to obtrude any constraints or restraints upon you. . . . If there is anything wanting which is within my power to give, do not fail to let me know it."[8]

In his response the next day, Grant wrote it would be "my earnest endeavor that you and the country shall not be disappointed." He was grateful for "the readiness with which everything asked for has been yielded, without even an explanation being asked. Should my success be less than I desire and expect, the least I can say is, the fault is not with you." These last words must have pleased Lincoln, plagued for years by generals who refused to accept responsibility for their failures.[9]

Grant then wrote to his wife Julia: "Before you receive this I will be away from Culpepper [sic] and the Army will be in motion. I know the greatest anxiety is now felt in the North for the sucsess [sic] of this move, and that anxiety will increase when it is once known that the Army is in motion," he wrote. "I feel well myself. [I] do not know that this is any criterion to judge results because I have never felt otherwise."[10]

THE GENERAL-IN-CHIEF AND his staff crossed the Rapidan and appropriated a house overlooking Germanna Ford as their headquarters. Following Grant over the pontoon bridges, VI Corps bivouacked around Grant's command center.

To avoid broadcasting his movements, Grant had forbidden correspondents traveling with the Army of the Potomac to telegraph reports to their newspapers; the articles had to be delivered by messenger. But after crossing the Rapidan unopposed, Grant was in an expansive mood, so that when a reporter asked him how long it would take him to reach Richmond—a theoretical question no one in Washington had dared ask—Grant surprised everyone by replying. "I will agree to be there in about four days—that is, if General Lee becomes a party to the agreement; but if he objects, the trip will undoubtedly be prolonged."[11]

IT WAS ROUGHLY sixty miles from the Rapidan to Richmond by way of the north-to-south "overland route"—so called because of what it was not: the roundabout Peninsular approach to Richmond from the southeast, attempted in 1862 by George McClellan, who failed to reach the Confederate capital from Fort Monroe on Chesapeake Bay by marching up the Virginia Peninsula between the James and York rivers. During three years of war, three Union generals—John Pope, Ambrose Burnside, and Joe Hooker—had mounted direct, overland campaigns, all ending in failure.

Grant had weighed crossing the Rapidan farther upriver, turning Lee's left, striking south toward Gordonsville and the Virginia Central Railroad, and then threatening Richmond from the west. Although this would have forced Lee to face the Army of the Potomac on open ground, it would have also exposed the Union army's supply line, as well as Washington. Moreover, Lee would have stood between Meade's and Butler's armies.

But by skirting Lee's right, the Army of the Potomac would remain between the Army of Northern Virginia and Washington, and it could obtain food, clothing, and ammunition from river depots in eastern Virginia—on the Rappahannock, the Pamunkey, and the James—supplied by ships and boats. On April 29, Grant had requested that one million rations and 200,000 forage rations be readied so that, when needed, they could be shipped to one of these depots. The plan's one, potentially daunting, drawback was the Wilderness, where few fields and roads broke up the unyielding density of its thickets, woods, and undergrowth. The Wilderness stood directly in the path of the Army of the Potomac.[12]

AT 9:30 A.M., Union signalmen on Stony Mountain intercepted a message sent from the Rebels' Clark's Mountain signal station. It was addressed to Richard Ewell, the Confederate Second Corps commander, by Lee's aide, Lieutenant Colonel Walter Taylor: "From present indications everything seems to be moving to the right, on Germanna and Ely's Ford roads, leaving cavalry in our front." At 1 p.m., the Union signal men reported to Meade's headquarters that Confederate forces were moving east from Orange Court House toward New Verdiersville. "Two brigades gone from this front. Camps on Clark's Mountain breaking up."

Upon receiving this information, Grant, sitting on the steps of his temporary headquarters overlooking the river, said, "That gives just the information I wanted. It shows that Lee is drawing out from his position and is pushing across to meet us." He dashed off a message to Burnside at Rappahannock Station: "Make forced march [with IX Corps] until you reach this place. Start your troops now in the rear, the moment they can be got off, and require them to make a night march. Answer." Burnside replied, "Will start column at once."

At 7 p.m., a Colonel George Sharpe sent a message to Meade's chief of staff, General Andrew Humphreys, informing him that a black boy just arrived from Gordonsville had seen Longstreet's corps starting toward the Wilderness. Lee's army was marching to confront the Army of the Potomac.[13]

ON THE CAMPAIGN'S first day, the Army of the Potomac committed a grave tactical error. While many high-ranking officers had fought at Chancellorsville exactly a year earlier and were well aware of the perils of operating in the Wilderness's green jungle, the army stopped its march on May 4 while still within the Wilderness's boundaries—when it might have easily gotten clear of them.

Humphreys's early drafts of the final order issued May 2, writes historian Gordon Rhea, show that he intended for the army to pass through the Wilderness on the fourth before halting. Humphreys had commanded a combat division at Chancellorsville and understood the region's snares and pitfalls. Extending the day's march by just five miles would have placed Meade's three infantry corps beyond the Wilderness and five miles from Spotsylvania Court House. But higher-ups overruled Humphreys.

The decision, wrote Humphreys, "was in consideration of the fact that it was not practicable in this region to move the great trains along the protected flank of the army simultaneously with the troops." The high command believed the wagon train would have been strung out and "too open during the forenoon of the fifth." Halting at mid-afternoon on May 4 "made the passage of the trains secure, and the troops would be fresher when meeting the enemy next day, of which there was much probability,"

Humphreys explained. Yet, the wagon train might have been held on the Rapidan's north shore for a day without much harm; each soldier carried with him ample food and ammunition.[14]

By stopping early on May 4, Grant and Meade handed Lee a glittering opportunity to strike at the massive Union army while it was still inside the claustrophobic Wilderness, a place that nullified Meade's overwhelming advantages in numbers and artillery. "It was a region in which the power of discipline almost disappeared, in which the personal influence of commanders was at a minimum, in which tactics were literally impossible," wrote Lieutenant Colonel Francis Walker, II Corps' assistant adjutant general. "Viewed as a battleground, [it] was simply infernal."[15]

For his part, Grant was immensely relieved that the army had reached the Rapidan's south shore without opposition or casualties. "This I regarded as a great success. . . . It removed from my mind the most serious apprehensions I had entertained, that of crossing the river in the face of an active, large, well-appointed, and ably-commanded army," he wrote.[16]

THAT AFTERNOON, SHERMAN reported to Grant that his 78,000-man Western army had marched that day into north Georgia. Franz Sigel's campaign in the Shenandoah Valley had started three days earlier. Benjamin Butler's 35,000-man Army of the James planned to sail from Fort Monroe up the James River on transports that night. Accompanied by a flotilla of warships, gunboats, barges and other vessels, the invasion force's immediate objective was City Point. Grant's grand strategy, unexampled in scope in this war or any other ever waged in North America, appeared to be unfolding as planned, involving a quarter-million Union soldiers spread over hundreds of miles.[17]

KNOWN AS GERMANNA Road before becoming Brock Road a few miles south of the Rapidan, the thoroughfare linked the river with Spotsylvania Court House fifteen miles away. The road was important because it was both lifeline to the river and corridor to Richmond for V and VI Corps.

Between the Rapidan and Spotsylvania, it intersected three narrow, forest-hemmed roads radiating eastward from Lee's headquarters at Orange Court House, twenty miles away: first, the Orange Turnpike, five miles south of the Rapidan, with the abandoned Wilderness Tavern located at the Germanna Road intersection; then, three miles south, the Orange Plank Road; and, finally, four miles south of that, Catharpin Road, which intersected Brock Road at Todd's Tavern.

Gouverneur Warren's V Corps made its camp near Wilderness Tavern, and Warren sent General Charles Griffin's division west on the Orange Turnpike to guard his flank against Lee's troops, known to be marching east; Griffin camped a mile from the rest of the corps. Near V Corps was General Phil Sheridan's Cavalry Corps. VI Corps had stopped on the Germanna Road between V Corps and the river. II Corps, having crossed at Ely's Ford six miles below Germanna, traveled other roads to the southeast and spent the night on the old Chancellorsville battlefield, seven miles from its sister corps.

Wilson's cavalry division drove off a small Rebel cavalry force at Parker's Store on the Orange Plank Road, and he sent a patrol down the Brock Road toward Spotsylvania. No other encounters with the enemy were reported. Believing there would be ample time the next morning before Lee's corps appeared—if, in fact, Lee chose to dispute possession of Brock Road—Grant planned short marches on May 5 for the Army of the Potomac's three corps, in order to present an unbroken front facing west and to seal the three main roads feeding into Brock Road from that direction.[18]

SHERIDAN, THE FEISTY, small-statured commander of the Army of the Potomac's Cavalry Corps, had come East with Grant in March. Grant witnessed Sheridan's charge up Missionary Ridge the previous November, and he admired his aggressiveness and promptness. Grant had confidence in Sheridan, even though his new cavalry commander had led infantry divisions for nearly two years.

And so Grant readily agreed when Sheridan proposed that the next morning he take two of his three cavalry divisions, ride east a dozen miles or so, and smash up Fitzhugh Lee's planned review of his cavalry division near Fredericksburg, at Hamilton's Crossing, to be presided over by Virginia Governor William "Extra Billy" Smith. While this would leave just Wilson's division to patrol the Army of the Potomac's right flank, Sheridan's plan appeared sound to Grant. Neither of them knew that Fitz Lee had called off the review when the Army of the Potomac crossed the Rapidan. Lee had left Hamilton's Crossing, and was riding around the south side of Meade's army, firing off reports to his uncle, Robert E. Lee, describing the enemy's dispositions.[19]

LATE MAY 3, the Confederate lookouts on Clark's Mountain had noted heavy activity in the Army of the Potomac camps. By mid-morning May 4, they were able to report that the Yankees were crossing the Rapidan by the lower fords—Germanna and Ely's. By 11 a.m., A. P. Hill's Third Corps—Lee traveling with it—informed Richard Ewell, the Second Corps commander, "We are moving." An hour later, Ewell's corps, too, was under way.

Hill's corps, with 15,000 infantrymen—Richard Anderson's 7,500-man division remained behind to guard the upper Rapidan crossings—had to travel twenty-eight miles from its camp north of Orange Court House and astride the Orange and Alexandria Railroad, to reach the Wilderness; Ewell's 17,000 men, camped ten miles from the courthouse, near the Rapidan, faced an eighteen-mile march.

Starting from Gordonsville, ten miles south of Orange Court House, General James Longstreet's First Corps had farther to go than its sister corps—forty-two miles, a two-day march. His 10,000 men were fewer in number (just two of his three divisions were present) than Hill's and Ewell's corps, but they were the cream of the Confederate army. When the three corps came together in the Wilderness, they would comprise a formidable force: 66,140 infantrymen, artillerymen, and cavalry troopers.[20]

JUST AS HANCOCK's assistant adjutant general, Lieutenant Colonel Walker, had deplored the Union high command's decision to stop for the night in the Wilderness, so did General Edward Porter Alexander, Longstreet's artillery commander, lament Lee's slow start. He believed it was a mistake to keep the First Corps at its camp near Gordonsville past midday May 4. "I have always believed it to have been one of those small matters up on which, finally, hung very great & important matters," Alexander later wrote. In the Wilderness, he said, Lee's army had "the one rare chance of the whole campaign to involve it in a panic such as ruined Hooker on the same ground."[21]

Lee, however, was unwilling to presume that Grant would cross the Rapidan on Lee's right when there was the slightest possibility that he might move around Lee's left. If Lee had recalled Longstreet's corps from Gordonsville and guessed wrong, Grant, without opposition, might have struck at Lee's rear or marched to the Virginia Central Railroad, and thence Richmond.

WITH GENERAL JUBAL Early's division at its head, Ewell's Second Corps marched eastward at a deliberate pace on the macadam-surfaced Orange Turnpike toward the Wilderness. Lee had ordered Ewell to travel slowly to permit Hill's Third Corps, which had a greater distance to go, to draw abreast on the partially planked Orange Plank Road three miles to the south. Jeb Stuart's cavalrymen rode ahead of the Third Corps and General Henry Heth's leading division, Hill and Lee at its head. Lee explicitly warned the two corps "not to bring on a general engagement" until Longstreet joined them. With the enemy nearby in great numbers, this would prove impossible.[22]

Longstreet was the slowest to move on May 4. He had to gather the regiments that he had flung out on his left to guard against an upriver crossing by Grant's army. Then, Lee changed First Corps' orders: rather than marching to Richard's Shop and east on Catharpin Road before joining Hill's corps, he wanted Longstreet to proceed to Orange Court House and follow Hill's corps on the Orange Plank Road.

Longstreet protested that the plank road would become too congested, and he asked Lee to reinstate the original order; Lee obliged, routing Longstreet's corps back to Catharpin Road. The First Corps did not set out until 4 p.m., but it covered fifteen miles before stopping at Brock's Bridge on the North Anna River. Longstreet intended to get his men back on the road long before dawn on May 5 to make up the miles not marched on May 4. By day's end May 5, he hoped to be in position for a daybreak attack on May 6 in concert with Ewell and Hill down the three parallel roads.[23]

Traveling with Hill's corps on the Orange Plank Road, William Dame of the Richmond Howitzers reported that the Rebels were ebullient, despite being hungry and knowing that they faced long odds. "It was a fact, accepted among us, that General Lee was pushing as hard as he could go, for Grant's 150,000 with about 35,000 men; and yet, knowing all this, these lunatics were sweeping along to that appallingly unequal fight, cracking jokes, laughing, and with not the least idea in the world of anything else but victory. . . . It was the grandest moral exhibition I ever saw! For it was simply the absolute confidence in themselves and in their adored leader."[24]

Lee, Hill, and the Third Corps stopped at New Verdiersville, ten miles from Brock Road. That night, Lee again asked Davis to send more troops. "It is apparent that the long threatened effort to take Richmond has begun, and that the enemy has collected all his available force to accomplish it," he wrote. "Under these circumstances I regret that there is to be any further delay in concentrating our own troops." For the time being, Lee would have to fight with the men that he had.[25]

On the Orange Turnpike, Ewell and the Second Corps camped at Locust Grove, five miles from Wilderness Tavern, where Warren's V Corps had made camp. Jubal Early's division and Griffin's V Corps division were just three miles apart. Because the wall of vegetation between them absorbed the noise from their camps, neither was aware of the other's presence.

WHILE CAUTIONING EWELL to not bring on a "general engagement," Lee wanted Ewell and Hill to make contact with Grant's army and fix it in place so that Lee could launch a general attack when Longstreet arrived. In his orders for May 5, Lee told Ewell to be ready to move early in the morning. "The general's [Lee's] desire is to bring [the enemy] to battle now as soon as possible," wrote his aide, Lieutenant Colonel Walter Taylor. If the Union army marched east toward Fredericksburg, Ewell was to fall on its rear; if it advanced west on the Orange Turnpike, he must fight a defensive battle—and, if necessary, pull back to the entrenchments the army had dug at Mine Run five months earlier.[26]

The Confederates were pleased that Grant had stopped in the Wilderness. Whether he knew it or not, he had chosen a battleground that favored a smaller, more mobile force. The Rebel veterans knew every path, stream, and road. "The Wilderness was our favorite fighting ground," wrote General Alexander, Longstreet's artillery chief. "The enemy's enormous force of artillery was there only in his way. Never was a better chance offered General Lee, & never was a chance more quickly snapped at."[27]

The situation put Lee in "the best of spirits," wrote Lieutenant Colonel Armistead Long of Lee's staff. "He expressed himself surprised that his new adversary had placed himself in the same predicament as 'Fighting Joe' had done the previous spring." Lee spoke "very cheerfully" of the situation, wrote another aide, Lieutenant Colonel Charles Venable. "He expressed his pleasure that the Federal general had not profited by General Hooker's Wilderness experiences, and that he seemed inclined to throw away to some extent the immense advantage which his great superiority in numbers in every arm of the service gave him."[28]

Lee not only longed to attack the invaders, he absolutely had to, if he were to have any chance of smashing Grant's massive army and driving it back across the Rapidan River. The Army of Northern Virginia's commander knew that he could not fight a solely defensive strategy and expect to defeat Grant. But Lee's reasons for acting as he did in the Wilderness are not altogether clear; much of his correspondence from this period, which might have better explained his actions, was destroyed in the Richmond fires of April 1865.

It is known that Lee underestimated the size of the Union forces that he faced, believing that just 75,000 troops had crossed the Rapidan, when the number was nearly 100,000, with Burnside's 20,000-man corps less than a day's march away. Attacking Grant would be an act of both supreme confidence and desperation.[29]

II CORPS BIVOUACKED May 4 at a dismal place full of grisly memories and ghosts: the old Chancellorsville battleground of May 1863. "It is a region of gloom, and the shadows of death," observed David Craft, chaplain of the 141st Pennsylvania. Brigade commander Robert McAllister of II Corps, who had fought at Chancellorsville, wrote to his wife that he saw "the bones of our dead laying and bleaching on top of the ground," and in his letter enclosed wildflowers picked where his men had stood and fought. "The ground was made rich by the blood of our brave soldiers," he wrote.

The charred hulk of the Chancellorsville mansion loomed in the dusk sky over a blighted landscape of splintered trees, crumbling breastworks, and torn ground littered with sun-cracked cartridge boxes, battered canteens, pieces of rotted cloth, and broken artillery carriages. "The dead were all around us," wrote Wilkeson of the 11th New York Artillery. "Their eyeless skulls seemed to stare steadily at us."

It was there that Lee, menaced on two sides, had audaciously divided his army before the enemy and sent Stonewall Jackson on a daring flanking maneuver around the Army of the Potomac. Jackson caught the Yankees

napping, and took the fight out of "Fighting Joe" Hooker: the Union commander had ridden to the Rapidan's north bank while his army fought
desperately in muddy trenches on the south bank. Hooker's spring campaign ended in disaster, but the Army of Northern Virginia lost Jackson,
accidentally wounded by his own troops. The great commander's left arm,
amputated in a field hospital, was buried nearby; Jackson died miles away.

A veteran told recruits that wounded men had burned to death during
the fighting. "It was a ghastly and awe-inspiring tale as he vividly told it
to us as we sat among the dead." Lieutenant Morris Schaff wrote that in
a twenty-five-square-foot area "fifty skulls were counted, their foreheads
doming in silence . . . half-open graves, displaying arms and legs with bits
of paling and mildewed clothing still clinging to them."[30]

A Captain Murray, whose 124th New York lost 200 men in the battle,
saw his comrades stop in their tracks as they walked toward a stream to fill
their canteens. "The way was barred by the bleached bones of their dead
comrades." Murray and his mates were at the very spot where the regiment
had been decimated, and where he had been wounded. "Our dead were but
partially buried," he wrote to his father. "I found a skull where Shawcross
fell with a hole in the forehead just where he was shot. . . . It made my
heart sick to look over the ground." Craft wrote that their dead comrades
"seemed to have so quietly waited our coming to bury them." That night,
there was no singing in the camps.[31]

II CORPS WAS the largest, most famous, and hardest-fighting corps in the
Army of the Potomac. General Winfield Scott Hancock and his dependable
division commanders led the corps' eleven infantry brigades and eighty-one
regiments. On paper, II Corps consisted of 28,333 men, but subtracting
the sick and those recovering from wounds, 23,877 were actually present
for duty. The Philadelphia and Irish brigades were its best-known units. At
Gettysburg on July 3, 1863, they had anchored II Corps' line when it flung
back Pickett's charge. At Chancellorsville, the Irish Brigade was sent to drag
away the guns belonging to Hancock's division after nearly all the artillery
mounts were killed. Under intensive enemy fire, the Irishmen retrieved the
guns before the Rebels could capture them.

The only corps that had been with the Army of the Potomac from the beginning, II Corps had fought in every major action. Its trefoil-shaped badge

was called "the ace of clubs" and its battle cry was "Clubs Are Trumps!" By the end of the war, its losses would surpass all other Federal corps: roughly 40,000 of the 100,000 who served became casualties.

When III Corps was disbanded in March's army-wide reorganization, two divisions were folded into II Corps, one of them Hooker's former division—now the 3rd Division led by David Birney. The other was Gershom Mott's 4th Division. Generals Francis Barlow and John Gibbon, respectively, commanded the 1st and 2nd Divisions. Of the four division commanders, only Gibbon had led a division in II Corps before Grant's campaign.

Gibbon was regarded as the most competent of Hancock's division commanders, "steel-cold . . . the most American of Americans, with his sharp nose and up-and-down manner of telling the truth, no matter whom it hurts." Gibbon in fact had led II Corps twice at Gettysburg—when Hancock was sent to command I Corps and XI Corps during various emergencies. On Gettysburg's last day, Gibbon's division had stood squarely in the path of the Rebels' gallant but futile charge up Cemetery Hill. Gibbon was wounded while riding along the battle line under heavy fire.

Fearless, eccentric Francis Barlow was a Boston Brahmin who spent part of his childhood at Brook Farm, where Ralph Waldo Emerson was one of his teachers; his mother, Almira, was a close friend of Margaret Fuller. He was valedictorian of his 1855 Harvard graduating class and was practicing law in New York when the war began. By November 1861 he was a lieutenant colonel with the 61st New York. At Antietam, he commanded a brigade that slaughtered Rebels in the sunken road. Clean-shaven, pale, and slightly built, he was nicknamed "the Boy General" and was often seen dressed in a flannel, checkered shirt, threadbare trousers, and blue kepi, with a large cavalry saber at his waist. A Harvard classmate, Lieutenant Colonel Theodore Lyman of Meade's staff, thought he resembled "a highly independent mounted newsboy."

Barlow's men were skeptical about him at first, but they found him to be cool under fire, as well as a strict disciplinarian. They also learned to respect his volcanic temper. Barlow so despised shirkers and deserters that he would strike them with the flat of his big cavalry sword, or, when especially wrathful, curse, kick, and punch them. Barlow later wrote that he would have executed every man who, without good reason, fell out, or flinched in battle. "It would establish a discipline and a spirit which would have saved thousands of lives."

Barlow took over a division of XI Corps six weeks before Gettysburg. On the first day of that battle, A. P. Hill's corps crushed XI Corps, and Barlow was badly wounded and nearly captured while trying to rally his men. During his convalescence, he lobbied for a division in II Corps and got one.[32]

MORALE IN II Corps might have been better. Many former III Corps soldiers resented losing their corps identities and still defiantly wore their old corps insignia. Moreover, twenty-two regiments of three-year volunteers were due to muster out in June and July—worrisome to officers who feared the men might become hypercautious in combat with their enlistments ending.

Some casualty-depleted regiments were less than pleased with the replacements that were arriving. In April, the 20th Massachusetts, known as the Harvard Regiment, had received 200 Swiss and German recruits from Hamburg; most could not speak English, which required officers at first to conduct basic drill by example, without verbal orders.[33]

While II Corps had had more than its share of losses and dislocations, the inspiring Winfield Scott Hancock, one of the great heroes of Gettysburg, was a major reason that it remained as effective as it was. The son of a Pennsylvania lawyer, Hancock graduated from West Point in 1844 and had been in the army for twenty years. During the Peninsular campaign, General George McClellan, a fellow Pennsylvanian and impressed like everyone else by Hancock's majestic bearing, nicknamed him "The Superb." In battle, Hancock's "thundering voice" could be heard bellowing orders and encouragement. Off the battlefield, he was a genial man, and a fastidious one; every day, he put on a clean white shirt with gleaming cuff links.

At Chancellorsville, Hancock's division, while under a terrible artillery barrage, covered the army's retreat to the Rapidan. Hancock took charge of II Corps just in time for Gettysburg. During the first day's fighting on July 1, Meade also gave him command of the shattered I and XI corps. When those shell-shocked men saw Hancock, wrote General Schurz of XI Corps, "His mere presence was a reinforcement, and everybody on the field felt stronger for his being there." An awed officer said of Hancock, "I think that if he were in citizen's clothes, and should give commands in the army to those who did not know him, he would be likely to be obeyed at once." With the remnants of those two corps and his II Corps, Hancock organized the Union's crucial defenses on Cemetery and Culp's Hills.

Hancock's corps stood squarely in the path of the massive Rebel frontal assault on Cemetery Hill on July 3. During the bombardment preceding it, he rode slowly along his line encouraging his men, who were crouched behind the hill's low stone walls.

When the attack came, Hancock was wounded while rallying his dwindling force against the 11,000 attackers. A musket ball drove a nail and fragments from his wooden saddle pommel into his thigh—a spurting wound that a witness compared to "the stab of a butcher's knife." The bleeding was stanched by a tourniquet improvised from a knotted handkerchief and a pistol barrel, and Hancock remained on the field until the attack was repulsed. Disabled for months, Hancock returned to command II Corps at the end of 1863, but five months later he had not yet fully recovered. He usually traveled by ambulance; it was less painful than riding a horse, which he did only on the battlefield.[34]

THE CHANCELLORSVILLE VETERANS found the Wilderness the same as before: second-growth pines and black oak, growing thickly beside dogwood, hazel, chestnut, and among incredibly clotted undergrowth that hid the contours of the Wilderness's low ridges, knolls, ravines, and swamps. The dense, scrubby vegetation rose like a wall.

At the fall line between the piedmont and coastal plain, the Wilderness had once been virgin forest and fields. A Virginia colonial governor, Colonel Alexander Spotswood, mined iron in the area in the early 1700s; the old-growth forest was cut down to feed the iron and gold smelters. When the minerals finally played out in the early nineteenth century, dense, nearly impenetrable second growth had overspread the area.

Even beyond the old Chancellorsville battlefield, the desolate region dampened the soldiers' spirits. Veterans could not forget the screams of the wounded, the smell of men incinerated by brush fires, and the feeling of bafflement occasioned by Hooker's unexpected timidity and precipitate retreat—when more than one-third of his army had not fought at all.[35]

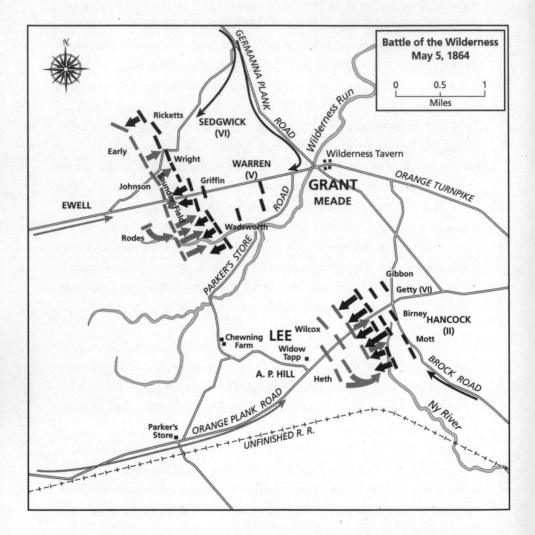

Battle of the Wilderness
May 5, 1864

0   0.5   1
Miles

Reflecting on the beginning of a new campaign, Major Henry Abbott of the 20th Massachusetts recalled that at Gettysburg the II Corps lost 45 percent of its men. "It will probably lose 50 percent this time, that is about 15,000," he wrote in a letter to his mother. "It makes me sad to look at this gallant regiment which I am instructing and disciplining for slaughter, to think that probably 250 or 300 of the 400 which go in, will get bowled out." John Perry, a surgeon in Abbott's regiment, anticipated being extremely busy in the days ahead. "No one seems to know what is to be done beyond marching, and that marching under Grant means moving toward the enemy."[36]

The high command knew that it faced a climactic fight. Grant believed that he could end the "standoff" in Virginia that had lasted three years. "The two armies had been confronting each other so long, without any decisive result, that they hardly knew which could whip," he wrote.

And so Grant came to the momentous realization that in order to triumph, individual victories and defeats must necessarily matter less to him than they had to his predecessors Hooker, Burnside, Pope, and McClellan. One defeat had been reason enough for each of them to abandon his strategy and withdraw to safety.

Grant was neither shrewder, nor more perceptive than they, but he was readier to take risks and he possessed a quality that they did not—perseverance, forged in the failures and misfortunes of his civilian life.

He might be just what the unlucky Army of the Potomac needed. Win or lose, Grant would go ahead. The romantic chivalry with which the war had begun had vanished in the red gore of Gettysburg and Chickamauga, replaced by simple mathematics: the ruthless application of greater numbers, firepower, and logistics to slowly destroy the Confederate army while moving inexorably southward—described by Grant's aide, Lieutenant Colonel Horace Porter, as "a moving siege."[37]

2

Thursday, May 5, 1864, Early Morning
Orange Plank Road

OUTSIDE A DERELICT market known as Parker's Store, Union cavalrymen saddled up at daybreak. Their smoking campfires were the only blemishes on the clear, dew-scrubbed morning, which betrayed no hint of the horrors to come on this day.

James Wilson, the 3rd Cavalry Division commander, was one of Grant's few generals from the Western Theater. The goateed Wilson was just twenty-six and had never led cavalry, having served on Grant's staff and as director of the new cavalry bureau in Washington, where he had excelled.

He had been given a critical job: to monitor the three main roads feeding into Brock Road from the west for signs of Lee's army. The assignment had fallen to him by default. Phil Sheridan's two other cavalry divisions were riding in the opposite direction, toward Fredericksburg, in the hope of striking the Rebel cavalry while it was conducting a dress review at Hamilton's Crossing. But the review had been cancelled, and Sheridan's troopers were embarked on a wild-goose chase.

Meade had ordered Wilson to ride to Craig's Meeting House on Catharpin Road, the southernmost of the three thoroughfares he was assigned to watch. "He will keep out parties on the Orange pike and plank roads," Meade's orders had said.[38]

But Wilson had not left any troopers on the Orange Turnpike; in fact, he had conducted no reconnaissance there. With Griffin's division bivouacking on the turnpike, Wilson had seen no need. He had ridden a few miles south to the next east-west thoroughfare, Orange Plank Road, and had camped at Parker's Store.

Before leaving for Craig's Meeting House, eight miles away on back roads through shadowy, thicket-choked woods, Wilson ordered Lieutenant Colonel John Hammond to remain behind with 500 troopers from his 5th New York Cavalry and watch the plank road.

Hammond and his men rode west on the plank road—and straight into A. P. Hill's Third Corps, which had left its camp at New Verdiersville before daybreak. Confederate cavalry and long columns of sinewy, deeply tanned men in gray were streaming down the plank road, with the sun glinting off their musket barrels. Robert E. Lee, Hill, and Stuart rode at the head of 15,000 men in two divisions.

Hammond was aware that if Hill's corps reached Brock Road, it would cut the Army of the Potomac in half and wreck Grant's offensive as it was just beginning. Nearly 100,000 Union troops were within ten miles of the vital Brock Road–Orange Plank Road crossroads, but, for all practical purposes, 500 mounted New Yorkers stood the best chance of stopping the Rebels from occupying it.

The incredibly mismatched forces collided west of Parker's Store. With their Spencer repeating rifles blazing, Hammond's troops began waging a tenacious delaying action, some of them fighting dismounted and dodging from tree to ditch to thicket. Hammond sent couriers to warn Meade. All the while, Confederate General William Kirkland's infantry brigade pushed the Yankees steadily back to Parker's Store. Fires left untended by Wilson's men spread to the nearby woods, flames leaping into the sky.[39]

UNKNOWN TO THE adversaries, their furious firefight was under observation by the lead brigades of General Gouverneur Warren's V Corps. Early that morning, Meade had sent V Corps down a primitive road connecting the Orange Turnpike with Parker's Store, four miles away, to take up a position on the plank road. VI Corps, which had bivouacked between the turnpike and the river, was going to replace V Corps on the turnpike, while II Corps, proceeding down other roads from the Chancellorsville mansion, would seize the Catharpin Road–Brock Road crossroad and march west to Craig's Meeting House, Wilson's destination.

Meade did not believe that Lee would attack the Army of the Potomac on the Brock Road; he thought Lee would instead reoccupy his old defensive positions at Mine Run, on the plank road west of Parker's Store, and wait for Meade to attack him there. And so Meade intended to menace Lee frontally at Mine Run with V and VI Corps on the turnpike and plank roads, while II Corps, to their south, marched out Catharpin Road and looped around Lee's right flank.

Meade had seriously underestimated Lee and had based the day's battle plan on a false premise.

Setting out at 5 a.m. from its camp near the Lacy house, General Samuel Crawford's division led the V Corps down narrow, overgrown Parker's Store Road toward the plank road. Behind Crawford came the division of fifty-six-year-old James Wadsworth, a wealthy New York landowner and politician, and a proven warrior. Griffin's division, arrayed along the turnpike, was to fall in behind Crawford and Wadsworth and serve as their rearguard. Warren's resourceful pioneers "cut alley-ways through the thickets with axes and hatchets," transforming the backwoods trail into a serviceable road for a large army corps. They widened it to twenty feet, built bridges, and straightened its turns. Even so, the dense woods crowded the road, and there was little room for maneuvering.[40]

When Crawford's men reached the Chewning farm, on a hill fortuitously overlooking the Orange Plank Road, they were stunned to see Union cavalry furiously battling Rebel infantrymen at Parker's Store. Crawford was in an ideal position to smash Hill's left flank with a surprise attack. Should he proceed, he asked Warren?

ON THE TURNPIKE, the division of General Charles Griffin, a crusty Mexican War veteran and Indian fighter, was not in a heightened state of alert at its bivouac a mile west of Wilderness Tavern. His division, and the rest of V Corps for that matter, was under the impression that Wilson's troopers were patrolling to the west and would alert them if Rebels were sighted. But Wilson's men were miles away and the turnpike west of Griffin was unguarded.

Around 6 a.m., as Griffin prepared to enter Parker's Store Road behind Wadsworth, his pickets reported a dust cloud to the west on the turnpike. They then saw mounted men—it was the 1st North Carolina Cavalry— followed by lanky, long-striding Confederate infantrymen from General Edward "Allegheny" Johnson's division—the lead elements of Richard Ewell's Second Corps.

Griffin alerted Warren, who ordered him to send a force to assess the Rebels' strength. The 18th Massachusetts cautiously advanced on the right of the pike and the 83rd Pennsylvania on the left, reaching an abandoned cornfield, part of the Saunders's farm. They watched Rebel foot soldiers stream down the turnpike and disappear into the woods ahead, on either side of the road. Gunfire raked Griffin's reconnaissance force, and eighteen-year-old Private Charles H. Wilson of the 18th Massachusetts became the campaign's first battle death. The Confederates were present in force, Griffin informed Warren. Griffin's men dug in at the edge of Saunders's Field and waited for instructions.

"I do not believe that Warren ever had a greater surprise in his life," wrote Meade's ordnance officer, Lieutenant Morris Schaff, who was with Warren when he received the news. "His thin, solemn, darkly sallow face was nowhere lightened by even a transitory flare."

Indeed, Warren, a fussy man who liked limericks, decidedly lacked gravitas. One officer judged him "a lightweight, although a good soldier and engineer officer." Theodore Lyman of Meade's staff wrote, "Fancy a small, slender man, with a sun-burnt face, two piercing black eyes, and withal bearing a most ludicrous resemblance to cousin Mary Pratt!"[41]

But during the second day at Gettysburg, the alertness of Warren, then Meade's chief engineer, saved Little Round Top and, consequently, Meade's fortifications on Cemetery Hill. Discovering that Little Round Top was undefended, Warren urged Meade to rush troops to the vital point. As a brigade jogged up the rocky promontory, Warren helped push two guns to the summit, just in time to repel the first attacks by a Rebel division.

A grateful Meade named Warren temporary commander of II Corps when Hancock received his painful wound during Pickett's charge. Warren proved himself up to the job at Bristoe Station, where he baited a trap and bloodied Hill's corps when it fell into it. In 1864, he assumed command of V Corps during the army reorganization; his predecessor, George Sykes, who had succeeded Meade to the command, had been criticized for slowness during the Mine Run campaign.[42]

When Warren informed Meade that Confederate infantry were advancing on the turnpike, Meade suspended the march to Parker's Store and stopped Hancock's II Corps at the Brock Road–Catharpin Road crossroad.

Nonetheless, Meade was still not convinced that Lee intended to strike Meade's army on Brock and Germanna roads. "I think the enemy is trying to delay our movement, and will not give battle," he wrote Grant, "but of this we shall soon see. For the present I will stop here."[43]

Meade instructed Warren to turn around Crawford's and Wadsworth's divisions and, in concert with Griffin, attack the Rebels on the turnpike. He ordered VI Corps, on Germanna Road north of Warren's corps, to send troops to reinforce Griffin.

Although acting on the supposition that Lee was going to attack, Meade believed that "Lee is simply making a demonstration to gain time," he wrote Grant at 9 a.m. At about the same hour, New York *Times* correspondent William Swinton overheard Meade telling Warren and other officers, "They [the enemy] have left a division to fool us here, while they concentrate and prepare a position towards the North Anna; and what I want is to prevent those fellows from getting back to Mine Run."[44]

ORDERED TO WITHDRAW from the Chewning Farm to the Orange Turnpike to participate in V Corps' planned attack on the Rebels, Crawford
hesitated. He continued to report on developments on the plank road and
sought clarification of his orders. "Shall I abandon the position I now hold
to connect with General Wadsworth, who is about a half a mile on my
right?"

Warren curtly replied, "You will move to the right as quickly as possible." A member of Warren's staff, Major Washington Roebling—the future builder of the Brooklyn Bridge—who had joined Crawford, instantly
grasped the importance of his position at the farm. To no avail, he urged
Warren to reconsider. "It is of vital importance to hold the field where General Crawford is," he wrote. "Our whole line of battle is turned if the enemy
get possession of it." Roebling urged Crawford to send a regiment to try to
connect with the Union cavalry on the plank road, but the 5th New York
was suddenly pushed back, and the opportunity was lost.[45]

GRANT WAS STILL at Germanna Ford, waiting for Ambrose Burnside's
IX Corps to cross the Rapidan, when he received Meade's report that the
Rebels were coming. Grant shot off a response that clearly illustrated the
difference between him and his predecessors in the East, whose actions
were characterized by caution, prudence, and slowness.

"If any opportunity presents itself for pitching into a part of Lee's army,
do so without giving time for disposition," he wrote. Deciding not to wait
for Burnside, but to leave him a message instead, Grant left Germanna Ford
to join Meade and prod him to move quickly to the attack.[46]

DURING THEIR WEEKLY meetings in Washington with Grant in March
and April, Lincoln and Halleck had undoubtedly discussed Meade's lack of
aggressiveness—Gettysburg and Mine Run being fresh in their memories.
But they were aware that the problem was bigger than Meade; it was insti-
tutional. It was said that the Army of the Potomac was unlucky, but luck
had little to do with it.

The major problems were a congenital balkiness that frustrated the execution of the army's best offensive plans; excuse-making and unceasing
demands on the War Department by its top generals; and a fatal inability

to react quickly and intelligently to changed circumstances. Moreover, the army had never had a commander who could anticipate what Lee would do.

The result, concluded Morris Schaff of Meade's staff, was "the lack of springy formation, and audacious, self-reliant initiative." The army, he wrote, had lacked "skillfully aggressive leadership" in its youth, and had instead been trained "into a life of caution, and the evil of that schooling it had shown on more than one occasion." General James Wadsworth believed the cause might be the regular army officers' enduring "West Point [notion] of Southern superiority. That sometimes accounts for an otherwise unaccountable slowness of attack."[47]

Whatever the reasons, it was understandable that with such a dubious tradition the Army of the Potomac lacked offensive victories. Its few triumphs were defensive: Antietam, insofar as the outcome of Lee's offensive was his retreat; and Gettysburg, where Meade had beaten back Lee's repeated attacks. After Meade failed to interdict Lee in his retreat to Virginia, a seething Lincoln had reportedly muttered, "If I had gone up there I could have whipped them myself."[48]

Lincoln, Halleck, and the war secretary, Edwin Stanton, fervently hoped that Grant would spur the Army of the Potomac to move quicker and hit harder. Grant, aware of these expectations, was determined not to miss any opportunity to strike at Lee.

GRANT NEVER INTENDED to fight a battle inside the Wilderness, wrote Meade's chief of staff, Andrew Humphreys. He planned just the opposite, and the orders for May 5 reflected this aim: to push the army to the southwest in the hope of engaging Lee in more open country and not in the suffocating woodland. But with the Confederates pouring down the turnpike and plank road, a Wilderness battle had now become "unavoidable, not a matter of choice," wrote Humphreys.[49]

Sometime between 9 a.m. and 10 a.m., Grant joined Meade at the turnpike crossroad five miles south of Germanna Ford. They discussed Warren's imminent attack and rode to the top of a knoll near the crossroad's northwest corner to see what was happening; but they could not see the armies' movements below; miles of dense woods cloaked the unfolding drama.

The generals set up adjacent camps nearby. Across the road was a farmhouse belonging to the Lacy family; it became the army's command center.

Grant sat down on the ground with his back to a tree and began coolly whittling a stick, not bothering to take off the yellow-brown thread gloves that he had worn with his dress uniform the previous day. He whittled and smoked cigars while steadily reading updates and issuing orders. By day's end, the gloves would be in shreds.

Meade's staff officers couldn't help but steal glances at the general of the army as he sat there whittling imperturbably; to Meade's staff officers, Grant was a striking contrast to the splenetic Meade. But Grant was not just idly whittling; his mind was ranging over strategic possibilities. "He never made known his plans far in advance to any one," wrote Porter, Grant's aide. "It was his invariable custom to keep his contemplated movements locked up in his own mind to avoid all possibility of their being mentioned."[50]

WITH HIS VESTIGIAL dragoon's moustache from his prewar frontier cavalry service, Richard Stoddert Ewell, bald, sharp-nosed, and pop-eyed, appeared oddly birdlike, and as befitted one with such a singular appearance, he was a notorious eccentric. He ate cracked wheat in an attempt to control his chronic dyspepsia. He lisped in a falsetto voice. He had lost his left leg below the knee in 1862 during the Second Manassas campaign, and affected nonchalance about his wooden leg and crutches. His "flea-bitten gray" horse, Rifle, Ewell's men observed, "was singularly like him—so far as a horse could be like a man."

While recuperating from his wound, the forty-six-year-old bachelor married his widowed first cousin and childhood friend, Lizinka Campbell Brown, a domineering woman who accompanied Ewell on his campaigns. For all his physical and biographical quirks, Ewell had been an extremely effective division commander under Stonewall Jackson, and he now commanded the late Jackson's Second Corps.

Ewell's men, however, soon noticed after his return from convalescent leave that he was a changed man; he was not the decisive, aggressive leader of before. "We were of the opinion that Ewell was not the same soldier he had been when he was a whole man—and a single one," wrote a Second Corps lieutenant, Randolph McKim. He might have once been an excellent division commander, but Gettysburg revealed him to be an irresolute corps commander: his failure to storm Cemetery Hill on the battle's first day deprived the Confederacy of a momentous victory.[51]

Early May 5, Major Robert Stiles, a Second Corps artillery officer, was leading his battalion eastward on the Orange Turnpike when, at a forest crossroad, he encountered Ewell crouched over a small campfire, boiling coffee. Stiles asked Ewell if he could tell him what his orders were.

"Just the orders I like," Ewell replied, "to go right down the [turnpike] and strike the enemy wherever I find him."[52]

BUT WHEN EWELL'S corps encountered Griffin's skirmishers near Saunders's Field, Lee reconsidered. Ewell's aide and stepson, Major Campbell Brown, had brought Lee the tidings of the first contact on the turnpike. Lee told Brown to inform Ewell that "if the enemy were found in large force, he did not want a general engagement brought on till Longstreet cd [sic] come up. . . . If the enemy advanced & showed a willingness to fight he preferred falling back to our own position at Mine Run. Above all, Gen. E. was not to get his troops entangled, so as to be unable to disengage them, in case the enemy were in force."[53]

Lee was struggling with the dilemma posed by his army's advance along separate, parallel roads, with none of the corps supporting the others. How to seize control of the two-to-three-mile gap of dense woodland between the turnpike and plank road—thereby connecting the flanks of the divisions on those roads—would become a priority and a headache for both sides. Until he found a solution, Lee wished to keep Hill's and Ewell's corps advancing more or less in step, while withholding them from a major battle until Longstreet arrived.

When the Army of Northern Virginia consisted of just two corps commanded by Jackson and Longstreet, Lee had routinely given them wide latitude in executing his orders; their successes affirmed his trust in them. Lee had continued the policy after he reorganized the army into three corps and Ewell and Hill were promoted from division to corps command. Consequently, his instructions to his corps commanders, Brown noted, "in fact will allow them to do almost anything provide only it be a *success*."[54]

THE WILDERNESS'S OBDURATENESS and the Army of the Potomac's congenital sluggishness delayed Warren's attack for six hours. Turning around on the narrow Parker's Store road was an ordeal for Wadsworth's and Crawford's divisions. In the dark woods, field officers were forced to use compasses to reorient their units. Cursing soldiers pushed through dense thickets that tore at their hands and faces and ripped their clothing.[55]

At noon, Meade, who had ordered the attack at 7 a.m., rode to the knoll with Grant, who was growing more impatient by the minute, to see if anything was happening. Grant, who had seen nothing like this in the West, told Warren to attack immediately.

An hour later, when still there was no attack, Grant, perhaps fearing that Lincoln's worries about Meade's cautiousness were coming to fruition, barbedly said to Meade that the Army of the Potomac appeared to be reluctant to fight. Stung, Meade turned to Warren and growled, "We are waiting for you."[56]

In truth, division commander Charles Griffin *was* reluctant to attack on the turnpike. Horatio Wright's division from VI Corps had not yet arrived at Saunders's Field, and General Romeyn Ayres, a Griffin brigade commander, friend, and former West Point classmate, rightly feared that a Rebel attack would crush his open flank. Griffin sided with Ayres, and when Warren saw the situation firsthand, he had to agree.

But by 1 p.m., Meade, rebuked by Grant once already, would brook no more argument from Warren; Griffin must attack immediately, with whatever supporting troops were on hand—at this point, just Wadsworth's division on Griffin's left.

Full of foreboding, Griffin sent his division into action. Wadsworth's men struggled forward through the woods on his left. Nearly useless were Warren's two other divisions—Crawford's, stuck in the woods and struggling to advance from the Chewning Farm area, and Robinson's, in reserve a mile away and idle.

THE CONFEDERATES WERE ready for them. The delay had given Ewell's divisions ample preparation time, and Ewell was now clear about his orders. Campbell Brown had returned to Lee after the first skirmish to tell him that Ewell planned to fall back to Mine Run if pushed. Lee told Brown that he had "misinterpreted" what he had said previously—"that he only meant us to fall back, in case we could not hold our position." Informed of his new orders, Ewell told Brown that "he could hold his ground with ease against any force, so far developed, & sent me to tell this to Gen. Lee."[57]

Griffin's brigades raced across Saunders's Field toward the woods where the Rebels waited. Bullets began falling into the dry soil, kicking up small clouds of dust. It reminded Private Theodore Gerrish of the 20th Maine of "heavy drops of rain falling just before the shower comes in full force."

The storm came soon enough. "A red volcano yawned before us and vomited forth fire, and lead, and death. Our lines staggered for a moment," and then Gerrish and his comrades slammed into the defenders. "Rifle barrels touched [and] the ground shook with the roar of musketry"; men cheered, swore, shouted, and prayed.

Sartell Prentice, an officer of US regulars in Ayres's brigade, described how sheets of Confederate musket fire from the woods swept scythe-like from left to right across the advancing Union troops—the Rebels firing in turn, regiment by regiment, from one flank to the other. Two revolutions were made without great effect; the third pass began as the brigade reached the edge of the wood. "How grim and severe it seems now, in its slow, sure movement, and awful in effect! The men fall in groups of eight and ten, and leave great gaps in the line," Prentice wrote.[58]

General Humphreys discerned something "sublime" in the "rising and falling sounds of [the vast] musketry fire that continually swept along the lines of battle, many miles in length." But the men charging through the Rebel fire saw only death, not sublimity. "As we ran shouting across the field many of our comrades fell on the right and on the left," wrote Corporal Norton Shepard of the 146th New York of Ayres's brigade. "It seemed almost impossible that any one should escape the storm of leaden hail."

Yet, half of Shepard's regiment reached the woods—a tangled place, they quickly learned, "where nothing could be seen a hundred feet away. . . . A colonel could not know of the whereabouts of all his regiment, and a general had no standing. It was a wild and disconnected battling of regiment with regiment, of company with company, without plan, or purpose, or knowledge or result," wrote Prentice.

Enough Yankees survived the dash to drive out General John Jones's brigade of Virginians—many of them recent conscripts. Jones was killed while attempting to rally his men.[59]

To Griffin's left, Wadsworth's three brigades—those of Lysander Cutler, James Rice, and Roy Stone—plunged blindly into the wall of vegetation, and appeared to have been swallowed up by the swampy woods, thickets, and the "champion mud hole of mud holes." Regiments lost contact with one another, coordination among the brigades became impossible, and the enemy was, for all practical purposes, invisible.

Smoke and the dense forest shut out the sunlight and made it impossible for men to see more than a few yards. "The only guide to the locality of the opponent was the noise of the scrambling through the network of briers and floundering through the mud and water," wrote a member of Stone's brigade. Officers consulted pocket compasses to establish their location and determine where to place their lines. "A change of position often presented an operation more like a problem of ocean navigation than a question of military manoeuvers [sic]," observed Grant's aide, Porter.

Volleys of musketry drowned out the crackling and splashing, the gunfire amplified by the trees, which also created an echo effect that unnerved even hardened combat veterans. An officer of the 150th Pennsylvania, part of Stone's brigade, said they "quailed before the leaden blast which cut and stripped the young pines as if a cyclone had swept over them. . . . It was a fearful experience."[60]

The woods' absorption of Wadsworth's division meant that Griffin had little protection on his left flank, while his right flank remained completely exposed, because VI Corps had not yet arrived. The very situation that Griffin and Ayres had tried to warn Warren about had now transpired.[61]

Confederate reinforcements poured into the woods where Jones's brigade had foundered. Robert Rodes's and Edward "Allegheny" Johnson's divisions appeared on Jones's left, flanking Ayres's brigade and preventing Horatio Wright's VI Corps division from reaching him.

And then Ayres was flanked on his left when the brigade beside him advanced too fast, and the 1st North Carolina from Johnson's division slipped behind it. In a broad ravine bisecting Saunders's Field, men fought with clubbed muskets and bayonets, and the North Carolinians captured two Union guns and scores of Yankees.

Griffin's attack collapsed under the combined pressure of Rodes and Johnson, and a "perfect stampede" occurred. To avoid being trampled by the fleeing Yankees, the North Carolinians jumped into the Saunders's Field ravine. "This vast herd of fleeing Federals came rushing through and over us without firing a gun or speaking a word," wrote Colonel Hamilton Brown.[62]

Unbeknownst to Griffin, Warren, and Wadsworth, their attacks, while poorly conceived and disjointedly executed, had pressed two of Ewell's divisions, those of Johnson and Rodes, nearly to the breaking point. When Jones's brigade broke for the rear around them, Ewell and the commander of his reserve division, Jubal Early, tried unsuccessfully to stop the men's flight.

EARLY SUMMONED HIS best brigade, General John Gordon's Georgians, to retrieve the situation. Thin and ramrod-straight, Gordon grew up on a plantation, became a lawyer and, when the war began, was operating a north Georgia coal mine with his father. Although Gordon had never received military training, he was a natural combat leader. His troops were in the thick of the fighting at Seven Pines, Malvern Hill, Antietam (where he was wounded five times), and Gettysburg.

Gordon brought up his brigade in compact marching order, and it breasted the waves of retreating Rebels like a ship cleaving stormy seas. The side of the road, the Georgians noticed, was strewn with packs of playing cards, discarded by Rebels repenting their sinful ways before going into combat.[63]

Ewell, stressed and excitable, rode up to Gordon and said, "General Gordon, the fate of the day depends on you, sir." Gordon replied, "These men will save it, sir."[64]

Gordon instantly counterattacked with one regiment to give him time to organize the rest of his brigade. Hat in hand, Gordon rode along the front of his brigade before sending it in. "Soldiers, we have always driven the enemy before us, but this day we are going to scatter them like the leaves of the forest." A member of his brigade summed up his men's feelings for Gordon: "He's the most prettiest thing you ever did see on a field of fight. It'd put fight into a whipped chicken just to look at him."

The Georgians plowed through the center of an advancing Union brigade; it was Lysander Cutler's fabled "Iron Brigade," doughty Western troops identifiable by their black slouch hats. They had attacked along the southern edge of Saunders's Field and helped break Jones's brigade, but had then gotten tangled in the thickets and woods. Perplexed at finding Gordon's brigade among them, the Yankees continued advancing on both sides of Gordon's men. Gordon described the situation as "both unique and alarming"—alarming because the Georgians potentially faced double envelopment and capture.

But then Gordon had a wildly inventive idea about how to transform a dire situation into one redounding to his advantage. He ordered his men to halt, and then issued a string of crisp orders that realigned the brigade into a single column, with his men standing back-to-back, perpendicular to the flanks of the Iron Brigade. Gordon ordered the two outward-facing wings forward simultaneously. With a shout, the Rebels drove the Iron Brigade from the field for the first time in its history.[65]

The Iron Brigade's precipitate retreat panicked the unit behind it— Colonel Andrew Dennison's reserve brigade of Robinson's division. The two brigades did not stop falling back until they reached the Lacy house on Germanna Road.

At the same time, Ewell's North Carolina brigade, commanded by Junius Daniel, was crushing another Wadsworth brigade, New Yorkers and Pennsylvanians led by James Rice. The North Carolinians attacked Rice's men in a jungle-like hollow. The disoriented Yankees followed their dazed comrades to the Lacy house, with Daniel's men in hot pursuit, all the way to the Lacy property. A battery of V Corps artillery, idle until now because of the dense woods, unlimbered and drove off the Rebel infantrymen.

GENERAL ARMISTEAD LONG, Ewell's artillery chief, wrote that in the jungle between the turnpike and plank road, "death came unseen; regiments stumbled on each other, and sent swift destruction into each other's ranks guided by the crackling of the bushes."[66]

Groping through the crepuscular light, the Yankees at times had to turn sideways to pass between the closely spaced trees wreathed in vines. "In that dismal Wilderness, in which a bird had scarce heart to peep there was . . . something oppressive in the dim light and strange quiet."[67]

Roy Stone's brigade of Wadsworth's division plunged into a swamp south of Saunders's Field, near where Cutler's and Rice's brigades had been routed. Rebels hidden in the thickets loosed a crashing musket volley as the Pennsylvanians foundered in the muck. Panicked by the sudden ambush, the 149th Pennsylvania fired into the backs of the 143rd Pennsylvania. The survivors fled the swamp.[68]

AT 2:30 P.M., an hour and a half after the offensive began, the Union troops were back where they began, licking their wounds. At the Lacy house, Wadsworth's three battered brigades were pushed into a defensive line to the left of Griffin's division, back in its entrenchments on the east side of Saunders's Field. Crawford's division, which had seen little action all day, was recalled from Chewning's Farm as Rebel regiments closed in. Its rearguard fight up Parker's Store Road was the division's major action of the day.

Warren, Griffin, and Ayres had been right: no attack should have been made until Wright's division could protect Ayres's flank. Grant's and Meade's impetuosity, and the uncoordinated attacks that followed, had forestalled any possibility of success. Thousands of men had fallen dead or wounded for no gain.

Never one to hide his feelings, Griffin rode to Meade's headquarters to rage at his superiors. "Stern and angry," he subjected Grant, Meade, and their staffs to a withering tirade. He had obeyed his orders, shattering a brigade of Ewell's corps and driving it three quarters of a mile. But with Wright's division not supporting his right, he said, and Wadsworth forced back on his left, both flanks were exposed, and he had been compelled to fall back, a pointless disaster.

Lyman, of Meade's staff, wrote that Griffin's outburst implied "censure on Wright and apparently also on his corps commander, Warren." Grant's chief of staff, John Rawlins, "considered the language mutinous and wished him put under arrest." Grant, who had stopped whittling to listen to Griffin's harangue, appeared to agree. "Who is this General Gregg?" he asked Meade. "You ought to arrest him." This time, Meade was the unruffled one. He began to button Grant's coat for him, saying, "It's Griffin, not Gregg; and it's only his way of talking."[69]

EVEN AFTER GRIFFIN's rant about the tardiness of Wright's division, it had not appeared on Griffin's right. The movement would take an incredible six hours—two hours for Thomas Neill's brigade from Getty's division to re-inforce Wright, and four more hours for the assembled task force to march the mile and a half from Spotswood Plantation to Saunders's Field, a march that normally might have taken an hour.

The road was narrow and overgrown, and the surrounding terrain ideal for ambush: crisscrossed by knife-like ridges and streams, gullies, and swamps. Rebels from Edward "Allegheny" Johnson's brigades bushwhacked Wright's men at every opportunity as they crept single-file through the dreadful landscape. "As our line advanced, it would suddenly come upon a line of gray-coated rebels, lying upon the ground, covered with dried leaves, and concealed by the chaparral, when the rebels would rise, deliver a mur-derous fire, and retire."

The Rebels set fire to the woods, incinerating men from both armies who were incapacitated by their wounds. There were other horrors, too. Thomas Hyde, a VI Corps staff officer, had just dismounted to fix his horse's bit when a cannonball beheaded a nearby soldier. "The head struck me, and I was knocked down, covered with brains and blood. Even my mouth, proba-bly gaping in wonder where that shell would strike, was filled. . . . I was not much use as a staff officer for fully fifteen minutes."

About 3 p.m., Colonel Emory Upton's brigade from Wright's division at last reached Saunders's Field and fell in beside V Corps. Fighting erupted along the line and deep into the woods to the north, where the rest of Wright's men had taken up positions. The musketry at times was so intensive that it became "one continuous roll of sound." The attacks and counterattacks produced high casualties and no measurable advantage for either side.

Sedgwick requested assistance from Ambrose Burnside's IX Corps, which was idle in Wright's rear. For some reason, Grant, who alone had the authority, never ordered it into action, yet another lapse on the turnpike on this day. Some historians later judged the day's poor coordination of units to be the worst in the Army of the Potomac's history.[70]

THE DEEP GULLY in the middle of Saunders's Field had become both sanctuary and prison for hundreds of Yankees and Rebels, wounded and whole. The wallow provided safety from alert snipers who would pick off any enemy soldier who carelessly exposed himself. The many able-bodied men trapped there could not safely rejoin their units without drawing fire.

The men's plight was briefly relieved by a comical incident, which began with a Yankee and Rebel taunting one another, and then agreeing to fight it out with fists on the turnpike, with the winner making the loser his prisoner. The shooting stopped when the men emerged from the gully. When they removed their coats in full view of both sides and began trading punches, the enemy troops began loudly cheering their respective champions. "The Johnny soon had the Yank down who surrendered, and both quietly rolled into the gulley." The shooting resumed.[71]

EWELL'S SECOND CORPS had repulsed all of Meade's attacks, inflicting heavy losses on the enemy. Ewell had done precisely what Lee had asked of him; he had held his position and tested the enemy's strength without committing himself to an all-out battle. His men had fought splendidly, and Ewell and his generals had led them well. Three brigade commanders, however, were out of commission: Jones, shot dead while calmly watching the approaching enemy from horseback; and John Pegram and Leroy Stafford, wounded. Pegram would survive, but Stafford would die three days later at the Spotswood Hotel in Richmond.[72]

As the afternoon shadows lengthened, Ewell repositioned his men and extended his line farther to his left. The Rebels improved their works west of Saunders's Field, and in the woods north and south of the turnpike. The fighting flared and receded; the Rebels held fast.

When Longstreet's First Corps joined the rest of Lee's army—Lee hoped it would be that night—the Second Corps would be ready to attack.

3

Thursday, May 5, 1864, Late Morning
Orange Plank Road

THREE MILES TO the south, a separate battle raged on the Orange Plank Road, wreathed in gray gunsmoke and thick, black smoke that billowed from crackling fires in the woods. Henry Heth's men from A. P. Hill's corps continued to steadily push the 5th New York Cavalry eastward down the plank road.

By 10:30 a.m., the situation had become perilous. Just a mile behind the Union troopers was Brock Road; if Hill's men seized the crossroad, they would isolate Hancock's II Corps to the south from V and VI corps, which were then preparing to attack Ewell along the turnpike.

Aware that if the plank road emergency was not quickly addressed, the Confederate Third Corps might wreck the Virginia campaign before it began, Meade pulled George Getty's VI Corps division out of Wilderness Tavern and sent it quick-timing south down Brock Road to the crossroad. He also redirected Winfield Scott Hancock's II Corps to the junction. It would take Hancock longer to get there because the lead brigades of his corps were already two miles past Todd's Tavern and headed west down Catharpin Road to carry out Grant's original plan of interposing itself between Lee's army and Richmond. Hancock would now have to turn around his 23,000-man corps—no easy feat—and send it pounding north on Brock Road, to the junction four miles away.[73]

When he received Meade's instructions, Getty had just sent one of his brigades to Saunders's Field to aid Griffin's beleaguered division. Told to hurry to the support of an understrength cavalry regiment under attack by Rebel infantry columns, Getty, an efficient, able career Army officer—and a West Point classmate of Ewell and William T. Sherman—got his 6,000 men on the road quickly.

A mile from the junction, Getty and his staff heard heavy firing and galloped ahead. They arrived as Hammond's 5th New York Cavalry troopers came boiling out of the plank road "like a flock of wild geese," as a Getty staff officer observed. Right behind the cavalrymen were Rebel skirmishers. With their rapid-firing Spencer repeating rifles, Hammond's New Yorkers, often fighting dismounted, had waged a textbook defensive battle for five hours against a powerful Confederate force. At a cost of just 79 of its 500 men, the 5th New York, it appeared at the moment, had saved the Army of the Potomac from disaster.

It was now up to Getty and his staff, who had barely beaten Hill's men to the crossroad, to preserve Hammond's strategic victory. With their headquarters flag snapping in the breeze amid the gunsmoke, the mounted officers stood their ground against the advancing Rebels. "The presence of my small retinue, consisting of my staff and orderlies, standing firmly at the point in dispute, although under fire, served to delay their advance for a few minutes," Getty wrote.

It was long enough for Getty's lead brigade, sprinting the last hundred yards or so, to reach their commander and throw a volley into the enemy. The Confederates recoiled, leaving the road and nearby fields strewn with their dead and wounded, some of them found thirty yards from the crossroad, "so nearly had they obtained possession of it," wrote Getty.

Confederate prisoners, surprised to learn they had been fighting a regiment and not a brigade, told Getty's men that they belonged to Heth's division, the vanguard of Hill's corps. Getty placed his men in defensive positions and hoped that Hancock's troops would soon arrive. For two hours, the dense woodlands surrounding the crossroad yielded no clues as to what would happen next.[74]

As SOON AS the Yankees crossed the river, Robert E. Lee's men had expected to "fall upon them with the speed of lightning and with tremendous power," wrote Lee's adjutant, Colonel Walter Taylor. He did not understand why the Union high command might believe otherwise. "It was, indeed, a bold movement, but, strange to relate, it appears not to have been expected by the enemy."[75]

At first light that day, Hill's Third Corps had broken camp ten miles away at New Verdiersville. Hill's two divisions, led by Heth and Cadmus Wilcox, soon reached their old Mine Run works. The troops anticipated taking up their former positions there. But when they did not stop, someone shouted, "Mars Bob is going for them this time," and the men erupted in cheers and Rebel yells.[76]

Around 8 a.m., when they were just three miles from Brock Road, Heth's infantrymen clashed with Hammond's New Yorkers at Parker's Store. The Union troopers' fierce resistance made Heth cautious. He remembered well how his division's fight with General John Buford's Union cavalry in Gettysburg on July 1, 1863, had ignited the bloody, three-day battle in which he had been severely wounded; on July 3, the division he now commanded had charged Cemetery Hill alongside George Pickett's division.

Obeying Lee's instructions to not bring on a general engagement, Heth slowed the advance. Two miles further, the Confederate infantrymen came to a small farm belonging to a Widow Tapp on the north side of the road. There they halted. In the clearing were a small house, a corncrib, and a log stable in the northwest corner of the field. Lee and Hill made their head-quarters on the Widow Tapp's property and unlimbered First Corps' guns in the clearing.[77]

In the Tapp field, Lee, Hill, and Jeb Stuart were resting and discussing their next move when out of the woods to the north emerged a line of blue-uniformed skirmishers. Mere yards from the Yankees lay potentially the greatest prize of the war.

Lee rose and walked rapidly toward the plank road, calling for his adjutant, Taylor. Stuart stood and stared at the interlopers, while Hill remained seated. "We were within pistol shot," wrote Colonel William Palmer, Hill's chief of staff, "when to our surprise the Federal officer gave the command 'right about' and disappeared in the timber, as much alarmed at finding himself in the presence of Confederate troops as we were at their unexpected appearance."[78]

The Yankees' appearance prompted Lee to act on his growing concern about the gap between the turnpike and the plank road. Obviously, there were bluecoats in those woods that might either menace Hill's left flank or Ewell's right, which was unprotected as he fought his separate battle on the Orange Turnpike.

On Lee's orders, Wilcox's division plunged into the solid mass of vegetation to connect Hill's forces with Ewell's and to root out any enemy troops between the two corps. At the same time, Lee sent Heth's division ahead on the plank road toward Brock Road, less than a mile away, to make contact with the enemy without bringing on a general engagement until Longstreet arrived. Heth's men advanced cautiously on both sides of the plank road. Not long after Wilcox's men disappeared into the woods, there was an explosion of gunfire on the plank road. The Yankees were attacking.[79]

AT 3:30 P.M., to the relief of Getty and his brigade commanders, Hancock's vanguard troops, out of breath from jogging nearly a mile, appeared at the Brock Road–Orange Plank Road crossroad. II Corps' lead divisions began forming on Getty's left and digging breastworks on the west side of Brock Road, which was "very narrow and heavily wooded on both sides," in the crossroad area.

Meade and Grant had grown impatient as the afternoon hours passed without major action on the plank road. Soon after Hancock's men began arriving at the junction, Meade directed Getty to attack at once, with or without II Corps. When Hancock arrived, he was to pitch in with a division on Getty's right, one on his left, and the remaining two in reserve. Grant wished to initiate the battle on the plank road as he had done on the turnpike.

Both armies were now witnessing for the first time Grant's swarming offensive style; never before had the Army of the Potomac displayed such relentless aggressiveness.[80]

Getty's assault struck Heth's Rebels as they advanced toward the crossroad behind lines of skirmishers. The Confederates instantly took defensive measures, barring the road, their lines extending far into the dark woods on either side of it.

With a loud cheer, Getty's three brigades attacked, pushing back the center of the Confederate line. Colonel Lewis Grant's Vermont Brigade led the assault and paid dearly for it; flame jetted from dense lines of Rebels, overlapping the Vermonters on three sides. Private Wilbur Fisk's regiment, the 2nd Vermont, lost 264 men. "Along the whole length of the line I doubt if a single tree could have been found that had not been pierced several times with bullets," wrote Fisk, whose clothing and cap were perforated.[81]

This was John Perry's first exposure to the Rebel yell. The 20th Massachusetts surgeon professed to "have never, since I was born, heard so fearful a noise. . . . It is nothing like a hurrah, but rather a regular wildcat screech. Each shell that burst over the heads of our men was followed by one of these yells, and the sound was appalling."[82]

Two of Hancock's divisions joined Getty and the three divisions advanced together. Grouped in the middle of the road, Union artillery blasted the Rebel defenders. Repeated attacks, followed by a massive Confederate counterattack at 5:30 p.m., littered the ground with the dead and wounded from both armies.[83]

BETWEEN THE JUNGLE-LIKE vegetation and the smoke from the intensive musketry and wildfires, the Yankees charging into the woods were lucky to see a dozen paces before them—until sheets of enemy musketry lit the way for them, often to instant death or a lingering one. Many of the survivors never saw the enemy. It was "a wrestle as blind as midnight," wrote Lieutenant Colonel Badeau, Grant's military secretary. General John Gibbon

...u it as "literally fighting in the dark for the possession of certain ...oads."[84]

The wall of vegetation concealed a jumbled landscape: low, accordion ridges, separated by streams, gullies, and swamps. The Rebels, who had marched, bivouacked, and fought in the Wilderness many times during the war, knew it intimately. Poor maps were no aid to the Yankees' already imprecise understanding of the area. Thus, for the moment, the terrain favored Heth, mitigating the severe disadvantage under which he operated—his 7,500 men facing three attacking divisions numbering 17,000 troops. "Such woods, if you have one line which is to remain stationary and on the defence, are an advantage; but if you attack, or if you must relieve one line with another, it is the worst place in the world," wrote Lieutenant J. F. J. Caldwell of the 1st South Carolina. Captain Henry Clay Albright of the 26th North Carolina said the trees and undergrowth grew so thickly that it was "almost impossible for a body of troops to move in any direction and form a line."[85]

At the height of the fighting, the 11th North Carolina lay down behind "a line of dead Federals so thick as to form a partial breastwork, showing how stubbornly they had fought and how severely they had suffered," wrote Colonel W. J. Martin, the regimental commander.[86]

"A butchery pure and simple it was, unrelieved by any of the arts of war," wrote J. M. Waddell, historian for the 46th North Carolina, of the primordial fighting in the woods, without benefit of artillery or cavalry. "It was a mere slugging match in a dense thicket of small growth, where men but a few yards apart fired through the brushwood for hours." The 46th North Carolina lost 201 of its 340 men.[87]

A New York *Tribune* reporter outside the woods was unable to see the actual fighting, but he could plainly see its effect, in surreal detail. "The wounded stream out, and fresh troops pour in. Stretchers pass out with ghastly burdens, and go back reeking with blood for more."[88]

Mott's division on Getty's left became disoriented in the undergrowth—where saplings were packed together so closely "that it was only by pushing them apart that a man could make his way through them"—and lost unit cohesiveness. Little more than a mob, Mott's men were unable to effectively return fire, as powerful volleys from Heth's division in the woods tore through them, shattering their ranks. They withdrew in confusion.[89]

Hancock, on horseback and in agony from his unhealed Gettysburg wound, was juggling multiple crises. Getty was nearly out of ammunition; Hancock sent John Gibbon's division to his relief. When Hancock was told that Mott's division had "broken, and is coming back," Hancock raised himself up in his saddle and roared, "Tell him to stop them!" and galloped off to personally rally Mott's men on Brock Road.[90]

Colonel Charles Weygant, commander of the 124th New York, wrote that some of Mott's men fell in with his regiment and Hobart Ward's brigade of Birney's division, and together they advanced on the Confederates. The seesaw battle began to tilt in the Yankees' favor. "Slowly but steadily they retired before our fresh and withering fire, contesting every foot of ground. We soon began to pass over their dead and wounded, but we left the ground strewn with not a few of our own men."[91]

Red-bearded, muscular General Alexander Hays, a personal friend of Hancock and Grant, was shot in the head and killed instantly while readying his brigade to attack on Getty's right. Earlier in the day, he had written a premonitory letter to his wife:

> This morning was beautiful, for
> Lightly and brightly shone the sun,
> As if the morn was a jocund one.
>
> Although we were anticipating a march at eight o'clock, it might
> have been an appropriate harbinger of the day of the regeneration of
> mankind; but it only brought to remembrance, through the throats
> of many bugles, that duty enjoined upon each one, perhaps, before
> the setting sun, to lay down a life for his country.[92]

Theodore Lyman, Meade's liaison to Hancock, wrote of Hays, "A braver man never went into action, and the wonder only is that he was not killed before, as he always rose at the very head of his men, shouting to them and waving his sword." Grant was "visibly affected" by the news of his friend's death and was silent for a time. When he finally spoke, he said Hays was "a noble man and a gallant officer. I am not surprised that he met his death at the head of his troops; it was just like him. He was a man who would never follow, but would always lead in battle."[93]

ATTACK MADE Lee repent his decision to send Wilcox's division
into the woods to connect with Ewell's right flank on the turnpike. Lee recalled him to the plank road. Alfred Scales's North Carolina regiments and
Samuel McGowan's South Carolinians had just reached Chewning's Farm
when they turned around; they got to the plank road first, Wilcox with
them. The combatants, he wrote, "could not be seen, the rattle of musketry
alone indicating where the struggle was severest, and the points to which
reinforcing brigades should be sent." To some Rebels the musketry sounded
like a house falling down. As Wilcox's division went in, wrote a North Carolinian, the woods "roared like fire in a canebrake."[94]

Hill launched a furious counterattack. Led by Scales's and James Lane's
two North Carolina brigades, the Rebels drove back Hancock's and Getty's
men all the way to Brock Road, even seizing part of the Union breastworks
that Hancock's men had dug there. Then, John Gibbon's division swung
into action, driving back the Confederates. For what seemed like hours,
the enemies slaughtered one another at close range. Heth, who thought the
assault would break the Yankees, afterward conceded that it was a mistake.
"I should have left well enough alone."

Alarmed by the close call, Lyman grimly wrote Meade, "We barely hold
our own; on the right the pressure is heavy. General Hancock thinks he
can hold the plank and Brock roads . . . but he can't advance." He added a
postscript: "Fresh troops would be most advisable."[95]

Hearing this news about Hancock, whom Grant was starting to value
as a real fighting general, Meade dispatched two V Corps divisions—John
Robinson's reserve division and Wadsworth's men, licking their wounds
at Lacy House—down Wilderness Run. He planned for the 15,000-man
task force, when it emerged from the woods on the plank road, to strike
Hill's left flank and relieve the pressure on II Corps. It was the very action that Crawford and Washington Roebling had vainly recommended
that morning from Chewning's Farm. Ironically, Roebling was assigned to
guide Wadsworth.

Hancock's situation on the plank road was not nearly as perilous as
Lyman had described it. With the arrival of Gibbon's and Barlow's divisions, Hancock had 33,000 men at his disposal, more than twice as many
as Hill's 15,000. It was Lee, not Grant, who should have been concerned—
and he was.

HILL'S THIRD DIVISION, 7,500 men led by General Richard Anderson, had already left the upper Rapidan crossings to join Hill. But where were Longstreet's 10,000 men?

About 6 p.m., Lee sent an aide, Major Charles Venable, to find the First Corps and direct it to march cross-country from Catharpin Road to the plank road and come up behind Hill as quickly as possible.

After Hancock's powerful force struck Hill a fifth time, Lee dispatched a second messenger, Major H. B. McClellan of Jeb Stuart's staff, to prod General Charles Field, the irascible, one-legged commander of John Bell Hood's former division that was leading Longstreet's advance. McClellan found Field and the First Corps—five hours behind schedule and ten miles from Hill—camped near Richard's Shop on Catharpin Road. He relayed Lee's instructions: Field must speed up the march.

Field irritably informed McClellan that Longstreet planned to resume the march at 1 a.m. and, moreover, he refused to accept McClellan's verbal orders to start before then. Fuming, McClellan returned to Lee, informed him of Field's response, and requested written orders. But Lee recognized that they would probably not reach Field until nearly 1 a.m. anyway, and he allowed Longstreet's marching orders to stand.[96]

REPORTS OF LARGE enemy formations moving through the woods toward the plank road had persuaded Grant that Ewell had sent a division to aid Hill. He ordered Warren, with his remaining divisions, to attack Ewell on the turnpike, alongside Wright's VI Corps brigades. But he was mistaken; they were Wilcox's troops from Hill's Third Corps, recalled to help Heth stop the energetic Yankee attack on the plank road. Grant, however, believed that he saw an opportunity to strike Ewell when he was vulnerable.

Wright's 7,000 men attacked, but Warren elected not to, further marring his reputation on a day when he had already attacked five hours late. Warren also calculatedly underreported V Corps' severe losses in the hope of avoiding Meade's and Grant's criticism. He reportedly told his adjutant, Lieutenant Colonel Frederick Locke, "It will never do, Locke, to make a showing of such heavy losses."

Wright's unsupported attack only added to the body count. Everywhere his men were repulsed. One VI Corps brigade, Truman Seymour's, was butchered while attempting to flank Ewell's left. When the heavy fighting ended, flames from wildfires and the screams of wounded men supplanted the roar of musketry. In a field in front of the 5th Maine of Wright's division, a wounded bluecoat beseeched his comrades for help as flames closed in on him. Two tried to aid him and were shot by Confederates. Then, a Union sergeant took deliberate aim and put the wounded man out of his agony.[97]

Sixteen-year-old Private Frank Wilkeson witnessed many desperate scenes on this day when, eager to see action, he left his idle artillery battery and went to the front. All day, Wilkeson fought alongside veteran infantrymen, who instructed him on the fine points of musketry.

A Union rifleman near Wilkeson, shot in the leg, turned to limp to the rear. But after a few steps, "he kicked out his leg once or twice to see if it would work." He examined the wound, returned to the ranks and resumed firing. Then he was hit in the arm, but after determining that the wound was minor, he continued fighting. Wilkeson said to him, "You are fighting in bad luck today. You had better get away from here."

The man had just turned to respond to Wilkeson when his head jerked, and he fell, shot through the jaw. He got up and "a tiny fountain of blood and teeth and bone and bits of tongue burst out of his mouth. . . . He cast his rifle furiously on the ground and staggered off."

When the fighting ebbed, Wilkeson saw a soldier with two broken legs lying on the ground "with his cocked rifle by his side and his ramrod in the hand, and his eyes fixed on the front. I knew he meant to kill himself in case of fire." Wilkeson also watched "battle-field ghouls" loot the bodies of the dead, turning their pockets inside out in search of money and valuables.[98]

Tramping through the woods between the two battlegrounds, the V Corps task force, with Wadsworth's men in the vanguard, followed Wilderness Run, a stream that sometimes paralleled Parker's Store Road. They were nearing the plank road, hoping to smash Hill's left flank before nightfall.

Rebel skirmishers spotted them and reported the news to Hill—who cast about for infantrymen to stop the Yankee thrust against his left flank. He came up empty-handed; all of Heth's and Wilcox's regiments were fighting on the plank road.

The only available unit was a 150-man detachment, the 5th Alabama Battalion, which had been assigned to round up stragglers and guard federal prisoners. Hill threw them into a skirmish line, instructed them to rush the Yankees shrieking the Rebel yell as loudly as possible—each side had "yelled" the other out of position in the dense woods many times—and sent off the tiny unit to stop two Union divisions.

Firing rapidly, the Rebel battalion struck the lumbering Union task force with shocking swiftness. The woods amplified their shrill battle cries. Unable to estimate the attackers' numbers, Wadsworth's men lost their nerve. Colonel Roy Stone's brigade, which earlier that day had foundered in a swamp and ignominiously fled before blazing Rebel musketry, went to pieces again before the screaming Alabamans. Amid the brigade's undignified flight, Stone's horse became spooked and fell on him. A brigade positioned behind Stone's running men stopped them at bayonet point. As darkness fell, Wadsworth ordered his division to entrench for the night; it was less than a hundred yards from Hill's left flank.[99]

FOR THREE HOURS, Hill's 15,000 men had fought toe-to-toe with up to 40,000 Yankees on the plank road and had repulsed repeated explosive attacks—a singular achievement. Hill's commanders, however, knew that their brigades were close to breaking. Every man was engaged; no reserves remained. W. M. Graham vividly recalled coming up with the 26th Mississippi to relieve fought-out Rebels on the firing line and finding "some dead, some lying flat on the ground. Still others squatting had been firing at close range on level ground until they had exhausted their ammunition."

Colonel William Palmer, Hill's chief of staff, passed Jeb Stuart and Lee's aide, Colonel Venable, as they sat on their horses listening to the increasing roar of battle on the extreme right. Palmer heard one of them exclaim, "If night would only come!"[100]

By contrast, Meade's chief of staff, General Andrew Humphreys, believed that just one more hour of daylight would enable the Union army to achieve a great victory on the plank road.[101]

BUT THE DAY ended before the Union forces could realize Humphreys's hope. In the smoking woods, the fighting ebbed, and finally ceased, except for outbreaks of shooting on the skirmish lines, which lit the inky black-ness with "flashes of musketry, as if with lightning," a New York officer observed.[102]

Tens of thousands of exhausted men lay down on the blood-sodden ground, often in the company of mangled corpses and wounded men living out their last hours. "We lay upon the ground surrounded by dead and dying rebel soldiers," wrote Captain Rufus Dawes of the Iron Brigade's 6th Wisconsin. "The sufferings of these poor men, and their moans and cries were harrowing. We gave them water from our canteens and all aid that was within our power."[103]

Indeed, the enemies' lines were so close together in places and the woods were so dark that soldiers blundered into one another's camps and were captured. "We sought water at the same streams or springs with the Con-federates, neither knowing the presence of the other, or friend from foe, until accidentally discovered," wrote Captain Robert Carter of the 22nd Massachusetts.[104]

AWAY FROM THE furious battles on the turnpike and plank road, the armies' cavalry forces had fought their own private battle on Catharpin Road. Obedient to orders, Union General James Wilson's division, with-out General John Hammond's 5th New York Cavalry, left Parker's Store at daybreak and rode southwest seven miles to Catharpin Road to serve as the vanguard for the advance of Hancock's II Corps. But Lee's attacks diverted II Corps to the plank road, leaving Wilson with no one behind him.

Although he did not know it, Wilson was operating in an information vacuum, unaware that Hancock was not coming, or that his messages were not reaching Meade because the plank road was full of Confederates.

Reaching Craig's Meeting House on Catharpin Road, Wilson's men suddenly ran into Confederate General Thomas Rosser's Laurel Brigade. "It was practically a head-on collision on a forest road, in which both parties bore themselves gallantly, making all the noise they could," Wilson later wrote. Wilson knew Rosser quite well; at West Point, the Illinois native and the Texan had been roommates for four years.[105]

Fighting with sabers, pistols, and Spencer repeating rifles, and supported by horse artillery, the Yankees initially drove the Laurel Brigade before them. But Rebel reinforcements arrived, and Wilson pulled back to Craig's Meeting House. There, he learned that none of his couriers had been able to get through to Meade.

Wilson now recognized that his understanding of his situation was dangerously incomplete. Prudence dictated a withdrawal to Todd's Tavern on Brock Road. Between Catharpin Road and the plank road was a "blind road," little more than a backwoods path, that crossed Catharpin Road farther east. With Rosser pushing rapidly eastward on Catharpin Road, Wilson hastened to get ahead of him to prevent him from reaching Brock Road. It was close, but Wilson got there first.

When no reports from Wilson reached them, Meade and Phil Sheridan, the Cavalry Corps commander, sent David Gregg's cavalry division to Todd's Tavern. Gregg, Sheridan's only experienced division commander, reached the rundown buildings at Todd's Tavern early in the afternoon. When he learned about Wilson's desperate situation, he sent a pair of regiments under General Henry Davies Jr. galloping off to aid him. Two miles west of the tavern, Davies's men struck the vanguard of Rosser's brigade and drove the Rebels across the Po River, enabling Wilson's exhausted troopers to reach safety.

In his report to Meade that night, Sheridan complained that too many troopers were tied down guarding supply trains. "Why cannot infantry be sent to guard the trains and let me take the offensive?" Sheridan wrote. It was a complaint that Meade had heard before from Sheridan, who wanted his corps to act as the army's mobile strike force.[106]

The Union and Confederate cavalrymen might as well have been fighting in another country for all the good they did the tens of thousands of foot soldiers slaughtering one another on the plank road and the turnpike. Wilson had never led cavalry in combat, or infantry for that matter, and his inexperience showed. He had fallen down in every respect: not scouting the turnpike, leaving only the 5th New York Cavalry on the plank road, and failing to clear Catharpin Road.

By contrast, the Confederate cavalry had proven useful in an important respect: by driving Wilson from Catharpin Road, it had effectively screened Longstreet's approach. While Grant might know that the First Corps was marching to join Lee, he did not know where it was.[107]

But Grant was convinced that Longstreet would reach Lee sometime during the night, and so he was eager to go into action early the next morning before the Rebels did. Grant ordered the attack to begin at 4:30 a.m.

Warren's and Sedgwick's corps would assault Ewell's divisions along the turnpike, while Hancock, with Getty's division, would attack Hill on the plank road. Wadsworth's division, entrenched in the woods between the roads, was to strike Hill's left flank.

Two divisions of Ambrose Burnside's IX Corps, which had been idle all day, were to set out at 2 a.m. for Wilderness Tavern; march into the gap between the turnpike and plank road, severing Hill from Ewell's corps; and then turn into Hill's rear. Hancock's strike along Hill's front, while Wadsworth and Burnside hit his flank and rear, would destroy the Confederate Third Corps, followed by Longstreet's First Corps whenever it arrived.

It was an audacious plan. If launched on time at 4:30 a.m. at all points simultaneously—never accomplished during the day that had just ended, a day of frantic, piecemeal attacks involving seven of the army's fifteen divisions—the Army of the Potomac, on the campaign's third day, might realize its objective of destroying Lee's army. Drawing upon every available resource, Grant summoned to the front "all train guards, as well as every man of your command capable of bearing arms," including inactive artillerymen, who would fight as foot soldiers.

But Meade, after conferring with his corps commanders, objected to the early hour set by Grant. "It will be difficult, owing to the dense thicket in which their commands are located, the fatigued condition of the men rendering it difficult to rouse them early enough, and the necessity of some daylight, to properly put in reinforcements." He urged Grant to push back the starting time to 6 a.m.

To Grant, it undoubtedly sounded like the Army of the Potomac was reverting to its old habit of procrastination, which he, Lincoln, and Halleck wished to exorcise. He consented to delay the offensive 30 minutes, until 5 a.m. "He is afraid that if delayed until 6 o'clock the enemy will take the initiative, which he desires specially to avoid," a Grant aide replied to Meade.[108]

The mood at Grant's headquarters "was as hopeful as it had been in the morning," wrote Lieutenant Colonel Badeau, although there was an undercurrent of concern about the ongoing efforts to recover the wounded still in the woods. Grant was "calm and confident." He described the day's fighting as "struggling through thickets and fighting for position. . . . [It] has not been much of a test of strength," with Longstreet and Burnside absent. "I feel pretty well satisfied with the result of the engagement," said Grant. Lee, he said, had struck at the Army of the Potomac's flank in the hope of driving it back across the Rapidan, as he had during previous campaigns, "but in this he has failed." Lee had never faced a relentlessly aggressive opponent like Grant, nor had Grant met one like Lee.[109]

WHILE GRANT WAS planning to take the fight to Lee, Lee intended to take it to Grant. "Be ready to act early in the morning," Lee told Ewell during the evening of May 5. Whether that meant attacking the Yankees' right or left depended on circumstances, and the arrival of 22,500 more Rebels—more reinforcements than Burnside would bring Grant. Besides anticipating that Longstreet's corps and Anderson's division—together totaling 17,500 troops—would soon reinforce Hill, Lee expected the brigades of Generals Stephen Ramseur and Robert Johnson, and six other regiments—up to 5,000 men in all—to join Ewell's corps on the turnpike. Nonetheless, even with these reinforcements, the Confederates would still find themselves at a nearly two-to-one numerical disadvantage.[110]

In a letter written that night to War Secretary James Seddon, Lee reported that General John Jones was dead and that General Leroy Stafford was dying. He summarized Ewell's repulse of Warren's uncoordinated attacks, and Hill's gritty stand on the plank road, where he "successfully resisted repeated and desperate assaults. . . . By the blessing of God we maintained our position against every effort until night, when the contest closed." Maintaining the army's position on two roads three miles apart until Longstreet could join it had been Lee's goal; he had accomplished it through Ewell's sharp, energetic generalship and the stubbornness of Hill's men.[111]

NORMALLY HIGH-STRUNG AND energetic, A. P. Hill tonight was ill. His chronic prostatitis was flaring up, and the pale, frail-looking corps commander was drained, feverish, and in pain. Hill epitomized the warrior general who led from the front. His fast-marching "Light Division" had been the exemplar of Stonewall Jackson's corps; its timely arrival at Antietam in September 1862 saved Lee from defeat. Amid high expectations, in May 1863 Hill was given command of the new Third Corps, but his added responsibilities had dulled his slashing boldness.

On this night, Hill's divisions were scarcely in better shape than he. Spent by hours of kinetic combat, Heth's and Wilcox's men had collapsed wherever they happened to be when the fighting stopped, after somehow battling nearly 40,000 enemy soldiers to a draw. "None of the brigades seemed to be in line—some regiments isolated entirely from their brigades—in fact, no line at all, but just as they had fought," wrote Lieutenant Octavius Wiggins of the 37th North Carolina. Roughly a half-mile from Brock Road, the Rebel regiments and brigades were mixed up and aligned at incongruous angles, "like a worm fence." Slender rations were distributed; each man in the Richmond Howitzers received two crackers and a handful of sugar.[112]

Heth asked Hill to allow him and Wilcox to sort out their brigades and place them in a line of battle spanning the plank road; the Yankees would surely attack early in the morning, he said. Hill irritably replied that Longstreet's First Corps would be up in a few hours to relieve the Third Corps before that happened.

"The men have been marching and fighting all day and are tired. I do not want them disturbed," Hill told Heth by way of dismissal. Still troubled, Heth twice more returned to Hill's tent to implore Hill to allow him and Wilcox to reorganize their lines. During Heth's last visit, Hill snapped, "Damn it, Heth. I don't want to hear any more about it. The men shall not be disturbed." Wilcox took up the matter with Lee who, more graciously than Heth, attempted to reassure Wilcox that Hill's corps would "be relieved before day" by Longstreet's corps and Anderson's division.[113]

Hill and his staff nervously awaited Longstreet's arrival. "We could not sleep," wrote Colonel Palmer, "but waited for news of Longstreet; for we knew that at first blush of the morning the turning attack on our right would open with overwhelming numbers, and, unsupported, the men must give way."[114]

When the eastern sky turned pewter gray on May 6, Longstreet was not there.

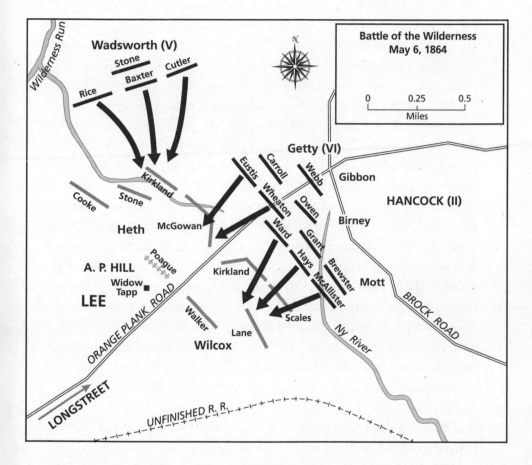

Battle of the Wilderness
May 6, 1864

0   0.25   0.5
Miles

Wadsworth (V)

Stone
Baxter   Cutler
Rice

Kirkland

Cooke   Stone

Heth

McGowan

A. P. HILL

Poague

Widow
Tapp

LEE

Getty (VI)

Carroll
Eustis   Webb
Wheaton   Gibbon
Owen

Birney

HANCOCK (II)

Ward   Grant

Kirkland   Hays   Brewster
McAllister   Mott

Walker   Lane   Scales

Wilcox

BROCK ROAD

Ny River

ORANGE PLANK ROAD

LONGSTREET

UNFINISHED R. R.

Wilderness Run

4

Friday, May 6, 1864, 4:30 a.m.
Orange Plank Road

AT THIS HOUR, Lee had envisioned Longstreet and Hill, with Anderson's division also having come up, launching a massive attack. The First Corps' 10,000 soldiers would be charging down Orange Plank Road, and Hill's 20,000 men would be sliding into the gap north of the road and connecting with Ewell.

Instead, the veil of night fell away in tense silence to reveal a spring morning that might have been delightful but for the fuliginous air, the splintered trees, and the dead and wounded lying everywhere. A. P. Hill's men, neither dug in nor properly aligned, could hear the Yankees' low voices as they checked their weapons and ammunition. The unfulfilled promise of Longstreet's arrival during the night filled them with deep apprehension.

On their left, Hill's troops heard a distant crash of gunfire. It was Richard Ewell's Second Corps attacking eastward on the turnpike, preempting V and VI Corps' scheduled attack at 5. Lee hoped that Ewell could seize Wilderness Tavern ridge and sever the Union army from the Rapidan—if it might be done "without too great a sacrifice." That was left to Ewell's judgment. Lee's discretionary orders had ignited Stonewall Jackson's creative brilliance when he commanded the Second Corps, but Ewell was not Jackson. The Union defenders threw back Ewell's assault, and two VI Corps divisions immediately counterattacked, only to be driven back, too. The battle on the turnpike subsided into hours of skirmishing.[115]

IT WAS NOW daylight, and Colonel William Palmer, Hill's chief of staff, was crouched beside a fire next to the guns at the Widow Tapp's when he saw Longstreet riding across the field toward him. Relief flooded him. Hill had ridden off to inspect the gap between his corps and Ewell's, but Palmer knew Longstreet well from their previous service and rose to shake his hand. "Ah, General, we have been looking for you since 12 o'clock last night," Palmer said. "We expect to be attacked at any moment, and are not in any shape to resist." Longstreet's reply—that he had ridden ahead but his troops had not yet come up—was drowned out by a roar of musketry on the plank road.

It was a shock, but not a surprise. Four Union divisions were bearing down on Hill's two depleted ones. As Longstreet galloped away to bring up his troops, Hill rushed back from his reconnaissance. "As far as we could see the road was crowded with the enemy moving forward," wrote Palmer.

As usual, Hancock had attacked on time. At 5 a.m., three divisions of II Corps and George Getty's VI Corps division swept westward on the plank road and along both sides of it.

On their right, Wadsworth's division was crashing through the woods toward Hill's left flank, linking up with David Birney's II Corps division and forming an irresistible wave. "The woods were blue with the enemy," wrote Captain R. S. Williams, whose regiment, the 13th North Carolina, barely avoided envelopment and capture.

The Rebel brigades, still jumbled and misaligned from the previous day's fighting, crumbled under the Union hammer blows. "We will give them one volley before we go," Colonel C. M. Avery told his 33rd North Carolina. They fired just as a powerful Union volley slashed through them, mortally wounding Avery and killing and wounding many others. "The men were willing to fight, but had no chance, 'twas confusion worse confounded," wrote Lieutenant Octavius Wiggins of the 37th North Carolina, which, without firing a shot, was borne rearward by the Union tide.[116]

"General Hancock went in punctually, and is driving the enemy handsomely. Some prisoners. Nothing from Longstreet," reported Lieutenant Colonel Lyman, whom Meade had sent to Hancock to provide timely updates.

Frank Wilkeson, the wayward teenage gunner from New York, was striding through the woods alongside Hancock's men, a musket in his hands. He saw dead Confederates everywhere. Their raggedness, their meager rations, and their inferior arms staggered him. "The direful poverty of the Confederacy was plainly indicated by its dead soldiers," Wilkeson wrote.[117]

Hancock, looking as magnificent as ever on horseback, was "wreathed in smiles" as he watched his shock troops pour down the plank road, overrunning every Rebel regiment in its path. To Lyman, he crowed, "We are driving them, sir; tell General Meade we are driving them most beautifully; Birney has gone in and he is just cleaning them out be-au-ti-fully." Hancock's face darkened when Lyman reported that just one of Burnside's four divisions had come up. "I knew it!" Hancock cried. "Just what I expected. If he could attack *now*, we would smash A.P. Hill to pieces!" Later, Grant, too, expressed annoyance with Burnside's tardiness, but lateness was a Burnside signature.[118]

Hancock, Wadsworth, and Wright drove A. P. Hill's corps a half mile, all the way to the Widow Tapp's farm. Lee, watching in mortification, tried to rally the Confederates. As General Samuel McGowan's South Carolina brigade streamed past, Lee cried, "My God, General McGowan, is this splendid brigade of yours running like a flock of geese?" McGowan replied, "General, these men are not whipped. They only want a place to form, and they will fight as well as they ever did." A lieutenant in that brigade, J. F. J. Caldwell, said Lee spoke "rather roughly to us," but "there was no panic and no great haste; the men seemed to fall back from a deliberate conviction that it was impossible to hold the ground, and, of course, foolish to attempt it."

Lee's army had faced no crisis of this magnitude since Antietam. Lee and Hill were acutely aware that if the unfolding disaster could not be checked, the Army of Northern Virginia's destruction was at hand.[119]

Some of the broken Confederate regiments and brigades attempted to re-form around Lieutenant Colonel William Poague's twelve guns at the Widow Tapp's farm. The four batteries had become Hill's last redoubt. A former artilleryman, Hill ordered double shots of canister to be fired obliquely across the road, over the heads of the Confederates. His chief of staff, Colonel Palmer, balked, fearing that Rebels might be hit, too. "General Hill said it could not be delayed, the guns must open," Palmer wrote. With Hill helping crew one of the guns, they "did terrible execution," the road being "packed with Federal troops."

The cannon fire transformed the swarming Yankees into blood-splashed blue heaps. The salvo startled everyone, for both armies' guns had been largely inactive the previous day.

Then the gunners swung their instruments of slaughter to the left and shredded Wadsworth's men as they emerged from the woods; the bluecoats withdrew in confusion. But all the while, Yankee riflemen were picking off Poague's gunners as the Union battle line lapped at the batteries. From a clearing behind the guns, Lee agitatedly watched the incredibly suspenseful drama through a miasma of smoke. Preparing for the worst, he sent Lieutenant Colonel Walter Taylor, his adjutant general, back to Parker's Store to ready the trains to move farther to the rear.[120]

LONGSTREET WAS LATE, but he was known for his slowness in getting into position—and for his strong, reliable leadership once he got there. Lee valued Longstreet's advice, and his First Corps was Lee's best fighting unit. A member of West Point's Class of 1842, he was a full-bearded, burly six-footer, whose stolid appearance suggested his methodical, even meticulous approach to things, as well as his core of stubbornness. Longstreet's record of accomplishments over the past eight months was a mixed one. At Chickamauga, his attack on the Union army of former West Point classmate William Rosecrans had won the battle. But in the months that followed in eastern Tennessee's cold forests, his corps had foundered badly.[121]

In marching to the Wilderness, Longstreet's lean, much-traveled veterans had to march farther, and they had started later than Lee's other two corps. Leaving their camps near Gordonsville about 4 p.m. on May 4, they embarked on a more than twenty-four-hour forced march that covered twenty-eight miles.

Late on May 5 they reached the end of their endurance, and the dusty, weather-beaten men halted at Richard's Shop on Catharpin Road after passing "freshly killed" Union cavalrymen—casualties from James Wilson's fight earlier that day with Thomas Rosser's Laurel Brigade. They were still ten miles away from Hill's beleaguered corps, but Longstreet wanted them to rest a few hours before resuming their march at 1 a.m. on May 6. He intended to reach Hill by daybreak. Longstreet's decision to stop, although necessary, was very nearly disastrous for the Army of Northern Virginia.

That night, Lee's aide, Major Charles Venable, brought new orders to Longstreet from Lee: to "strike across" from Catharpin Road to the plank road, and come up behind Hill. "The change of direction of our march was not reassuring," Longstreet wrote. More than that, it portended a numbing, night-long test of stamina. During the too-brief rest period, the Palmetto Sharpshooters' band serenaded its South Carolina brigade commander, General Micah Jenkins; Jenkins would be dead by the next evening.[122]

Under "a very fair late risen moon," a guide sent by Lee led the corps down a faint road, little more than a bridle path, "overgrown by the bushes, except the side tracks made by the draft animals and the ruts of wheels which marked occasional lines." So that his corps could travel faster, Longstreet left his artillery and supplies behind on Catharpin Road. In the utter darkness of the woods, the men cursed, sweated, "floundered and fell." During one stretch, the road disappeared altogether, and the head of the column lost its way; the march stopped while the guide hunted for the lost path. This "was about the only rest we got. The men were already worn out by their forced march of the day before," wrote D. Augustus Dickert of Joseph Kershaw's division, "and now they had to exert all their strength to its utmost to keep up." When the guide again found the path, he managed to lead Longstreet's panting men to the plank road.[123]

IT WAS DAYLIGHT, and they were on the plank road, Kershaw's and Charles Field's divisions marching side-by-side eastward, eight abreast. They hastened to make up for lost time. "We walked fast and double quick as much as we could," wrote a South Carolina soldier. Another Rebel described the pace as "a turkey trot." At Parker's Store, Longstreet's Rebels pricked their ears at the sound, directly ahead, of furious musketry and cannon fire, and adrenaline surged through them. The corps jogged the last two miles to the Tapp farm as the sun, a lurid "blood red," rose before them.[124]

They came "swinging down the Orange Plank road at a trot," Field's division on the left and Kershaw's on the right. An artilleryman at the Tapp farm shouted, "Look out down the road. Here they come!" William Dame, a private in the Richmond Howitzers, wrote, "We were driven nearly wild with excited joy, and enthusiasm by the blessed sight of Longstreet's advance division coming down the road at a double quick." Someone shouted, "The old war horse is up at last. It's all right now." As the lead regiments swept by, "We yelled ourselves nearly dumb to cheer them," wrote Dame.[125]

As they neared the Tapp field, Longstreet's men met knots of battle refugees and then came upon a scene of panic, confusion, and desperation. The First Corps determinedly pressed ahead, like a ship through heavy seas of walking wounded, men on litters, and unwounded stragglers. "Is this Lee's army?" some of Longstreet's men called tauntingly to the retreating Rebels. Hill's men were embarrassed to be found in this condition by Longstreet's corps after having fought so valiantly the day before, wrote Colonel Palmer of Hill's staff.[126]

GENERAL JOHN GREGG'S Texas brigade—the 1st, 4th, and 5th Texas, and the 3rd Arkansas—was famously aggressive, a reputation earned with spilled blood under John Bell Hood's command. The brigade reached the Tapp farm first.

Lee's countenance, reflecting his despair over the collapse of Hill's corps, was miraculously transformed when he saw Longstreet's men jogging into the Tapp field.

"The Texans cheered lustily as their line of battle, coming up in splendid style, passed by Wilcox's disordered columns, and swept across our artillery pit and its adjacent breastwork," wrote Lee's aide, Charles Venable.

Lee, red-faced with emotion and moved by the Texans' spirit, welcomed them with rare effusiveness. "Texans always move them!" he shouted, evoking "a yell [that] rent the air that must have been heard for miles around," wrote Robert Campbell, a courier for Gregg. "I would charge hell for that old man," another courier told Campbell. A member of Field's staff remarked on Lee's unusual demeanor: "Never did I see him so excited, so disturbed. . . . He was almost moved to tears."

Lee spurred Traveller through an opening in the trenches and joined the Texans' line as they began to advance toward Hancock's divisions. When they saw that Lee intended to attack with them, the Texans slowed and shouted, "Go back, General Lee! Go back! We won't go unless you go back." They knew that Lee was irreplaceable, and that his loss would devastate the Confederacy.

But Lee's blood was up and he wasn't listening. His eyes were focused on the front. A sergeant seized Traveller's bridle rein. Gregg remonstrated with Lee. Then, Venable called Lee's attention to Longstreet, who sat his horse on a nearby knoll. Lee, who had been looking for Longstreet, reluctantly joined him there as Venable took Longstreet aside to relate what had just happened. "With affectionate bluntness," Longstreet persuaded Lee to move farther to the rear.

During his brief reversion to the warrior that he was at his core, Lee conveyed to his men part of his own fighting spirit—not that they really needed it. "Every man felt that the eye of the commanding general was upon him, and was proud of the opportunity of showing him that his trust in his men was not misplaced," wrote Walter Taylor, Lee's adjutant general.[127]

Behind the Texans came General Evander Law's Alabama brigade, commanded by Colonel William Perry; Longstreet, in his long-running feud with Law, had placed Law under arrest. Lee rode up to them and asked, "What troops?" They replied, "Law's Alabamans," to which Lee responded, "God bless the Alabamians."[128]

As the First Corps got ready to attack from behind Poague's belching guns, Longstreet rode his horse at a walk down the line, telling each company, "Keep cool, men, we will straighten this out in a short time—keep cool." Lieutenant Colonel Moxley Sorrel, Longstreet's assistant adjutant general, believed that the First Corps during these minutes displayed its utmost "steadiness and inflexible courage and discipline" in "the simple act of forming line in that dense undergrowth, under heavy fire and with the Third Corps men pushing through to the rear through the ranks."[129]

The First Corps was now in a battle line thrown across the plank road, barring the further advance of Hancock's onrushing troops. Hill's men, at last relieved of the Yankees' killing pressure, re-formed behind Longstreet's divisions. Longstreet's men advanced and met the Yankees pressing toward the Tapp farm with "a cool and murderous fire" and "we heard the old rebel yell. . . . I don't think I ever listened to a sweeter sound," wrote a North Carolinian in Hill's corps. Others picked up the battle cry, and like a wave, it rolled "down the line and back again, and our line took up the refrain."

The counterattack began in earnest. "Here, I honestly believe, the Army of Northern Virginia was saved!" enthused J. F. J. Caldwell, a lieutenant in the South Carolina brigade whose retreat had provoked Lee's chastisement. A North Carolina officer wrote that Longstreet's corps "saved our army from defeat and possibly from annihilation." Herman Melville was inspired to write in "Armies of the Wilderness" of Longstreet's dramatic arrival: "Look, through the pines what line comes on? / Longstreet slants through the hauntedness!"[130]

Kershaw's division pushed ahead on the south side of the plank road, while Gregg's 800 Texans and Arkansans walked the point of Field's division north of the road. Crashing through the dense undergrowth, the Texas Brigade smashed into Wadsworth's ranked brigades—perhaps 7,000 men in all—now comprising Hancock's right flank. The Texans stopped the three Union brigades cold, but at a terrible cost: in just ten minutes, half of them were killed or wounded. When Hancock's Yankees ran down the road to cut them off, Gregg withdrew what remained of his brigade.

General Richard Anderson's division of Hill's corps reached Widow Tapp's after Longstreet. Anderson's men had marched ten miles that morning from New Verdiersville. Although they belonged to Hill's corps, Lee threw them into the powerful attacks on Wadsworth's division that were being delivered by General Henry Benning's Georgians and Law's Alabamans—Longstreet's brigades—who had swarmed to the Texas Brigade's aid. David Holt of the 16th Mississippi wrote that the Rebel attackers overran the Yankee skirmishers. "They seemed so perfectly at our mercy that it was a pity to shoot them." Then the Mississippians reached the Union first line. "Their line ceased to be, leaving the ground strewn with men in blue, some crying, some dying, some still and some begging for water."

Wadsworth's men could not withstand the ferocious assaults. They were "driven back, and badly scattered, a large portion of them taking the route over which they had marched the night before" to the Lacy house, and the rest retreating on the plank road.[131]

UP AND DOWN the plank road, the Union assault troops staggered under the smashing blows delivered by Longstreet's divisions. "Our men fell by scores. Great gaps were struck in our lines," wrote the artilleryman-turned-infantryman Frank Wilkeson. "The men wavered badly. They fired wildly. They hesitated." Wilkeson said officers stood behind their men, saying, "'Steady, men, steady, steady, steady!' as one speaks to frightened and excited horses." The Confederate bullets "swished by in swarms. It seems to me that I could have caught a pot full of them if I had had a strong iron vessel."[132]

Private Lewis Fisk of Getty's division wrote, "Oh how discouraging it is to lose ground before the enemy. So much hard fighting, and so many killed and wounded for nothing." A comrade who had been loading and firing as fast as possible was shot in the chest, exclaiming, "I am killed," as he took a step toward the rear and then fell dead on top of Fisk.[133]

Lyman of Meade's staff witnessed the Rebel onslaught and the Union line's retreat, "slowly but mixed up—a hopeless sight. . . . They have no craven terror—they have their arms, but, for the moment, they will not fight, nor even rally. Drew my sword and tried to stop them, but with small success."

Among them was Private Fisk, who in falling back found himself with stragglers from another division. "I began to consider myself a straggler, too," he wrote, admitting to feeling "shamelessly demoralized." But after having some coffee and hardtack, Fisk returned to his regiment.[134]

GETTY'S DIVISION, SHOT up during the intensive fighting the day before, was supposed to get a breather this morning, holding a place in Hancock's second line. Longstreet's counterattack threw it back into combat. Hancock sent two of Getty's three brigades running to aid Wadsworth, leaving just Colonel Lewis Grant's Vermont Brigade in Hill's former breastworks on a low rise south of the plank road. When David Birney's and Gershom Mott's divisions crumbled in confusion before Kershaw's powerful attack, Grant's Vermonters suddenly found themselves on the firing line.

From their defensive positions, Grant's men hurled back repeated charges by Kershaw's three brigades, and when Wadsworth retreated, exposing the brigade's flank, it bent the right side of its line to repel attacks from that quarter as well. When the fighting ebbed around 8 a.m., the Vermont Brigade still clung to its position.[135]

FOUR UNION BRIGADES on Hancock's left were idle during the three hours of desperate combat on the plank road. Informed the previous night that Longstreet was coming down Catharpin Road to flank his left, Hancock preemptively sent Barlow's division and much of II Corps' artillery south on Brock Road—all under the command of John Gibbon, "cool as a steel knife, always, and unmoved by anything and everything."

But Gibbon had no one to fight. Even when Longstreet appeared on the plank road, Hancock's worries were not allayed; only Kershaw's and Field's divisions were present. Where was Pickett's division? And Anderson's division of Hill's corps was absent. Jeb Stuart's cavalry, active near Catharpin Road's junction with Brock Road, prevented Phil Sheridan's troopers from finding out the answers. Firing heard near Todd's Tavern and a column of infantry approaching from that direction only heightened Hancock's anxiety.

But the gunfire was only General David Gregg's cavalry division at Todd's Tavern, tilting with Rosser's Laurel Brigade. The infantrymen turned out to be several hundred Union convalescents coming from Chancellorsville. As for Pickett's division, it was on duty in Richmond. Anderson's division was rejoining Hill's corps on the plank road. The Confederate formations so dreaded by Hancock were no more than phantoms.[136]

As LONGSTREET's FIERCE counterattack was reaching a crescendo just after 7 a.m., Hancock asked Meade to send reinforcements. Ambrose Burnside's IX Corps, hours behind schedule, was just then arriving at the Lacy house. "Your dispatch just received, informing me that I can have a division from Burnside in case of absolute necessity," Hancock wrote. "They are pressing us on the road a good deal. If more force were here now I could use it; but I don't know whether I can get it in time or not." Meade immediately sent General Thomas Stevenson's IX Corps division to the plank road. Hancock, although still worried that he might be flanked via Catharpin Road, at last ordered Barlow's idle division into action south of the plank road.[137]

However, Barlow's division did not attack. Gibbon and Barlow—two of the army's most aggressive commanders—later swore that they never received Hancock's order. Evidently they were believed, because a week after the battle, Grant recommended Gibbon for promotion to major general. The lost order meant that 7,000 troops that might have stemmed Longstreet's counterattack and renewed Hancock's offensive remained inactive all morning long.

Ulysses Grant later wrote that Hancock and his command might have exploited the collapse of Hill's corps to devastating effect—if they had in fact been able to see it. As Lee had known, the Wilderness's nearly impenetrable vegetation was the Confederates' great ally.[138]

WHEN THE FRENZIED attacks and counterattacks on the plank road had spent themselves at 10 a.m., Lee and Hancock occupied roughly the same positions they had held before Hancock's attack five hours earlier. The Yankees had lost their early gains, and the Confederates had recouped their early losses.

When the fighting began at 5, Hancock commanded half of the Army of the Potomac's infantry divisions—more than 40,000 men from six divisions culled from all three corps, including his own. The arrival of Thomas Stevenson's division from IX Corps gave Hancock seven divisions from four Army corps, or about 50,000 men.

But Longstreet's and Hill's five divisions with 32,000 men had momentum on their side. The smaller Rebel divisions were also nimbler and more familiar with the Wilderness. Size was not an advantage in the dense woods. During the numerous attacks and counterattacks, the Union lines were sometimes so gridlocked that ammunition could not reach the front.[139]

The lull enabled both sides to reconstitute the brigades and divisions scattered throughout the swamps, smoldering woods, and thickets around the plank road. The enemies attended to their wounded, replenished their ammunition, and improved their fortifications, no one believing that the day's fighting was over.

HILL AND HIS staff dismounted at the Chewning farm, where his two divisions entered the woods between the turnpike and the plank road seeking Ewell's right flank.

They arrived just as a line of Union infantry emerged from the woods, like the previous day at the Tapp farm, when Hill was with Lee and Jeb Stuart. This time, the Yankees did not recoil; they continued to advance toward the Confederate officers. Hill quietly instructed his staff to mount their horses and to leave at a walk. Their feigned nonchalance enabled them to escape. A Rebel brigade dispatched to the farm rounded up the Yankees.

The wayward Yankees had been caught earlier in a Rebel surprise attack on two of Burnside's divisions probing along Parker's Store Road to get behind Hill. Stephen Dodson Ramseur's North Carolina brigade drove the Union infantrymen back a half mile, scooping up hundreds of prisoners, clothing—and copies of the Bible in the Ojibwa language belonging to Native Americans from the 1st Michigan Volunteer Sharpshooters.[140]

As HILL'S DIVISIONS poured into the woods between the two roads, Longstreet and Lee were planning a fresh attack on Hancock's troops, massed on the plank road. General William Wofford, who commanded a brigade of Georgians in Kershaw's division, believed that Hancock's left flank was vulnerable. A surprise flank attack at the same instant that Longstreet and Lee frontally assaulted Hancock might shatter the Union lines, enabling the Confederates to seize the Brock crossroad, Wofford said.

Lee assigned General Martin L. Smith, the Army of Northern Virginia's chief engineer, to scout the area. Smith followed an unfinished railroad bed partially concealed by lush foliage—the line was to have linked Orange Court House and Chancellorsville—until he emerged on Hancock's exposed left flank. No one saw him. Smith excitedly reported his findings to Longstreet and Lee, and they decided to proceed with Wofford's plan. Ironically, Union commanders had contemplated using the railroad bed to flank the Rebels with one of Barlow's brigades, but never acted on the idea.

Longstreet selected his assistant adjutant general, Lieutenant Colonel Moxley Sorrel, to lead the daring flank attack. "Colonel, there is a fine chance of a great attack by our right," Longstreet told his staff officer. "If you will quickly get into those woods, some brigades will be found much scattered from the fight. Collect them and take charge."

Sorrel, a twenty-six-year-old former clerk for a railroad bank with no formal military training, had never led troops in combat; he was thrilled to be given the opportunity. He selected four brigades for the mission: those of Wofford and George Anderson from Longstreet's corps; and William Mahone's and John Stones's brigades from Hill's corps. About 11 a.m., Smith guided the task force along the railroad cut to the spot where he had beheld Hancock's exposed flank.

On the plank road, Kershaw's and Field's divisions began firing heavy volleys into the Yankee line while Sorrel's four brigades moved into attack positions. Then, the 4,000 shock troops "raised the old rebel yell and went on them like a duck on a june bug," wrote a Georgia veteran. Arrayed six lines deep, they shattered Gershom Mott's II Corps division, which had broken the day before. Colonel Paul Frank's brigade—sent by Barlow to Hancock earlier that morning—was the next to crumple under Sorrel's assault.

Waves of panicked bluecoats plunged through the Union brigades to their right, and they, too, began to dissolve. The chaos rippled through Hancock's formations, which retreated for the second time that morning.

"A stand was attempted by a reserve line of Hancock's, but it was swept off its feet in the tumultuous rush of our troops, and finally we struck the Plank Road lower down," Sorrell wrote.

Lieutenant Colonel Charles Weygant thrust his 124th New York "Orange Blossoms" into the Confederates' path in the hope of at least slowing them, as the flash of Rebel musketry lit the forest "like heat lightning from a cloudy horizon." "I might as well have tried to stop the flight of a cannon ball, by interposing the lid of a cracker box," wrote Weygant. "The next moment the Sons of Orange were caught up as in a whirlwind, and broken to fragments; and the terrible tempest of disaster swept on down the Union line, beating back brigade after brigade, and tearing to pieces regiment after regiment, until upwards of twenty thousand veterans were fleeing."

Union officers planted their regimental colors on every piece of high ground that they found and attempted to rally their men around them, but the colors were swept away by running Yankees. Sorrel led his swarming gray-clad attackers through dense stands of trees and swamps, with the Yankee brigades falling like dominoes. As Hancock acknowledged to Longstreet after the war, "You rolled me up like a wet blanket."

Sorrell's men reached the plank road, joining Longstreet's two divisions, and creating a colossal traffic jam. While the way to Brock Road lay open to the Confederates, their disordered formations on the plank road foreclosed the possibility of their making a quick assault to wrest the crossroad from the Yankees.[141]

AMID THE CONFUSION, General James Wadsworth, whose V Corps division had crumbled under the assaults of Longstreet's Texas, Georgia, and Alabama brigades, became irrational. At age fifty-six, Wadsworth, a Harvard-trained New York lawyer, was the second-oldest division commander in the Union army and also a "political general"; he was an important asset to the Lincoln administration in New York, where his father had been the largest landowner in the state. Lincoln appointed Wadsworth to general rank in August 1861 and, because he was patriotic and independently wealthy, Wadsworth chose to serve without pay. In 1862, Wadsworth was the Republican candidate for New York governor; he refused to leave the army to campaign, and he lost.

Wadsworth gathered the remnants of his division in the woods north of the plank road, joining Stevenson's IX Corps division, which had just arrived from the Lacy house. Rebel attacks, however, were slowly pushing them back. Happening upon General Alexander Webb's II Corps brigade just north of the plank road, Wadsworth peremptorily demanded that Webb leave his men, find four regiments from somewhere on his left and reinforce another II Corps division. Roving Webb's lines, Wadsworth became angry when he saw the 20th Massachusetts lying prone behind field works. He ordered it to attack; the regiment's commander, Colonel George Macy, protested that Webb had ordered him to hold his position. An attack, Macy knew, would be suicidal. Wadsworth threatened Macy with insubordination charges if he refused.

The 20th Massachusetts heroically attacked, led personally by Wadsworth, waving his sword. Wadsworth's horse was wounded, and as it careered wildly into the Confederate line, Wadsworth was shot in the head and captured. When they realized who their prisoner was, his captors took him to a field hospital, after divesting him of watch, sword, money, and glasses. Someone gave Moxley Sorrell Wadsworth's map. "It was a good general map of Virginia, and of use afterwards," he wrote.

Wadsworth lingered in a large hospital fly-tent for two days without regaining consciousness. Curious Confederate soldiers looked in on the multi-millionaire Northerner dying in enemy country, "not a friend to hear his last farewell or soothe his last moments by a friendly touch on his pallid brow," wrote Captain D. Augustus Dickert, who was one of Wadsworth's visitors.

When the report of Wadsworth's death reached the White House, Lincoln felt a personal loss. "No man has given himself up to the war with such self-sacrificing patriotism as Genl Wadsworth," said the president, adding that Wadsworth was "actuated only by a sense of duty which he neither evaded nor sought to evade."[142]

Wadsworth's assault was as disastrous as Macy had predicted; the 20th Massachusetts was nearly wiped out. Of the 533 men that went in, 114 returned fifteen minutes later.[143]

IT WAS NOON, and Longstreet, his staff officers, and Generals Kershaw and Micah Jenkins rode together at the head of Longstreet's two marching divisions. They were exultant. The flanking attack had been a success, and Longstreet's men were poised to deliver the coup de grâce that Stonewall Jackson had been ready to dispense a year ago, just a few miles away, when he was shot by his own men. Now Lee's army might exorcise the ghost of Jackson that haunted the Army of Northern Virginia with a spectacular tactical victory, just six hours after looking disaster in the eye.

Martin Smith had conducted a second reconnaissance along the unfinished rail line. Proceeding past where Sorrel had attacked, he found a place where the Rebels might cross Brock Road and flank Hancock's corps, now behind its breastworks along the road. Longstreet liked the idea of a second two-pronged attack, virtually identical to the first, only this time targeting the vital crossroad itself. Smith was placed in command of the new task force, to be led by Wofford's Georgia division.

Jenkins's South Carolina brigade of Field's division, which had seen little action that morning, would spearhead the frontal attack on the plank road. The frail 28-year-old was in a buoyant mood as he rode beside Longstreet. "I am happy," Jenkins told Longstreet. "I have felt despair of the cause for some months, but am relieved, and feel assured that we will put the enemy back across the Rapidan before night." They were Jenkins's last words.

At the conclusion of Sorrel's earlier attack, the 12th Virginia had outdistanced the other regiments and entered the woods north of the plank road, intending to strike Wadsworth's left flank. But upon finding themselves unsupported, the Virginians turned around to recross the road and join their brigade. They wore new, dark gray uniforms that in the dim light looked blue. As the Virginians emerged from the woods, their comrades across the plank road mistook them for the enemy—and opened fire.

With the worst possible timing, Longstreet and his entourage at that very moment rode between the two regiments, and the swarm of bullets struck them instead. Jenkins fell mortally wounded; a captain and an orderly were killed instantly.

Longstreet was shot in the neck, the Minie ball exiting through his right shoulder. "The blow lifted me from the saddle, and my right arm [thereafter, largely paralyzed] dropped to my side, but I settled back to my seat, and started to ride on, when in a minute the flow of blood admonished me that my work for the day was done."

Kershaw shouted a drawn-out "F-r-i-e-n-d-s!" and the Rebels ceased fire, aghast at what they had done when they saw Longstreet's staff officers lifting him to the ground. The nightmare of a year and three days earlier, just three miles away, was happening again. "A strange fatality attended us!" wrote Lieutenant Colonel Walter Taylor, Lee's aide. "Jackson killed in the zenith of his successful career; Longstreet wounded when in the act of striking a blow that would have rivaled Jackson's at Chancellorsville."

Longstreet's aides propped him against a tree. "He was almost choked with blood," wrote Sorrel. Longstreet blew "bloody foam" from his mouth before saying, "Tell General Field to take command, and to move forward with the whole force and gain the Brock road." He sent Sorrel to Lee to report what had happened and to urge him to continue the attack.

They moved Longstreet to an ambulance, around which artillery Major Robert Stiles found the general's staff "literally bowed down with grief." As Stiles peered inside, Longstreet's eyelids cracked opened a slit to reveal "a delicate line of blue between them." Longstreet carefully lifted his blood-soaked undershirt from his chest, held it up a moment, "and heaved a big sigh."[144]

Lee received the news stoically but sorrowfully, undoubtedly feeling himself transported back a year earlier to the awful loss of Jackson. Captain Francis Dawson of Longstreet's staff wrote, "I shall not soon forget the sadness in his face, and the almost despairing movement of his hands, when he was told that Longstreet had fallen."[145]

The wounding of Longstreet "seemed actually to paralyse our whole corps," wrote Edward Porter Alexander, the First Corps' artillery chief. Lee and Field reassessed Longstreet's attack plan. Sorrel's brigades and Field's and Kershaw's divisions remained intermingled on the plank road as shouting red-faced officers tried to sort them out.

In the opinion of Lee and Field, the units were too tangled up to carry out Longstreet's plan. If they had been ready to attack immediately, Field believed, they would have routed Hancock, but they were not. "Neither could move without interfering with the other," he wrote. Realistically, even if Longstreet had not been wounded, it would have been difficult, if not impossible, for him to immediately assault the Brock Road positions. About 1 p.m., Lee suspended the attack.

Others, however, believed that this was a mistake and that the army might have been able to cripple Grant's offensive. "But for Longstreet's fall, the panic which was fairly under way in Hancock's corps would have been extended and have resulted in Grant's being forced to retreat across the Rapidan," wrote Alexander. Walter Taylor, Lee's assistant adjutant general, also believed Longstreet would have "rolled back" Hancock's wing and forced the Yankees to recross the Rapidan.[146]

But as Longstreet later drily observed, "General Lee did not care to handle the troops in broken lines," and rearranging them in the tangled woods would have consumed "several hours of precious time." By then, the opportunity to strike a decisive blow would have passed.[147]

THE WOODED GAP between Orange Plank Road and the Orange Turnpike haunted Grant as it had Lee and Hill, who had sent Wilcox's division to link Hill's corps with Ewell's Second Corps on the turnpike, but then had hastily recalled it when Hancock attacked. Grant had a similar plan for Burnside, who was supposed to occupy the woods and connect Hancock with Warren's V Corps.

This was a critical element of Meade's and Grant's offensive plan for the day. Burnside was to have operated alongside Wadsworth's division, beginning at 5 a.m. Wadsworth would veer left to strike Hill's flank while Burnside plunged straight ahead through the woods. Warren was to have attacked west on the turnpike. But Warren, who had ignored orders to attack the previous day, had not gone into action on this morning either. Burnside was not on Warren's left anyway.

And so Grant and Meade drafted a new plan for Burnside. Now, rather than plowing through the woods between the two main roads, he was to march down Parker's Store Road and slip behind Hill on the plank road.

But at Chewning's Farm, Hill's divisions, which Lee had sent from the plank road to connect with the turnpike, blocked the way. Burnside stopped.

At 11:45 a.m., General John Rawlins, Grant's chief of staff, prodded Burnside: "Push in with all vigor so as to drive the enemy from General Hancock's front and get in on the . . . plank road at the earliest possible moment." He irritably added, "Hancock has expected you for the last three hours, and has been making his attack and disposition with a view to your assistance."[148]

By midday, the negligible IX Corps involvement in the morning's fighting revived memories of Burnside's "genius of slowness." He was hours late attacking at Antietam, and he led the Army of the Potomac during the Fredericksburg debacle. Today, his slowness severely tested everyone's patience. Hancock's assistant adjutant general, Lieutenant Colonel Francis Walker, wrote in disgust, "While the Confederates had brought three new divisions into action, Burnside had not borne a finger's weight upon the fight."[149]

GRANT HAD BEGUN the day with a singular breakfast: sliced cucumber doused in vinegar, taken with a cup of strong coffee. As his aide, Horace Porter, observed, Grant "ate less than any man in the army; sometimes the amount of food taken did not seem enough to keep a bird alive." Then Grant lighted the first of the twenty-four cigars that his servant had put in his pockets; by day's end, he would smoke them all.

When still nothing happened on Burnside's front, Grant dispatched Porter in the early afternoon to prod Burnside to "move without a moment's delay, and connect with Hancock's right at all hazards." Porter found Burnside's troops flailing through the dense undergrowth and wetlands between the roads, struggling to form a line. Seated beside the road, their commander was being served a sumptuous lunch.

"A champagne basket filled with lunch had been brought up," wrote Porter, "and at his invitation I joined him and some of his staff in sampling the attractive contents of the hamper." When it came to dining, Burnside was Grant's polar opposite, which was just fine with Porter. Burnside was a firm believer, Porter wrote, in "the recognized principle of experienced campaigners, who always eat a meal wherever they can get it."[150]

FINALLY, AT 2 P.M.—nearly seven hours behind schedule—Burnside attacked with three brigades. They struck two brigades of Alabamans and Floridians that had lost heavily in that morning's fighting and drove them back to their breastworks along a wet swale. The attack swept up to and over part of the Rebel fieldworks, where the enemies fought frenziedly, with casualties high on both sides. After what seemed to them like days, but was really only one hour, Burnside's men withdrew to the swale's other side. The exhausted blue and gray brigades were content for the moment to hold their positions facing one another.

Lyman of Meade's staff urged Hancock, dug in on Brock Road but not under attack, to go to Burnside's aid, but Hancock refused. "He said with much regret that it would be to hazard too much, though there was nothing in his immediate front. . . . We were obliged to listen to Burnside's fighting without any advance on our part," Lyman later wrote.[151]

Meade advised Hancock to rest his men until 6 p.m., "at which time a vigorous attack made by you, in conjunction with Burnside, will, I think, overthrow the enemy. I wish this done." But Hancock made it clear that he did not want to attack again that day. "The present partially disorganized condition of this command renders it extremely difficult to obtain a sufficiently reliable body to make a really powerful attack," he replied to Meade.[152]

Hancock wouldn't have to; Lee had made new plans.

THE WOUNDING OF Longstreet had frozen the contemplated two-pronged assault on Hancock's jumbled brigades, now behind their Brock Road breastworks. Had the First Corps attacked immediately, Hancock's corps, even behind breastworks, likely could not have held.

But Lee had been uneasy about attempting it because of the disordered state of the First Corps brigades after Sorrel's flank attack. He still planned to attack that day, just not at that moment. He began re-forming the brigades into battle lines, perpendicular to the plank road, believing that one more attack would break Hancock.

In the woods and the afternoon heat, realigning the Rebel brigades took hours—hours that Hancock's men used to deepen and fortify their entrenchments, to expand the cleared area in front of them, and to rest. "In an incredibly short space of time Hancock's command was substantially re-formed, re-supplied with ammunition, and ready for action," wrote Lieutenant Colonel Weygant of the Orange Blossom Brigade.[153]

JUST AFTER 4 P.M., Field's and Kershaw's Confederate divisions began advancing toward Hancock's three lines of what were now chest-high log breastworks. Bristling with abatis, the field fortifications commanded a broad, cleared reach that the Rebel assault troops would have to cross under intensive musket fire and the salvos of a dozen cannons.

These would have been daunting enough obstacles for an attacking force with a large numerical advantage, but the Confederates faced long odds—4 to 1, minimally. Lee abandoned the flanking element of Longstreet's attack plan, and placed his full, nearly irrational faith in the First Corps' ability to prevail in a frontal assault. It appeared to be suicidal to send 10,000 attackers against more than 40,000 enemy troops protected by sturdy field fortifications.

Even after three years of war, generals still deprecated the force-multiplying power of well-constructed fortifications, which heretofore were usually built *after* a battle to protect a position. The weeks ahead would convince both armies that breastworks were tactical imperatives.

Just as at Gettysburg Lee had sent George Pickett's division up Cemetery Hill, so Lee now tried to break the Union center on Brock Road. "They hurled their columns, massed in close formation, right in our front with a terable [sic] onset," wrote brigade commander Robert McAllister. Corporal John Smith of the 19th Maine lay with his comrades behind the breastworks when the Confederate First Corps, with bugles blaring, came charging in a battle line out of the woods. An artillery battery poured canister into the Rebel ranks, and "when the enemy got near enough we opened fire and while in some places Longstreet's men planted their colors on our works, in about fifteen minutes those not killed went back howling."[154]

The battle lasted more than fifteen minutes—more like an hour. Charging into withering musketry and cannon fire that swept the cleared area in front of the breastworks, the Confederates dropped to the ground thirty yards from the works and fired back.

A wildfire, ignited by bursting shells, spread from the woods to part of the log breastworks immediately south of the crossroad, and the late Micah Jenkins's brigade seized it. Amid flames "literally licking the legs of the combatants," and pine smoke driven by the wind into their faces, the three Yankee brigades defending the fortifications withdrew, coughing and blistered, enabling Jenkins's Rebels to briefly take control of the section of breastworks.[155]

Hancock's men instantly responded and, for the first time, artillery played an important role in the Wilderness fighting. As the Confederates converged on the breach in the Union fortifications, Captain Edwin Dow's Sixth Maine battery opened fire with shell and case-shot, "bursting them just over the first line of works, which were on fire, and shot their flag down five times." More Rebels emerged from the woods on Dow's right and front, and his men raked them with double-shotted canister. Then, two II Corps brigades, commanded by Colonels John Brooke and Samuel Carroll, rushed to the smoldering, blackened logs, and shot down and chased away the Rebels there. Outside the works, the ground was "literally covered with the mangled bodies of their dead and dying," wrote an officer of the 124th New York. "The whole forest was now one mass of flame and . . . burning underbrush." Some of the wounded Confederates were "roasted to death," wrote Corporal James Donnelly of the 20th Massachusetts, although desperate efforts were made to rescue them.[156]

Alexander, the First Corps' artillery chief, believed that the Rebel assault lacked the élan that had stimulated Longstreet's attacks that morning. It "ought never, never to have been made. It was sending a boy on a man's errand. It was wasting good soldiers whom we could not spare." Walker, Hancock's assistant adjutant general, agreed that the attack "was not made with great spirit; nor was the response from our side very hearty." Twelve hours of combat had sapped both armies.[157]

It was the Army of Northern Virginia's last major attack of the war.

GRANT CANCELED HIS plan for Hancock and Burnside to attack at 6 p.m., but not before Burnside returned to action with two divisions, nearly bagging the Alabama and Florida brigades that he had earlier mauled. General Nathaniel Harris's Mississippi brigade came to their rescue and helped the beleaguered Alabama and Florida brigades repel successive attacks by Burnside, but not before scores of Rebels were made prisoners.

The Union troops marveled at the enemy prisoners' ragamuffin clothing and appearance. "Indeed, it was pathetic, to note their knapsacks of woven carpets with coverlets and patchwork quilts and braided carpets used as blankets," wrote William Hopkins of the 7th Rhode Island. "The men themselves were lank, yellow, long-limbed, weather-beaten, rough-haired fellows, but they were terrible soldiers, possessing the hardihood of wild animals."[158]

An older Rebel from Gregg's Texas brigade, shot in the shin late in the day and left behind, was asked by his Yankee captors what he thought of the battle. "Battle be ——!" he said. "You Yanks don't call this a battle, do you? At Chickamauga there was at least a rear. . . . It's all a —— mess! And our two armies ain't nothin' but howlin' mobs!"[159]

THREE MILES AWAY, it had been quiet on the turnpike since the Rebel attack and two VI Corps counterattacks early that morning. During one counterattack, Truman Seymour's brigade tried to turn the Confederate left flank. John Pegram's well-entrenched men, practically invisible in the lush undergrowth, eviscerated the attackers. A Southerner, William W. Smith, wrote, "The men enjoyed the novelty of fighting behind breastworks," where "a general spirit of hilarity prevailed." He noted that a comrade had exclaimed, "Say, boys, isn't this the mos'est fun for the leas'est money?" The bloody repulse of Seymour's troops dampened enthusiasm for further Union attacks. Gouverneur Warren, unwilling to lose men for no tangible gain, forbore sending his V Corps into either counterattack.[160]

In his instructions to Ewell, Lee had proposed that he attack the Union right and interpose his Second Corps between the Yankees and the Rapidan—if he saw an opportunity to do so. If that were impossible, Ewell must be ready to reinforce Hill on the plank road.

Ewell had neither flanked nor reinforced. Instead, his 17,000 troops had spent the day strengthening their defenses and waging a low-grade firefight that occasionally rose to a crescendo before subsiding once more to desultory skirmishing. Ewell's men held their positions while firing thousands of rounds of ammunition and keeping five Union divisions out of the plank road fight, but otherwise Ewell accomplished nothing.

After the Rebel attack on Hancock's Brock Road breastworks was beaten back, Lee again pressed Ewell to do something, perhaps wondering if the relative silence on the turnpike was another sign, as it had been at Gettysburg, of Ewell's incipient irresolution. Preoccupied all day with directing

Hill's and Longstreet's corps on the plank road, Lee now asked whether Ewell's corps could do anything to relieve the pressure on Longstreet and Hill—perhaps attacking the Union right flank, as Lee had suggested earlier that day. But Ewell and his advisor and division commander, Jubal Early, had decided that morning that the Yankee defenses were too formidable for any attack to succeed.

GENERAL JOHN GORDON, Early's most promising brigadier, had been urging an attack all day, but was rebuffed each time by Early and Ewell. At dawn, scouts had told Gordon that Grant's extreme right ended a short distance away and was "wholly unprotected," while Gordon's line extended beyond it. Gordon sent other scouts to verify the report and to determine whether Union reserve units were posted nearby. "The astounding information was brought that there was not a supporting force within several miles of it," Gordon wrote.

He went to see for himself. Indeed, everything the scouts had said was "correct in every particular"; nothing guarded the enemy's right flank. "The Union soldiers were seated on the margin of the rifle-pits, taking their breakfast." The sight amazed Gordon "and filled me with confident anticipation of unprecedented victory."

But when Gordon informed Early and proposed hitting the Yankees' right, Early replied that cavalry scouts had reported that Burnside's IX Corps occupied positions behind the Union VI Corps. It did not, Gordon told him. "He [Early] was not perceptibly affected by the repeated reports of scouts," wrote Gordon, "nor my own statement that I myself had ridden for miles in rear of Sedgwick's right" without seeing any other Yankee units. Ewell upheld Early's decision to not act.

For the next nine hours, from 8 a.m. until after 5 p.m., with the roar of the plank road fighting in the distance, Ewell's men lay comparatively idle behind their breastworks—while Gordon alternately advocated his plan to Early and Ewell and quietly seethed over their refusal to act upon it.[161]

Late in the afternoon, however, after the failed Confederate frontal assault down the plank road, Gordon's plan suddenly found favor. Exactly why is unclear. In his report, Ewell wrote that he personally reconnoitered the Union right later in the day and found that it was completely unsupported. In his memoirs, Early wrote that sometime during the afternoon "it had been ascertained that Burnside had gone to Grant's left," and that it was he who urged Ewell to carry out Gordon's plan.[162]

In his *Reminiscences*, published in 1903, after the other principals had died, Gordon furnished a more dramatic narrative: Lee riding to Ewell's headquarters to prod him into action; there learning that Gordon had been advocating an excellent plan all day that had been spurned again and again; and then, after hearing out Early and Gordon, tersely ordering Ewell to carry out Gordon's plan.

However, accounts do not agree on whether Lee even visited Ewell's headquarters. If he did, Lee might have simply apprised Ewell of the repulse on the plank road and urged Ewell to reconsider an attempt to turn the Union right. This could have spurred Ewell to conduct his reconnaissance and to reconsider Gordon's proposal. Because it appeared after the deaths of anyone who could dispute it, Gordon's version should be met with skepticism. It smacks of self-aggrandizement, and rather incredibly suggests wanton dereliction by Early and Ewell.[163]

Late in the day, Gordon and his Georgians finally received permission to attack the Union's dangling right flank, the domain of John Sedgwick's VI Corps. Sometime that afternoon, General Robert Johnston's brigade of North Carolinians from Robert Rodes's division had taken a position on Gordon's left, so that the Rebel line overlapped the Union flank to an even greater extent. When Gordon launched his assault, Johnston's brigade would follow Gordon's to scoop up Yankee prisoners.[164]

ABOUT 7 O'CLOCK, Gordon's Georgians suddenly appeared on Grant's right flank. It was a tremendous shock to Truman Seymour's brigade, still recovering from its drubbing that morning. When Gordon's brigade emerged from the woods and attacked with piercing shrieks, Seymour's men, facing the wrong way, were in the act of resting, cooking, and eating, with their weapons stacked and blankets spread on the ground. The Yankees fled, "almost as quickly as partridges could. It was like shooting birds on the wing," wrote George Nichols of the 61st Georgia.

Dr. Daniel Holt, a surgeon with the 121st New York, was swept up in the rout, with the Rebels "driving us like scared sheep . . . a promiscuous skedaddle from right to left and from front to rear." His horse galloped off, with Holt ignominiously running after it and barely avoiding capture. Johnston's brigade rounded up hundreds of prisoners, including Seymour, captured while attempting to rally his men. His brigade's defeat was complete in just five minutes.[165]

Gordon's men burrowed deeper into the Union flank, next sweeping through Alexander Shaler's brigade. It suffered the same fate as Seymour's brigade, and Shaler joined Seymour as a prisoner. "There was practically no resistance," wrote Gordon. "There could be none. . . . There was nothing for the brave Federals to do but to fly." Charles Page, a New York *Tribune* correspondent, described the attack as "like a torrent rolling and dashing in living waves, and flooding up against the whole VI Corps." General John Sedgwick, tried to rally his corps, crying, "Boys, don't run! I will stay here with you and get you out."[166]

Stampeding men from the shattered regiments raced through the woods toward army headquarters a mile and a half away, arriving "in an incredibly short time" to breathlessly announce that the Rebels had broken VI Corps. "Aides came galloping in from the right, laboring under intense excitement," wrote Horace Porter, "talking wildly and giving the most exaggerated reports of the engagement." In the growing pandemonium, ambulances and commissary wagons collided and overturned, and horses ran wild.

Through it all, Grant remained unruffled, skeptical of the wild accounts blurted by excited couriers arriving on galloping horses. Reacting to the real emergency, he and Meade placed the rest of VI Corps into a new line to better resist the flank assault.

The exaggerated reports and warnings began to irritate Grant. When a staff officer told him that if the Union right collapsed, the army would also lose its supply trains, Grant snapped, "When this army is defeated and when I am driven from this line, it will be when I have so few men left that they will not want any trains."

When an overwrought general exclaimed that Lee was poised to cut off the army from the Rapidan, Grant lost his temper. "Oh, I am heartily tired of hearing about what Lee is going to do," he said. "Some of you always seem to think he is suddenly going to turn a double somersault, and land in our rear and on both of our flanks at the same time. Go back to your command, and try to think about what we are going to do ourselves, instead of what Lee is going to do." The chastised officer slunk off in silence.[167]

Colonel Emory Upton hustled two regiments from his brigade into Gordon's path, but they were broken up. The brigade next in line, Thomas Neill's, was able to turn its right flank in time to face Gordon's thunderbolt and slow it down, while simultaneously fending off frontal attacks by yet another Rebel brigade, John Pegram's. Timely reinforcements and disarray in the now jumbled Confederate ranks slowed the attacks' velocity.

Darkness ended the fighting. Gordon's, Johnston's, and Pegram's brigades withdrew.

Yet, in a short period, the Rebels had seized 600 Union prisoners, killed and wounded hundreds more, and had shaken up the entire Union right flank. "Had daylight lasted one half-hour longer, there would not have been left an organized company in Sedgwick's corps," Gordon wrote, with some hyperbole. If Gordon and Ewell had that morning launched simultaneous flank and frontal attacks amid the crisis on the plank road, Grant's army might have suffered a major defeat.[168]

As THE WOODS around them burned, Yankees and Rebels labored to improve their breastworks in anticipation of a resumption of the battle the next morning. The two square miles west of the Brock Road–Orange Plank Road crossroads abounded in horrors. "Every bush seemed hung with shreds of blood-stained clothing. It was as though Christian men had turned to fiends, and hell itself had usurped the place of earth," wrote Porter.

Dead men lay everywhere, in every attitude and every state of dismemberment. Dr. John Perry, the 20th Massachusetts's surgeon, reported "walking over rows of dead bodies piled at times two and three deep, as they lay in lines, exactly as if mowed down."

As wildfires lit the night sky, the survivors heard wounded men crying for help. "The dead were roasted in the conflagration," wrote Porter. "The wounded, roused by its hot breath, dragged themselves along, with their torn and mangled limbs, in the mad energy of despair, to escape the ravages of the flames." Many did not. The Army of the Potomac's medical director later estimated that 200 men were burned alive.[169]

GRANT HAD SEEN nothing like the past two days. Even Shiloh, bad as it was on the first day, had ended in victory. The Battle of the Wilderness, he would write the next morning to Henry Halleck, had ended in a draw. "We can claim no victory over the enemy, neither have they gained a single advantage," Grant wrote. "The enemy pushed out of his fortifications to prevent their position being turned, and have been sooner or later driven back in every instance."[170]

Grant's chief of staff, John Rawlins, later said that after Gordon's surprise attack on the Union right flank was stopped, Grant went to his tent "and throwing himself face downward on his cot, instead of going to sleep, gave vent to his feelings in a way which left no doubt that he was deeply moved." James Wilson, the cavalry division commander, recounted the story in his biography of Rawlins. Wilson wrote that the general-in-chief's staff had never seen him lose his composure as he did that night. But Porter wrote that he looked in on Grant minutes after he entered his tent and found him fast asleep; his memoirs do not mention the episode that Wilson described.[171]

Apocryphal or not, the anecdote illustrates the tension and concern that gripped the Union high command on the night of May 6. It disturbed Grant that although Lee had been driven back from his full-throated attack on Grant's army, he had not backed down. Grant remarked to Meade that General Joseph Johnston would have retreated after two days of such fighting. "He recognizes the difference of the Western rebel fighting," wrote Theodore Lyman, who witnessed the conversation.[172]

As Grant sat quietly by his fire that night, chewing on a cigar, slumped in an army chair, hat pulled low, coat collar pulled high, the possibility of failure surely occurred to him. How else could it have been for a man who had failed as a farmer, who had struggled mightily to feed and clothe his family, and who had been forced to admit his failure to his father and gratefully accept a clerk's job in the family leather goods store?[173]

Grant had company by the fire—journalist Sylvanus Cadwallader, who was troubled by the failure of two days' heavy fighting to produce a Union victory. When Grant noticed Cadwallader, he threw off his introspection and began discussing a range of subjects unrelated to the war. After a while, Cadwallader proposed that they get some sleep. Grant smiled, the journalist wrote, and, before entering his tent, remarked that Lee had given his army "sharp work."[174]

A piece of good news reached Grant that day: Benjamin Butler's Army of the James had reached City Point, at the confluence of the James and Appomattox Rivers, and had then advanced to Bermuda Hundred between Petersburg and Richmond. From Bermuda Hundred, Union troops might sever the Richmond and Petersburg Railroad, a principal supply line to the Confederate capital.[175]

WHILE GRANT BROODED by his campfire near Wilderness Tavern, Lincoln in Washington sleeplessly paced the White House corridors in his long robe, "his hands behind him, great black rings under his eyes, his head bent forward upon his breast." He was anxious to receive news—any news—from the front. At all hours of the day and night, the president would stride across the White House lawn to the War Department to haunt the telegraph office. It was a tense time for many in Washington. "There is an impression that we are on the eve of a great battle and that it may already have commenced," Navy Secretary Gideon Welles wrote in his diary on May 6.

But no reports had reached Washington since the Army of the Potomac crossed the Rapidan. The army had moved away from the railroad lines, and telegraph lines had not yet been strung. When a congressman asked Lincoln what Grant was doing, the president responded with humor: "I can't tell much about it. You see, Grant has gone into the Wilderness, crawled in, drawn up the ladder, and pulled in the hole after him, and I guess we'll have to wait till he comes out before we know just what he's up to."[176]

But on the night of May 6 the president's patience was at an end, and he summoned Charles Dana, the assistant war secretary and former journalist, to the White House. Lincoln asked Dana to travel to Grant's headquarters and report to him what was happening. Dana left that night with a 100-man cavalry escort on a train to Alexandria. By the afternoon of the next day, Dana was riding into Grant's camp. He remained with Grant during the weeks that followed.[177]

While Dana was en route to Grant's headquarters, New York *Tribune* correspondent Henry Wing was headed north with the first news of the Wilderness fighting. That day, Wing had sought Grant's permission to try to get through to Washington, and Grant had approved his plan—while also giving Wing a private verbal message for Lincoln alone.

The odds were against Wing. The roads and woods between the Rappahannock and the Potomac teemed with Confederate guerrillas and cavalry. But Wing was young, twenty-four, and he was a combat veteran who had been wounded in the leg and had lost two fingers at Fredericksburg. Wing pretended to be a Southern sympathizer who was on his way to tell John Mosby's partisans about Lee's victory in the Wilderness. One band of Rebels didn't believe him and took Wing into custody, but he slipped away.

Reaching a Union outpost, Wing wrote a dispatch that was sent on the government telegraph line to the War Department. Wing had news from the front, his message said. War Secretary Edwin Stanton personally responded, asking Wing where Grant was. Wing told Stanton he would tell him everything, if he agreed to allow him to send 100 words of copy to the *Tribune*. Stanton ordered the outpost commander to arrest Wing unless he gave him news from the front; Wing refused.

Then, to everyone's surprise, Lincoln came on the line and accepted Wing's terms. The president even suggested that Wing write a longer account for his newspaper to better inform the public. Wing dictated a half-column dispatch to the *Tribune*, and Lincoln sent the special train that had taken Dana to Alexandria to fetch Wing. Wing arrived at the White House about 2 a.m. on May 7.

Led into a room where a large map of Virginia covered the wall, Wing pointed out the armies' locations to Lincoln, Welles, and other officials, and described what he had seen of the battle. After answering their questions, he requested a private meeting with the president.

When they were alone, Wing said that he had a message from Grant. Lincoln stooped to bring his eyes level with Wing's. "What is it?" he whispered to Wing. Wing replied, "General Grant told me to tell you, from him, that, whatever happens, there is to be no turning back." Lincoln impulsively wrapped his arms around Wing and planted a kiss on his forehead.[178]

5

Saturday, May 7, 1864
The Wilderness

THE COMBATANTS AWOKE as gray light began leaking through a miasma of fog and smoke reeking of charred flesh. The soldiers were red-eyed, muddy, and smoke-smudged after two days of their savage "blind wrestle." Less than a mile apart, each side waited for the other to attack. "There lay both armies, each behind its breastworks," wrote Theodore Lyman of Meade's staff, "panting and exhausted, and scowling at each other."[179]

The night terror a fading memory, Grant was his usual impassive self this morning. Refreshed by a few hours of sleep, the general-in-chief, seated outside his tent near the Orange Turnpike crossroad opposite Wilderness Tavern, watched as James Wilson, the former Grant aide and now a cavalry commander, rode up and dismounted. Discerning the purpose of Wilson's visit from his anxious expression, Grant said, "It's all right, Wilson; the Army of the Potomac will go forward to-night."[180]

Shocking casualties and Longstreet's and Gordon's flank attacks might have briefly unnerved Grant, but he remained determined to continue the campaign. The previous afternoon, he had discussed with his staff a plan to march around Lee's right flank and interpose the army between Lee and Richmond, and he had asked Henry Wing to tell President Lincoln there would be no turning back. Now, he was informing Wilson the campaign would resume that night.

Grant's decision was enormously important, because each time that the Army of the Potomac had previously crossed the Rapidan, it had soon retreated. But the leader of this fourth offensive was different from his predecessors, although no one outside of Grant's inner circle—much less Lee and the Army of Northern Virginia—knew what he was going to do.[181]

Full morning arrived, and there was no assault by either army. "The silence was strange and oppressive, after the terrible and continuous roar of the last two days," wrote Adam Badeau, Grant's aide and military historian.[182]

Both armies had lost heavily: Grant's army, 17,666 killed, wounded, and captured; the Army of Northern Virginia, 11,033. The Orange Plank

Road battles accounted for most of the losses. There, Hancock had lost 5,100 men; Wadsworth's V Corps division, about 2,000; and Getty's VI Corps division, 3,000—fully 10,000 of Grant's casualties. Lee, too, had lost 10,000 men on the plank road: 7,000 from Hill's corps and 3,000 from Longstreet's. Of battles lasting more than one day, only Gettysburg and Chickamauga had been bloodier.[183]

Some units had been nearly annihilated. The 2nd Vermont had lost two thirds of its men May 5 when it and Getty's division stopped Hill's corps from capturing the plank road crossroad. "All of our former battles put together have not reduced our ranks like this one, and the end is not yet," lamented Private Wilbur Fisk.

The Texas Brigade had lost 550 of its 800 men during Longstreet's counterattacks on the plank road May 6. The dead Texans were buried there with separate headstones beneath an oak tree to which was nailed a sign that simply read, "Texas Dead—May 6, 1864."[184]

As the day grew warmer and dustier, sharpshooters began targeting anyone who thoughtlessly exposed himself. Union and Confederate commanders sent out skirmishers to try to ascertain one another's position and numbers in the hope of somehow divining the enemy's intentions. While they were at it, they looked for live, wounded comrades among the heaps of decomposing bodies that had begun to foul the air.

Both sides took the opportunity to bury the dead. John Casler of the 33rd Virginia wrote that at one spot in front of his brigade, "where the enemy had made a desperate charge on the 6th, we buried five hundred of them that lay in line as they fell." The Rebels were hungry; their rations were in their wagons. But the Yankees had ample hardtack and bacon in their haversacks, "and we would get them from the dead," wrote Casler. "I have been so hungry that I have cut the blood off from crackers and eaten them."[185]

A Confederate soldier claimed that the skin of dead Rebels shrank and turned yellow, while Yankee corpses swelled, turned purple, and stank; he attributed the difference to the "superior keeping of the Federal soldier."

A man in Captain Robert Carter's company of the 22nd Massachusetts who was wounded in both hips and had both legs amputated ended up being the charge of one side, then the other. After he was abandoned in a field hospital, Rebels briefly captured him, but then Union cavalry found the legless man just as a wildfire was about to incinerate him. In the ambulance, he said to a drummer boy, "Tell the boys that I did not lose my legs trying to get to the rear."[186]

AFTER THE FIGHTING ended on May 6, surgeons worked into the night at the field hospitals, amputating shattered limbs and dressing the wounds of "men wounded in every conceivable way, men with mutilated bodies, with shattered limbs and broken heads." Severe wounds were inflicted by the musket-fired, .58-caliber, soft-lead bullets that "mushroomed" when they struck. Abdominal wounds were usually fatal; the bullets tore up the intestines. When they struck bones, they smashed them to splinters, and amputation was usually the course of treatment. Many of the wounded died in hospitals, and half of those who survived were never again fit for duty.

Near the front, each regiment's medical officer gave emergency care and shuttled the seriously wounded in one of his three ambulances to the field hospitals staffed by surgeons, about 500 yards behind the front. Farther back still was the division hospital, staffed by a surgeon in charge, three operating surgeons, nine assistant surgeons, and male nurses.

Sometimes the frazzled surgeons meted out rough justice while treating the wounded. The teenage artillerist, Frank Wilkeson, witnessed an example of this after helping a man with a foot wound to a field hospital. After chloroforming the soldier, the surgeon examined his foot. "The cowardly whelp!" he cried, when he saw that the entry wound was blackened with powder, evidence that it was self-inflicted. Without hesitation, the surgeon took off the man's leg below the knee. When the soldier awakened, "I will never forget the look of horror," Wilkeson wrote, when he realized that his leg was gone. Yet, Wilkeson approved of the surgeon's draconian act. "The utter contempt of the surgeons, their change from careful handling to almost brutality when they discovered the wound was self-inflicted, was bracing to me."

At midnight, the surgeons were ordered to stop work. The wounded were loaded into ambulances and army wagons and moved to the old Chancellorsville battleground. The tents were re-erected, the men still needing surgery were unloaded from ambulances, and the surgeons resumed their work.

John Perry, a surgeon with the 20th Massachusetts, wrote that he had slept only a couple of hours during the previous forty. "My face is black with dirt and perspiration, clothes soiled and torn almost to pieces," he told his wife Martha.[187]

Eventually, the wounded were transported to Fredericksburg. The jolting trip, over rutted roads, took a day and a half. Every jerk of the wagons, each packed with nine to twelve men, elicited a chorus cries and curses. The leaky wagon beds spattered the roads with fresh blood from sutures that burst during the jarring ride.

The residents of Fredericksburg, who had been shot, bombarded, and plundered during years of war, watched in horror as the wagons bearing their cargo of misery streamed into the city. "The churches were filled first, then warehouses and stores, and then private houses, until the town was literally one immense hospital," wrote George Stevens, a surgeon with the 77th New York.[188]

Army quartermasters in Washington were caught off-guard; orders had stipulated that the wounded were to be taken to Rappahannock Station, and thence by railroad to Washington hospitals. No provision had been made to stock Fredericksburg with food and supplies, and just forty surgeons had accompanied the thousands of wounded men.

The result was "such wretchedness and suffering as we had never before seen," wrote Mrs. Charles A. L. Sampson of the Maine Soldiers' Relief Association. The wounded men, she wrote, lacking even blankets, covered the counters and floors of Fredericksburg's shops. Promising that supplies would arrive soon, aid workers did what they could to cheer up the men—as opposed to "the most malignant spirits" exhibited toward them by many Fredericksburg residents, forced to admit them into their homes.[189]

The sight of semi-starved soldiers lying on bare floors shocked Clara Barton, the "angel of the battlefield." And then, when she learned that Union officers were refusing to open Fredericksburg's grandest mansions to the wounded, she went straight to her patron in Washington, Senator Henry Wilson of Massachusetts. Wilson took up the matter with War Secretary

Stanton, threatening a Senate investigation. Stanton promptly dispatched Quartermaster General Montgomery Meigs and his staff to Fredericksburg with orders to open up the homes and seize the city's food. Meigs put crews to work repairing the railroad so that the wounded could be evacuated from Fredericksburg to Washington.[190]

When the war began, Barton, a diminutive New Englander, had left her job as a copyist at the US Patent Office to succor wounded and ill Union soldiers in the field. At the same time, Dorothea Dix, a crusader for the mentally ill, had organized an Army nursing corps modeled on Florence Nightingale's volunteer organization from the Crimean War.

Barton would have met Dix's criteria for her nurses: plain, modest women over thirty years old, required to wear austere black or brown dresses. Barton, however, did not want to work for the dedicated but notoriously autocratic Dix—or, really, for anyone; she was a loner. Working with a few assistants, Barton began collecting donated items and taking them to the front, where she and her assistants handed out bandages and dressings and aided the surgeons.

After Second Manassas, Barton brought soup and food to the wounded at an aid station and assisted in their care for days before leaving on the last train as the Rebels moved in. Barton continued in her ad hoc role at Fredericksburg. "The number of wounded has exceeded anything in history," she wrote to her brother David. Eventually, 142 contract surgeons, 194 reserve surgeons, and 775 medical students and nurses were dispatched to aid the army medical staff at Fredericksburg.[191]

THE ARMIES HAD fought to a stalemate: Grant had failed to crush Lee; Lee had failed to drive Grant from the field, much less back over the Rapidan.

During the tense standoff on May 7, the battle's result was not immediately apparent. The blind fighting in the dense woods and swamps, the wildfires, and the appalling losses conspired to obscure the outcome. Most of the participants could agree that it had been "a private's battle," fought under conditions that hobbled both armies—and by no means a battle of maneuver directed by generals. Artillery had proven nearly useless, evidenced by the high proportion of bullet wounds. Newspaper correspondent

William Swinton wrote, "It is impossible to conceive a field worse adapted to the movements of a grand army." Theodore Lyman described the battle as "a scientific 'bushwhack' of 200,000 men."

While the troops steeled themselves for renewed fighting, Rebel leaders lamented the lost opportunities for a smashing victory that had briefly been theirs. The wounding of Longstreet, who had until then outperformed all the generals of both armies, was "an undisguised blessing to Grant's army," wrote Lieutenant Colonel Weygant of the Orange Blossom Brigade.

Edward Porter Alexander wrote that May 4th would have been Lee's day if Hill and Ewell had begun marching early in the morning and not at noon. Conversely, "May 5th was Grant's day," wrote Alexander. "Every hour of its daylight was to him a golden opportunity to crush an inferior enemy which had rashly ventured within his reach."[192]

Longstreet's timely arrival on the plank road early May 6 had spared Lee's army from a catastrophic defeat. Lee, more than Grant, felt the pinch of fighting two uncoordinated battles on parallel roads three miles apart. Despite their efforts, neither general was able to join his forces on the two roads to form a single battle line.

Winfield Scott Hancock's II Corps excepted, the Army of the Potomac had moved haltingly. Grant planned bold, powerful movements, but got tardy, piecemeal attacks, and May 5th's potential was squandered. The army failed to utilize its overwhelming numerical advantage and, in fact, was sometimes fortunate to avoid defeat.

Meade's ordnance chief, Morris Schaff, expressed the bewilderment felt by many of the soldiers over not having beaten Lee. "Two days of deadly encounter; every man who could bear a musket had been put in; Hancock and Warren repulsed, Sedgwick routed, and now on the defensive behind breastworks; the cavalry drawn back . . . thousands and thousands of killed and wounded . . . the air pervaded with a lurking feeling of being face to face with disaster. What, what is the matter with the Army of the Potomac?"[193]

But even with the sloppy staff work and the poor coordination of the attacks, the blue-coated assault troops, coming in relentless waves, had sometimes daunted even Lee's confident Rebels. "There was something

remorseless even in Grant's mistakes," observed British military historian
C. F. Atkinson in his study of Grant's campaign.

ALTHOUGH A BLOODY tactical draw, the Wilderness was a strategic triumph for Grant, because when the fighting ended, Grant retained the initiative. For the first time during the war, Robert E. Lee had been forced to
go on the defensive, lest his army, having lost 11,000 men during two days
of fighting, be further depleted of irreplaceable troops.

In his report, Grant wrote, "It was evident to my mind that the two days'
fighting had satisfied [Lee] of his inability to further maintain the contest
in the open field, notwithstanding his advantage of position, and that he
would await an attack behind his works." Henceforth, Lee would prosecute
a defensive strategy—and do it superbly—hoping to prolong the war until
the North grew weary enough to seek peace.[194]

In the span of three days, the war in the East had changed irrevocably; it
was the major turning point of the war.

ON MAY 7, the cavalry battle shifted to Todd's Tavern after Meade re-
leased most of Sheridan's corps from the duty of guarding the trains. Sheridan had earlier told Meade that infantrymen could just as well protect the
wagons, and now Meade assigned a division from IX Corps to that task.
Sheridan was free "to detach any portion of your command for offensive
operations," Meade wrote.[195]

This was good news for Sheridan, who was determined to drive Fitzhugh
Lee's and Wade Hampton's cavalrymen from Todd's Tavern. On May 6,
after hours of bitter fighting that had no impact on the roaring plank road
battle and no clear winner, Meade pulled back all of Sheridan's cavalrymen
to the old Chancellorsville battleground in the mistaken belief that the Confederates had turned Hancock's left flank. The Rebel cavalrymen promptly
seized the Furnace Road, Todd's Tavern, and Piney Branch Church. The
Union cavalry's efforts that day were wasted. "The points thus abandoned
had to be regained at a heavy cost in killed in wounded, to both the cavalry and the infantry," Sheridan wrote. "Much blood was shed and many
valuable lives were lost in retrieving the error," wrote Major James Kidd.[196]

Sheridan sent David Gregg's and Alfred Torbert's divisions to clear the Todd's Tavern area—the latter under the temporary command of General Wesley Merritt, because Torbert was disabled by a spinal abscess. Wilson's battered division was left behind with the trains to rest.

At Todd's Tavern, Fitz Lee's dismounted men fought from behind log barricades as Merritt's brigades closed in from the north and Gregg's from the east. Before he was caught in the pincer movement, Lee withdrew a mile south on the Brock Road. Splitting his force, Sheridan sent Colonel Irving Gregg's brigade across Brock Road toward Corbin's Bridge on Catharpin Road to attack Hampton's division. Seeing that the Rebel cavalrymen held excellent high ground, Irving Gregg's men withdrew to Todd's Tavern, posted artillery and dug earthworks—just in time to repel an attack by Hampton and troopers from the division of General W. H. F. "Rooney" Lee, a son of Robert E. Lee.

A mile away, Merritt's three brigades fought Fitz Lee's hard-bitten troopers on foot in the hot woods. The Rebels had rapidly erected new barricades after abandoning the ones at Todd's Tavern. Sheridan described the battle as "an exceedingly severe and, at times, fluctuating fight."

The Yankees' rapid-firing Spencer repeaters set the barricades on fire and forced the Confederates to again withdraw—to new, hurriedly built rail barricades. "For a half hour there was one of the hottest fights between the opposing brigades of dismounted cavalry that occurred during the war," wrote a cavalryman with the 4th Virginia. At nightfall, flames licked the sky and Fitz Lee's hard-pressed Rebels had not been dislodged. "My command fought most gallantly," wrote Lee, "and night found them holding every part of their hastily constructed rail breastworks."

Sheridan recalled all of his troopers to open fields east of Todd's Tavern, leaving Brock Road and the woods on either side of it littered with blue-coated dead.[197]

His report to Meade pronounced the day's fighting to be a triumph. "Our cavalry behaved splendidly," he wrote, and "drove" the enemy. True insofar as it went, his claim was also profoundly disingenuous; he had failed to clear Brock Road, which portended major difficulties for the Army of the Potomac. Fitzhugh Lee's troopers still barred the way.[198]

IN HIS BRIEF report to General Henry Halleck, Grant had described the result of the two days' fighting to be no better than a draw. But as his natural optimism returned early May 7, Grant began to feel better about the battle. While not a "positive victory," he told his aide, Horace Porter, at breakfast, the Rebels had only reached the Union lines twice with their many attacks. By May 8 he would be telling Halleck that the battle was "decidedly in our favor."

Buoying Grant's confidence was his plan to steal a march on Lee. Grant was most comfortable in the role of aggressor; it gave him control of the situation. If all worked as planned, the Army of the Potomac would capture Spotsylvania Court House, ten miles south of the Wilderness—Todd's Tavern being midway between the two points—and stand between Lee and Richmond. Grant saw two advantages to this: preventing Lee from beating Grant to Richmond and crushing Benjamin Butler's army on the James River, and forcing Lee to leave his breastworks and fight in the open.

In orders issued at 6:30 a.m. on May 7, Grant directed Meade to prepare to march south that night. Warren's V Corps would travel down Brock Road behind II Corps' entrenchments at the plank road crossroad. Hancock's men would hold its position there, and then follow Warren. Using roads east of Brock Road to speed the march, Sedgwick's VI Corps would also head south, with Burnside's IX Corps falling in behind it. "All vehicles should be got out of hearing of the enemy before the troops move, and then move off quietly."[199]

LEE DID NOT believe that Grant would withdraw across the Rapidan; engineers had pulled up the Germanna Ford bridges. He prepared to act quickly no matter what Grant did, although he thought it probable that Grant would march directly south toward Spotsylvania Court House, for it was what Lee would have done. Roads radiated from the town, and it sat on a ridge between the Ni and Po Rivers—narrow, but deep and steep-sided rivers that were difficult to cross except over bridges. The surrounding countryside was heavily timbered, but broken up by clearings. "It was a much better country to conduct a defensive campaign in than an offensive one," Grant would later write.

That day, May 7, Lee ordered his artillery commander, General William Pendleton, to cut a new road through the forest behind the Rebel positions between the plank road and Catharpin Road. The new road would have a single purpose: so that the First Corps, on the Confederate far right, might move quickly southward if Grant did. Lee's chief engineer, General Martin Smith, had mapped this route in April while planning for contingencies during this campaign.

Lee told his cavalry commander, Jeb Stuart, to watch for any enemy movement toward Spotsylvania. Later in the day, Lee visited Ewell's corps on the turnpike. He instructed Ewell to closely watch Sedgwick's VI Corps and report any change in its position. Lee did not want to be taken unawares when Grant began to maneuver.[200]

Lee stopped at A. P. Hill's headquarters at the Chewning farmhouse while returning to his headquarters at the Tapp farm. As he and Hill sat on the porch talking, Hill's chief of staff, Colonel William Palmer, was upstairs, studying the Union positions on Brock Road through a telescope poking through the roof. Palmer had a fine view of Grant's headquarters near Wilderness Tavern. "In a field near the headquarters was a large park of heavy guns, and as I looked these guns moved into the road and took the road to our right, their left," Palmer wrote.[201]

When Palmer clattered downstairs to report that the Union artillery were moving south, Lee had just the information that he needed; he was now certain that Grant was going to Spotsylvania. He directed the First Corps to withdraw from its positions when it grew dark, prefatory to an all-night march down Pendleton's new road. Ewell's Second Corps would follow.[202]

Earlier in the day, Lee had named General Richard Anderson, who led a division in Hill's Third Corps, to assume temporary command of the First Corps while Longstreet recovered from his wound. Lee had had three division commanders in mind for the position—Jubal Early and Edward Johnson of the Second Corps, and Anderson. Before choosing one of them, Lee had asked Moxley Sorrel, Longstreet's adjutant general, which one would be the best fit for the First Corps; it was important to Lee because the corps was unquestionably the best in the army. Sorrel said Early was probably the most able of the three, but because of his irascibility, he was unpopular with the First Corps. Johnson, he said, was not known in the corps, but Anderson had once commanded a division there; the men would be satisfied with him. Although Lee preferred Early, he appointed Anderson. William Mahone assumed command of Anderson's division in his absence.[203]

ON THIS DAY, too, Grant and Lincoln resolved a sticky command problem in the Department of the Gulf when Lincoln agreed to replace General Nathaniel Banks as field commander. It was a victory for Grant, whose exasperation over Banks's failed Red River campaign had moved him to urge Banks's removal. The campaign's failure had broad repercussions: it delayed Grant's plan to seize Mobile and prevented 30,000 troops temporarily assigned to Banks from being returned to William Sherman in time for his Georgia offensive.

Lincoln had resisted removing Banks because he was an old friend and he had powerful congressional allies who could damage Lincoln politically. But the president and Grant had compromised: Lincoln agreed to relieve Banks of field command, but to retain him as the department's administrator. General Edward Canby became field commander.[204]

THAT NIGHT, THREE Union army corps quietly withdrew from their positions. II Corps remained behind its breastworks on Brock Road to shield the marching formations. The troops had not been told where they were going, and they were irritable, dusty, tired, and unhappy; naturally, many of them assumed that they were being withdrawn across the Rapidan River. That was what the Army of the Potomac always did after fighting Lee in northern Virginia. Sedgwick's VI Corps and Burnside's IX Corps marched east toward the old Chancellorsville battleground, while Meade's V Corps stopped at Brock Road. If they were ordered to march north or east, the soldiers believed, the campaign was over.

But when V Corps turned south on Brock Road, the men's spirits instantly rose. Grant, Meade, and their entourages rode to the front of the column, and it began to pass behind the sleeping men of Hancock's corps. The news spread that Grant was moving on to Richmond. Hancock's men sprang to their feet and rushed to the roadside. "Wild cheers echoed through the forest. . . . Men swung their hats, tossed up their arms, and pressed forward to within touch of their chief, clapping their hands, and speaking to him with the familiarity of comrades," wrote Grant aide Horace Porter. "On to Richmond!" they shouted. "Pine-knots and leaves were set on fire, and lighted the scene with their flickering glare," wrote Porter. "The night march had become a triumphal procession for the new commander."

The men were ordered to stop cheering, but they continued to loudly proclaim their approval. The Rebels, believing that it was the prelude to a night attack, replied with "a furious fusillade of artillery and musketry, plainly heard but not felt by us," wrote Grant.

The scene was repeated when VI and IX Corps reached Chancellorsville and likewise turned toward Spotsylvania. "The men began to sing," wrote Private Frank Wilkeson, the New York artilleryman. "That night we were happy." The general-in-chief was pleased by the men's display of "greatest enthusiasm. . . . It indicated to them that they had passed through the 'beginning of the end' in the battle just fought."[205]

It was more than just the turning point of the war. General William T. Sherman, who was conducting his own campaign in Georgia, described Grant's decision to press on to Spotsylvania Court House as "the supreme moment of his life."[206]

THAT NIGHT, TOO, the First Corps stepped back from the Confederate right. The Third Corps took its place in the line. A. P. Hill's tired men lay down in the darkness among scores of sleeping figures that daytime would reveal to be dead Yankees.

Anderson's nearly 10,000 men were supposed to march a short distance south on the newly cut road, rest for a few hours, and then resume their march no later than 3 a.m. But there was a problem with the plan—one that would prove to be incredibly lucky for the Rebels. "I found the woods on fire and burning furiously in every direction," Anderson wrote, "and there was no suitable place to rest."

Consequently, Anderson decided to march all night—and to rest when the corps neared its objective. It was slow going on Pendleton's road, lit by the raging fires. The road was dusty and dotted with tree stumps that tripped up the men, whose patience and stamina were already being tested by the slow pace, heat, road dust, and falling embers. They were soon coated in white dust and ash. Calvin Collier of the 3rd Arkansas observed that the Texas Brigade, whose May 6 counterattack on the plank road had cost it half its men, was distinguishable in the darkness by the white bandages worn by its many walking wounded. Upon reaching Shady Grove Church Road, the First Corps did not stop, but turned southeast toward Spotsylvania Court House.[207]

REBELS REPORTED THAT VI and IX Corps were withdrawing to Chancellorsville, and a rumor started that Grant was abandoning the "overland" route to Richmond. It was wishful thinking, but the story inspired someone to begin the Rebel yell on the Confederate right. Anderson's men raised it after calling for "three cheers for General Lee." The sound traveled along the line to Lee's extreme left flank, near the Rapidan.

"At first, heard like the rumbling of a distant railroad train, it came rushing down the lines like the surging of the waves upon the ocean, increasing in loudness and grandeur, and passing, it would be heard dying away on the left in the distance," wrote a soldier in the 26th North Carolina. Twice more, the weird, high-pitched battle cry made its way from one end of the Confederate line to the other. "The effect was beyond description," wrote a South Carolina lieutenant.[208]

Lee was beginning his first defensive campaign with 11,000 fewer men than he had three days earlier, and without his "Old Warhorse," Longstreet, and five other generals who had been killed or wounded. But the Army of Northern Virginia's morale remained high.[209]

6

Sunday, May 8, 1864
Brock Road, The Wilderness

FITZHUGH LEE WAS the toast of Richmond society that winter. A rakish twenty-eight-year-old with a droll sense of humor, Lee began showing up at parties with a wind-up doll—a mock-up of a black boy, elegantly dressed. "Fitz Lee sings corn-shucking tunes, and the toy boy dances," wrote the diarist Mary Chesnut. "He is the delight of Richmond salons."

At West Point, Fitz Lee was his uncle's antithesis. While Robert E. Lee had famously graduated without a single demerit, Fitz Lee annually skirted the red line of automatic dismissal for his many demerits. A carouser and mediocre student, Lee graduated in 1856, ranked forty-fifth among his class's forty-nine students.

In 1859, Second Lieutenant Fitz Lee of the 2nd US Cavalry had taken an arrow through his right lung during a fight with a Comanche brave; Lee barely survived, but the Comanche did not.

In 1861, soon after the war began, Jeb Stuart promoted Fitz Lee to brigadier general. Lee became one of Stuart's ablest lieutenants, steadily growing in judgment and experience under Stuart's guidance.[210]

On the smoke- and dust-choked road to Spotsylvania Court House during the night of May 7–8, Fitz Lee demonstrated how a small, mobile force might delay, frustrate, and thwart a large army's progress on a narrow road hemmed by choking vegetation. Lee's cavalry division saved the Army of Northern Virginia.

AFTER THE CHEERING stopped and the troops' exhilaration over marching south had abated, Grant's 100,000-man army settled into a draining, irritating, stop-and-go slog down jammed roads in the dark. V Corps slipped behind II Corps' breastworks on Brock Road while VI and IX Corps, which some Rebels thought were marching toward Fredericksburg, filled Piney Branch Road to the east. Later, the corps would fall in behind V Corps on Brock Road.

Road dust and wildfire ash soon coated the endless columns. Whenever there was a halt, many men stepped out of line and instantly fell asleep on the ground by the roadside, getting to their feet when the line began to move again. The 121st New York of VI Corps battled boredom by kicking a skull as they marched through the old Chancellorsville battleground; some of the soldiers wondered whether the deceased would have minded; when they tired of the game, one of them tossed the skull into a pile of leaves beside the road.[211]

WHEN MEADE REACHED Todd's Tavern, he saw two of Phil Sheridan's Cavalry Corps divisions—Gregg's and Merritt's—bedded down where

Sheridan had left them after their day-long fight with Fitz Lee on Brock Road. Meade flew into a rage. Why weren't they securing Brock Road ahead of the infantry, and where was Sheridan? Merritt and Gregg said they had no orders, and Sheridan was at his headquarters several miles away. The previous afternoon, Meade had specified how each corps was to proceed— except for Sheridan's Cavalry Corps, ordered only to watch the army's right flank and "keep the corps commanders advised in time of the appearance of the enemy." Meade's instructions to Sheridan suggest that he had no role in mind for the Cavalry Corps during one of the Army of the Potomac's most important operations.

Meade drove the cavalrymen out of their bivouac around Todd's Tavern and onto the road. He sent Gregg west to block Catharpin Road at Corbin's Bridge, and Merritt south on Brock Road toward Spotsylvania Court House. To Merritt, Meade wrote, "It is of the utmost importance that not the slightest delay occur in your opening the Brock road beyond Spotsylvania Court-House, as an infantry corps [V Corps] is now on its way to occupy that place." Meade did not ask where Sheridan's third division was. In fact, Sheridan had sent James Wilson's troopers by another route to seize Spotsylvania and to hold it until the infantry arrived.

After ordering the two cavalry divisions onto the already clogged Brock Road, Meade, without giving further thought to the gridlock that he had inadvertently caused, repaired to the log tavern for a few hours' sleep. But first, he fired off a curt note to Sheridan: "I find Generals Gregg and Torbert without orders. They are in the way of the infantry and there is no time to refer to you. I have given them the inclosed [sic] orders, which you can modify to-day after the infantry corps are in position."[212]

Sheridan, in his tent at Alrich's, southeast of Chancellorsville, did not issue orders for Gregg and Merritt until 1 a.m. on May 8, four and a half hours after V and VI Corps had begun moving to Spotsylvania—and about the time that Meade had rousted the cavalry divisions from Todd's Tavern. This was more than odd; it suggested that Sheridan had not even seen Meade's orders to the other corps commanders, issued at 3 p.m. the previous day. Sheridan's orders to Gregg and Merritt, rendered moot before he even wrote them, said: "Move at daylight on the morning of the 8th, for the purpose of gaining possession of Snell's bridge over the Po River, the former

[Gregg] by crossing at Corbin's bridge and the latter by the Block House [between Block House Bridge and Spotsylvania]." After seizing Spotsylvania, Wilson was to join Gregg and Merritt at Snell's bridge, Spotsylvania's southern approach.[213]

Sheridan would later claim that Meade had wrecked his plan, although when Meade arrived at Todd's Tavern, Merritt and Gregg had no orders. If his plan had been carried out, Sheridan would assert, there would have been no need to fight for Spotsylvania Court House; the Union army would have captured it before the Rebels arrived. Adam Badeau, Grant's aide, supported Sheridan's hypothesis. "Every avenue to Spottsylvania [sic] would have been closed to the rebel army," he wrote.

However, by waiting until daylight to ride, Gregg and Merritt would have been too late, with Fitz Lee blocking the Brock Road, and the First Corps marching toward the Block House. "The presence of Fitzhugh Lee's cavalry on the Brock road, and Hampton's cavalry and Longstreet's corps on the Shady Grove road, settled the question as to who should first hold the Court House with infantry, whatever might have been the disposition of our cavalry," concluded General Humphreys, Meade's chief of staff.[214]

The Union army's latest operational gaffe would bear grave consequences.

WHILE GRANT, MEADE, and their staffs rested at Todd's Tavern, the bold flanking movement coagulated in epic traffic jams on the narrow farm roads issuing from the Wilderness. It was nearly 6 a.m. before the two cavalry divisions were untangled from the V Corps' vanguard and Warren's men were able to resume their march south from Todd's Tavern.

In the meantime, frayed tempers snapped; shouting matches erupted; confusion and miscommunication reigned. On nearby Piney Branch Road, wagons, horses, and marching men were hopelessly jumbled; VI Corps advanced a mere four miles in eight hours. Had staff officers directed traffic and kept men, horses, and supplies moving, the army might have beaten Lee's army to Spotsylvania. But they did not.

At one point, Brock Road was blocked for an entire hour while two cavalry regiments brawled. The veteran 3rd Pennsylvania Cavalry was countermarching to Brock Road after taking a wrong turn when it encountered a new cavalry regiment. The veterans spontaneously leaped from their exhausted horses to commandeer the newcomers' fresh mounts. The greenhorns put up a fight, but when the dust cleared, the Pennsylvanians possessed the newcomers' horses.[215]

Meade and Warren did nothing to speed things along. While Meade slept at Todd's Tavern, Colonel Charles Wainwright, V Corps' artillery chief, found Warren and his staff with division commander John Robinson a mile and a half south of Todd's Tavern, "all quietly eating their breakfast, waiting for Merritt to open the way with his cavalry." Highly irritated by their passivity, Wainwright wrote, "I certainly thought then that both Warren and Meade were not pushing matters as much as they ought, considering how important it was to reach Spotsylvania Court House before Lee. . . . I feel sure that had our column been properly pushed we might have got up to Merritt at least an hour before daylight."[216]

THIS WAS JEB Stuart's last great day; the actions of his 8,800 men in six brigades would shape the battles of the next two weeks. While Fitz Lee's two brigades blocked Brock Road, three brigades shielded First Corps, and Rosser's Laurel Brigade galloped to Spotsylvania Court House.

As the Union columns inched southward on Brock Road, Fitz Lee's brigades under Generals Lunsford L. Lomax and William Wickham spent the night bushwhacking the Yankees. The Rebel cavalrymen felled trees that blocked the road and, when the Yankees lit lanterns to illuminate their tree-removal efforts, the Confederates picked them off from the dark woods. Then, Captain P. P. Johnston's horse artillery battery would suddenly blaze from the darkness with shell and canister, driving the Yankees to take cover while the gunners fell back with Fitz Lee's men.

WHEN MEADE'S CURT message reached Sheridan's cavalry headquarters earlier that morning, Sheridan leaped onto his towering jet-black horse, Rienzi, and rode off to join Merritt and his division on Brock Road.

Reaching the head of Warren's column, Sheridan found the 12th Massachusetts in the vanguard, waiting for Merritt to clear the road. A member of the 12th wrote that "a solitary horseman" emerged from the forest and approached the regiment's adjutant, asking the unit's name. He ordered it to deploy to the left of the road, and the regiment behind it to deploy to the right. "By whose order?" asked the adjutant. "The figure raised the flapping brim of his felt hat, and answered with the single word, 'Sheridan!'" When the two regimental commanders rode up to receive the orders directly from Sheridan, he repeated them with "each sentence being bitten off with a 'Quick! Quick!'" The skirmish lines pushed ahead two miles, until becoming entangled with Merritt's troopers and the trees felled by Fitz Lee's men.[217]

As light crept into the eastern sky, Warren at last sent John Robinson's division to put steel into Merritt's snail-like advance. The Union infantrymen compelled Fitz Lee's men to fall back from their first-line barricade to a second line, and finally to withdraw to open ground two miles from Spotsylvania.

On a low ridge known as Laurel Hill, the Rebel cavalrymen threw up a fence-rail barricade and dug entrenchments that slashed across Brock Road. By 8 a.m., they were dug in and ready to fight again. All night long, Fitz Lee's men had held their own against the more numerous Yankee cavalry, but the young general knew that they could not withstand an attack by the numerous Yankee infantrymen that he knew were coming down the road. Fitz Lee sent couriers to find Anderson's First Corps. Come quickly, Lee's message to Anderson said.[218]

ON THE STREETS of Spotsylvania Court House, Wilson easily dispersed Rosser's Laurel Brigade, sent by Stuart to seize the village crossroad. Dozens of Rebels were made prisoners. Wilson was unaware that the situation had changed, and that Merritt and Gregg would not be joining him. At 9 a.m., he reported to Sheridan, "Have run the enemy's cavalry a mile from Spotsylvania Court-House. Have charged them through the village. Am fighting now with a considerable force, supposed to be Lee's division. Everything all right."[219]

Sheridan was worried about Wilson. Because Meade had overridden Sheridan's plan, Wilson was now isolated and faced possible annihilation if he remained in the village. Sheridan sent a courier pounding off to find him and tell him to get out of there.

The situation was changing rapidly in Spotsylvania. Fitz Lee sent a regiment to drive out Wilson, but the Confederate cavalrymen failed. Wilson, who could see Fitz Lee's fieldworks barring Brock Road, decided to attack Lee's rear and break the barrier to Grant's march to Spotsylvania. Colonel John McIntosh's brigade had begun the assault when Wilson learned that a large infantry force was approaching. He recalled McIntosh. "Just at this juncture," wrote Wilson, "an officer of General Sheridan's staff arrived with an order . . . directing me to withdraw immediately." Wilson led his division to Alsop's House two miles northwest of Spotsylvania.[220]

FIRST CORPS WAS enjoying its first rest since leaving its lines several hours earlier. It had marched all night down a crude road full of tree stumps and lined by raging wildfires—nine miles altogether. Unlike Merritt's troopers on the Brock Road, Anderson's men had not faced snipers or sudden volleys from the woods, but the march had been arduous enough. The tree stumps had repeatedly tripped up the Rebels in the dark, and they had sweated throughout the hot night. In daylight they resembled ghosts, covered as they were in dust and ash.

After reaching Shady Grove Church Road and marching southeast a distance, they stopped in a field near the Block House Bridge over the Po River for a breakfast of bacon, hardtack, and peanut coffee. They had earned their rest; Spotsylvania Court House was just three miles away, and the corps was hours ahead of schedule. After an hour's respite, the corps resumed its march; Kershaw's division led it over the Po at Block House Bridge.

Heralds of trouble ahead began to arrive. First, "an old Virginia gentleman, bareheaded and without his shoes, riding in haste towards us," reported that the Rebel cavalry was holding Brock Road, but that Union infantry were preparing to attack, wrote Captain D. Augustus Dickert. Kershaw ordered his brigades forward double-quick. Then, a cavalryman from Fitz Lee's division galloped up, shouting, "Run for our rail piles; the Federal infantry will reach them first, if you don't run."[221]

"Our men sprang forward as if by magic," Dickert wrote. Soon, they were sprinting up the backside of Laurel Hill. Jeb Stuart, conspicuously sitting astride his horse while sometimes drawing fire, calmly placed them in fighting positions alongside Fitz Lee's 3,000 troopers. They arrived just in time to see bluecoats in "a column, a gallant column, moving towards us." By just a minute, First Corps had won the race to Spotsylvania.[222]

A brigade of Robinson's V Corps division emerged from the woods into a broad open field that sloped gently upward to Fitz Lee's field works and entrenchments. Stuart ordered the Rebels to hold their fire until the Yankees drew nearer.

ALL NIGHT LONG, Sheridan's troopers had made little progress against Fitz Lee's cavalrymen, but Warren now believed that with his infantrymen leading the way, he could smash through the barricades barring the army's way to Spotsylvania. "The opposition to us amounts to nothing as yet," he confidently informed General Andrew Humphreys at 8 a.m. Dressed in his best uniform, Warren made a point of telling Humphreys that he would lead the advance personally, and "if anything happens to me, General Crawford is the next officer in rank."

Robinson had fought in nearly every battle in the East, and he did not like the tactical situation that he saw through his binoculars: upward-sloping open ground ending in a densely wooded hillcrest crowded with Confederates behind barricades. He advised Warren to wait until his other brigades arrived, but Warren instead ordered Robinson to attack immediately.[223]

Expecting to fight weary Rebel cavalrymen armed with carbines, Robinson's lead brigade was shocked when it met "a terrible fire of infantry and artillery" that chased it back down the slope. "It was a very sad surprise" for the Union troops, wrote Private William Dame of the Richmond Howitzers. The retreating Yankees collided with a brigade coming up behind it, and they became a mob desperately trying to escape the whistling Minie balls and slashing fire from Stuart's horse artillery batteries.[224]

More Rebels from Anderson's division were arriving every minute and taking places behind the Laurel Hill works. Robinson attacked again, leading a newly arrived brigade; General Charles Griffin, with part of his division, attacked with him. Musket fire flashed from the long Confederate line. Robinson went down with a bullet in the knee, and his brigade fell back, followed by Griffin's men.[225]

The First Corps' artillery batteries arrived. Stuart personally positioned them behind and along the sides of Laurel Hill. Pointing to a field covered in blue-uniformed troops and their ambulances and wagons—units of V corps—Stuart said, "Boys, I want you to knock that all to pieces for me."

The bombardment caught the Yankees by surprise. "We could see men running wildly about, teamsters, jumping into the saddle, and frantically lashing their horses—wagons, ambulances, ordnance carts, battery forges, tearing furiously in every direction," wrote Dame, who helped man one of the Rebel guns. One wagon struck a stump and flew through the air, team and all, landing on a low fence rail, which it crushed and rolled over. Warren's gunners fired back. "The air seemed full of . . . bursting shells, jagged fragments, balls out of case-shot—it sounded like a thousand devils, shrieking the air all about us," wrote Dame. The duel lasted three hours.[226]

EVEN AFTER RECEIVING Warren's report and being told that infantrymen from Anderson's division had been taken prisoner, Meade remained unconvinced that more than cavalry held Laurel Hill. In a note to Grant accompanying Warren's report of the failure of his second attack, Meade wrote, "I hardly think Longstreet [Anderson] is yet at Spotsylvania." The failure wasn't due to Confederate infantrymen having reached the scene, wrote Meade, "but I fear the morale of his [Warren's] men is impaired."[227]

There was truth in this, but morale wasn't the problem. Warren's men were physically drained; they had marched all night and fought all morning without sleep or food. Moreover, the prospect of charging a fortified position across open ground had a depressing effect on tired, hungry men. They grumbled that their commanders threw them in piecemeal, without attempting a concerted attack, and got good men killed for nothing. Captain Wainwright, the artilleryman, observed, "Our men did not go in today with any spirit; indeed, it is hard work to get any up after marching all night."[228]

Warren wanted to make no more attacks that day. "I have done my best, but with the force I now have I cannot attack again unless I see very great weakness on the enemy's left flank. . . . I incline to think . . . that if I let the enemy alone he will [attack] me. I cannot gain Spotsylvania Court-House with what force I have."[229]

Meade could not have disagreed more. If all of V and VI corps were thrown into an attack, he believed, the Rebel position, defended by one understrength corps, would surely crack. At 1:30 p.m. he wrote to Warren, "Sedgwick's whole corps is sent to join you in the attack on the wing. . . . It is of the utmost importance the attack of yourself and Sedgwick should be made with vigor and without delay."[230]

MEADE'S SHARP REPLY changed Warren's thinking. "I feel the less apprehension of an attack than I did after considering the matter from my own point of view. The rebels are as tired out as we are." But the Rebels could conserve their small reservoir of energy by lying behind field works, while Warren's and Sedgwick's weary men were struggling through dense woods and undergrowth to get into line for their assault.

As testimony to the troops' bone-deep fatigue, as well as to the glacial attack preparations, nearly five hours were consumed in readying V and VI Corps to try to dislodge the Rebels from Laurel Hill. Theodore Lyman, Meade's aide, rode down Brock Road to where Warren, Sedgwick, and Horatio Wright, a VI Corps division commander, were deep in conversation. Lyman "was struck by their worn and troubled aspect. . . . In fact the sudden transition from a long winter's rest to hard marching, sleepless nights, and protracted fighting, with no prospect of cessation, produced a powerful effect on the nervous system of the whole army."

Meade had refused to name either Warren or Sedgwick as operational commander; instead, Meade said, they should cooperate "and see what can be done." Warren, who had once been Meade's chief of staff and was accustomed to speaking to him bluntly, ranted: "I'll be God d——d if I'll cooperate with Sedgwick or anybody else. You are the commander of this army and can give your orders and I will obey them; or you can put Sedgwick in command and he can give the orders and I will obey them; or you can put me in command and I will give the orders and Sedgwick will obey them; but I'll be God d——d if I'll cooperate with General Sedgwick or anybody else."

While the Yankees slowly made their attack preparations, the Confederates improved their entrenchments, and the rest of First Corps moved into the battle line, with Richard Ewell's Second Corps right behind Anderson's men.[231]

Meade and Grant inspected Warren's and Sedgwick's lines, and were displeased to see that the troops were digging in—not exactly the hallmark of Grant's aggressive style. Perhaps for this reason or the long delay in attacking, Grant rode to an exposed position and sat there on his horse as bullets nicked the trees around him and shells occasionally exploded nearby. Meade joined him, in an unspoken test of nerve and nonchalance, as their staffs uneasily sat their horses. "I almost fancy Grant felt mad that things did not move faster, and so thought he would go and sit in an uncomfortable place," wrote Lyman. The tableau ended when Meade ordered Lyman to show Grant to the new headquarters. "Oh! With what intense politeness did I show the shortest road!" recalled Lyman.[232]

ROBERT E. LEE had been up since well before dawn. Early in the morning, he had set out for Spotsylvania Court House when Wade Hampton reported that his best scout, Channing Smith, had seen V Corps on the road to Todd's Tavern. Now certain that Grant was marching south and not to Fredericksburg, Lee had ordered Ewell to move the Second Corps to Shady Grove Church, following in Anderson's tracks. "Anderson by this time is at Spotsylvania Court-House and may need your support," Lee told Ewell.[233]

The Confederate commander had another piece of urgent business to attend to: A. P. Hill. No longer able to ride because of acute pain from his prostatitis, the slender, high-strung Third Corps commander notified Lee that he must temporarily relinquish his command. Lee quickly appointed Jubal Early to Hill's place, and John Gordon, Ewell's gifted brigade commander, to command Early's division in the Second Corps. During his two weeks' convalescence, Hill never left his corps, lying in an ambulance parked behind the line.[234]

In three days, two of Lee's corps had changed commanders. Moreover, Generals John Jones and Micah Jenkins had been killed, General L. A. Stafford mortally wounded, and Generals Henry Benning and John Pegram seriously wounded. It meant that Lee had to shoulder even greater tactical responsibility than before.

At 2:30 that afternoon, after arriving at Spotsylvania, Lee informed War Secretary James Seddon that his army had prevented Grant from reaching the crossroad village. "General R.H. Anderson with the advance of the army repulsed the enemy with heavy slaughter and took possession of the Court-House. I am the more grateful to the Giver of all victory that our loss is small."[235]

BY THE TIME Warren and Sedgwick completed their elaborate attack preparations, it was nearly 6 p.m., and the shadows were deepening in the woods.
The Confederate First Corps occupied two and a half miles of strongly
fortified entrenchments and, just as the Union attack began, Robert Rodes's
division arrived from Second Corps. It had endured a miserable, draining
march—men fainted in the ranks—through dust, smoke, and flames from
the burning woods, and the warm May weather.

Robert E. Lee immediately sent Rodes's men to the right to stop a Union
flanking attempt. In confused fighting in the woods in the gathering darkness, General Charles Griffin's division pushed back Rodes's men and took
some prisoners before the Rebels counterattacked. Captain Robert Carter
of the 22nd Massachusetts wrote that in the forest gloom, "there was no
time to reload, men threw down their arms, and 'went in rough and tum-
ble' where fists were freely used." Another of Griffin's regiments became
isolated at the edge of a swamp, fighting hand-to-hand. "Men fought with
desperation. Hungered, fatigued, discouraged, they were goaded to frenzied madness," wrote the historian for the 118th Pennsylvania.

It was in vain; Meade's attack failed to break the Confederate lines. General Humphreys, Meade's artillery commander, observed that the assault
was "only partial, and not determined and vigorous. The ground was new
to everyone, and the troops were tired." With resignation, Grant wrote,
"Warren led the last assault one division at a time, and of course it failed."[236]

Twenty-four hours of maneuvering, marching and fighting had gone for
naught; Grant had failed to capture Spotsylvania Court House. Lee's army
stood between Grant and Richmond. Phlegmatic as always, Grant did not
reveal what must have been his acute disappointment. Instead, he, Meade,
and their staffs and generals immediately began planning their next gambit.

Luck and pluck had enabled the Army of Northern Virginia to beat
Grant to Spotsylvania by a whisker. The good luck was the burning woods,
which goaded General Richard Anderson's First Corps to march all night
without rest. The pluck of Fitz Lee's troopers, whose roadblocks and am-
bushes on Brock Road delayed the Union march for hours, gave the First
Corps time to reach Laurel Hill and stop V Corps' piecemeal attacks.

For all that, the Union army might still have reached the crossroad village first if the march were not so badly coordinated, and if the generals had

communicated a sense of urgency. They did not. Staff officers might have eased the gridlock on the roads if they had been sent to direct traffic; they were not. It was made worse when Meade turned out Sheridan's two cavalry divisions onto Brock Road. Meade's decision to have Merritt clear the road while Warren's infantrymen followed was just as misbegotten.

Now the Army of Northern Virginia blocked the Union army's path with better fortifications than anything seen in the Wilderness, and its defenses were becoming more impregnable by the hour.

CHAPTER 3

The Red Hour

SPOTSYLVANIA COURT HOUSE

I propose to fight it out on this line if it takes all summer.

—ULYSSES GRANT[1]

We have met a man this time, who either does not know when he is whipped, or who cares not if he loses his whole army.

—A CONFEDERATE SOLDIER DESCRIBING GRANT[2]

This army cannot stand a siege. We must end this business on the battlefield, not in a fortified place.

—ROBERT E. LEE[3]

Rank after rank was riddled by shot and shell and bayonet-thrusts, and finally sank, a mass of torn and mutilated corpses.

—HORACE PORTER'S DESCRIPTION OF
THE BLOODY ANGLE FIGHTING[4]

1

Monday, May 9–Tuesday, May 10, 1864
The Rebel Redoubt

REMARKABLY, AFTER ALL that happened over the previous four eventful days—the Wilderness bloodbath, the race to Spotsylvania Court House, and the fighting there by two exhausted armies—both Lee and Grant sounded optimistic in reports to their respective governments.

"We have succeeded so far in keeping on the front flank of [Grant's] army, and impeding its progress, without a general engagement," Lee wrote to President Jefferson Davis, "which I will not bring on unless a favorable opportunity offers, or as a last resort."[5]

Although he remained sanguine about his army's prospects, Lee's losses had forced him to radically change his tactics. The man whom General Henry Heth described as "the most belligerent man in his army"—whose first inclination had always been to attack—now had to fight defensively.[6]

In less than one week, Grant, arguably "the most belligerent man" in blue, had changed the war's paradigm with his relentless onslaught by waves of bluecoats. Neither Lee nor Grant had ever faced an opponent as tough-minded and tenacious as each other. Lee's objective was now to seize the initiative somehow and strike Grant's army a mortal blow; Grant's was to retain the initiative and keep applying pressure to Lee until his army crumbled to pieces.

From his new headquarters at Piney Branch Church, a couple of miles east of Todd's Tavern, Grant wrote to General Henry Halleck, the Union army's chief of staff, "It is not yet demonstrated what the enemy will do, but the best of feeling prevails in this army, and I feel at present no apprehension for the result."

While Davis and Lee still believed that Grant's goal was to capture Richmond, Grant was telling Halleck something else. Besides destroying Lee's army, he remained determined to "form a junction with General Butler as early as possible. . . . My exact route to the James River I have not yet definitely marked out."[7]

Grant did not betray his dissatisfaction with the Army of the Potomac's leadership, its mistakes and poor communication, and its lack of focus—or his unhappiness about Lee's having reached Spotsylvania first. But his staff knew how he felt. Adam Badeau, an aide, wrote, "Though disappointed, Grant was not discouraged. He lost no time in criticizing or complaining, but at once attempted to repair the situation."[8]

WITH LONGSTREET AND Hill disabled, and Ewell's performance in the Wilderness suspect, Lee became the Army of Northern Virginia's de facto field commander. He began rising at 3 a.m., when he breakfasted by candlelight, and then rode to the lines. He spent the day there, organizing the army's defensive positions and shifting units around.[9]

Better than just about anyone in the Confederate army, Lee knew how to build entrenchments. Before the war, Lee was among the cream of the Corps of Engineers, having spent more than two decades supervising army projects around the country. They included improving defenses along the Narrows in New York, as well as in Virginia and Maryland, and reversing the silting of St. Louis harbor.

Upon becoming commander of the Army of Northern Virginia in June 1862, Lee built fortifications east of Richmond to withstand attacks by George McClellan's army, then marching up the Peninsula. When his troops grumbled that digging was unsoldierly, Lee pointed out that the Roman legions had built roads and fortifications, some of which had survived nearly two millennia. "There is nothing so military as labor," Lee wrote, "& nothing so important to an army as to save the lives of its soldiers."

Through the first two and a half years of war, the armies dug in *after* battles, not before, and only when the enemy remained within striking distance. This changed in late November 1863 at Mine Run, when Lee's men dug fieldworks along their entire front in anticipation of an assault. Because the works were so formidable, George Meade cancelled the attack by his massed army.[10]

Now, at Spotsylvania, Lee and his top officers, including his brilliant chief engineer, General Martin Smith, put the Rebel army to work building what would be the most daunting field fortifications yet seen during the war. Meade's chief of staff, Andrew Humphreys, described them as being "unknown to European warfare and . . . new to warfare in this country."[11]

This was a slight overstatement, for there was nothing new in the fortifications' elements, but there was ingenuity in their combinations—the result being that they were nearly impregnable. There were slashings to deny concealment, and bayonet-like abatis to entangle attackers. Head logs atop the breastworks shielded the defenders and provided them with firing ports. And traverses were built at the ends of the entrenchments to repel enfiladers.[12]

"With such intrenchments as these, having artillery throughout, with flank fire along their lines wherever practicable . . . the strength of an army sustaining attack was more than quadrupled, provided they had force enough to man the intrenchments well," wrote Humphreys. If Humphreys was correct, the Rebels held a strong advantage when arrayed behind fortifications.[13]

THE SOLDIERS OF both armies were relieved to have left behind the claustrophobic Wilderness for more open country. They savored the terrain north of Spotsylvania, with its hills and ridges, and mixture of farms, fields, and dense woods of oak, hickory, and blooming dogwoods.[14]

Lee advantageously used the high ground that his army occupied between the Po and Ni Rivers to bar the way to Spotsylvania and its web of roads pointing toward Richmond. His left was two and a half miles long, and held by Anderson's First Corps; it faced northwest and rested on the Po. His right, occupied by the Third Corps under Early's command, was two miles long and faced east from a ridge separating the two river valleys. Trees and undergrowth largely concealed the works from the Yankees.[15]

Between the two wings, however, lay an anomalous salient that was about two-thirds of a mile wide and three-quarters of a mile deep. The Rebels called it the "Mule Shoe" and the Yankees referred to it as the "Salient," but it would soon become known by the gruesome nickname "Bloody Angle."

Ewell's Second Corps occupied the Mule Shoe, and his men "did not like it at all," wrote William Seymour, a Louisiana captain in General Edward Johnson's division. Every veteran instantly recognized that it was exposed to attack on three sides; moreover, just 200 yards away lay dense woods where Yankees might hide until the moment they began sprinting for the Rebel lines.

"It was so liable to be enfiladed by artillery and would be a dangerous trap to be caught in should the line be broken on the right or left," Seymour wrote. But the salient also rested on a hill, and herein lay the Rebels' dilemma: if ceded to the Yankees, the high ground would give the Yankees a commanding position from which to bombard the Rebels with their batteries. Lee and his chief engineer, Smith, disliked the bulge in their lines, but conceded the greater importance of holding the high ground. Moreover, Ewell assured them he could ably defend it.[16]

GRANT'S KNOWLEDGE OF the Rebels' sprawling positions north of Spotsylvania was inexact and flawed—and unlikely to improve soon. Phil Sheridan's Cavalry Corps had left that morning on a mission to destroy Jeb Stuart's mounted divisions, leaving Grant with just a few cavalry regiments for reconnaissance.

Grant's decision to dispatch Sheridan's men was a spontaneous one, although not as capricious as it might seem. It was precipitated by a fiery argument that erupted between Sheridan and Meade after Meade peremptorily issued orders to two of Sheridan's cavalry divisions during the overnight march to Spotsylvania, disrupting Sheridan's plans—about which neither Meade nor Sheridan's cavalry generals had any knowledge at the time.

Sheridan and Meade were both hot-tempered, and it had been a long, difficult night; both men had slept little. Sheridan was still fuming over Meade's supposed overriding of his orders, and Meade was angry with Sheridan, believing that his troopers had slowed the army's march and enabled Lee to reach Spotsylvania first.

Around noon on May 8, Meade summoned Sheridan to his headquarters. Meade "had worked himself into a towering passion" over the Cavalry Corps' performance, wrote Grant's aide, Horace Porter, who was present when Sheridan arrived. Meade "went at him hammer and tongs, accusing him of blunders, and charging him with not making a proper disposition of his troops, and letting the cavalry block the advance of the infantry."

Sheridan had long resented Meade's use of the cavalry to guard the army's supply trains rather than as an independent strike force tasked with fighting the enemy cavalry and cutting his supply lines. Meade's reprimand ignited a profanity-laced tirade from the peppery Irishman. It was Meade, Sheridan hotly asserted, who had mixed up the cavalry and infantry on Brock Road by countermanding Sheridan's orders, and who had also imperiled Wilson's division by stranding it at Spotsylvania Court House without support.

"Sheridan declared with great warmth," wrote Porter, "that he would not command the cavalry any longer under such conditions, and if he could have matters his own way he would concentrate all the cavalry, move out in force against Stuart's command, and whip it." Sheridan stalked out of Meade's tent. Eyewitnesses to the donnybrook were amazed by Sheridan's tirade and his language, "highly spiced and conspicuously italicized with expletives."

Meade stormed over to Grant's tent to report Sheridan's insubordination. But Grant did not respond in the way that Meade had expected. After silently listening to Meade's outraged retelling of their conversation and Sheridan's declaration that he could whip the Rebel cavalry, Grant replied, "Did Sheridan say that? Well, he generally knows what he is talking about. Let him start right out and do it."[17]

Meade had lost the argument, but he wasted no time brooding over it. Later on May 8, Sheridan received new orders to "immediately concentrate your available mounted force, and . . . proceed against the enemy's cavalry." Major James Kidd of the 6th Michigan Cavalry wrote that in the Army of the Potomac, "it had long been a settled article of belief that Stuart was invincible." Phil Sheridan aimed to change that settled opinion.[18]

EARLY THE NEXT morning, May 9, Sheridan and the Cavalry Corps rode down the Telegraph Road, which linked Fredericksburg and Richmond. His 9,800 troopers rode four abreast at a walking pace of four miles per hour, as though they were on a Sunday ramble. The thirteen-mile column included thirty-two guns, forage for the horses, and a long wagon train containing supplies and ammunition. "It was a glorious sight," wrote artilleryman George Marsh. "The long even lines of cavalry obliquely descending the slope showed boldly against the summer green. Over all hotly shone the sun. My eye could not tire with gazing."

This raid was unlike any previous Union cavalry foray—in which the raiders would ride rapidly through the countryside, avoiding the enemy as much as possible, never fighting unless forced to. By contrast, Sheridan "went out with the utmost deliberation, looking for trouble—seeking it—and desiring before every other thing to find Stuart and fight him on his native heath," wrote Major Kidd.

Before setting out, Sheridan had told his three division commanders, "We will give him a fair, square fight; we are strong and I know we can beat him. . . . I shall expect nothing but success." Sheridan later wrote that he intended to challenge Stuart to "a cavalry duel behind Lee's lines, in his own country."[19]

WHILE SHERIDAN THREATENED Richmond from the north, Benjamin Butler menaced the Confederate capital from the south. Butler's offensive on the James River had begun well with his efficient seizure of City Point and advance to Bermuda Hundred, just six miles from the Richmond and Petersburg Railroad, which linked the two cities. Grant's April 2 orders to Butler had stated that "Richmond is to be your objective point and that there is to be co-operation between your force and the Army of the Potomac."[20]

A flotilla of Union warships transported Butler's 33,000 men up the James River from Fort Monroe. There were gunboats, transports, barges, armed tugs, hospital and cargo ships, and six ironclads. The Stars and Stripes fluttered from every vessel, their decks teeming with waving soldiers as the tugs' whistles shrieked. On the hurricane deck of his flagship, the *Greyhound*, Butler loudly exhorted the fleet forward. "Give her all the steam you can, Captain!" he shouted. One soldier described the sight as "one of the finest and most stirring scenes imaginable."[21]

Under Butler's command were X Corps, led by Quincy Gillmore; XVIII Corps, commanded by William F. "Baldy" Smith, who had built the "Cracker Line" that brought supplies to besieged Chattanooga; and August Kautz's cavalry division. To all appearances, it seemed that the droopy-eyed, rotund general's army was poised to sever one of Richmond's lifelines while menacing both Petersburg and Richmond.

But the Army of the James was less than it seemed. XVIII Corps had not seen action for months, and X Corps had failed in its attempt to capture Charleston, South Carolina, and had been defeated at Olustee, Florida. Butler's army also had more political generals than any army in the war; just

30 percent them had matriculated at West Point, compared with 80 percent for the Army of the Potomac. In *Army of Amateurs*, author Edward G. Longacre wrote, "In many respects, the Army of the James was the preeminent civilian army of its day."

Although comparatively deficient in formal military training, Butler's army surpassed Meade's army in other respects—although none that necessarily made it fight better. It was more progressive, with the Union army's largest contingent of black soldiers; Butler was an ardent advocate for the blacks. It was innovative, too: Butler experimented with machine guns, and his army pioneered the use of mobile dressing stations.[22]

Butler was without a doubt the avatar of Union political generals. His ascent had seemed unlikely in 1860 when, as Massachusetts's leading conservative Democrat, he had first supported Jefferson Davis, and then John Breckinridge, for president. But when war broke out he became a brigadier general in the Massachusetts militia where, at the head of the 8th Massachusetts, he had thwarted attempts by Rebel sympathizers to isolate Washington during the war's early days. Lincoln rewarded Butler with general rank in the Union army—the first volunteer general so promoted.

While commanding Fort Monroe, Virginia, in 1861, he had lost the Battle of Big Bethel, but he had also conceived an inspired policy governing the treatment of escaped Southern slaves. By declaring them wartime "contraband"—subject to seizure just like enemy horses, supplies and weapons—and refusing to return them to their masters, Butler laid the groundwork for Lincoln's Emancipation Proclamation.

In New Orleans in 1862, Southerners nicknamed him "Beast Butler" and put a bounty on his head because of his sometimes harsh actions as military governor. Yet, Butler restored order in the city, and established public health practices that reduced yellow fever cases to record-low numbers.[23]

After becoming general-in-chief, Grant had sought Butler's transfer or demotion, believing him unfit to command an army. Political considerations, however, compelled Lincoln and Stanton to keep Butler. Then, Grant had proposed leaving Butler as titular commander of the Department of Virginia and North Carolina, while placing Smith in operational command. Lincoln and Stanton endorsed Grant's plan, but Butler refused to go quietly, so the idea was shelved.[24]

In sending Gillmore and Smith to Butler's command, Grant hoped that their combat experience might compensate for Butler's deficiency. What Grant did not anticipate was that Gillmore and Smith would neither get along with one another nor work smoothly with Butler. From the beginning of the campaign, the three generals bickered and threw blame on one another.

Butler had a brief opportunity to attack Richmond when it was especially vulnerable. Upon reaching Bermuda Hundred on the evening of May 5, a courier sent by Elizabeth Van Lew, who operated a Union spy ring in Richmond, informed Butler that Richmond was nearly unprotected. The Confederate command had sent units from Drewry's Bluff to Lee, and reinforcements coming from North Carolina had not yet arrived.

Butler later claimed that he wanted to assault Drewry's Bluff that night, under a full moon. "The men all had two days' rations in their haversacks ... and they could easily get there by daylight." But Smith and Gillmore opposed the plan. Butler wrote. "One of them intimated that he should feel it his duty to refuse it even if it were ordered." Butler did not order the attack. Gillmore and Smith later denied having rejected Butler's plan.[25]

BUTLER'S CHANCE TO overwhelm Richmond was fleeting. Recognizing that the capital city was imperiled, War Secretary James Seddon called on all Richmond men able to bear arms to report for duty to defend the city, and he recalled furloughed soldiers for "temporary organization." Additional troops were summoned from the Carolinas, Florida, and Georgia. "We are in the very crisis of our fortunes, and want every man," wrote Seddon. When Lee asked Davis to send him reinforcements, Davis replied that he could not. "We have been sorely pressed by the enemy on the south side."[26]

Seddon and Davis sent for General P. G. T. Beauregard to take charge of defending Petersburg and Richmond. Beauregard had been reassigned to oversee the coastal defenses in South Carolina and Georgia after having fallen out of favor with Davis. But Davis and Seddon now needed him.

If Butler had immediately seized the railroad and struck at Petersburg and Richmond, he might have compelled Lee to march to Richmond's defense or, minimally, to send troops from his army.

But it was not Butler's nature to act quickly. An excellent administrator, he was a cautious field commander at best; his greatest success was the amphibious landing at Hatteras Inlet, North Carolina, in 1861. He now reverted to form. Rather than move swiftly to achieve his objectives, Butler marched to Bermuda Neck, half the distance between Bermuda Hundred and the railroad, and dug in. The James and Appomattox Rivers, just four miles apart at the Neck, secured Butler's flanks while his entrenchments defended his front.

Butler finally ordered two brigades to cut the railroad, but one of them waited eight hours before advancing, and the other did not march at all. When it finally came, the thrust, such as it was, was turned back by 600 Rebels rushed to the line by General George Pickett, famed for his doomed attack at Gettysburg. Pickett was supposed to have already left Richmond to rejoin Lee's army, but he had remained behind after Beauregard wrote from North Carolina that he was ill and could not take the field.

The next few days were a test of Pickett's nerves, still frayed by his Gettysburg experiences. Operating with a hodgepodge of troops arriving daily from the south, Pickett improvised a plan to counter Butler's predictable attempts to capture the turnpike and railroad between Richmond and Petersburg. It was Pickett's good fortune that aggressive, sharp-tongued General D. H. Hill was currently without a command, and had volunteered to serve as an aide-de-camp to Beauregard. Beauregard sent the North Carolinian to Pickett, who immediately gave him command of two brigades dug in along the turnpike.

On May 7, Butler marched to the turnpike with five brigades, and D. H. Hill and his two brigades flung them back. Butler spent May 8 strengthening his entrenchments in case Lee bottled up or defeated Grant in the Wilderness and could then send reinforcements to Richmond.

Butler's position at Bermuda Neck was easy to defend, wrote General John Barnard, the Army of the Potomac's chief engineer, sent by Grant to inspect Butler's position. But Barnard told Grant the Confederates had entrenched along an equally strong line opposite Butler's, making it difficult for Butler to march from his lines toward the turnpike and railroad line. Barnard said it was "as if Butler was in a bottle. He was perfectly safe against an attack; but . . . the enemy had corked the bottle and with a small force could hold the cork in its place."

On May 9, Butler emerged from his entrenchments with half of his army, intending to march on Petersburg. If he captured the city, he could then turn his full attention to Richmond. In an exceptionally miserable performance by the Army of the James, Butler's men approached a small Confederate force dug in on the south side of Swift Creek, three miles north of Petersburg. To the astonishment of the Union generals, the creek was unfordable, and after a pointless exchange of long-range gunfire, Butler's men returned to Bermuda Neck, having failed to capture the railroad, the turnpike, or Petersburg.

Butler sent Stanton an upbeat, not altogether honest appraisal of his operations through May 9. It was true, as he wrote, that General August Kautz's cavalry had burned railroad bridges below Petersburg, delaying the arrival of some Rebel units from the Carolinas. But his description of his clash with D. H. Hill's two brigades strayed from the facts. "That portion which reached Petersburg under Hill I have whipped to-day, killing and wounding many and taking many prisoners, after a severe and well-contested battle. General Grant will not be troubled with any further reenforcements to Lee from Beauregard's force."

Meanwhile, Confederate brigades continued to reach Petersburg from the Carolinas, having bypassed the ruined railroad bridges. From Petersburg, the Rebels used the railroad to shuttle troops under Butler's nose, north to the Drewry's Bluff fortifications. Less than a week after Butler's arrival at Bermuda Hundred, twelve Confederate brigades—20,000 Rebels—had assembled south of the James. Beauregard, recovered from his illness, planned to go on the offensive soon against the Army of the James.[27]

OUTSIDE SPOTSYLVANIA, THE break in the action shakily extended to midday May 9. Then, that afternoon was in some ways worse than the four previous days of killing and movement. Sudden eruptions of artillery fire, and the steady, deadly attrition from sharpshooters grated on everyone's nerves. Along the approaches to Laurel Hill, Union troops retrieved the dead and properly buried them. But even in that there was no respite from the snipers and gunners.

A Pennsylvania soldier, Alfred Thompson, and his comrades were digging a grave as the chaplain conducted services when a Confederate round landed so close to them "that the number of auditors was perceptibly diminished."[28]

One death that occurred that day plunged the Army of the Potomac into mourning.

General John Sedgwick, the commander of VI Corps, was a fifty-year-old bachelor who had made the army his family and home; he was arguably the most beloved general in the Army of the Potomac. Sedgwick was adjusting his lines that morning when he noticed that his infantry overlapped part of an artillery battery. Sedgwick was an artillerist by profession, and he felt compelled to personally correct the problem, although his chief of staff, General Martin T. McMahon, warned him that every officer who had exposed himself in that area had been shot.

When Sedgwick saw that the sharpshooter fire was causing some of the artillerymen to duck, he laughed. "What! Men dodging this way for single bullets!" he said. When a man passing in front of Sedgwick flinched at a bullet's passage, Sedgwick said teasingly, "Why, my man, I am ashamed of you, dodging that way. They couldn't hit an elephant at this distance."

At that moment, another bullet came in, whistling shrilly, and struck with a dull thud. Blood streamed from a hole beneath Sedgwick's left eye, and he fell, taking McMahon with him. "A smile remained upon his lips, but he did not speak," McMahon wrote.[29]

Henry Thomas of the 12th Georgia wrote that Sedgwick was more than a half mile from the Rebel picket line when Sergeant Charles Grace, "a fine shot," killed him. Grace was armed with one of the Confederate Army's scope-mounted Whitworth sharpshooting rifles, accurate to 2,000 yards. The Whitworth's hexagonal bullets made a whistling sound in flight.[30]

Horace Porter, Grant's aide, had just met with Sedgwick and Grant, when Grant sent him after Sedgwick to discuss another matter. The general's lifeless body was being carried away when Porter reached his headquarters, where his men appeared numbed by a "sense of grief akin to the sorrow of personal bereavement."

Porter carried the news to Grant. "For a few moments he could scarcely realize it and twice asked, 'Is he really dead?' The shock was severe and he could ill conceal the depth of his grief." Grant said the loss to the army was "greater than the loss of a whole division of troops." Theodore Lyman of Meade's staff wrote that Sedgwick was "a pure and great-hearted man, a brave and skillful soldier. From the commander to the lowest private he had no enemy in this army." Wrote Doctor Daniel Holt, surgeon for the 121st New York, "This is an awful loss to us. We had learned to love and obey him as faithful, dutiful children." When the report of Sedgwick's death reached the Lincoln administration, Navy Secretary Gideon Welles said, "The death of no general officer during the war could be more depressing, I apprehend, than this."[31]

VI Corps got a new commander, General Horatio Wright, while V Corps lost a division—John Robinson's, mangled by the May 8 attacks on Laurel Hill. Its brigades were parceled out to the other three divisions in V Corps. Robinson was wounded in the left knee during one of the attacks and his leg was taken off. He never returned to field duty.[32]

BENT OVER HIS maps at his headquarters at Piney Branch Church on May 9, Grant thought he had found a way to flank the Confederates. Their left rested on the Po River, which flowed southeast before turning sharply south along the west side of Laurel Hill, around a wedge of low-lying woods. It was a strong position because the Yankees would have to cross the river twice to reach the Confederate left, but Grant believed for this reason the Rebels would not expect an attack here. It would be inconceivable to the Rebels that Grant's troops would attempt to cross the Po twice. The Po wasn't wide, but it was swift and its banks were steep-sided. The Yankees would have to ford or bridge the river to make their first crossing. But for their second river passage, the Union troops could use the Block House Bridge.

Earlier in the day, a division of General Ambrose Burnside's IX Corps, which missed the Laurel Hill fighting, had marched down the Fredericks-burg Road toward Spotsylvania Court House. Commanded by Orlando Willcox, the division crossed the Ni River and dug in just a mile and a half northeast of Spotsylvania, where it was joined by Thomas Stevenson's division.

IX Corps had stumbled upon a weak spot in Lee's right flank, where Burnside's corps extended a half-mile beyond the Confederate positions.

It was a huge opportunity—if only Burnside's generals had recognized it and pressed on; scarcely any enemy troops stood between them and Spotsylvania.

Lee, however, immediately grasped the menace posed by IX Corps and rushed a division from Third Corps to the area. His swift reaction inadvertently planted the suspicion in the Union command that Lee was shifting troops to the right. "The enemy are now moving from our immediate front either to interpose between us and Fredericksburg or to get the inside road to Richmond," Grant reported to Halleck.[33]

Grant had badly misread the situation. When he should have sent Burnside's corps fast-marching through the weak Confederate right flank, Grant did just the opposite: he assumed that the Rebel *left* had been weakened, and was now vulnerable to attack. With Sheridan's Cavalry Corps riding toward Richmond, Grant and Meade had no way to acquire accurate information about Lee's dispositions.

GRANT EXPLAINED HIS new plan to Meade and General Winfield Scott Hancock. II Corps had been idle since the bloody fighting on the Orange Plank Road on May 6. During the nighttime march to Spotsylvania, Hancock's battered corps had remained behind its fortifications at the plank road crossroad, guarding the army's right flank. It was now bivouacked around Todd's Tavern.

Hancock was the Army of the Potomac's promptest and hardest-hitting corps commander, and Grant wanted Hancock and his corps to begin the mission on the Po River immediately. At 4:30 p.m. on May 9, three of II Corps' four divisions—Gershom Mott's would remain behind to guard the trains and aid Burnside if needed—began wading and walking across fallen trees to the Po's south bank. Nearby engineers erected three bridges to enable the crossing of the corps' artillery.

Nighttime came as the Union column reached Shady Grove Church Road, a short distance west of the Block House Bridge. In a dispatch at 10 p.m., Hancock reported that the bridge was intact and lightly guarded, but he did "not think it wise" to attempt a nighttime crossing. Meade told him to wait until daylight. "We were in a very delicate position," wrote adjutant J. W. Muffly of the 148th Pennsylvania, being "across the left flank of Lee's

Army, but separated from it and from the remainder of Meade's Army by the Po River."[34]

While Hancock's men rested, Lee, apprised that Union infantry columns threatened Block House Bridge, started the Third Corps' other two divisions on an overnight march from the Rebels' extreme right flank to its left flank.

After misinterpreting what was occurring on Burnside's front, Grant had erred a second time in ordering Hancock to begin his movement so late in the day—too late, as it turned out, to strike Lee's left flank that day.

SUNRISE THE NEXT morning, May 10, presented a dismaying sight to Hancock and his three divisions: freshly dug Rebel entrenchments on a rise east of Block House Bridge, manned by thousands of gray-clad infantrymen supported by a dozen guns. William Mahone's Third Corps division had arrived overnight and dug in.

The Confederates did nothing when Hancock sent men to reconnoiter their positions, evidently confident that their position was unassailable.

Hancock reached the same conclusion. "After a careful survey had been made," he wrote, "I concluded not to attempt to carry the bridge." Instead, he sent reconnaissance forces downriver to look for another crossing point. Colonel John Brooke's brigade discovered a shallow place a half-mile below Block House Bridge, and sent the 66th New York to the east bank, where it encountered an extension of Mahone's line, held by entrenched infantry and artillery.[35]

Another probing force, two regiments led by Major James Briscoe, encountered something far more alarming: Henry Heth's Third Corps division. While Mahone's division had remained at Block House Bridge, Heth had crossed the Po farther to the south and now threatened Hancock's rear.

Grant was losing hope that he could turn Lee's left flank on the Po River, but Horatio Wright had given him another idea. Wright reported that Confederates were pulling away from the VI Corps front opposite the Salient, apparently to help parry Hancock's advance on the Po.

To Grant, this signified that Lee might also be weakening his Laurel Hill defenses in order to deal with Hancock. Even though his intelligence about what Lee was doing was virtually nonexistent, Grant thought that he might outfox him: he would scrap Hancock's mission, and instead attack Laurel Hill, where the Rebel forces, he was convinced, had been drawn down.

Grant ordered Hancock to return to the Laurel Hill approaches with two of the three divisions that had crossed the Po, and to lead a massive frontal assault on Laurel Hill beside Warren's corps. "The assault is to be conducted by Hancock in person," wrote Assistant War Secretary Charles Dana, who was with Grant. "Whether Lee's entire army is here, or whether any part has been detached to Richmond, is a question concerning which we have no positive evidence."

Dana was right about that. Worse, though, Grant's intelligence was terribly wrong; the Confederates had not removed any troops from Laurel Hill.[36]

GENERAL FRANCIS BARLOW's II Corps division drew the dangerous job of remaining south of the Po as a decoy. Barlow's presence, Grant believed, would prevent Mahone's and Heth's divisions from leaving the Po to reinforce Laurel Hill.

While this might give Grant an advantage when attacking Laurel Hill, it put Barlow in a tight spot. As Heth's infantrymen advanced against the Union infantrymen under the dense forest canopy, Mahone's artillerymen at Block House Bridge shelled Barlow's forward field works along Shady Grove Church Road.

Learning of Barlow's plight—unsupported and with his back to the Po—Meade sent Hancock back over the river to extricate Barlow and his men. The "Boy General"—the nickname given Barlow by his friend and former Harvard classmate Theodore Lyman—reluctantly began pulling back his two advanced brigades, led by Colonels Brooke and Paul Frank. "A prettier field for such a contest was rarely to be found in that land of tangles and swamps," regretfully wrote Francis Walker, Hancock's assistant adjutant general.

The combative Barlow, attired in his trademark flannel checked shirt, blue pantaloons and cap, with a large cavalry saber dangling from his waist, certainly preferred to stand and fight at the head of one of the best fighting divisions in the Army of the Potomac. His command had emerged from the Wilderness relatively intact, while Heth's had suffered severe losses. "It seemed a pity to interrupt the fight that was imminent; and had it been left to the vote of Barlow and his brigadiers the duel would have come off," observed Walker.

Barlow's withdrawal under fire was more harrowing than standing and fighting would have been. Colonels Nelson Miles's and Thomas Smyth's brigades threw up defensive positions on a hill on the river's south bank, as Heth's division pounced on Brooke's and Frank's brigades with "loud yells, delivering a terrible musketry fire." "The combat now became close and bloody," wrote Hancock. Frank's brigade was driven back, but Brooke's men repelled the attack, and two subsequent ones, as the woods around them caught fire, spreading to their fieldworks. They withdrew toward the river.

For some reason, Barlow's order to withdraw to the Po's north bank never reached the 148th Pennsylvania, which found itself nearly alone on the south bank, facing Heth's advancing regiments. "Our men were falling like game before hunters, and still no relief and no orders," wrote Adjutant Muffly. Faced with death or capture, Colonel James Beaver ordered the regiment to withdraw down a ravine toward the bridges.

Smoke from the burning woods "choked, blinded and stifled us to a most exasperating extent," wrote Muffly. To reach the Po, they had to run a gantlet of flames while under heavy musket and artillery fire. Terrified horses pulling an artillery piece dragged the gun between two trees, wedging it fast. Despite the artillerymen's strenuous efforts to pull it free, the gun remained stuck and had to be left behind—the first gun ever lost by II Corps. Two hours later, the Pennsylvanians crossed the river, after losing 167 men.[37]

When his division reached safety, Barlow fired Colonel Frank, because of his brigade's hasty retreat and reports that he was drunk. His replacement was Colonel Hiram Brown of the 145th Pennsylvania, known for his singing ability and his dog, Spot.[38]

Edward Porter Alexander, the Confederate First Corps' artillery commander, knew why Hancock's flanking movement failed. "It had been a mistake to send Hancock across the Po at such a late hour in the afternoon. Night intervened before he could accomplish anything, and it disclosed his plan."[39]

Had Hancock waited until early May 10 to cross the Po and marched to the Block House Bridge in one fluid movement—before Lee could send reinforcements—"there appears to be every reason to conclude that the Confederate left would have been turned and taken in rear, while the Fifth Corps attacked it in front," wrote Andrew Humphreys, Meade's chief of staff.[40]

The bold thrust at Lee's left flank had failed because of hasty execution, lack of coordination, and Grant's abrupt change of plan in favor of a frontal attack. His new plan would be tested in the lengthening shadows on Laurel Hill's approaches.

2

Tuesday, May 10, 1864, Afternoon
Laurel Hill

ALL DAY, WARREN'S infantrymen had eyed with dread the long, open approaches to the concealed Rebel breastworks along Laurel Hill. V Corps had been bloodied during a large-scale probe there earlier that day, and its men knew they were going back up the hill soon.

That morning, Warren sent two divisions "to ascertain where the enemy's main line of battle is. I want them well pressed to drive back his covering force if it can be done," Warren told General Samuel Crawford and Lysander Cutler. He hoped to expose weaknesses in the Confederate positions. The divisions had gotten close enough for Crawford to report, "Our troops suffer in their present position severely," and had then withdrawn—after sustaining hundreds of casualties and finding no chinks in the Confederate defenses.[41]

About the same time, VI Corps, on Horatio Wright's first full day of command after Sedgwick's death, probed the center of the Confederate lines, in the vicinity of the Salient. Wright suspected it was not as strongly defended as previously, causing Meade and Grant to conjecture that enemy troops from Richard Ewell's Second Corps might have been sent to the Rebel left to counteract Hancock's movement on the Po.

Based on these fragmentary reports—comparable to the blind man trying to identify the elephant—Grant decided to attack all along the line at

5 p.m. with all four of his infantry corps: II and V Corps at Laurel Hill; VI Corps at the Salient; and, on the Union left, Mott's II Corps division and IX Corps. "Do it with vigor and with all the force you can bear. Do not neglect to make all the show you can as the best co-operative effort," Grant's order read. Surely, the Rebel defenses would buckle at some point along the five-mile front, Grant believed.[42]

EARLY THAT MORNING, Grant had mounted Jeff Davis. It was going to be a long day in the saddle, and Jeff Davis, confiscated from the Mississippi plantation of Jefferson Davis's son, Joe, was Grant's smoothest-riding horse.

Grant's headquarters was moved from Piney Branch Church to a glade a mile nearer the center of the Union line. There, Grant wrote a brief report to General Henry Halleck in Washington that lacked his previous messages' ebullience, but reflected his determination to persevere.

"The enemy hold our front in very strong force and evince a strong determination to interpose between us and Richmond to the last," he said, adding, "I shall take no backward steps." He needed more supplies and provisions and 5 million rounds of ammunition—fifty rounds each for 100,000 men.

"We can maintain ourselves at least, and, in the end, beat Lee's army, I believe," Grant wrote.[43]

That day, he received good news from two fronts. He was encouraged by Benjamin Butler's report that his operations on the James River would interdict further reinforcements to Lee from Beauregard. Grant also learned that Sherman had driven the Rebels from Tunnel Hill, between Ringgold and Dalton, Georgia.

He dispatched couriers to the four infantry corps with an announcement of these developments to be read to the men, with instructions to permit "no cheering by the men."[44]

HANCOCK, WHO WAS Warren's senior in rank, had been assigned to lead the 5 p.m. attack on Laurel Hill. But when Hancock had to recross the Po to extricate Barlow's beleaguered division, Warren went to Meade and Grant and persuaded them to move up the Laurel Hill attack by one hour. "The opportunity for attack immediately is reported to be so favorable by

General Warren that he is ordered to attack at once, and Gibbon [Hancock's division commander] is directed to co-operate with him," Meade wrote just before 4 p.m. The opportunity was undoubtedly favorable to the ambitious Warren, who would be in command of the attack instead of Hancock. Warren put on a dress uniform for the occasion.[45]

Warren with good reason believed that his reputation had been tarnished because of his corps' performance in the Wilderness, on Brock Road on May 8, and now, at Laurel Hill, where every attack had failed. Capturing Laurel Hill would elevate his profile in the Army of the Potomac to the heights that followed his heroics at Little Round Top and, to a lesser extent, his quick thinking at Bristoe Station.

However, Warren's insistence on an earlier attack threw the timetable out of kilter. Then, Grant delayed VI Corps' attack by Colonel Emory Upton and twelve picked regiments on the center of the Rebel line from 5 p.m. to 6 p.m. Gershom Mott's II Corps division and two divisions of Burnside's IX Corps were still scheduled to go into action at 5 p.m. The all-out attack initially scheduled at 5 p.m. had become three uncoordinated attacks between 4 p.m. and 6 p.m.

MANY OF WARREN'S infantrymen were convinced before they even jumped off that the attack was doomed; some of them had unsuccessfully stormed Laurel Hill three times on May 8, and that morning, their reconnaissance in force had been driven back. In low spirits, V Corps gloomily prepared to try again to seize the hill from the well-entrenched Rebels.

The pessimism infected the top echelons. General John Gibbon, whose II Corps division would attack on Warren's right, thought the likelihood of success to be "entirely out of the question." The veteran artilleryman and combat leader, wounded at Fredericksburg and Gettysburg, had introduced the Iron Brigade's trademark black hats when he was its commander. Gibbon protested to Warren that his men would have to advance through "a dense piece of woods where dead cedar trees were scattered about, their stiff ragged arms standing out like so many bayonets." The woods, he said, would throw his division into disarray.[46]

Warren was unwilling to reject Gibbon's concerns out of hand, and so they rode together to Meade's headquarters. After Gibbon had restated his objections, Meade told his generals that it was Warren's decision to make. Gibbon glumly observed, "The latter seemed bent upon the attack with some idea that the occasion was a crisis in the battle of which advantage must be taken." He returned to his command, "in a place where I could exercise no control over it," and waited for Warren to send forward more than 20,000 men.[47]

LONGSTREET'S FIRST CORPS, now led by Richard Anderson, had occupied Laurel Hill since racing to Fitz Lee's rescue on the morning of May 8. The nearly 10,000 Rebels had tirelessly labored to improve their breastworks and entrenchments until they were now nearly unassailable. They relished the new sensation of fighting from behind solid defensive works. "This was the first time we had ever fought behind real, artificial cover," wrote Adjutant R. T. Coles of the 4th Alabama of Field's Division. "Behind it the men felt safer than in the open; consequently their aim was more deadly."[48]

That morning, after the Confederates had driven back the probing attacks by Crawford's and Cutler's divisions, the Alabamans had scavenged the muskets and cartridge boxes of the Union dead and wounded and distributed them inside their lines, until each man had four or five. Lacking repeating rifles, the Rebels now had "a very good substitute—several loaded ones to each man."[49]

BEFORE THE ATTACK commenced, the Yankees hugged the ground while Confederate batteries pounded their positions. Then, with a loud cheer, they leaped from their breastworks onto the long hill—and into a hurricane of musket fire, which "whipped the sand like a switch." Confederate artillery tore jagged holes in the advancing Union lines. "We were using double shot of canister nearly every time," wrote William Dame of the Richmond Howitzers, "on masses of men at short range; the infantry fire was rapid and deadly."[50]

CORPORAL JAMES DONNELLY and the 20th Massachusetts were ordered to rush the Confederate works without stopping to fire. Even before leaving their entrenchments, they knew it was hopeless. As Donnelly and his comrades started up the hill, heavy Confederate volleys carved huge gaps in their formation. Most of the men lay down or returned to the breastworks. "A large number were killed and wounded, mostly killed, as when they arose they were struck in the head."[51]

THE CONFEDERATES, STANDING four or five deep behind their breastworks, were able to efficiently pour heavy musket fire into the Yankees without letup because they had a system. The men in front fired continuously, tossing their empty muskets behind them and instantly being given freshly loaded weapons. Officers and men reloaded the empty muskets and handed them forward, wrote Coles of the 4th Alabama. "Often the officers would only take time in their haste to bite cartridges, insert [them] in the muzzle, and with a quick sharp blow of the butt of the piece on the ground send the cartridge home"—without even pausing to use a ramrod.[52]

Dame's artillery battery "swept the front clear of the enemy. We piled up more canister, and waited again."[53]

Blue-clad forms carpeted the hillside—the dead and wounded. The musketry ignited the carpet of pine needles on the ground, and soon fires raged in the dry timber. Just as in the Wilderness, some of the wounded burned to death, in screaming agony, with their comrades powerless to aid them.[54]

The blue wave ebbed; the attack had failed. At the assault's zenith, some Union troops had almost reached the abatis before withdrawing with heavy losses.

Rather than growing discouraged, Grant and Meade decided to double down. Convinced that Lee had to have weakened his defenses somewhere to repulse Hancock's attack on his flank, they believed the Rebel line would surely buckle with one well-placed blow. They ordered another attack on Laurel Hill.

BURNSIDE, WHO OCCUPIED the Union army's easternmost sector, had found the Confederate Achilles heel on Lee's right flank, but he did not know it. His orders called for him to reconnoiter his front in force, and if he saw an opening, "to attack with vigor." But vigor was not part of Burnside's character; he was a cautious, slow-moving general, described as "an odd figure, the fat man!" Moreover, he never realized that he had in fact turned

Lee's right flank. Grant later wrote with regret, "He [Burnside] had gained his position with but little fighting, and almost without loss."

All day on May 10, IX Corps had faced only Wilcox's depleted division of A. P. Hill's Corps, dug in between Burnside and Spotsylvania Court House. Burnside slowly pushed south on the Fredericksburg Road until his corps was just a quarter mile from Spotsylvania Court House.

It evidently did not occur to either Burnside or Grant, miles away watching the Laurel Hill attacks, that Lee had stripped Burnside's sector—not Laurel Hill or the Salient—of the divisions that opposed Hancock's corps on the Po River. As evening approached, Burnside was pulled back one mile to connect with VI Corps on his right. Grant later blamed himself for the failure.[55]

At Rappahannock Station in November 1863, Emory Upton had led his men in a nighttime sprint toward the Rebel lines in which not a shot was fired. The tactic caught the Confederates by surprise; he overran their lines, and they fell back in confusion. Now, the goateed twenty-four-year-old, an 1861 West Point graduate, was poised to employ the same tactic again—but on a larger scale, with twelve regiments against the Salient.[56]

Upton must have been a persuasive man, because Horatio Wright, the VI Corps commander, as well as Meade and Grant, were won over by his plan during their meeting the night of May 9. They made his assault the centerpiece of the attack on the Confederate center the next day. It would be supported by a simultaneous attack on Upton's left by Mott's division that, if all went well, would strike the Confederate line as Upton's men were overrunning it.

Upton personally selected the twelve regiments that would carry out the attack—the 5,000 men came from four brigades—and carefully tutored each regimental commander in his unit's role. They would quickly advance in a mass formation of four lines, three regiments to each, along a rough woodman's road before crossing a 200-yard open area between the tree line and the enemy defenses, without stopping to fire a volley. Speed and surprise were essential. After penetrating the Confederate line, the lead regiments would wheel to the left and right to keep the breach open, while the regiments behind them pushed forward.

A Meade engineering officer, Captain Ranald Mackenzie, and General David Russell, the commander of a sister brigade of Upton's, had selected the assault's target: a slight bulge in the western side of the Salient, a section occupied by General George Dole's Georgia Brigade. The Rebel works were deep and well-fortified, with firing ports protected by head logs. Abatis and traverses, as well as a second line of breastworks, made them even more formidable.[57]

UPTON'S 5 P.M. attack, postponed until 6 p.m., was delayed again until 6:30.

On Upton's left, Mott inexplicably was not informed of the change. At 5 p.m., his two brigades attacked as originally scheduled. Unsupported and alone, Mott's men stepped into a gale of musket and artillery fire from Richard Ewell's brigades. The Yankees fell back in disarray. Colonel Robert McAllister deplored his division's performance. "We were repulsed when we ought to have been successful," he told his wife Ellen. He blamed the failure on the division's short-timers, weeks away from being discharged after three years' service. They "do not fight well. I am sorry to say that in our Division we have too many of this kind."[58]

Just as Mott had not been informed that Upton was attacking later, so was Upton kept in the dark about Mott's premature attack; Upton still believed that Mott would protect his flank when his men charged the Salient.

While Burnside dithered on the army's left flank, Hancock returned to Laurel Hill from rescuing Barlow's division—and to orders from Meade to attack Laurel Hill when Upton launched his assault at 6:30. But even that attempt at coordination became problematic; a false report of an enemy movement against the Yankees' right flank delayed Hancock's attack. When it finally began, it would be 7 p.m.—a half-hour after Upton went in. The day's record of sloppily coordinated, piecemeal attacks would remain unbroken.

UPTON'S ATTACK PREPARATIONS appeared to be shaping up quite well. The plan was sound, and the objective had been reconnoitered by not only Mackenzie and Russell, but also by Upton and the regimental commanders. For thirty minutes beforehand, Union artillery plastered the Salient.

Then, at 6:35 p.m., Upton's twelve regiments emerged from the tree line, and "with a wild cheer and faces averted, rushed for the works." "Attention battalions! Forward, double quick! Charge!" Upton shouted.

Adam Badeau, a Grant aide who witnessed the attack, wrote, "The men seemed inspired from the start." A "sheet of flame" burst from the Rebel lines. "The rebels mowed down the men with awful effect," wrote Private Wilbur Fisk of the 2nd Vermont, "but the advancing line was not checked." Bullets "rattled like hailstones among the trees over our heads," as Upton's men raced ahead, grappled their way through the abatis and reached the Confederate breastworks without stopping to fire.[59]

The Confederates did not budge from their works. They sat in their pits "with pieces upright, loaded, and with bayonets fixed, ready to impale the first who should leap over. The first Union shock troops to climb over the parapet were riddled by Rebel musket fire. Others held their weapons over their heads and fired down into the enemy fortifications, or hurled their bayoneted muskets like javelins.

As their commanders shouted, "Forward! Forward!" the bluecoats swamped the Rebels, who fought tenaciously with clubbed muskets and bayonets until they were killed, wounded, or made prisoners. Upton's men surged into the second line of breastworks and captured the Rebel batteries. But when the Yankees wheeled around the guns to pour canister into the Confederates, they discovered that when the gunners withdrew, they took the rammers with them, rendering the guns useless.[60]

So far, the attack had unfolded just as Upton had predicted. After over-running the Rebel works, the two lead regiments, the 121st New York and the 96th Pennsylvania, had veered to the right and charged the Rebel battery, now in the Yankees' hands. The 5th Maine had cleared out the enemy to the left. The second wave had paused to unleash volleys that flickered like heat lightning in the heavy smoke.

Upton had broken the Rebel lines and had made an opening for Mott's division to exploit. Grant ordered Mott to attack a second time, but intensive Confederate artillery fire stopped his division's advance almost immediately, and it hastily retreated. "Mott's men . . . behaved abominably," wrote Theodore Lyman, Meade's aide. "They broke almost before getting under fire." It now occurred to Upton that while his attack had succeeded, his troops had crawled out on a limb.[61]

THE CONFEDERATE COMMAND reacted instantly. Lee started for the broken defenses to rally the men, but his staff remonstrated with him that it was too dangerous. He replied, "Then you must see to it that the ground is recovered." Lieutenant Colonel Walter Taylor, Lee's adjutant general, galloped to the front. "I found a pandemonium of excitement and confusion."

Ewell rode up behind the 45th North Carolina and shouted, "Don't run, boys; I will have enough men here in five minutes to eat up every damned one of them!" Indeed, Ewell threw into the fight all or parts of three North Carolina brigades and a brigade of Alabamans. Then, John Gordon's Georgia brigade, now commanded by General Clement Evans, also went in. The Georgians recaptured the batteries, the gunners returned with their rammers, turned around the guns "and commenced pouring canister into the ranks of the retreating foe," forcing them to seek protection behind the first line of captured breastworks. There, Upton's men continued to fight stubbornly, but they were now outnumbered.[62]

RELUCTANTLY, GRANT ORDERED Upton to withdraw. His men refused. "The officers and men of his command were so averse to giving up the advantage they had gained that I withdrew the order," wrote Grant. He tried to hurry Hancock and Warren into action on Laurel Hill in the hope of relieving the pressure on Upton. At last, under pressure from Ewell's counterattacking brigades, Upton's regiments began to fall back—all except the Vermont troops, who insisted they could hold the enemy works.

When Upton personally ordered them to retreat, the Vermonters refused, telling him to send ammunition and rations "and we can stay here six months." "The men wept when they were commanded to abandon the lines they had won," wrote Badeau. The VI Corps commander, General Horatio Wright, asked Grant what he should do about his stubborn Vermonters. Grant replied, "Pile in the men and hold it." When Wright returned to the front, however, he learned that the Vermont troops had finally withdrawn, two hours after the assault began.[63]

Upton lost 1,000 of his 5,000 men, and the Rebels 1,200 men—100 of them killed when overrun in the first line of breastworks; several hundred others, mainly Doles's Georgians, were made prisoners. "Upton had gained an important advantage," wrote Grant, "but a lack in others of the spirit and dash possessed by him lost it to us."

The problem was larger than that, though; leadership at the highest levels had failed Upton. Rather than relying entirely on Mott's undersize division to exploit Upton's breach, other VI Corps units might have supported his attack, but they were not used. Grant told Wright to "pile in the men," but only as an afterthought.

And rather than attack both the Salient and Laurel Hill, Grant would have been better served to concentrate on one point. "To assault at two points instead of one only is to double the loss while halving the chance of victory," wrote Walker, Hancock's assistant adjutant general. Charles Wainwright, V Corps' artillery commander, agreed. "I cannot help thinking that one big, well-sustained attack at one point would have been much more likely to succeed." When the fighting ended May 10, the Union army had lost 4,100 men—half of them from Hancock's corps.

Grant, however, was pleased with Upton's success. Puffing on a cigar, he said, "A brigade today—we'll try a corps tomorrow." Exercising his new authority to reward officers on the field for gallantry, Grant made Upton, who had been wounded in the fighting, a brigadier general "on the spot."[64]

That night at Grant's headquarters, Boston newsman Charles Carleton Coffin found the general-in-chief to be unusually candid and talkative. "We have had hard fighting today, and I am sorry to say we have not accomplished much," he told Coffin. "We have lost a good many men, and I suppose that I shall be blamed for it."

But Grant then added, "I do not know any way to put down this rebellion and restore the authority of the Government except by fighting, and fighting means that men must be killed. If the people of this country expect that the war can be conducted to a successful issue in any other way than by fighting, they must get somebody other than myself to command the army."[65]

"I HARDLY KNOW what to think of the wholesale slaughter in storming breastworks so well manned and stubbornly defended," surgeon Daniel Holt jotted in his journal that night. This had been Holt's hardest day of the campaign. He and two other surgeons worked through the night treating 350 men wounded during Upton's assault. And for an hour, bullets and artillery shot and shell flew through their field hospital "as thick as hail."

"One man was shot a second time while in my arms dressing his wound, and expired," Holt wrote. "I wonder why we were not killed."[66]

FLUNG BACK THREE times already at Laurel Hill, the Union troops awaited the sunset attack with dread. General Samuel Crawford and his staff walked along the line of his V Corps division, with Crawford "gesticulating in an excited manner," and wringing his hands—neither gesture confidence-inspiring. And then, in an anguished tone, he burst out, "This is sheer madness. I tell you this is sheer madness and can only end in wanton slaughter and certain repulse."[67]

Crawford's prediction was dead on. General Hobart Ward's brigade from II Corps made a good showing, crossing 300 yards of open ground, and despite being hit by swarms of "whizzing, whistling bullets" from the right, left, and center, pushed forward. "The heavy, dark lines of attack came into view, one after another, first in quick time, then in a trot, and then with a rush toward the works," a Confederate writer noted. Upon reaching the earthworks on the Rebel left, the Yankees overran part of the Texas Brigade, weakened by its heavy losses in the Wilderness. Moreover, the Texans had no bayonets at the very moment they needed them most. But "desperate fighting" by the Texans and an adjacent brigade and timely canister fire finally drove out the attackers, who found themselves without support on either side. The Texans, who had regarded bayonets as useless and had stopped carrying them, were never without them afterward.

It was over in thirty minutes. For Ward's brigade, the defeat was "complete and most disastrous." Other brigades got off more lightly because they were quicker to fall back. Assistant War Secretary Charles Dana observed the debacle from Warren's lines. The attack, he wrote to Stanton, "was executed with the caution and absence of comprehensive ensemble which seem to characterize [Warren]." Lyman was condemnatory: "Warren is not up to a corps command. . . . He cannot do it, and the result is partial and ill-concerted and dilatory movements."[68]

The Rebels still held their six-mile line as night fell on May 10. Many hundreds of dead and dying Union soldiers lay bleeding on the ground beneath the frowning Confederate breastworks on Laurel Hill. There, a Yankee from Maine called out, "Can you pray, sir? Can you pray?"

Moved by the man's entreaties, a Confederate chaplain and Major Robert Stiles, who was a minister's son and a First Corps artilleryman from Georgia, knelt beside the mortally wounded man. Stiles took his hand and told him to recite after him, "God have mercy on me, a sinner, for Jesus Christ's sake," and "all will be well with you." The man repeatedly recited the words with the greatest of intensity until life left him.[69]

AFTER UPTON'S ATTACK, Lee again inspected the Salient, or Mule Shoe, as Lee's men called it. A mile wide at its base and three-quarters of a mile deep, it jutted toward the Union lines. In devising what have been called the first "fully developed" fieldworks in North America, Lee had utilized the high ground between the Po and Ni Rivers to ingenious effect. The Mule Shoe, however, was the one blemish on the masterful defensive work. Lee had never liked it; it contradicted the tenets of military engineering because of its vulnerability to attacks from three sides. But on the other hand he could not allow the Yankees to make it a platform for their artillery.

Johnson's division had constructed it at night, without lights, under the supervision of Captain William Old, Johnson's aide-de-camp. To discourage enfilading fire, they had built numerous high traverses—essentially log-enclosed bays that were head high, three to four feet thick, and 20 feet long—behind the parapet. They had cleared a field of fire in front of the parapets and built abatis facing the enemy. But they could do nothing about the woods just 200 yards away that had hidden Upton's men until the moment of attack, or the ravine just 50 yards away that could shelter attackers. The engineers had done their best, and it had not been enough.

Having seen what Upton had accomplished, Lee considered abandoning the Mule Shoe. He wanted new fortifications, a mile long, built across its base. Lee told himself that he would withdraw Johnson's division to the new line when it was completed.[70]

ALL DAY LONG May 10, Lee had parried the Union army's clumsy lunges toward Spotsylvania Court House. As though operating on a vast chessboard, he had sent two Third Corps divisions opposite Burnside's corps to the Po River to thwart Hancock, leaving just one division facing IX Corps.

In so acting, Lee had accurately divined Burnside's timidity. With his remaining two corps manning strong, elevated fortifications, Lee was able to repel the fumbling Union attacks against Laurel Hill and the Salient.

As a Confederate band struck up "Nearer, My God, to Thee," and a Union band answered by playing the "Dead March" from Handel's *Saul,* Lee sat down to write orders and reports. Lee described the eventful day to Jefferson Davis, War Secretary James Seddon, and General Braxton Bragg in messages that ended with the words, "Thanks to a merciful Providence our casualties have been small."

However, Lee's orders to Ewell conveyed his anxiety about the Mule Shoe, especially "that part which seemed so easily overcome this afternoon." Ewell's men must restore and strengthen the line during the night, Lee said. He suggested that they dig a ditch and throw up an abatis outside the breastworks to slow future attacks. He concluded with a wry observation about Grant: "Perhaps General Grant will make a night attack as it was a favorite amusement of his at Vicksburg."[71]

To Jefferson Davis, Lee wrote, "Every attack made upon us has been repelled and considerable damage done to the enemy. With the blessing of God, I trust we shall be able to prevent Gen. Grant from reaching Richmond, and I think this army could render no more effectual service." A letter the same day by Lee's aide, Lieutenant Colonel Charles Venable, to his wife was equally sanguine. "I think that Grant will soon give it up & go back to Washington. His losses have been enormous."[72]

The enemy bands changed genres from funereal to patriotic. The Confederate band played "Bonnie Blue Flag," the Yankee band replied with "The Star-Spangled Banner," and then the Confederates played "Home, Sweet Home," which evoked cheering from both sides, "such a one as was never heard among the hills of Spottsylvania [sic] county before or since."[73]

3

Wednesday, May 11, 1864
Near Richmond

THE "BEAU SABREUR" was in a hurry. Jeb Stuart, the South's most revered cavalryman, had initially doubted Phil Sheridan's intentions on May 9, when Sheridan and his 9,800 troopers had ridden four abreast south on the Telegraph Road, guns and supply wagons in tow. The column, thirteen miles long, proceeded at a majestic four miles per hour. Stuart had never seen anything like it. It was as though Sheridan were daring him to attack him. Was it a trick? Would Sheridan turn northwest and strike at Lee's rear at Spotsylvania, or did he intend to ride into Richmond?

JAMES EWELL BROWN Stuart came from a Virginia family with a long military history. His father had fought in the War of 1812, and his great grandfather had commanded a regiment during the Battle of Guilford Courthouse in 1781. At West Point, Stuart's classmates bestowed the sardonic nickname "Beauty" on the stocky, barrel-chested, blunt-featured young man. He graduated in the Class of 1854 with his friend George Washington Custis Lee, the oldest son of Robert E. Lee, West Point's superintendent at that time.

In 1859, Stuart happened to be at the War Department in Washington as reports of a slave uprising at Harper's Ferry trickled in. Stuart was dispatched to Arlington to summon Colonel Robert E. Lee to duty. Volunteering as an aide, Stuart accompanied Lee to Harper's Ferry. It was Stuart who delivered the surrender demand to the uprising's leader, John Brown, and Stuart who signaled its rejection, triggering the government attack on the incendiaries. He kept Brown's Bowie knife as a souvenir.

In May 1861, Stuart reported to Colonel Thomas Jackson—after First Manassas, better known as General "Stonewall" Jackson—for duty in the Confederate Army. Both of them being able soldiers, devout Christians, and teetotalers, they got along splendidly. Jackson gave Stuart command of a cavalry regiment. Promotions came quickly for Stuart as his reputation for boldness soared. Full-bearded, ruddy, robust, and flamboyant, he lived in camp like a knight errant, surrounding himself with musicians and singing along with them. He dressed the part, too: red-silk-lined cape, yellow sash, golden spurs, and a black ostrich plume in his hat. As his list of exploits grew, he was celebrated throughout the South in song and verse, with good reason.

Stuart had led the war's first great cavalry raid, a grand ride around General George McClellan's army on the Peninsula that provided Lee with valuable intelligence that he put to use during the Seven Days battles. His cavalry circled Burnside's army at Fredericksburg in December 1862, and when Jackson was mortally wounded at Chancellorsville, Stuart assumed temporary command of his corps. But at Gettysburg, he arrived two days late, depriving the Rebel army of its eyes and ears. The failure caused him to slip in Lee's estimation.

More consequential, however, was the slow, steady erosion of Stuart's Cavalry Corps—from casualties, worn-out horses, and its unchanging military doctrine and technology. While Sheridan's troopers had been issued repeating rifles, Stuart's were still armed with muzzle-loaded rifles with a maximum firing rate of four rounds a minute.

Moreover, the Union cavalry, first under General Alfred Pleasanton, and now under Sheridan, had steadily improved. The Yankee troopers were not only more numerous, but they had better leaders, tactics, and equipment than before.

Probably the key factor in the Union cavalry's performance was the Spencer repeating rifle, a "force-multiplier" when used by dismounted troopers. With it, a cavalryman could fire seven shots successively by working the lever action. By replacing empty tube magazines with preloaded ones, a trooper might fire twenty-one rounds in a minute. While their 100-yard effective range could not compete with infantry muskets that could hit targets accurately at 300 yards or more, the repeating rifles gave Sheridan's men a tremendous firepower advantage over Stuart's cavaliers.

The cavalry would never have received Christopher Spencer's invention had it not been for Lincoln, who was fascinated by technology and routinely test-fired rifles on the open ground south of the White House. Lincoln's Ordnance Bureau chief, General James Ripley, had rejected the Spencer, but Lincoln reversed Ripley's decision.

In the Confederacy, however, no one had challenged Robert E. Lee's rejection of repeating rifles. Lee thought they wasted too much ammunition. Moreover, requiring soldiers to load a rifle after each shot, he believed, "makes the man to value his shot, and not to fire till he is sure of his aim."[74]

GENERAL WILLIAM WICKHAM'S cavalry brigade shadowed Sheridan from the outset, keeping Stuart, at Spotsylvania Court House, apprised of his movements. It was not difficult to keep pace with Sheridan, whose strategy was simple: "a slow and steady march, straight toward the confederate capital, all the time in position to accept battle should Stuart offer it." A choking cloud of dust hung in the calm air above the column, coating the riders with a gray patina. When Sheridan left the Telegraph Road at the Ta River, angling southwest toward Beaver Dam Station, that was enough for Stuart. Stuart gathered up three of his brigades and rode hard sixteen miles south, joining Wickham near the North Anna River.[75]

Stuart was concerned about Sheridan's route. Just across the North Anna was Lee's forward supply depot at Beaver Dam Station. And nearby, Stuart's wife Flora and their two children were staying at the plantation home of Dr. Edmund Fontaine.

Just as Stuart had feared, George Armstrong Custer's Michigan Brigade—nicknamed the "Wolverines" and part of Sheridan's Cavalry Corps—crossed the North Anna and turned northwest toward the Rebel depot on the Virginia Central Railroad. In aggressiveness and flamboyant dress, the twenty-four-year-old general was a Yankee counterpart of Stuart, whom he had fought and repulsed at Gettysburg. He was a striking figure with his drooping mustache and reddish-blond ringlets, broad-brimmed hat, and red necktie.

With loud yells, Custer's men barreled into Beaver Dam Station, scattering the small Rebel force and liberating 400 Union captives from the Wilderness who were on their way to prisons in Richmond. Then, Custer's men and troopers from Thomas Devins's brigade turned their attention to the mountains of Confederate rations, medical supplies, and weapons that were to succor Lee's army if it fell back to the North Anna, but that now would not.[76]

Ordered to fill their haversacks, Custer's men stuffed them with bacon, flour, molasses, sugar, meal, liquor, and medical supplies. They burned everything else: 200,000 pounds of bacon, 1.5 million rations, the rest of Lee's medicines, and the station itself. To complete the scene of ruination, thunder and lightning crashed and sizzled, and rain fell in torrents. The cavalrymen turned to the railroad tracks and the telegraph wires—Lee's communication line to Richmond—and wrecked more than eight miles of railroad and telegraph lines. Custer's men fired artillery shells through the boilers of the two locomotives at the station and destroyed three trains and ninety wagons. "With the blazing buildings in front of us, the drenching rain falling, the thunder pealing overhead, and the blinding flashes of lightning, the situation can be better imagined than described," wrote Alonzo Foster of the 6th New York Cavalry.[77]

The low clouds glowed from the inferno set by Custer's wrecking crews. The reflected flames were visible from the Fontaine house, where Jeb Stuart's family anxiously wondered whether the Yankees would ride there next.[78]

In destroying three weeks' worth of food stockpiled for the Army of Northern Virginia, Sheridan had accomplished more than any of his predecessors during the previous three years.[79]

THE NEXT MORNING, May 10, Stuart rode into the ruined village of Beaver Dam Station as Sheridan's rearguard was pulling out; the Union Cavalry Corps had spent the night in the area. Before resuming his mission of heading off Sheridan north of Richmond, Stuart went to see Flora.

She came out of the house and they talked quietly in the yard, Stuart remaining mounted. Before riding away, he bent down and kissed her. The parting would be their last. As they rode south, Stuart told his aide, Major Reid Venable, that he did not expect to survive the war.[80]

Later that morning, Stuart warned General Braxton Bragg in Richmond that Sheridan had left Beaver Dam Station and was riding toward the Rebel capital. "I am pursuing him closely. I think he will cross between Hanover Junction and Richmond, but it will be well to be prepared for him in the defenses at Richmond."[81]

Sheridan's men felled trees behind them as they traveled south. Finding the way blocked, Stuart split his force—a questionable decision when his total strength was less than half of Sheridan's. Most of Stuart's men took a wide southeastern route to the Telegraph Road in the hope of getting in front of Sheridan before he reached Richmond. James Gordon's brigade continued to follow the Yankees.

Stuart's unease grew throughout the day. He warned Bragg that Sheridan's force was large "and if attack is made on Richmond it will be principally as dismounted cavalry, which fight better than the enemy's infantry." That night, he confessed in another report that as yet, "there is none of our cavalry from this direction between the enemy and Richmond." Near

Hanover Junction, his weary men lay down to rest for a few hours. Stuart planned to decamp around midnight to beat Sheridan to the crossroad where the Telegraph Road intersected the road that Sheridan was traveling—a place called Yellow Tavern.

With a small rearguard, Sheridan forced Gordon to keep his distance throughout May 10, while the rest of the Cavalry Corps enjoyed a quiet day as it proceeded at a stately pace through the riotous springtime countryside. "So leisurely was it that it did not tax the endurance of men or horses," wrote Major Kidd of the 6th Michigan. "There was a steadiness about it that calmed the nerves, strengthened self-reliance, and inspired confidence." The Cavalry Corps camped that night near Ground Squirrel Bridge on the South Anna River, twenty miles from Richmond.[82]

On Wednesday, May 11, Stuart's troopers were in the saddle riding south at 1 a.m. Around daybreak, they reached Ashland. One of Sheridan's brigades was there, having just burned a train and ripped up tracks. There was a cavalry fight, with both sides claiming victory. At 8 a.m., Stuart's men reached Yellow Tavern. Yankee cavalrymen were nowhere in sight.

With a supreme effort, Stuart had accomplished what he had set out to do: he had successfully interposed his cavalry between Sheridan's cavalry and Richmond.

"I intersect the road the enemy is marching on at Yellow Tavern, the head of the turnpike," Stuart wrote to General Bragg. "My men and horses are all tired, hungry and jaded, but *all right*." Stuart intended to defeat Sheridan in battle and force him to retreat.[83]

FROM THEIR ENTRENCHMENTS at Bermuda Hundred between Petersburg and Richmond, Benjamin Butler's men could hear train whistles on the Richmond and Petersburg Railroad and Rebel infantry marching on the nearby turnpike. Freshly arrived Confederate troops from the Carolinas and Georgia were moving north.

The previous day, May 10, Butler had abandoned his drive on Petersburg when he learned that Meade's army had moved south from the Wilderness. Butler's orders from Grant had stated that his primary objective should be Richmond; Butler moved quickly now to prove his determination to fulfill his mission. He sent General Alfred Terry's X Corps division to seize the Richmond and Petersburg Railroad.

Near Chester Station, the Yankee division collided with two Rebel brigades that General Robert Ransom had led south from Drewry's Bluff. After a vicious hand-to-hand fight, Ransom withdrew, leaving Terry's men in possession of the field and, more importantly, the railroad linking Petersburg and Richmond. Small though it was, the victory would be Butler's only triumph of this campaign.

And then, after gathering up their wounded and destroying a stretch of railroad tracks, Terry's troops withdrew from the railroad to their lines in Bermuda Hundred, forfeiting what they had won. "I am afraid there has been a fine opportunity for decided advantages lost here," wrote a Union officer.[84]

YET BUTLER'S THRUST toward Richmond threw a scare into Confederate officials, their nerves still raw from the Army of the James's sudden appearance at Bermuda Hundred. At that time, they had summoned troops from the Carolinas, Georgia, and Florida, and Davis had turned down Lee's request for reinforcements at Spotsylvania. After Terry's clash with Ransom's brigades at Chester Station, alarm bells and whistles kept Richmond residents on edge through the long night of May 10–11. Colonel Josiah Gorgas, the ordnance commander in Richmond, went to War Secretary Seddon's office at 5 a.m. after a short, fitful sleep and "found him laboring under the impression that the last hours of Richmond were at length numbered." Many civilians evidently thought so, too. Mrs. Alexander Lawton, the Confederate quartermaster general's wife, wrote in her diary, "Many ladies sat up all night, dressed in their best clothes with their jewelry on," ready to flee the city if necessary.

And then, amid the excitement over the Chesterfield Station fight came the reports that Sheridan's Cavalry Corps was less than twenty miles north of Richmond, riding south without serious opposition. City militiamen were hustled from the south side of Richmond into trenches on the city's north side to face the new, graver crisis.[85]

YELLOW TAVERN, SIX miles north of Richmond, was an abandoned stagecoach station whose faded yellow exterior suggested its name's origin. From the crossroad, on a straight line to Richmond, ran Brook Turnpike, a macadamized road. Before and behind a thin skirt of woods on a bluff,

Stuart had positioned his two brigades—William Wickham and his four regiments, and Lunsford Lomax and his three—parallel to the road down which Sheridan was marching. Stuart hoped to smash Sheridan's column with a powerful blow to its flank.

Possibly believing that his men and horses, which had seen hard use through the night, would be too exhausted for a mounted charge—or perhaps Stuart was fatigued himself and not thinking clearly—he made a critical error: he dismounted his cavalry. The immediate effect was to sharply reduce his fighting force; as many as one in four troopers, along with orderlies and slaves, were required to hold the horses so their comrades could fight on foot. With just 3,000 men on hand, after having sent Gordon's brigade to harry Sheridan's rear, Stuart's fighting force numbered no more than 2,500 after his men were dismounted. Sheridan's force outnumbered Stuart's more than three-to-one.

A cavalry charge on Sheridan's flank now being out of the question, Stuart's men would have to fight defensively as infantrymen, placing them at an additional disadvantage: while they were armed with single-shot carbines, Sheridan's troopers had seven-shot Spencer rifles.[86]

SHERIDAN INITIALLY LAUNCHED probing attacks on both ends of Lomax's line, and then Wesley Merritt's division seized the Brook Turnpike between Stuart and Richmond. Stuart sent his aide, Major Henry McClellan, to General Bragg in Richmond, urging him to march out of the city and attack Merritt's rear. Meanwhile, Stuart's batteries shelled Merritt's brigades.

Sheridan, described as "calm, unruffled," took his time scouting the battleground as he awaited the arrival of the rest of his corps. While Stuart's troopers had been riding most of the night, Sheridan's cavalrymen had enjoyed a good rest. "Never were men and horses in better condition or spirits for battle than were Sheridan's troopers," wrote Major Kidd.[87]

At 4 p.m., Custer's Wolverine Brigade—some regiments mounted, others dismounted, and supported by James Wilson's division—attacked the left side of Stuart's line. The assault began at a walking pace, then became a dash. Stuart's line began to give way.

Stuart leaped onto his horse, General, and rallied the 1st Virginia Cavalry, just as Custer's mounted troopers slammed into it. The Virginians threw back Custer's first attack, but the Wolverines' second attack overwhelmed them. Bluecoats swarmed through the line, shredding the defenders with their rapid-fire carbines.

One of Custer's dismounted troopers, forty-eight-year-old Private John A. Huff of the 5th Michigan, formerly a top marksman in Berdan's Sharpshooters, shot Stuart with a .44 caliber pistol from ten to fifteen feet away. The bullet struck him under the right ribs.

Stuart's hat flew off and he clasped his side. "Oh, the general! The general!" his troopers cried. Aides kept him from falling, tried unsuccessfully to control his plunging horse, and then moved him to a calmer mount. Finally, they lowered him to the ground and propped him against a tree.

Fitz Lee and an ambulance arrived. "Go ahead, old fellow," Stuart told Lee, who was next in command. "I know you'll do what is right." As he was being lifted into the ambulance, he saw some of his men running to the rear. "Go back! Go back!" he cried. "Do your duty as I've done mine. I would rather die than be whipped!"

But Stuart was dying and his cavalrymen were whipped; Custer and Wilson had broken the Rebel left, and Sheridan's brigades were driving the Confederate troopers toward Ashland and Richmond.[88]

NOTHING NOW STOOD between Phil Sheridan's Cavalry Corps and the war's great prize, the Confederate capital. In one afternoon, his troopers had beaten the once invincible Confederate cavalry and mortally wounded its iconic leader.

The dusty column rode through Richmond's exterior defenses after scattering a small militia force. The Yankees could hear church bells tolling the news of the city's gravest peril of the war: the enemy was a mere three miles from Richmond's center, and every available citizen, young and old, was needed to man the city defenses.

Sheridan, however, did not plan to capture Richmond; he knew that he could not hold the city when thousands of nearby Rebel infantrymen could counterattack within hours. He intended to cross the Chickahominy River, join Butler's army, and obtain supplies. "When Stuart was defeated the main purpose of my instructions had been carried out," Sheridan later wrote. He led his troopers down the Mechanicsville Road toward the Chickahominy bridge north of Richmond.[89]

The Rebels had mined the road with trip-wired shells—primitive improvised explosive devices—which the horses detonated, wounding both riders
and mounts. Sheridan ordered two dozen prisoners brought up, and they
were forced to crawl ahead of the cavalry column on their hands and knees
to find the trip wires, follow them to the shells, and disarm them.

The delay bought time for Fitz Lee and what cavalry he could gather to
build field works and barricade the Chickahominy bridge. The Yankees
would have a hard time forcing a crossing.

In Richmond, General Braxton Bragg and Jefferson Davis had collected
more than 4,000 city militiamen and 3,500 infantry regulars from the
Drewry's Bluff area and were pursuing Sheridan's troopers, slowed by 625
wounded and 200 to 300 prisoners. To add to Sheridan's problems, wind-
driven rain lashed the bluecoats.[90]

Sheridan consulted his maps and sent a brigade to reconnoiter the upriver Meadow Bridge. The scouts reported that it was lightly defended and,
while the main bridge had been destroyed, the railroad trestle was intact.

Under fire from two Rebel guns and dismounted cavalry, two of Custer's
regiments managed to cross the railroad bridge on foot in the torrential
rain. They "tiptoed from tie to tie, watching the chance to make it in
the intervals between shells." Once across, they deployed as skirmishers
and drove back the defenders on the north bank to their breastworks and
pinned them there, while their comrades laid planks over the rails and ties
for the wagons.

Meanwhile, Sheridan's rearguard, Wilson's division, was being driven
back toward the river by Bragg's improvised force. Sheridan roved the battle
line, encouraging his troops. "We have got to whip them! We can do it and
we will!"

Gregg's division, hiding in a ravine, suddenly raked the Rebels with volleys of Spencer repeater fire that flashed down the road like sheet lightning.
Then, Wilson counterattacked and broke Bragg's line. The Rebels retreated
to their Richmond breastworks.

Their way now clear, the Cavalry Corps crossed the Chickahominy,
making camp on May 12 near Gaines's Mill. Sheridan triumphantly wrote
that his men had inflicted on the Confederate cavalry "the most thorough
defeat that had yet befallen them in Virginia."[91]

JEB STUART WAS taken to the home of his brother-in-law, Doctor Charles Brewer, who lived on Grace Street in Richmond. A crowd kept quiet vigil outside, as visitors came and went; one was Jefferson Davis. To Davis's solicitous questions, Stuart said that he felt "easy, but willing to die, if God and my country think I have fulfilled my destiny and done my duty." The war's greatest cavalry leader died at 7:38 p.m. on May 12.[92]

When Robert E. Lee was informed of Stuart's death, he covered his face with his hands and went to his tent to grieve. To a staff officer who entered later, Lee said, "I can scarcely think of him without weeping!" In General Orders No. 44 announcing the death to the army, Lee wrote, "Among the gallant soldiers who have fallen in this war General Stuart was second to none in valor, in zeal, and in unfaltering devotion to his country."[93]

THE MORNING OF May 11, Grant appeared confident at the mess table as he ate his breakfast—such as it was. He "made his entire breakfast of a cup of coffee and a small piece of beef cooked almost to a crisp; for the cook had by this time learned that the nearer he came to burning the beef the better the general liked it," wrote his aide, Horace Porter.

Congressman Elihu Washburne of Illinois, Grant's friend and longtime patron who had traveled with Grant's headquarters during the campaign's first week, was returning to Washington that morning. His cavalry escort arrived around 8 a.m. Before departing, Washburne told Grant that when he reached Washington, he planned to brief Lincoln and Stanton on his experiences with the army. Did Grant have any messages to relay?

Indeed, Grant did. As he sat in a camp chair in front of his tent, smoking a cigar, he used Washburne as a sounding board for what he wanted to tell Lincoln, Stanton, and Henry Halleck. The army was making good progress, Grant told Washburne, "but the campaign promises to be a long one, and I am particularly anxious not to say anything just now that might hold out false hopes to the people."[94]

Grant went to the camp desk inside his tent and wrote short letters to Stanton and Halleck in his fluent, epigrammatic style. To both men, Grant acknowledged that the army had lost "probably twenty thousand men" and eleven generals killed, wounded, or missing, but he said that Lee's losses were most likely higher. He asked Halleck to send reinforcements quickly.

"I am satisfied the enemy are very shaky, and are only kept up to the mark by the greatest exertions on the part of their officers, and by keeping them intrenched in every position they take."

To Stanton, he wrote, "We have now ended the sixth day of very hard fighting. The result to this time is much in our favor. Our losses have been heavy as well as those of the enemy." He closed with a striking sentence that would thrill Lincoln and his advisors and, days afterward, the Union when it was reported in Northern newspapers: "*I propose to fight it out on this line if it takes all summer* [emphasis added]."

Washburne slipped the letters into his pocket and left for the capital.[95]

IT WAS A trying time for the Lincoln administration. When there was initially no news from Grant, the suspense wore on Lincoln and his cabinet. Navy Secretary Gideon Welles wrote, "The intense anxiety is oppressive, and almost unfits the mind for mental activity." At times, Lincoln was unable to eat or sleep. After receiving bad news one day, he told Indiana Congressman Schuyler Colfax, "How willingly would I exchange places today with the soldier who sleeps on the ground in the Army of the Potomac."[96]

When the casualty list from the Wilderness finally arrived, it made matters worse. Colfax encountered Lincoln as he gloomily paced a hallway, hands clasped behind his back. "As he looked up, I thought his face the saddest one I had ever seen. He exclaimed: 'Why do we suffer reverses after reverses? Could we have avoided this terrible, bloody war? Was it not forced upon us? Is it ever to end?'" To Illinois Congressman Owen Lovejoy, the president said: "The war is eating my life out. I have a strong impression that I shall not live to see the end."

The president grieved when he saw wounded soldiers being transported in wagons through Washington's streets to army hospitals. One evening, while riding past a long line of ambulances with his friend, Isaac Arnold, Lincoln said, "Look yonder at those poor fellows. This suffering, this loss of life is dreadful."[97]

Indeed, Lincoln slept little and, when Mrs. Lincoln was out of town, he sometimes forgot to eat. His weight steadily dropped, and his aides worried about his health. John Hay recalled Lincoln visiting the aides' room one night in his nightshirt. When Hay complimented him on "the amount of underpinning he still has left . . . he said he weighed 180 pounds. Important if true."

Several times a day, the president walked across the yard between the White House and the War Department to read the latest war news in the telegraph office. It was a refuge from the office-seekers who besieged him in the White House, but Cabinet members and congressmen knew where to find him if needed.

Lincoln would read through the recent messages, kept in a drawer, until he came upon a telegram that he had already read, invariably saying, "Well, boys, I am down to the raisins." (A favorite Lincoln story was about a girl who overate at her birthday party and began vomiting. Her parents called a doctor. The child had eaten raisins for dessert, and when the doctor saw them come up, he said that she was out of danger, because she was "down to the raisins.") Sometimes, Lincoln remained at the telegraph office all night, telling stories to the young operators, who lived in an adjoining room, while incoming messages were being deciphered.[98]

For Lincoln, Grant's message—*"I propose to fight it out on this line if it takes all summer"*—was a lifeline after so many years of disappointment. "Hope beamed on his face" when he again met Congressman Colfax. "Grant will not fail us now," he said, "he will fight it out on that line, and this is now the hope of the country."

ON THE NIGHT of May 11, a crowd gathered on the White House lawn to celebrate reports—wildly exaggerated ones—of Union victories in the Wilderness and near Spotsylvania Court House. "There was something like delirium in the air," wrote Noah Brooks, the Sacramento *Daily Union's* correspondent. "Everybody seemed to think that the war was coming to an end right away." Even congressmen were caught up in the excitement and were prolonging their session so that they could "be in at the death" of the Confederacy.

At nine o'clock, Lincoln emerged from the White House and stood bare-headed beneath the portico, as "a great crowd of cheering citizens" surged around him to hear his words. He spoke optimistically about Grant's campaign and told them of his vow to "fight it out on this line." The audience loved it. "For a time it appeared as if most people thought Grant would close the war and enter Richmond before the autumn leaves began to fall," wrote Brooks.[99]

While the Washington crowds cheered, the Richmond people gathered in the churches for prayer meetings. "We take great comfort in them," wrote diarist Judith McGuire. "We feel strengthened by the prayers of so many good people. . . . We feel that the Lord will keep the city."[100]

"HOW NEAR WE have been to this thing before and failed," Lincoln told John Hay. "I believe if any other general had been at the head of that army it would have now been on this side of the Rapidan. It is the dogged pertinacity of Grant that wins."

Amid the climactic campaign of the war and a pending reelection campaign, the painter Frances Carpenter was busy composing a portrait of Lincoln reading the Emancipation Proclamation to his Cabinet. Carpenter had been living in the White House since February, and Lincoln had permitted him to temporarily convert the state dining room into his studio.

Carpenter hoped the portrait—on the grand scale of nine-by-fourteen feet—would capture one of the great moments in the nation's history. After three months of sittings by the president and his cabinet members, Carpenter, Lincoln, and his advisers were entirely at ease with one another, and so it was not presumptuous of Carpenter to ask the president his opinion of Grant.

"The great thing about Grant," replied Lincoln, "is his perfect coolness and persistency [sic] of purpose. I judge he is not easily excited—which is a great element in an officer—and he has the *grit* of a bulldog! Once let him get his 'teeth' *in*, and nothing can shake him off."[101]

GRANT STRIPPED THE army for action. He instructed Meade to send back to Belle Plain, the great Union depot northeast of Fredericksburg, "every wagon that can be spared, retaining here only [that] sufficient to move what ammunition and other stores that cannot be carried on the person." Reserve artillery might also be sent away, Grant told Meade, adding, "This however I leave to your own discretion."[102]

Indeed, even as Grant incrementally assumed tactical control of the Army of the Potomac, he strove to preserve the pretense of Meade remaining in charge. Meade had no illusions about his diminishing role. He told senators visiting the war zone: "At first I had maneuvered the army, but that gradually, and from the very nature of things, Grant had taken control; and that it would be injurious to the army to have two heads." A newspaperman charitably described Grant's and Meade's relationship: "Grant does the grand strategy, and [Meade] the grand tactics." But Grant increasingly was doing both.[103]

Assistant War Secretary Charles Dana characterized Meade as "an intellectual man," a pleasant companion when not preoccupied, "but silent and indifferent to everybody when he was occupied with that which interested him." Dana thought Meade lacked boldness, self-confidence, and "tenacity of purpose. . . . As soon as Meade had a commander over him he was all right, but when he himself was the commander he began to hesitate."[104]

"A BRIGADE TODAY—WE'LL try a corps tomorrow," Grant had said after Emory Upton broke into the Salient with 5,000 men late May 10. Ultimately, the attack failed because no reinforcements were sent, and because the Rebels quickly plugged the hole in their line.[105]

Confederate Edward Porter Alexander described May 11 as "a day of bitter sharpshooting & angry artillery practice." The constant sniping and shelling allowed no respite for soldiers weary after seven days of marching and fighting. Major William Fowler, an adjutant in V Corps, wrote home in a letter: "We are completely used up, officers and men being overpowered by fatigue and excitement. . . . The strain is intense and wearing. All of us have grown a year older during this week."

For Grant, it was a day for planning a fresh assault on the Salient, utilizing the tactics that had carried Upton's men through the Confederate defenses: a swift approach to the enemy line by a compact column; no firing until the line was breached. But instead of 5,000 men attacking, Grant intended to raise the ante to 20,000 men. They would come from his hardest-hitting corps—Winfield Scott Hancock's II Corps.

GRANT WANTED HANCOCK's three divisions to march that night behind V and VI corps, traveling from the far right of Grant's six-mile battle line to its left. Massing in the woods opposite the Salient, Hancock's men would attack at 4 a.m. on May 12 in columns—as Upton had—while Burnside's IX Corps on their left launched a simultaneous assault. Warren's V Corps and Wright's VI Corps would remain opposite Laurel Hill, ready to charge forward if any Rebel defenders began moving to the Salient. "There is but little doubt in my mind that the assault last evening would have proven entirely successful if it had commenced one hour earlier and had been heartily entered into by Mott's division and the Ninth Corps," Grant wrote to Meade.[106]

II Corps' fourth division was Gershom Mott's, unjustifiably blamed by one and all for the final failure of Upton's attack. Wright disdained even having Mott's men on his left flank. "They are not a support; I would rather have no troops there!" he ranted to Meade. In just a few days, Mott's undersized division would be downgraded to a brigade and assigned to David Birney's division.[107]

ABOUT 10 P.M., Hancock's men pulled out of the line, after first piling more wood on their fires so that the Rebels would believe they were settling in for the night. As rain steadily fell, II Corps set out cross-country for its staging area, a spot on the map labeled "Brown House." Lieutenant Colonel George Mendell, a II Corps engineer, guided by compass. It was a "hard, wearisome" march in the rain and through fields, woods, and swamps for men who had slept little in days.

The soldiers' boots filled with water when they waded the rain-swollen streams; there was no time to empty them on the forced march. Whenever the column stopped, the men dropped to the ground and fell asleep instantly, rising when the column began moving again.

One man fell asleep on a fence rail, pitched off it, and broke his neck. "In less than ten minutes from the time the unfortunate man sat down on the fence, his comrades were digging his grave," wrote Colonel Charles Weygant of the 124th New York. Even the horses were weary, he said. "Seized by the same irresistible desire to close their weary eyes, and with their noses almost touching the ground, [they] would weave to and fro like drunken men."[108]

It was just as taxing for Hancock's division commanders, frustrated by their ignorance of the Confederates' position, or the size of their force, or, for that matter, even where their guide was leading them. Francis Barlow, whose division would lead the attack, tried without success to obtain more information. At last, "the absurdity of our position—that we were proceeding to attack the enemy when no one even knew his direction, and we could hardly keep on our own legs—appealed to me very much." The New York lawyer laughed so hard at the ridiculous situation that he nearly fell off his horse. Turning to Lieutenant Colonel Charles Morgan, his inspector-general, Barlow said, "For heaven's sake, at least face us in the right direction so that we shall not march away from the enemy and have to go round the world and come up in their rear."

Barlow's division reached the Brown House around midnight, the men filing into positions behind the picket line 1,200 yards from the Rebel entrenchments. Inside the Brown House, Barlow huddled with Hancock and the other II Corps division commanders, John Gibbon, Birney, and Mott.

Other than knowing they were less than a mile from the enemy line, they knew no more than Barlow. Lieutenant Colonel C. B. Comstock of Grant's staff was to have scouted the ground the previous afternoon, but he got lost in the woods and did not reach the area until it was nearly dark. Rebel skirmishers made it impossible for him to conduct a reconnaissance.

When his questions about the terrain yielded no answers, Barlow exasperatedly asked, "Well, have I a gulch a thousand feet deep to cross?" The reply was: "We do not know." The generals did the best that they could; they marked the line of attack on a map, along a compass line connecting the Brown House with the McCoull House, a large white house inside the Confederate lines on the other side the Salient. A bit more information came from Lieutenant Colonel Waldo Merriam of the 16th Massachusetts, who had participated in Mott's May 10 attack and had gotten close to the Rebel works. In response to Barlow's questions, Merriam sketched the Confederate defenses, as he understood them anyway, on a wall.

Barlow left the meeting looking uncharacteristically glum. A Barlow aide, Lieutenant John Black, wrote, "I never remember seeing General Barlow so depressed as he was on leaving Hancock's headquarters that night; he acted as if it was indeed a forlorn hope he was to lead."

Afterward, Barlow met with his brigade commanders, and on the damp ground, by the "flickering light of a lantern," he sketched a rude map of the

Rebel defenses and explained each brigade's role. He left them without any of his usual exhortations, such as, "Make your peace with God and mount, gentlemen. I have a hot place picked out for you today." Instead, for the first time before a battle, Barlow handed his valuables to a friend for safekeeping in case he did not return.[109]

Brigade commanders formed II Corps' assault troops into double columns and ordered them to shed coffee cans and other accouterments that might rattle. The horses were sent to the rear. The men spread their ponchos on the wet ground and lay down to rest for a couple of hours.[110]

A FEW MILES away, inside a church in Spotsylvania Court House that served as General Henry Heth's headquarters, Robert E. Lee was telling his generals that he believed the Yankees were going to retreat that night to Fredericksburg. Generals Cadmus Wilcox and Rooney Lee, a cavalry leader and the commanding general's son, reported that Burnside had withdrawn north of the Po River on Lee's right and that Federal wounded were being sent to Belle Plain. Lee believed this portended a movement of some kind by Grant, and he did not want to be caught flat-footed.

Lee had badly misread what in fact were preparations for a massive attack. Burnside had shifted his divisions so they could support Hancock's attack on the Salient at first light the next morning. The transfer of wounded to Belle Plain was Grant readying the army for action.

But Lee evidently did not consider an all-out assault to be a possibility; otherwise, he would not have deliberately weakened his defenses. He had ordered his artillery chief, General William Pendleton, to ready all of his guns for instant movement—and before nightfall to withdraw any artillery in forward positions where it would be difficult to maneuver in the dark. Consequently, most of the Mule Shoe's guns, which would have had to travel down a narrow road through dense woods, had already been removed. This left General Edward Johnson's division in the Mule Shoe without artillery, just as 20,000 enemy troops were poised to attack his breastworks.

During the meeting, several officers criticized Grant for squandering men in futile attacks on the Rebel breastworks. Lee disagreed. "Gentlemen, I think that General Grant has managed his affairs remarkably well up to the present time."

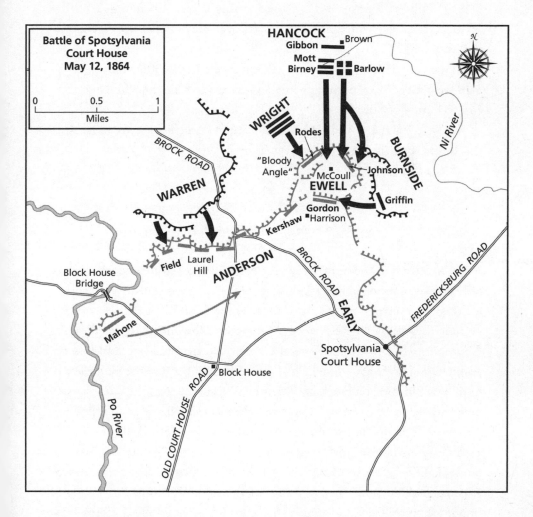

Battle of Spotsylvania
Court House
May 12, 1864

0   0.5   1
Miles

Lee longed to go on the offensive, if only Grant would give him an opening. "We must attack these people," he said.

A. P. Hill, who was present at the meeting despite his illness, replied, "General Lee, let them continue to attack our breastworks; we can stand that very well."

Supporting Hill's viewpoint, Heth interjected that 300 of Burnside's men were killed that morning while attacking Heth's entrenchments, at a cost to him of one dead.

Rising to leave, Lee said, "This army cannot stand a siege. We must end this business on the battlefield, not in a fortified place."[111]

4

Thursday, May 12, 1864
The Bloody Angle

EVEN IN THE rain and mud, forty-year-old Winfield Scott Hancock looked tall and handsome on horseback this morning in his immaculate white shirt, looking every inch his nickname, "Hancock the Superb." But as usual when he rode these days, "I suffer agony," he wrote. The gunshot wound from Gettysburg remained unhealed—the bullet had driven a nail and bits of pommel into his thigh—and he had put on weight because the pain forced him to ride in a wagon much of the time. Even so, "He was the finest figure on horseback in either Army. . . . He was the incarnation of war and the embodiment of patriotism," wrote Joseph Muffly of the 148th Pennsylvania.[112]

II Corps had lost nearly one-fourth of its men in the Wilderness battles, but its fighting spirit was intact, and it remained Grant's elite corps. Since crossing the Rapidan, Grant had repeatedly chosen II Corps for the most important missions. Compared with the army's other corps, II Corps was the picture of dependability and efficiency. For this reason, Grant had once more turned to Hancock's men to deliver a pile-driving blow to the bulge in Lee's battle line.[113]

Rain had fallen all night long, and a thick fog hugged the ground as the black sky faded to leaden gray. At 4 on a clear morning, there would have been enough daylight for II Corps to see its way to the Salient, but not today. Although it irked him to do so, Hancock, a stickler for punctuality, postponed the attack until visibility improved. Thirty-five minutes later, at 4:35 a.m., he decided that his men could see well enough, and he launched the assault.

The troops were instructed to advance silently: no cheering or firing until they reached the Rebel parapet. "Let silence—dead silence—be the awful menace! And break it only with the bayonet!" Colonel John Brooke, a brigade commander in Barlow's division, told his regimental leaders.

Barlow's division, in two thickly massed columns—one writer described the formation as a "double-column fist"—would lead, emerging from the black woods to cross a broad clearing. From the advance's starting point, the ground sloped down to a stream before ascending to the Rebel line. All around were thick woods. On Barlow's right was Birney's division, which had a swamp in its path. Gershom Mott's small division formed behind Birney, and John Gibbon's division was in reserve.[114]

Hancock galloped along the line, waving his sword to urge his men forward. In the weak light, the four lead assault brigades appeared as a solid blue rectangle. As they advanced at "quick time," they made a rustling sound like water flowing over rocks. Orders were conveyed in whispers. "There was something weird . . . in the hooting of owls as the dark figures of men moved through the pines," wrote a soldier in the 17th Maine.[115]

Hidden by the fog, Hancock's shock troops advanced a half-mile without any shots fired by either side. They then encountered a thin line of Rebel pickets, who appeared stunned by the sudden appearance of dense formations of Yankees. "There was a little pattering of bullets," Barlow wrote, and "a few of our men [were] on the ground." The attackers crested a low hill. On the other side of a cleared area spanning a few hundred yards, they could see the heaped red dirt of the enemy works on a ridge ahead.

The Yankees "rolled out a tremendous cheer" and began to run across a field toward the entrenchments, with Brooke's and Nelson Miles's brigades leading. They tore away the Rebel abatis with eager hands, "crawling through and tumbling over the mass of material that was piled in front of the breast-works." The second line of brigades mingled with the first. "All line and formation was now lost, and the great mass of men, with a rush like a cyclone, sprang upon the intrenchments and swarmed over," swinging clubbed muskets and bayonets.[116]

GENERAL EDWARD "ALLEGHENY" Johnson's Rebels had passed a wet night in their muddy trenches. Like Hancock's corps, they, too, were exhausted after three days of digging and fighting with little sleep or food. Around midnight, pickets reported large formations of enemy troops moving along their front—Hancock's men arriving at the Brown House. Scouts and officers warned Johnson that the enemy was preparing to attack.

Johnson put his command on alert and sent his adjutant general to Richard Ewell to seek the return of the artillery removed from his lines the previous evening; just two guns remained at the Mule Shoe. Ewell did not grant Johnson's request. He told the adjutant that Lee was certain Grant would move at any time. So Johnson rode to Ewell's headquarters to plead his case personally, and the corps commander relented, promising to return the artillery immediately. For unknown reasons, Johnson's artillerymen did not receive the order until 3:30 a.m. When they did, they limbered the guns and moved out "with extraordinary speed," wrote Pendleton, Lee's artillery chief.

The guns were within sight of the Mule Shoe when the Confederates heard the Yankees coming through the woods, making a noise "like the roaring of a tempestuous sea." With loud cheers, Hancock's men emerged onto the 200 yards of cleared ground that lay before Johnson's line. The Rebels were momentarily transfixed by the spectacle. "As far as the eye could reach, the field was covered with the serried ranks of the enemy, marching in close columns to the attack."[117]

The famed Stonewall Brigade, in the toe of the Salient, and its three sister brigades opened fire on the charging formations of bluecoats, but to their horror, they discovered that the steady rain had soaked the powder in their preloaded muskets. Weary as they were, they had neglected to check their rounds. The sound of popping percussion caps, followed by silence, traveled up and down the line.[118]

AND THEN, HANCOCK's shock troops were swarming over the breastworks. Amid a ferocious hand-to-hand fight—clubs, fists, and bayonets—the Union regiments pushed past the defenders and captured the two guns before they could fire more than two shots apiece, and seized "the whole 20 guns coming in at a gallop," before they were fired even once.

"The storm had burst upon us," wrote Major Robert Hunter, a Confederate staff officer. An Irish Brigade officer ran through a Confederate color-bearer with his sword. A Rebel shot a Yankee and then threw down his musket, calling out, "I surrender." He was instantly shot dead. Private Henry Bell of the 116th Pennsylvania leaped over the works and shouted, "Look out, throw down your arms, we run this machine now."

It certainly appeared that way, at least initially. Nelson Miles's brigade struck the Salient's east side, defended by Colonel William Witcher's Virginians, and was briefly repulsed at bayonet-point—until Brooke's brigade joined him. Then, Witcher's breastworks were flooded with bluecoats. "The 50th [Virginia] was overwhelmed and the Union tide flowed over it," wrote the regiment's historian. The attackers spilled into the adjoining trenches on Witcher's right, and they bagged the 1st North Carolina, all but thirty of them. Then, it was General George Steuart's turn. His brigade was surrounded, and Steuart was taken prisoner.

Not all of the Rebels were ready to fight; some were caught sleeping in their blankets. When called upon to surrender, one crawled out from under his tent fly and said, "Oh, well, that is all right boys; don't get excited. Just let us get our coats on, and we will go to the rear."[119]

To the left of Witcher's brigade in the Salient, the 900 men of James Walker's Stonewall Brigade watched as the mass of Yankees approached. "The figures of the men seen dimly through the smoke and fog seemed almost gigantic, while the woods were lighted by the flashing of the guns and the sparkling of the musketry," wrote a Confederate lieutenant. The Virginians used the traverses—log mini-fortresses at right angles to the entrenchments—to slaughter the Yankees pouring into their trenches, but were forced back from one traverse to the other. Union numbers were too great for the fabled brigade; it shattered. The Yankees seized the abandoned Rebel guns, swung them around, and opened up on the fleeing Confederates. The rest were surrounded and captured. The Stonewall Brigade ceased to exist that morning.[120]

IN THE MULE Shoe's apex, Allegheny Johnson stormed back and forth with his hickory walking stick, exhorting his men to stand and fight. His division was arguably the most famous in the Army of Northern Virginia.

Stonewall Jackson had commanded it, its nucleus being the brigade that bore his name. On this black, rain-soaked morning, Johnson's four brigades were beaten to pieces around him as Hancock's brigades poured through breaches in the Salient like seawater through a crumbling dike, enfilading the Rebel defenders and taking them from the rear before they could change position. One by one, Johnson's brigades were crushed: Witcher's, Walker's, Steuart's, and Colonel Zebulon York's. In his frustration, all that Johnson could do was rail and strike at the swarming bluecoats with his stick. He would later write with some bitterness, "The main attack would have been repulsed had any artillery [been] on the line which could have possibly swept the ground over which they advanced."[121]

Stonewall Jackson's old division disappeared under the "irresistible wave" of Yankees, who took 2,000 to 3,000 prisoners, including Generals Johnson and Steuart. The bluecoats scooped up thirty colors and pursued the fleeing survivors.[122]

Johnson and Steuart were taken to Grant's headquarters, where Meade and Hancock were sorting through battle reports. When Hancock saw Johnson, an old friend, he extended his hand. "General Johnson," said Hancock, "I am glad to see you." Tears streaming down his face, Johnson took Hancock's hand. "General Hancock, this is worse than death to me," he said. Theodore Lyman of Meade's staff wrote that Johnson was "terribly mortified and kept coughing to hide his nervousness." Meade and Grant shook Johnson's hand, and General Seth Williams, Meade's assistant adjutant general, took him to breakfast at the officers' mess, a routine courtesy bestowed on captive generals by both sides.

But Steuart, who Lyman said "behaved like a donkey," was not invited to the mess. When Hancock offered his hand to the thirty-five-year-old Maryland native, Steuart recoiled, saying, "Under existing circumstances, Sir, I cannot take your hand." Hancock irritably retorted, "Under any other circumstances, Sir, it would not have been offered." Instead of getting breakfast, Steuart was cast into the rain to make his way with the other prisoners "on foot to Fredericksburg, for his pains, with the mud ankle deep!"[123]

As Major Hunter galloped to the rear to inform Lee of the unfolding disaster, Colonel John Crocker's brigade from Birney's division was crashing into the Salient's left side, defended by Junius Daniels's North Carolina brigade. Daniels alertly repositioned his men at right angles to their trenches, so that they could fire into the Yankees as they tried to take possession of them. Behind the kneeling North Carolinians, two Virginia batteries pounded the advancing enemy with shrapnel and canister; a red mist filled the air. "This combined fire . . . was more than flesh could stand and it was not possible for them to reach our line," wrote Major Cyrus Watson of the 45th North Carolina.

It was the Yankees' first setback in what otherwise had been an unadulterated triumph, and now another problem developed: too many troops were crowded into too confined an area. In just one hour, the crisply massed formations, so effective during the initial attack, had become almost a mob in the chaotic hand-to-hand fighting. And more troops were arriving by the minute, with Hancock sending in everything that he had, including Gibbon's reserve division. Men were crammed up to forty deep in some places along the quarter-mile-long battlefront, and unit cohesion was breaking down.

Barlow asked Hancock not to send more men to the Salient. "My troops are in great disorder, but I am working hard and will soon have them under organization," Hancock wrote to Meade. To General Williams of his staff, Hancock was more candid. "I must get a line [in] order first, or I may have trouble, before pressing on. I have used all the men through the woods nearly, and they have lost their organization."[124]

Nonetheless, Hancock's men managed to seize a second line of entrenchments before pushing ahead toward Spotsylvania Court House. But when they entered a wooded area behind the Salient's apex, large numbers of the attackers began falling to the ground, hit by Rebel musket and cannon fire, whose volume was rapidly growing.

The gunfire came from General Robert D. Johnston's counterattacking brigade, positioned in reserve directly behind the Salient. "Into the breach the brigade [Johnston's] went, the morning fog being so thick that at ten paces one could not distinguish friend from foe, and was subjected to an enfilading fire from right and left. In less than fifteen minutes after going into action five officers were killed," wrote a member of the 5th North Carolina. A soldier in the 12th North Carolina wrote that it was "one of the bloodiest scenes of the war. The ground was strewn with the dead and dying of the regiment and the brigade."

Johnston's men stopped the Union advance in the dark woods, where every soldier seemingly fought alone, all order gone. "At every step a life was lost—a man went down. . . . The air was thick and hot with flashing, smoking, whirling missiles of death," wrote a soldier from the 12th New Jersey. A Union comrade wrote that Rebel musket volleys "mowed down the boys like grain on the bloody field."[125]

GRANT'S HEADQUARTERS ERUPTED in "shouts and cheers which made the forest ring" when Hancock's first reports arrived. "Our men have the works," Hancock wrote at 5 a.m. A little later: "Prisoners come in rapidly; probably over 2,000." At 5:55 a.m., when the intensive Rebel gunfire in the woods behind the Salient's center had stopped II Corps' advance, Hancock wrote, "It is necessary that General Wright should attack at once. All of my troops are engaged." Meade replied, "Your good news is most welcome. Burnside attacked at the appointed hour. Wright is ordered in at once on your right. Hold all you get and press on."[126]

Through it all, Grant sat in a camp chair near a smoking campfire, wrapped in his overcoat, calmly analyzing the reports and devising ways to complete Hancock's triumph. Only when Hancock reported that 2,000 prisoners had been taken did Grant become animated. "That's the kind of news I like to hear," he said. Lieutenant Colonel Porter, his aide, wrote that capturing prisoners "amounted to a passion with him."[127]

LEE HAD BEEN working since 3 a.m. at his headquarters. Upon hearing the crashing musketry and artillery fire that heralded Hancock's attack at 4:35, Lee mounted Traveller. He was riding toward the sound of gunfire when Major Hunter galloped up to report that the Yankees had broken through at the Mule Shoe.

The Army of Northern Virginia was in mortal danger of being split in half.

Lee had committed a rare mistake—interpreting Grant's sending his wounded and artillery to the rear as a prelude to a movement away from the Spotsylvania front, either to Fredericksburg, or around the Confederate

General Ulysses S. Grant, general-in-chief of the Union Army. *Library of Congress.*

General Robert E. Lee, commander of the Army of Northern Virginia. *Library of Congress.*

"Five Dollar Bill" portrait of
President Abraham Lincoln.
Library of Congress.

Jefferson Davis, president of the
Confederate States of America.
Library of Congress.

General Henry Halleck, the Union Army's chief of staff. *Library of Congress.*

General George Meade, commander of the Army of the Potomac. *Library of Congress.*

An Army of the Potomac unit prior to the commencement of the Overland Campaign. *Library of Congress*.

The Army of the Potomac crossing the Rapidan River on a pontoon bridge on May 4, 1864. *Library of Congress*.

General A. P. Hill,
commander of the
Confederate Third Corps.
Library of Congress.

General Richard Ewell, commander
of the Confederate Second Corps.
Library of Congress.

GEN. LONGSTREET, C. S. A.

General James Longstreet, commander of the Confederate First Corps. *Library of Congress.*

Sketch by Alfred Waud of soldiers evacuating wounded as the woods burn. Waud reported that many wounded troops died in the flames. *Library of Congress.*

General Winfield Scott Hancock (seated), commander of the Union II Corps, with (left to right) division commanders Generals Francis Barlow, David Birney, and John Gibbon. *Library of Congress.*

General Gouverneur Warren, commander of the Union V Corps. *Library of Congress.*

Wounded soldiers outside a Fredericksburg hospital in May 1864. *Library of Congress.*

Burial detail at work outside a Union hospital in Fredericksburg in May 1864. *Library of Congress.*

Confederate prisoners of war at Belle Plain awaiting transport to Union prisons. *Library of Congress.*

General Philip Sheridan, the Army of the Potomac's Cavalry Corps commander whose aggressiveness made him one of Ulysses Grant's favorite generals. *Library of Congress.*

General J.E.B. Stuart, the famed Confederate cavalry commander who was Robert E. Lee's eyes and ears. *Library of Congress.*

General John Gordon, one of Robert E. Lee's most promising young officers. *Library of Congress.*

Alfred Waud sketch of the battle at the Bloody Angle. *Library of Congress.*

Sketch of the furious combat at the apex of the Bloody Angle near Spotsylvania Court House. *Library of Congress.*

Union Colonel Emory Upton, who won a rare battlefield promotion to general for leading an attack on the Salient on May 10. *Library of Congress.*

Confederate soldiers killed at Spotsylvania Court House. *Library of Congress.*

General Ulysses Grant leans over to examine a map held by General George Meade on May 21. The pews were appropriated from Massapponax Church. *Library of Congress.*

The canvas pontoon bridge laid over the North Anna River by V Corps near Jericho Mills. *Library of Congress.*

Sketch by Alfred Waud of the 7th New York Heavy Artillery attacking at Cold Harbor on June 3. *Library of Congress.*

The pontoon bridge that carried the Army of the Potomac across the James River in June 1864. *Library of Congress.*

General Ulysses Grant and his staff at his headquarters at City Point. *Library of Congress.*

The busy James River wharf at City Point in June 1864. *Library of Congress.*

Burial detail collecting the bones of soldiers killed at Cold Harbor. *Library of Congress.*

right in another lunge toward Richmond. His decision to withdraw the Mule Shoe's artillery had left the middle of his lines naked to attack. Too late, he had consented to the guns' return.

With his army facing possible annihilation, and two of his three corps commanders disabled by battle wounds and illness, Lee took personal command of the Army of Northern Virginia.

"Hold on!" he shouted to the troops fleeing the Mule Shoe. "We are going to form a new line. Your comrades need your services. Stop, men!" When exhortations failed, Lee tried scolding. "Shame on you, men, shame on you! Go back to your regiments!"[128]

Lee's blood was up. He rode ahead to where General John Gordon was organizing his division—formerly Jubal Early's and today the Second Corps' reserve—to counterattack the Salient. Gordon had already sent Johnston's brigade ahead to slow the Yankees until his other two brigades could attack.

Joining the center of Gordon's line at the Salient's base, Lee removed his hat and rode along the front of Gordon's line to inspire the men. It was the plank road and May 6 again, when Lee attempted to lead the Texas Brigade's counterattack against Hancock's corps. "The General's countenance showed that he had despaired and was ready to die rather than see the defeat of his army," wrote Isaac Bradwell of the 31st Georgia.

Gordon would have none of it. He spurred his horse to block Traveller, and grasped its bridle. "General Lee," Gordon said in a voice loud enough to reach his men, "you shall not lead my men in a charge. No man can do that, sir. Another is here for that purpose." He told Lee that if he, and not Gordon, led the attack, it would appear to be a rebuke to Gordon's ability and courage.

"These men behind you are Georgians, Virginians, and Carolinians. They have never failed you on any field. They will not fail you here. Will you boys?" said Gordon. His men roared back, "No, no, no; we'll not fail him."

Gordon shouted at Lee, "You must go to the rear!" Gordon's men made it a loud refrain, "General Lee to the rear, General Lee to the rear!" while crowding around Traveller and turning Lee's mount around. "They would have carried on their shoulders both horse and rider to a place of safety," wrote Gordon.[129]

"Forward! Guide right!" Gordon called out, and his 4,000 men surged toward the Salient to throw back the Yankee shock troops. It was 5:45 a.m., a little more than an hour after Hancock's initial assault. Gordon's brigades "raised a yell and made a most gallant charge in a dense fog," wrote George Nichols of the 61st Georgia, and were "mown down at every step."

Four ranks of Hancock's troops fired volleys into the counterattacking Rebels, breaking Gordon's vanguard. "It was no more, no less, than a slaughter," wrote a member of the 20th Massachusetts. And it was just the beginning.[130]

Two brigades of North Carolinians—Stephen Dodson Ramseur's from Robert Rodes's Second Corps division on the left, and James Lane's from Henry Heth's Third Corps division on the right—swung into positions on either side of Gordon and secured his flanks. As Armistead Long's batteries mowed down the Yankees "like grass before the scythe," Gordon's brigades, with Ramseur's and Lane's men, drove the Yankees back to the Salient and recaptured a section of it.

The broken ground, the thick clouds of gun smoke, and the fog dulled the attack's symmetry and organization, but the Confederates still slammed into the densely packed Union troops "with the fury of a cyclone." An epic melee erupted, with the combatants fighting "like demons" with bayonets, swords, pistols, and muskets.

Ramseur was wounded in the right arm, and he lost the first of the three horses that would be shot out from under him this day. The twenty-six-year-old general struggled to keep up with his brigade, his arm hanging uselessly by his side, as his men fought their way up the western Salient, driving the Yankees from the breastworks with bayonets—the only time during the war that the brigade used bayonets in combat. They recaptured the inner breastworks in the northwest angle, but paid dearly as the Yankees poured fire into them from their right.

GRANT'S ATTACK HAD badly smashed up Ewell's corps, and the excitable general was highly agitated. "In a towering passion, he hurled a terrible volley of oaths at the stragglers from the front, stigmatizing them as cowards," wrote Captain William Seymour of the Louisiana Brigade. The one-legged general had been a model of propriety since marrying, but his brave resolutions wilted in the heat of battle "and he swore with all of his old time vehemence and volubility."

When Lee witnessed Ewell slapping the backs of fleeing troops with the flat of his sword, he reproved him for his behavior. "How can you expect to control when you have lost control of yourself?" Lee asked Ewell. "If you cannot repress your excitement, you had better retire."[131]

GRANT NOW SENT his second wave—two divisions from Horatio Wright's VI Corps—against the Salient's west side. Thomas Neill's four brigades went in first; David Russell's four brigades were to pile in after Neill. More than 35,000 Union troops would soon be crowded into a half-square-mile area.

Meade ordered Gouverneur Warren to menace Laurel Hill with V Corps to prevent the Confederate First Corps from going to Lee's aid in the Salient. "Keep up as threatening an attitude as possible," Meade urged Warren.[132]

LEE AND HIS staff roamed the rear of the battleground, plucking brigades and sending them to places where they were desperately needed. Lee issued orders directly to the brigade commanders.

He pulled two brigades from William Mahone's idle division of Third Corps west of the Po River, leaving just one to guard the Rebel flank. They were sent to Robert Rodes's division on the west side of the Salient. Third Corps' other two divisions, on Lee's right, were busy fending off powerful attacks by Ambrose Burnside's IX Corps.

The previous night near the Po River, the weary men of the 16th Mississippi, who belonged to one of Mahone's idle brigades, had lain on the wet ground in the rain without supper, "with about as much comfort as a wet starving steer," wrote Private David Holt. The sound of gunfire had jolted them awake before dawn, as rain continued to fall.

A rider came pounding through the water and mud, asking for General Nathaniel Harris, a Vicksburg lawyer who commanded a brigade of Mississippians. What Holt had thought was a bundle of dirty rags lying in the pasture "moved and unwrapped and said, 'Here! I am General Harris!'"

After hurriedly reading the courier's note, Harris shouted a string of orders: fall in, move forward quickly, keep the ranks closed up. When asked what was wrong, Harris said Johnson's division had broken, and the Mississippians were going to take back the Mule Shoe.[133]

Mahone's other brigade, General Abner Perrin's Alabamans, was already under way, and Harris's Mississippians fell in behind them, quick-timing the four miles around Laurel Hill to the rear of the Salient. As the Mississippians arrived, Lee appeared and rode at Harris's side, directing his brigade to Rodes's position on the west side of the Salient.

The air became dense with whirring and whizzing projectiles as artillery shrieked and dug huge divots in the ground and Minie balls whistled around them. Traveller reared and, at that instant, a round shot passed beneath him. Harris's men implored Lee, "Go back, General! Go back! For God's sake, go back!" One or two of them grabbed Traveller's bridle and turned him around. Lee said, "If you will promise me to drive those people from our works, I will go back." The men roared out, "We will!" Colonel Charles Venable, Lee's aide, took charge of guiding the Mississippians, on the heels of Perrin's brigade.

It was a climactic moment. Firing pointblank into the massed Yankees, Harris's men surged into the breastworks to the right of Ramseur's troops and began driving out the invaders. Perrin's troops, who had sought shelter in the traverses from the showers of Minie balls, surged into the trenches. Perrin himself was wounded, however, and bled to death.

Waves of bluecoats crowded in so close that some Confederates had room only to shoot from the hip. Holt kept seven rifles within reach, firing each in turn while standing in ankle-deep mud and blood, with rain streaming off his cap and down his face "like buttermilk on the inside of a tumbler." He later wrote, "In that way I became a rapid repeater. I stood to my guns and shot carefully."[134]

BEHIND HARRIS'S BRIGADE came another brigade from Third Corps, pulled out of Cadmus Wilcox's division on Lee's right flank: Samuel McGowan's South Carolinians. Rebuked by Lee six days earlier when Hancock's men drove them down the plank road, they now flung back Hancock's troops as they charged in to support the Mississippians, winning vindication. "We advanced at the double-quick, cheering loudly," wrote Lieutenant J. F. J. Caldwell. The reinforcements were struck by the demoralization of the Confederate troops that had been fighting in the Mule Shoe since the first Union attack. "They seemed to feel that Grant had all the hosts of hell in assault upon us."[135]

Indeed, it seemed that way. In short order, General McGowan was shot in the arm, and his next-in-command also was wounded. The South Carolinians sloshed into trenches flooded by the heavy rain that still fell. "The wounded bled and groaned, stretched or huddled in every attitude of pain. The water was crimsoned with blood." Bullets filled the air in the front and on right flank, where the Yankees were firing across the traverses. The South Carolinians settled in for a long fight. "It was plainly a question of bravery and endurance now," Lieutenant Caldwell wrote. Lee's counterattacks had reduced Hancock's early gains to just a few hundred yards extending to both sides of the Salient's apex.[136]

Amid the chaos and carnage, General Rodes, whose Second Corps division had managed to cling so tenaciously to the Salient's west face, paced the rear of the supporting artillery on his restive black charger, "humming to himself and catching the ends of his long, tawny moustache between his lips."[137]

Lee had gone to a seemingly safer place just fifty yards from the courthouse. But the Union gunners found him there. A member of the 26th North Carolina saw shot and shell suddenly explode all around Lee. "As quick as a flash the members of his staff placed themselves around him to protect him with their own bodies," the soldier wrote. "The troops were visibly affected, as General Lee with his staff, still surrounding him, rode off."[138]

WHEN HANCOCK'S GUNS roared at 4:35 a.m., Simon Griffin's brigade of IX Corps attacked the lower east side of the Salient, the place where Ewell's hard-pressed men adjoined Jubal Early's Third Corps. Griffin was the tip of the spear that Burnside intended to thrust through the Rebel lines.

Simon Griffin's men struck James Lane's brigade of North Carolinians, and overran Lane's works in some places. It appeared that Griffin, with the weight of IX Corps behind him, might succeed. But then Gordon's counterattack brought Lane relief; so did the Third Corps brigades of Alfred Scales and Edward Thomas, hastily summoned by Early and sent to Lane's support. The Rebel counterattacks propelled Griffin's brigade into disorderly retreat.

Burnside's attack failed.

AT LAUREL HILL, Warren's V Corps was supposed to attack at 7:30 a.m., in order to prevent the Confederate First Corps from reinforcing the Rebels in the Salient. But at 8 a.m., there was no sign of activity from Warren's men. As the minutes ticked by without anything happening, Grant began to lose patience with the corps commander, with whom he had been displeased previously at Laurel Hill and in the Wilderness.

Grant demanded that Meade compel Warren to act. Meade wrote to Warren: "Attack immediately with all the force you can, and be prepared to follow up any success with the rest of your force." Warren protested, "Your order to attack immediately with my whole force leaves me no time to attack the key points first," but he added, "Your orders have been issued and reiterated."

Warren had good reason to drag his feet; by now, he knew—as did every man under his command—that further attacks against the daunting Laurel Hill entrenchments were destined to end in bloody failure. His men made a few spiritless attempts to move forward, each met by a gale of gunfire. "I cannot advance my men at present," Warren wrote to Meade.

At 9:15, Meade's chief of staff, General Andrew Humphreys, wrote to Warren: "The order of the major-general commanding [Meade] is peremptory, that you attack at once, and at all hazards, with your whole force, if necessary." To Grant, Meade wrote, "Warren seems reluctant to assault. I have ordered him at all hazards to do so." Grant replied, "If Warren fails to attack promptly send Humphreys to command his corps and relieve him."

When the campaign began, Grant had regarded Warren as a potential successor to Meade, but Warren now teetered on the brink of dismissal. Humphreys, who was Warren's elder by twenty years, might have felt a pang of sympathy for him. Whatever the reason, minutes after forwarding Meade's stern order, Humphreys wrote the general a milder note that began with the salutation, "Dear Warren." The note said: "Don't hesitate to attack with the bayonet. Meade has assumed the responsibility, and will take the consequences." It was signed, "Your friend, A.A. Humphreys."

Warren ordered his three division commanders into action. "General Meade reiterates his order to move on the enemy regardless of consequences," Warren told them. They attacked twice with vigor—both efforts repulsed. "My brigade commanders report they cannot carry the works,"

Lysander Cutler, who now commanded the late James Wadsworth's division, told Warren. "They are losing badly, and I cannot get them up the hill." Humphreys, dispatched by Meade to monitor Warren, concurred with Warren that further attacks would be futile, and suspended them. Satisfied by Humphreys's reading of the situation, Meade ordered Warren to send two of his divisions to reinforce the attacks on the Salient.

Despite Humphreys's affirmation of Warren's assessment of the Laurel Hill situation, Warren's reputation had suffered further damage. Adam Badeau of Grant's staff was scornful of Warren's "feebleness" that morning, and ticked off his sins: "an excess of caution, a delay in assuming the offensive, an indisposition to take tactical risks. . . . While he was cautiously manoeuvering [sic], the critical moment passed."

It is worth mentioning that Grant, Meade, and their staffs were more than a mile from Warren's lines when they insisted that he attack. As the armies' increased use of entrenchments foreshadowed those used fifty years later during World War I, so did the peremptory orders from distant high commands, without regard for the actual situation.[139]

THE SALIENT BATTLE'S opening acts had featured Grant's massive daybreak attack, followed by the Confederate counterattack and Lee's effective piecemeal reinforcement of his broken Second Division lines with Third Corps brigades. The furious counterattacks had largely driven Hancock's assault troops, impaired by their large numbers and loss of unit cohesion, out of the Rebel breastworks.

Ironically, Grant at last had managed to utilize his numerical superiority, and it turned out to be the wrong tactic for a half-mile front. By 7 a.m., all of II Corps and most of VI Corps were wedged into the cramped front. Instead of creating an irresistible force, Grant had created a traffic jam. "That corps [II Corps] was as broken by its success as it would have been by a heavier loss in killed and wounded," wrote C. F. Atkinson, a British military historian. Lee got better results by sending brigades, and not divisions, into the fighting; they did not get in one another's way.[140]

Despite the desperate counterattacks that had wrested the Salient from Grant's men, the Yankees had not withdrawn. Thousands of Union troops, with more arriving all the time, pressed up against the outside of the breastworks, waging a close combat of incredible fury with the Rebels on the other side. The crimson hours ahead inspired a new nickname for the Salient and Mule Shoe: the "Bloody Angle."

"THE FIGHTING NOW became desperate—our troops on the outside, theirs on the inside of the intrenchments." Ditches on both sides of the parapet steadily filled with bodies. Joseph Muffly of the 148th Pennsylvania described how the combatants "fired their guns full in each other's faces. They lunged at each other with bayonet thrust. They leaped upon the works and fired down among the maddened crowds on the other side. . . . They held their guns overhead and shot down into the enemy. . . . Hour after hour, all day long, they fought like demons," wrote Muffly. "It was a literal Saturnalia of blood."

The atmosphere was so filled with flying metal and torrents of rain that sometimes there seemed to be no air left to breathe. Dead and wounded men fell into oozing pools of knee-deep mud, blood, and gore, with the wounded sometimes pinned beneath the dead, and then by their fighting comrades, who used the bodies as a firing step.

A lieutenant in Perrin's Alabama brigade devised an efficient method for killing Yankees. Arranging his men, the lieutenant said, "Now you stand here, and as you see them come I will run the bayonet through them and pitch them over to you and you catch them." A soldier in the brigade later wrote, "I regard this day as the most dismal one I ever passed through."

Hancock's artillery officers positioned their guns on high ground and fired over his men's heads, plastering the Rebel trenches. A battery of the 1st Rhode Island Light Artillery poured canister fire into the enemy at close range, its gun carriages sunk ino the mud. In a short time, all but two of the battery's twenty-three officers and men were killed or wounded.[141]

"Like leeches we stuck to the work, determined by our fire to keep the enemy from rising up," wrote Private G. Norton Galloway of the 95th Pennsylvania that, with Emory Upton's brigade, had attacked the angle's west side around 6 a.m. Two brass cannons were brought up to fire at close range, but in minutes the officer was killed and the cannons stuck in the mud, unmanned. "Near at hand lay the horses of these guns, completely riddled."[142]

Amid the roar of musketry and cannon fire, a 19th Massachusetts sergeant, J. G. B. Adams, who commanded a company during the attack, began loudly singing "Battle Cry of Freedom." His comrades joined in, and then other regiments did, too, until the song was "made to echo over the hills."[143]

With bayonets, the combatants stabbed one another through gaps between the logs, and some of the Rebels swung hatchets taken from Union prisoners. Lieutenant John Black of the 145th Pennsylvania saw a seventeen-year-old in his company, after witnessing the death of an officer, throw his rifle like a spear, shouting, "'Take that you Rebel Son of a ——,'" striking the man who had fired the shot just above the heart, burying four inches of the rifle's muzzle in the man's chest. "He fell over backward with the gun sticking in him."

General John Gordon wrote that the enemy soldiers in the front ranks fought ceaselessly at arms' length, with comrades behind them passing them freshly loaded weapons. On the Confederate side of the breastworks lay mounds of men in gray; on the Union side, blue-clad dead and wounded. "As those in front fell, others quickly sprang forward to take their places," he wrote. "The bullets seemed to fly in sheets. Before the pelting hail and withering blast the standing timber fell. The breastworks were literally drenched in blood."

After a day of gunfire, Private Walter Raleigh Battle of the 4th North Carolina had become somewhat of an expert on the sounds made by Minie balls. He told his mother that some "put one in mind of some musical instrument; some sounded like wounded men crying; some like humming of bees; some like cats in the depth of the night, while others cut through the air with only a 'Zip' like noise." His regiment, part of Ramseur's brigade, spent much of the day on the west side of the Salient enduring deadly enfilading fire that seemed to find them wherever they sought concealment. "Men were killed while squatting just as low and as close to the breastworks as it was possible for them to get," wrote Battle, who had comrades killed on both sides of him. "It was a wonder to me that the last one of us was not killed."

Those who became casualties were trampled into the mud and slime. "The dead and wounded were torn to pieces by the canister as it swept the ground where they had fallen," wrote Private Galloway. "The mud was halfway to our knees. . . . Our losses were frightful."

For nearly twenty hours, without a break for food or sleep, the slaughter went on. "The rain poured down. Many of our men sunk down exhausted in the mud," wrote Colonel Robert McAllister, who commanded one of Mott's two brigades.[144]

LEE RODE ALL day through the rain and mud, shifting brigades to meet emergencies, rushing reinforcements to imperiled sectors. He now knew that his unease with the Mule Shoe had been justified. It *was* vulnerable to enfilading fire; it *was* exposed to possible attack from three sides. The question was what to do now?

After Emory Upton's breakthrough two days earlier, Lee had contemplated a new line a mile to the rear, at the base of the Mule Shoe. But it had seemed like too big of a job, and it had not been begun. Now he recognized that it simply had to be done. With both armies fighting to the death all along the Mule Shoe, it would be foolish to abandon it without having a place to fall back.

Lee ordered a new line dug at the base of the Mule Shoe. The Second Line, as it would be called, would take many hours to complete. Lee's men would have to hang on in the Mule Shoe until it was ready.

GRANT HAD BEEN on his little black horse, Jeff Davis, most of the day, too, inspecting the far-ranging battlefield to see the fighting firsthand. Cheers erupted whenever the troops saw their general-in-chief. Aides brought Grant dispatches and rode off with fresh orders.

While riding between the lines east of the Salient, Grant and his staff came upon the home of a woman who was living alone; her husband and sons were serving in the Union army. The woman was thrilled to see Yankees, and Grant and his aides stopped to talk to her. Before leaving, Grant made arrangements for her to receive food and supplies from the army, and he asked the War Department to send her news about her husband and sons.[145]

Grant had dispatched C. B. Comstock, his senior aide-de-camp, to accompany Burnside as his liaison. Since his failed attack five hours earlier, Burnside had been inactive on the Union left, while the battle at the Salient furiously raged. At 10 a.m., Grant wrote to Comstock, "How are things progressing on the left? Tell Burnside to push hard with everything he can bring into the fight." At 10:20, Grant impatiently ordered Burnside to send a division to Hancock and to "push the attack with the balance as vigorously as possible" against the east side of the Salient. Grant wanted to force Lee to move men from the Salient's apex to reinforce Early on his right. "Warren and Wright have been attacking vigorously all day," Grant reprovingly told Burnside, adding the spur: "See that your orders are executed."[146]

Burnside obeyed, but Lee had had the same idea: he ordered Early to attack Burnside's left flank, in the hope of compelling Grant to remove some of *his* troops from the Bloody Angle.

Both attacks failed.

MIDDAY ARRIVED, AND the rain pounded down, and the awful, primordial fighting in the Salient showed no signs of abating in ferocity. Rebel and Yankee units fought in relays, stumbling from the front line plastered with mud, their lips encrusted with powder from biting cartridges. Sliding down into a shallow ravine fifty yards from the breastworks, the Yankees replenished their cartridge boxes with ammunition brought to the front by mules. The men rested in the mud for a few minutes before returning to the blood frenzy. On the other side of the breastworks, lines of Rebels handed shelter halves full of cartridges forward to their front-line comrades. By day's end, the troops had fired hundreds of rounds apiece.

The two armies, by now little more than mobs, slaughtered one another by every possible means. The hopelessly intermingled Union regiments and brigades stood dozens deep along the breastworks' outer walls. The soldiers who fought there—many of them veterans of the major battles in the East—had never experienced anything like it. They would remember it until the day they died, during waking moments and in their dreams.

Grant's aide, Porter, wanted to see the fighting firsthand and received permission to go to the Salient, ostensibly to ensure that new orders Grant had issued were carried out. What he saw was "absolutely appalling."

"It was chiefly a savage hand-to-hand fight across the breastworks," Porter wrote. "Rank after rank was riddled by shot and shell and bayonet-thrusts, and finally sank, a mass of torn and mutilated corpses; then fresh troops rushed madly forward to replace the dead, and so the murderous work went on." He saw muskets fired "muzzle against muzzle," skulls crushed by clubbed muskets, men impaled by swords and bayonets. "Wild cheers, savage yells, and frantic shrieks rose above the sighing of the wind and the pattering of the rain, and formed a demoniacal accompaniment to the booming of the guns."

"Never since the discovery of gunpowder had such a mass of lead been hurled into a space so narrow," wrote Francis Walker of Hancock's staff. Concentrated musket and artillery fire splintered the breastworks' logs and rails until they resembled "hickory brooms." Trees were cut in half. "We had not only shot down an army, but a forest," wrote Porter.

During the afternoon, a large red oak tree, gnawed through by bullets to the point of collapse, crashed down on the parapet, injuring some Rebel soldiers.[147]

ON HIS WAY to ask Hancock to send Barlow reinforcements, Lieutenant John Black observed how wounded men tried to drag themselves to pools of water; those unable to move lay with their mouths open to catch the rainwater. At one sinkhole behind the Salient, rain and blood had collected until it brimmed with red water, and "around this were a hundred wounded men drinking and groaning."

As Black passed an officer who was going to the front, the man stopped him to ask a question. "But before he could speak, a shell took off that part of the head above his lower jaw, as smooth as if it had been cut with a knife." The officer fell, and as Black looked down at him, "the tongue was moving in its socket as if in the act of speaking—a horrible sight I can never forget."[148]

Black finally reached Hancock and delivered Barlow's request. Hancock said he would try to get reinforcements from VI Corps. Then, he told Black "to give my compliments to [Nelson] Miles and [John] Brooke and assure them that they may consider themselves brigadier-generals from today." They, as was Emory Upton two days earlier, were the beneficiaries of Grant's new policy of rewarding good work with battlefield promotions.[149]

While the battle roared in the distance, Grant and Meade incongruously whiled away a pleasant hour or so at the home of a Mrs. Armstrong, a Union sympathizer who invited them to lunch. "Meade was highly tickled at the fresh butter, though it was intolerably garlicky to my mind!" Theodore Lyman wrote in his journal.[150]

ANOTHER UNION ATTACK was planned late that afternoon. Horatio Wright envisioned a fresh assault on the Salient with unengaged units from his VI Corps and two divisions from Warren's V Corps. But when the troops were assembled and he saw that Warren's divisions amounted to no more than 5,000 men and his own troops just another 1,000, Wright had second thoughts. Not only did it appear that he had too few men to succeed, he also feared that if he failed, he might not be able to withstand a counterattack. "I have decided not to make the assault," he wrote to Meade's chief of staff, Humphreys, at 5:10 p.m. No more attacks were proposed that day, but the frenetic combat along the breastworks continued.[151]

WHILE THE MEN in the front ranks fought at close quarters, fifteen to thirty yards behind them, troops lay on the ground firing at the top of the breastworks at anyone who showed himself. Private Francis Wayne of the 1st South Carolina wrote to his mother that most of the men killed or wounded on the Rebel side of the breastworks were shot in the head. "I fought almost ankle deep in the brains & blood of our killed and wounded. . . . Sargt [Philip] Forc of our Co was killed just by me & his blood & Brains poured out on my right leg & Shoe. Such, is war *in reality*."[152]

Unsurprisingly, under the extreme circumstances, even good soldiers broke down and raised the white flag. One of Harris's Mississippians put his white shirt on his gun muzzle in a token of surrender, and the Yankees cheered. The soldier's comrades shouted, "Shoot him!" The man next to him did. It wasn't the last time that day that the Confederates shot comrades who tried to give up. One report said that about thirty Rebels were shot down when they leaped atop the parapet to surrender.[153]

Union mortar and artillery fire overshot or undershot the breastworks more often than not, but the occasional direct hit seared the memories of survivors. Private David Holt of the 16th Mississippi, who was fighting near the Salient's apex, watched as a round hit two nearby comrades, blowing one of them to pieces and removing the head of the other, without moving his body. With horrible fascination, Holt watched blood shoot upward from the beheaded soldier's neck, "high at first, but lower with each succeeding pulsation of the heart."[154]

Nighttime brought no respite. In the rain and in the darkness, the Rebels and Yankees continued to slaughter one another.

Around midnight, the firing ebbed at last. Lee sent orders for the Second Corps to slowly fall back to the new line that had been laboriously dug three-quarters of a mile to their rear. When the shooting stopped, the troops were able to hear the driving rain splashing on the water-logged ground and the cries of thousands of wounded men rising from the muddy fields and the trenches full of the dead.

The living, "black and muddy as hogs," sought food after not having eaten for more than twenty-four hours. Others simply lay down where they were and fell asleep. Holt napped with his head on a dead Yankee's leg to keep his face out of the bloody mud and water. He woke up after midnight as his comrades were withdrawing to the new line. They hadn't bothered to wake him because they thought he was dead. As he followed his comrades to the rear, Holt looked back on the place where his regiment had fought all day and all night. "I don't expect to go to hell, but if I do, I am sure that Hell can't beat that terrible scene."

When the Mississippians reached the new position, "we sat down on the wet ground and wept," Holt wrote. Then, they washed their hands and faces in pools of rainwater. As they gazed into one another's clean faces, they appeared "wan and bloodless" from fatigue and lack of nourishment.[155]

Everywhere, there was revulsion at the day of butchery. "I pray God, that I may never experience another such one" as the night of May 12, Private Creed Davis of the Richmond Howitzers wrote in his diary. "Oh God, will this war never end?" Captain Benjamin Justice of the Third Corps wrote to his wife in North Carolina, "I am heartily sick of blood & the sound of artillery & small arms & the ghastly pale face of death and all the horrible sights and sounds of war."[156]

DEFYING OVERWHELMING ODDS, Lee's troops had withstood 20 hours of relentless hammer blows by Grant's II and VI Corps on their flawed salient, "a wonderful feat of arms." Charles Venable of Lee's staff later wrote, "Gordon, Rodes and Ramseur were the heroes of this bloody day." Rodes's division numbered 6,000 at the most, and the brigades of Perrin, Harris, and McGowan added just 2,500 more. Yet they managed to hold off twice as many attackers and their artillery—"one continuous roll of musketry from dawn till midnight," wrote Venable. But other Lee units deserved credit, too. James Lane's North Carolinians disrupted the attack by Burnside's IX Corps on the Confederate right, preventing Yankee divisions from pouring into the east side of the Salient and splitting Lee's army in two. The Third Corps' counterattacks spoiled a second Burnside attack.[157]

Grant and Meade counted the Bloody Angle a victory. Assistant War Secretary Charles Dana wrote that night to Stanton, "The results of the day are that we have crowded the enemy out of some of his most important positions, have weakened him by heavy losses. . . . Our troops rest to-night upon the ground they have so victoriously fought for."[158]

That wasn't true. As Dana was writing those lines at army headquarters a mile from the front, the combatants continued fighting along the breastworks, still held by Lee's army.

The Yankees' failure to break the Confederate line had many fathers, beginning with Grant and Meade. After drafting the initial attack plan, Grant and Meade had left its implementation to subordinates. Had they zealously monitored events from a forward command post where they could efficiently receive reports and send orders, they might have rushed artillery to the Salient to break up Gordon's counterattack; they might have fed smaller units of reinforcements into the Salient, thereby alleviating the overcrowding that developed; they might have pushed Burnside to continue attacking the Confederate right flank.[159]

Hancock bears responsibility, too. After successfully penetrating the Salient and bagging thousands of prisoners, Hancock's divisions became commingled, Hancock was unable to restore cohesion, and his corps' initial gains and effectiveness were lost. "He could inspire, but apparently not control his soldiers," remarked Grant aide Adam Badeau. This had happened before, on the plank road. "One achievement requires physical courage and personal magnetism; the other, mental and moral power."[160]

However, assigning blame alone suggests that the Battle of the Bloody Angle was Grant's to win, that his army, but for command failures, should have won a great victory. This one-sided analysis shortchanges the Rebel army and its commanders, particularly Robert E. Lee.

The Confederacy's greatest general fought his greatest battle at Spotsylvania. The 57-year-old master engineer established bristling fortifications on the high ground between the Ni and Po Rivers in ingenious configurations—with the exception of the problematic Mule Shoe. In defending it, Lee avoided Hancock's error by dispatching one or two brigades at a time. Finally, Lee was at the front—too close to the danger, in fact—and was able to control his units' deployment and personally inspire his men when they counterattacked.

UNDER FIRE NEARLY twenty hours, Grant's men, numb with exhaustion, at first did not even notice that the Rebels had left the Salient. Every available Confederate had helped dig new entrenchments along the Salient's base. Already exhausted from the fighting that day, the men labored through a rainy night "so dark we could not see each other, and we so sleepy we could hardly stand up," wrote John Casler of the Stonewall Brigade.

The Second Line, as it was called, was completed at 3 a.m. on May 13, and the Rebels silently withdrew from the Salient before dawn and occupied the new works. At 5:30 a.m., Hancock informed Humphreys that his sharpshooters had advanced 800 yards into the Salient without finding anyone except a prisoner who told them "the enemy have gone." Humphreys ordered Hancock to push ahead. An hour later, Hancock reported that the sharpshooters had gone nearly a mile without seeing Confederate soldiers.

This was welcome news to the Union troops. "The first news which passed through the ranks the morning after the battle of Spottsylvania [sic] was that Lee had abandoned his position during the night," wrote Charles Dana, adding that the discovery "inspired the men with fresh energy, and everybody was eager to be in pursuit."

Union skirmishers discovered that the First Corps remained atop Laurel Hill, and that Jubal Early's Third Corps still guarded Lee's right flank. A short time later, around 9 a.m., patrols found Lee's Second Line, occupied by Ewell's Second Corps. "I have found the position of the enemy, and will send you a sketch of it directly," Hancock told Humphreys. The new enemy line, "as strong as the old one," said Dana—and probably even stronger, absent the previous line's bulge—connected the First Corps' right with Early's left flank.[161]

LATER THAT MORNING, the Northerners ventured into the Bloody Angle slaughterhouse. As burial details began their herculean task, the soldiers and officers that had fought the battle surveyed the torn and bloodied battleground with wonder, revulsion, and horror. The storms of bullets had shaved trees, shrubs, even grass down to the ground. Guns, bayonets, canteens, and cartridge boxes were scattered among the hundreds of bodies. Abandoned gun carriages and caissons were "sheeted with lead from striking bullets."

Atop the earthworks, Union soldiers found bodies that had been "shot through and through by friend and foe alike" so many times that they were no more than "a mangled mass of flesh and cloth." Captain Robert Carter of the 22nd Massachusetts wrote, "Putrid corpses, black and festering, lay all about us, repulsive and sickening." Many were unrecognizable, "appearing more like piles of jelly than distinguishable forms of human life." It was "one hideous Golgotha," wrote New York *Times* correspondent William Swinton.

Horace Porter saw Rebels piled four layers deep in places behind the breastworks, "ghastly" in their mutilation. "Below the mass of fast-decaying corpses, the convulsive twitching of limbs and the writhing bodies showed that there were wounded men still alive and struggling to extricate themselves from their horrid entombment."[162]

While touring the battlefield, Assistant War Secretary Dana leaned against a fence, on the other side of which was a muddy pool of water. "As we stood there, looking silently upon it, of a sudden the leg of a man was lifted up from the pond and the mud dripped off his boot. It was so unexpected, so horrible, that for a moment we were stunned." Dana summoned soldiers who rescued the man.[163]

Lieutenant Black of the 145th Pennsylvania helped Major Nathan Church of the 26th Michigan locate the body of a private killed in the battle. The private's parents had sent him an "elegant gold watch and chain." Before he attacked the Salient with Miles's brigade the private had asked Church to send the watch back to his father if he were killed. The dead man's comrades directed the two officers to the spot where they had seen him fall, which was fortunate, for they "would never have recognized it as having been a soldier. There was no semblance of humanity about the mass that was lying before us. The only thing I could liken it to was a sponge. I presume five thousands [sic] bullets had passed through it." After a careful search for the watch, Black and Church found just three links from the man's watch chain.[164]

There were bodies "as thick as corn hills . . . an officer's horse lying on five men, and two or three men were lying across the horse. . . . Their mouths, nose, eyes, hair, and the mutilated parts were full of maggots!" The Rebel trenches were full of dead men. Chaplain Alanson Haines of the 15th New Jersey could see muddy footprints where soldiers had stood on the bodies of their dead comrades and continued fighting. Later, "we passed a man sitting upon a stone, presenting a horrible appearance. His arms had been torn off, and his whole face was hanging in a bloody mass in front of him." Before the battle, Private Wilbur Fisk of the 2nd Vermont had secretly hoped, if he were die while a soldier, to be killed on the battlefield. He no longer wished for that. "After looking at such a scene, one cannot help turning away and saying, 'Any death but that.'"[165]

Burying the dead was difficult. Many of the bodies were so bullet-riddled, "bones cut up as fine as dust," that they disintegrated when moved. "Some lying between the lines are so completely riddled that it is impossible to raise them," surgeon Daniel Holt of the 121st New York said in a letter to his wife. "A hole has to be dug on the side of them and they rolled into it for burial. They were a complete jelly!" Burial details attempted to identify the Yankee dead and carve their names and unit numbers on ammunition boxes where they were interred. Captured breastworks were tipped onto the Rebel dead in the ghastly trenches full of red-tinged rainwater, or else dirt was shoveled onto their remains.[166]

Veterans had never seen anything like the fighting on May 12. Confederate General John Gordon, whose division had sutured the torn lines in the Bloody Angle, thought Chickamauga, Gettysburg, Chancellorsville, Antietam, and Shiloh bloody, too, "but to Spotsylvania history will accord the palm, I am sure, for having furnished an unexampled muzzle-to-muzzle fire; the longest roll of incessant, unbroken musketry." General Lewis Grant, commander of VI Corps' Vermont Brigade, believed that the battlefield on May 13 was "much worse than at Bloody Lane [Antietam]. There a great many dead men were lying in the road and across the rails of the torn down fences, and out in the cornfield; but they were not piled up several deep and their flesh was not so torn and mangled as at the 'angle.'"[167]

A small drama involving a wounded man on Laurel Hill occurred between the enemy lines as Edward Porter Alexander, the Confederate First Corps artillery commander, watched with one of his battery commanders, Lieutenant Colonel Frank Huger. The Yankee, who had lain on the ground since being wounded five days earlier, would sometimes sit up and try to "knock himself in the head with the butt of a musket—raising it up & letting it fall on him," wrote Alexander. "It hardly seemed possible that a man could really give himself a fatal blow in that way, but through the glass he now seemed to be dead." When the Yankees pulled out of the lines, Alexander and Huger went to check on the man. He was dead and had been stripped of his clothing.[168]

5

Friday, May 13, 1864
Spotsylvania Court House

RAIN FELL FOR a third day on May 13 as the adversaries rested, ate, and took stock. It was their first respite from combat since May 4, although not a pleasant one because of the mud and the stench of decaying bodies. Although no major fighting occurred, the musketry never ceased; sharpshooters expertly plied their murderous trade, and the skirmish lines occasionally erupted in gunfire.

Nine days after fording the Rapidan River, Grant's army had advanced fifteen miles and fought more than half a dozen battles, neither decisively winning nor losing any of them. Of the 120,000 men that had begun the campaign, more than 36,000 were either in army hospitals, on their way to Confederate prisons, or dead—about 30 percent of the army. The four Union army corps reported just 56,124 infantrymen present for duty.

When Grant expressed regret over the losses during a conversation with Meade, the second-in-command replied, "Well, general, we can't do these little tricks without losses."

In just one day, May 12, Grant had lost 9,000 men at the Bloody Angle. Nearly one-third of the casualties since May 5, about 11,500, had occurred in just one of Grant's corps—II Corps, his most dependable shock force, although at the current attrition rate not for long. Francis Barlow's division, which spearheaded the Bloody Angle attack, lost 1,430 of its 5,000 men. Just two days earlier, Barlow's division had also sustained heavy casualties on the Po River. VI Corps' 121st New York, which had gone in with Emory Upton on May 10 with 471 men, counted just 189 effectives three days later. Losses pared Gershom Mott's two-brigade division of II Corps to one brigade, and Hancock assigned it to David Birney's division. When Mott indignantly asked to be relieved of command, he was threatened with being mustered out of service. Mott accepted the demotion and remained with his brigade.

The Confederates had fared better numerically, although not proportionately. The Army of Northern Virginia had begun the campaign with 66,000 infantry, cavalry, and artillery troops, but about 20,000, or about 30 percent, were now gone—7,200 of them lost on May 12 alone. After the Bloody Angle fighting, Lee counted just 41,000 infantrymen. Nearly 8,400 of the Rebel losses had occurred in Richard Ewell's Second Corps, which had begun the campaign with 17,000 men; Edward Johnson's division, overrun during the initial attack on May 12, was left with just 960 of the 5,400 men that had begun the campaign on May 5. The wounded lay in field hospitals at Milford and Louisa Court House, prefatory to being sent on to Richmond's military hospitals.[169]

The survivors of the bloodbath remained surrounded by horrors that "no tongue can describe. . . . Dead and dying men by scores and hundreds lie piled upon each other," wrote surgeon Holt of the 121st New York. "Heaven only knows how much longer this battle will last, but I hope not many days. No doubt we shall at last be victims." The Rebels' stubbornness disturbed him. "The rebels fight like very devils! We have to fairly *club* them out of their rifle pits. We have taken thousands of prisoners and killed an army; still they fight as hard as ever."[170]

Oliver Wendell Holmes Jr., an aide to General Wright, told his parents that "these nearly two weeks have contained all of fatigue & horror that war can furnish—The advantage has been on our side but nothing decisive has occurred & the enemy is in front of us strongly entrenched."[171]

Walter Carter of the 22nd Massachusetts wrote to his father on the same day: "I just live, father, and that is about all." Half of the men in his regiment, he said, "have been shot away, and the rest are perfectly used up."

The Rebels maintained a high level of alertness. One of every three men in each unit stayed awake during the night, with the whole line rousted at 3 a.m. each day in case of a daybreak attack. Details from each unit cooked the rations in the rear at the wagon train and brought the food—cornbread and bacon—to their comrades. "We often ate the meat raw, and the bread . . . was generally sour on the second day," causing "most distressing" heartburn and diarrhea, wrote J. F. J. Caldwell of the 1st South Carolina.[172]

EVERY ASSAULT AT Spotsylvania by Grant's army had been repulsed or ended in stalemate, but Grant believed that he had badly hurt Lee's army and that one more all-out attack could smash Lee's lines.

Despite his losses, Grant took pride in the fact that he "did not lose a single organization, not even that of a company while we have destroyed and captured one division (Johnson's), one brigade (Doles's), and one regiment entire of the enemy," as well as more than thirty guns. Although careful not to make rash predictions, he hinted that the war might end soon. "The enemy are obstinate and seem to have found the last ditch." Writing to his wife Julia on May 13, Grant's description of the battle's outcome sounded even better. "The enemy was really whipped yesterday but their situation is desperate beyond anything heretofore known. To loose [sic] this battle they loose [sic] their cause."[173]

In a letter to Stanton, Grant recommended promotions to major general for Brigadiers Horatio Wright and John Gibbon; and to brigadier for Colonels Samuel Carroll, Emory Upton—whom Grant had awarded a battlefield promotion—and William McCandless. He requested that Winfield Scott Hancock, a brevet major general, be made a brigadier in the regular army and that Meade and William T. Sherman receive promotions to major general in the regular army. "General Meade has more than met my most sanguine expectations. He and Sherman are the fittest officers for large commands I have come in contact with," Grant wrote.[174]

Grant's generous praise of Meade followed a frank discussion with his staff about Meade's role. The aides had pressed Grant to no longer give orders through Meade, but to issue them directly. "Time was often lost in having field orders pass through an intermediary," they argued. Moreover, Meade's position "was in some measure a false one," because he would neither be held responsible for setbacks, nor get credit for successes. Furthermore, Grant's aides said, Meade "had an irascible temper, and often irritated officers who came in contact with him," which might have been the underlying reason for their lobbying effort.

Grant listened quietly, and when they had finished presenting their case, he said that if he assumed field command of the Army of the Potomac, he would necessarily neglect his broader responsibilities as general-in-chief: overseeing Benjamin Butler, Franz Sigel in the Shenandoah Valley, Burnside, and Sherman and the Western armies. Grant believed that Meade was "capable and perfectly subordinate, and by attending to the details he relieves me of much unnecessary work. I will always see that he gets full credit for what he does." The discussion ended.[175]

About the same time, Meade was writing to his wife, "By the blessing of God I am able to announce not only the safety of George [their son] and myself, but a decided victory over the enemy. . . . Our work is not over, but we have the prestige of success, which is everything, and I trust our final success will be assured."[176]

LEE WAS NOT discouraged, although it would have been understandable if he were. While the Army of Northern Virginia had held its own on the battlefield, it had suffered heavy losses—losses that would not soon be made good by reinforcements, because Jefferson Davis was holding them in Richmond to use against Butler's army. Lee's aide, Walter Taylor, wrote that morale in the army remained high, although the loss of the guns in the Bloody Angle had hurt the men's pride. They otherwise "are in good heart and condition, our confidence, certainly mine, is unimpaired. Grant is beating his head against a wall."

Lee had to absorb a slew of bad news on this day: Jeb Stuart had died in Richmond; Sheridan had cut the Richmond, Fredericksburg, and Potomac Railroad; and Butler's cavalry had severed the Petersburg and Weldon Railroad in two places south of Petersburg. The damage to the rail lines was repairable, although it slowed the movement of food and supplies to Lee's army and temporarily disrupted communications with Richmond from Georgia and the Carolinas.

But Stuart was irreplaceable, and his death was the hardest to bear; Lee grieved not only because his army was diminished by the loss of its best eyes and ears, but because he loved Stuart like a son. Lee acknowledged that he mourned not just Stuart's loss, but "the loss of our gallant officers and men, and [I] miss their aid and sympathy. . . . Praise be God for having sustained us so far."

Lee also had to patch up his command after the loss of more than a half dozen generals, most of them in the shattered Second Corps. Generals Edwin Johnson and George Steuart were captives; Abner Perrin and Junius Daniel were dead or dying; and James Walker, Samuel McGowan, Robert Johnston, and Stephen Ramseur had been wounded.[177]

If Lee was not discouraged, other Southerners were becoming so. A Confederate soldier wrote, "We have met a man this time, who either does not know when he is whipped, or who cares not if he loses his whole army." In Richmond, diarist Judith McGuire wrote after learning about Stuart's death, "Thus our young men, of the first blood of the country—first in character and education, and, what is more important to us now, first in gallantry and patriotism—fall one by one. What a noble army of martyrs has already passed away!"[178]

GRANT DID NOT want to give the Rebels time to catch their breath. Believing that Lee's army was close to collapse, Grant wished to quickly strike where Lee was not expecting a heavy blow to fall. From Spotsylvania Court House, the Fredericksburg and Massaponax Church roads angled like spokes to the northeast and east, respectively. Scouts reported the roads lightly defended by units from Third Corps. Here, Grant believed, was where the Union army should attack.

Orders went out to V and VI Corps, resting in positions around the Bloody Angle, to march that night—Warren's V Corps first, Wright's VI Corps behind it. The seven-mile movement to the southeast, with guides leading the troops behind Hancock's and Burnside's corps, would bring the 35,000 men to a place on Burnside's left. "Our march to-night is designed to bring us opposite the enemy's extreme right, on the road from Fredericksburg to Spotsylvania Court-House, there to form an assault before daylight behind the picket-lines of the Ninth Corps," Warren told his troops. Grant wanted to attack before 4 a.m., when the dim light would make it difficult for the Confederate artillery to zero in. While V and VI corps attacked from the northeast, II Corps would attack from the north.[179]

The movement began at 10 p.m. Few other night marches rivaled it in absolute misery—due to the rain, mist, and mud, compounded by the crypt-like darkness. The army followed a crude road cut through undergrowth-clotted woods and across fields transformed into bogs by three days of rain. Then, "a dense fog arose and covered the ground, so that not even the numerous fires that had been built to guide the column could be seen," wrote New York *Times* correspondent William Swinton. "The men, exhausted with wading through the mud knee deep and in the darkness, fell asleep all along the way." Daybreak found most of Warren's men still struggling through the muck to reach the attack line; just 1,200 "fagged-out men" got there in time.[180]

Grant called off the attack. Had the weather cooperated, he might have been able to strike Hill's corps with three Union corps before the Rebels could be reinforced. But the rain persisted; it continued to fall on May 15, 16, and 17. "The roads have now become so impassable that ambulances with wounded can no longer run between here and Fredericksburg," Grant wrote on the 16th. "All offensive operations necessarily cease until we can have twenty-four hours of dry weather."

GRANT ASSURED HALLECK that despite the poor weather, "the army is in the best of spirits and feels greatest confidence in ultimate success." He thanked him for the 6,000 reinforcements that were arriving from Washington—mostly heavy artillerymen unhappily transformed into infantrymen. "You can assure the President and Secretary of War that the elements alone have suspended hostilities and that it is in no manner due to weakness or exhaustion on our part," Grant told Halleck.[181]

When Lee saw that the Union army had slid to the southeast and occupied a new north-south line facing Third Corps, he reinforced A. P. Hill's men. The rain, however, flooded the roads and sent streams from their banks; combat operations were out of the question. The soldiers welcomed the lull after eight days of fighting, although musketry and cannon fire never entirely ceased.

"By a 'quiet day' I only mean comparatively so, for skirmishing is going on incessantly, and more or less wounded constantly coming in from the front, but there has been no attack on either side, nor any artillery firing on our side," Colonel Charles Wainwright, V Corps' artillery commander, wrote on the 15th.

Two exceptions occurred on the 14th. Emory Upton's brigade wrested Myers Hill from a small Rebel force. With its plantation buildings, the promontory was a fine observation post. But that afternoon, the Confederates returned with a larger force, expelled Upton, and very nearly captured Meade. Then, at sunset, a large Union brigade threw the Rebels off the hill.

On the same day, black troops from Burnside's IX Corps attacked part of the Third Corps' line and were repulsed—three times. Each time, the attack began with the command, "Remember Fort Pillow! Charge!"—recalling the reported massacre of black soldiers at the Tennessee fort. Private John Casler of the 33rd Virginia wrote that the enemy soldiers would dash forward a short distance, fire a volley, and then dash back to their breastworks. "Our line never fired a shot and the enemy soon retired."[182]

"WE SEEM TO have the luck to be engaged in all the battles from day to day," wrote brigade commander Robert McAllister of II Corps. "It is all one great battlefield for miles & miles. We know very little as to what we have done or what we have gained, further than that we have fought them from day to day. . . . It is fight, fight, everyday."[183]

But sometimes the soldiers unexpectedly displayed a tender side. John Worsham and his surviving comrades of the 21st Virginia, which was nearly annihilated during the first attack on the Mule Shoe, befriended four abandoned bunnies they found in a nest in the middle of their camp. The grizzled veterans treated the bunnies tenderly—possibly a reaction to the butchery the soldiers had just survived. "It was raining, and some wanted to make a house over them, others wanted to hold their oilcloths over them," Worsham wrote. "No one was allowed to touch them . . . When we left it was a sad parting."[184]

The interregnum gave Lee the time to school A. P. Hill in the finer points of commanding a citizen army. Hill, not yet recovered from his illness, or back to commanding the Third Corps, became angry when General Ambrose Wright's brigade botched a minor operation. He vowed to bring Wright before a court of inquiry.

Lee reminded Hill that the army had to rely on untrained officers much of the time. "These men are not an army," Lee said. "They are citizens defending their country. General Wright is not a soldier; he's a lawyer. I cannot do many things that I could with a trained army. The soldiers know their duties better than the general officers do, and they have fought magnificently. . . . You understand all of this, but if you humiliated General Wright, the people of Georgia would not understand. Besides, whom would you put in his place? You'll have to do what I do: When a man makes a mistake, I call him to my tent, talk to him, and use the authority of my position to make him do the right thing the next time."[185]

GRANT WANTED TO try one last time to smash Lee's lines at Spotsylvania. If the new attack failed, he intended to maneuver again around Lee's right flank.

When the rain stopped, II and VI Corps embarked on another exhausting night march, this time returning northward to the muck, stench, and wreckage of the Bloody Angle. Because Lee expected Grant to attack from the east along the Fredericksburg road, Grant planned to surprise him by striking the Rebel Second Line from the north. While IX Corps would attack from the east, as previously planned, Horatio Wright and Hancock would assault the Second Line. Grant and his generals believed that this was the Rebel army's secret Achilles heel.[186]

This time, at the appointed hour, 4 a.m. on May 18, Barlow's and Gibbon's II Corps divisions and Thomas Neill's VI Corps division—all three of them hard-hitters—were in position near the tip of the Bloody Angle.

On schedule, Union guns began pounding the Second Line and the east side of the Rebel defenses, at least what the artillerymen could see of them through the dense ground fog. Twelve thousand troops in muddy blue uniforms began advancing toward the Second Line through the Bloody Angle battlefield, while nearly 20,000 of Burnside's men surged toward the Rebel lines on the east side.

The Rebels, now expert in preparing defenses, had dug their breastworks along low ridges. Before attackers got to the obstructions in front of the Rebel trenches, they would first have to cross hundreds of yards of cleared ground. Burnside's men gazed at the killing zone with trepidation. "We felt that it was almost sure death to go down into and cross the field before us and up the slope on the opposite side," wrote Lynn Jackman of the 6th New Hampshire.

Both at the Bloody Angle and in front of IX Corps, unburied dead in advanced stages of putrefaction lay everywhere—a sight that became indelibly printed on the memories of many soldiers. "From where I stood and in front of a rebel rifle-pit, lay stretched in all positions, over fifty of our unburied soldiers, and within the pit, lying across each other, perhaps as many rebel dead," wrote Chaplain A. M. Stewart of what he saw when the 102nd Pennsylvania crossed the Bloody Angle. Men stuffed their nostrils with green leaves to block out the smell, which made some of them violently ill.[187]

The revolting smells and sights layered horror on the terror of imminent death. "We were obliged to pass directly over them [the bodies], and we did so as quickly as possible, for it was impossible to breathe in that locality," wrote Jackman.

The Confederate gunners, who had watched Grant's preparations, ignored the Union guns firing at them, instead zeroing in on the advancing infantrymen. They waited until the attackers reached "good canister range of our breastworks" before firing.

The effect was devastating. Corporal James Donnelly of the 20th Massachusetts and his comrades quick-timed through a whirlwind of bursting shells that "mowed lines of heads of[f] the bodies of our men." A shell burst stunned Connelly and knocked his rifle from his hands. His arm swung limply at his side, dripping blood. Shells struck the decomposing bodies, splashing the Yankees with chunks of rotted flesh.[188]

"Their artillery cut our men down in heaps," wrote Lieutenant Colonel Elisha Rhodes of the 2nd Rhode Island of the long sprint across the open ground inside the Bloody Angle. Cannon fire and musketry prevented VI or II Corps from penetrating even Ewell's outer defenses, although Barlow's division reached the slashings below the parapets and held on for an hour.

Burnside's troops, too, were unable to fight their way through the "furious fire of musketry and artillery." "Our grim 'Napoleons' poured upon them a murderous storm of iron which tore great rents in their ranks & drove them crippled & shattered from the field," wrote Captain William Seymour of the 6th Louisiana. Theodore Lyman, Meade's aide, wryly observed, "So far from being surprised, the rebels had spent the last days in strengthening their front."[189]

General Armistead Long, the Confederate Second Corps' artillery commander, proudly described the effect that "the murderous fire of canister and spherical case-shot" from his twenty-nine guns had in forcing Meade to suspend Wright's and Hancock's attack. "This attack fairly illustrates the immense power of artillery well handled," Long wrote in his battle report. Fifteen minutes later, Burnside's assault was stopped, too. Confederate reports put Rebel losses at "nothing," while Hancock, Wright, and Burnside sustained 1,500 casualties.

One of Long's battalion commanders, Major Wilfred Cutshaw, later wrote that the Confederates "could not believe a serious attempt would be made to assail such a line as Ewell had, in open day, over such a distance. Every one on the Confederate side felt that such an attack was reckless, and hopeless in the extreme. So when it was found that a real assault was to be made, it was welcomed by the Confederates as a chance to pay off old scores."[190]

AS HE RODE along a road lined with wounded men, Grant was forcefully reminded of the cost of his aggressiveness. A beardless youth, dying from a chest wound, attracted Grant's attention just as a staff officer galloped past, heedlessly splashing black mud in the wounded man's face. Grant reined up, "visibly affected." Seeing that he was going to dismount and attend to the man, Grant's aide, Horace Porter, leaped from his horse, ran to the soldier's side and wiped his face with his handkerchief. The man died minutes later. "There was a painfully sad look upon the general's face, and he did not speak for some time," Porter wrote.[191]

Disappointing dispatches awaited Grant when he returned to his headquarters. "It was a depressing day," wrote Lyman, Meade's aide. "Ill news from all sides; and the enemy securely on guard." Former Vice President John Breckinridge's Confederate division, with a battalion from the Virginia Military Institute, had defeated Franz Sigel's Shenandoah Valley army at New Market, and Sigel was withdrawing. Butler had been driven back from Drewry's Bluff to Bermuda Hundred Neck, and General Nathaniel Banks's army was retreating in Louisiana.

Grant had sent Sigel up the Shenandoah Valley to stop Confederate supplies from flowing through Staunton to Lee's army and Richmond. After Halleck forwarded the order to Sigel, he had warned Grant, "If you expect anything from him you will be mistaken. He will do nothing but run. He never did anything else." Familiar with Sigel's skittishness, Rebels in the Valley nicknamed him the "flying Dutchman." New Market was the last straw; Grant relieved Sigel. Stanton replaced him with sixty-one-year-old General David Hunter, an incremental improvement over Sigel. Banks had already been removed from field command and replaced by Edward Canby. By retreating to Bermuda Hundred Neck, Butler was neutralized as a threat to Richmond, "as if [he] had been in a bottle strongly corked," Grant ironically observed.[192]

GRANT HAD NOT broken Lee's defenses, and he knew that Lee would soon receive reinforcements from the armies that had defeated Sigel and Butler. "All of this news was very discouraging," he wrote.

But the ever-optimistic Grant believed that this was the perfect time for the Army of the Potomac to again maneuver—a sidle to the southeast, as he had attempted when trying to steal a march on Lee on May 7–8. The movement would flush the Army of Northern Virginia from its Spotsylvania entrenchments into the open, where Grant might destroy it. He had been weighing the plan for several days, wrote Assistant War Secretary Dana, but "he did not wish to try [it] till after this last attempt to get the enemy out of his stronghold by attacking it on one of its flanks."[193]

The last attempt had failed early May 18. Orders now went out to Hancock and Burnside to quietly withdraw from their lines before daybreak May 19 and shift southward to new positions where they would begin the sidle. The actual movement would occur that night, with II Corps striking out toward Richmond along the Fredericksburg and Richmond Railroad, marching as many miles as possible, and fighting any enemy forces sent to stop it.

Grant believed that that by sending II Corps ahead, he might lure Lee from his entrenchments to try to destroy it before support arrived. Of course, II Corps' isolation would be an illusion; Grant's other three corps would in fact remain within striking range. "If the enemy make a general movement to meet this, they will be followed by the other three corps of the army, and attacked if possible before time is given to intrench."[194]

"THE ARMY RECEIVED with joy the news of General Beauregard's success south of the James River," Lee wrote to the Confederate War Department an hour before Grant's attack on the 18th, but his army's high spirits and its repulse of the attack did not change Lee's sober view of the present situation. Lee still wished to attack Grant, but Grant's position, he told Jefferson Davis, "is strongly entrenched, and we cannot attack it with any prospect of success without great loss of men, which I wish to avoid if possible. . . . He has suffered considerably in the several past combats, and . . . his progress has thus far been arrested. I shall continue to strike him whenever opportunity presents itself."

Lee understood that the campaign's "importance . . . to the administration of Mr. Lincoln and to General Grant leaves no doubt that every effort and every sacrifice will be made to secure its success."[195]

The enemy armies' "most belligerent men" remained committed to destroying one another.

THE NEXT DAY, May 19, Lee saw an opportunity to go on the offensive, when scouts reported movement along the Union right. Lee surmised that Grant's troops, aligned northwest-to-southeast, were going to try again to swing around Lee's right flank, but he had to be sure. While Ewell's Second Corps had lost half of its 17,000 men in two weeks, it was best positioned to determine if the Yankees were moving south. If so, the Second Corps could march to the Fredericksburg Road and cut Grant's supply line.

Ewell was told "to demonstrate against the enemy in his front as [Lee] believed that Grant was about to move to our right and he wished to force his hand and ascertain his purpose," wrote Lee's aide, Lieutenant Colonel Walter Taylor. Ewell, however, thought a frontal attack "unwise," and persuaded Lee to permit him instead to probe the Union right flank with 6,000 men. Moving to the northwest and then turning northeast, the Second Corps crossed the Ni River. It then turned east, toward the Fredericksburg Road, the Union lifeline at the northern extremity of Grant's army.

ALL THAT LAY between the Rebels and the Fredericksburg Road were Union heavy artillery regiments that had never seen combat. They had been turned out of comfortable billets in the forts around Washington and Baltimore, issued muskets and supplies, and sent to the front to reinforce Grant. The day after the Bloody Angle fight, Halleck had promised to start 24,500 reinforcements—10,000 of them heavy artillerymen—on their way to Grant within 48 hours. Three days later, on May 16, Grant wrote to General Robert O. Tyler, in charge of the Washington artillerymen assembling at Belle Plain, "I want and must have the whole of your command here by tomorrow night at fartherest [sic]. . . . You must bring forward by that time, without fail, such as have arrived."

A West Point classmate of John Schofield and Phil Sheridan, the bespectacled Tyler had commanded a 130-gun artillery reserve that helped shatter George Pickett's frontal assault on Cemetery Hill at Gettysburg. Five regiments led by Tyler reached Spotsylvania the night of May 17–18 after long marches in the rain and heat. Tyler's 8,800 "foot artillerists," as they were called, joined II Corps as the new Fourth Division, going far to replenish the corps' losses of the previous two weeks. Hancock withheld Tyler's troops from the attack on the Second Line, but circumstance placed the "heavies" directly in the path of Ewell's corps on May 19.[196]

DAYS OF RAIN had turned the light Virginia soil into oatmeal, and Ewell did not want to risk getting his artillery stuck. He sent back his guns when the infantry angled off Gordon Road into the fields and woods. General Stephen Ramseur's brigade led the Second Corps straight toward the 4th New York Heavy Artillery positions around the Harris house. This unit had reached Hancock before Tyler's division, joining II Corps' regular artillery brigade.[197]

Under threatening skies, a Rebel skirmish line emerged from the woods directly in front of Captain A. C. Brown's company of 4th New York foot artillerists, followed by two battles lines, "closely massed with flags flying and officers on horseback. . . . It was a magnificent sight, for the lines moved as steadily as if on parade." Heavy rain began falling. The New Yorkers slowly withdrew, firing volleys into the Rebels as they struggled through a swamp. General John Gordon's brigades swung northward around the 4th New York and artillerists from the 1st Massachusetts and 2nd New York that were now fighting beside the 4th, and reached Fredericksburg Road. They swarmed over a wagon train laden with food and ammunition and began cracking open barrels of pork.

The gunfire alerted Meade and Grant to the peril on their right. Grant dispatched Horace Porter, who had been napping in his tent, to Tyler. Send every available unit, Grant ordered Tyler, to repel the attack and then drive back the Confederates, if possible. The artillery general told Porter that his men were "raw hands at this sort of work, but they are behaving like veterans." Meanwhile, David Birney's II Corps infantry division was on its way to the battlefield, along with Colonel Richard Bowerman's Maryland Brigade from V Corps.

Until they arrived, the artillerists would have to hold. The heavies' baptism by fire had begun.[198]

ON THEIR WAY to the front, the veterans had teased them unmercifully; in their clean blue uniforms, the newcomers looked like "holiday soldiers." "Their new uniforms and bright muskets formed a striking contrast to the travel-stained clothing and dull-looking arms of the other regiments," Porter noted. "The Johnnies will take the shine out of you, fellows!" the veterans called out to the newcomers. "Haven't you brought your feather beds along?"[199]

Tyler's 7th New York Heavy Artillery advanced through a wood under orders not to fire because its officers believed that another Yankee unit was in front of it. They were wrong.

As the artillerists emerged from the wood and began crossing a field, "the enemy appeared as if out of the ground and gave us a volley in our faces," wrote Lieutenant Fred Mather. "That fresh troops would break under such circumstances was natural and we did."

But they then halted, their officers re-formed them, and they attacked again, this time driving back the Rebels nearly half a mile.[200]

TYLER'S 1ST MASSACHUSETTS Heavy Artillery advanced along a farm road as if on a parade ground, elbow to elbow. As they entered woods, there was a crash of musketry and the air was full of Minie balls. "It was like a stroke of lightning from clear skies," wrote a Massachusetts soldier with astonishment. "In an instant the scene was transformed from peace and quiet to one of pain and horror." Shot eleven times, an officer tumbled from his horse, and the regiment instantly lost nearly 200 men.

The explosion of gunfire and the cries of the wounded froze the green troops. Veterans would have dropped to the ground to return fire, but the artillerists did not—and they took a beating.

Then, Ramseur's brigade attacked, "with the most terrific yells . . . firing as they came and wounding and killing our men at short range." The Rebels chased the traumatized Massachusetts troops to the top of a knoll, where their officers managed to calm them and restore order. By the end of the day, the 1st Massachusetts had lost one-fourth of its troops.

THE 1ST MAINE Heavy Artillery of Tyler's division and black soldiers from Edward Ferrero's IX Corps division—their first appearance in a major battle—threw Gordon's men off Fredericksburg Road, where they had been pillaging the wagon train.

Tyler's division and Ewell's corps slugged it out toe-to-toe, with Tyler's bounteous regiments giving him a 2,800-man advantage. Then, the veterans from the Maryland brigade and Birney's division arrived and pitched in alongside the heavies. Gordon and Ramseur were obliged to fall back.

Although outnumbered, the Rebels held their ground for the rest of the day. At twilight, Ramseur shouted, "Come, Yankees!" as the two sides exchanged cheers and Rebel yells. The shooting finally stopped about 10 p.m.

Surgeons noted an odd phenomenon among the wounded artillerists: in the 7th New York Heavy Artillery alone, thirty-six men sustained slight gunshot wounds to the hands. It was highly improbable that all of the wounds were accidental, or that they had been inflicted by the Rebels' long-barreled muskets. About half of the self-wounded later returned to duty, to endure their comrades' contemptuous remarks.

During the night, the Confederate Second Corps withdrew all the way to the Second Line, with 900 fewer effectives.[201]

Theodore Lyman wrote that the "heavies'" fought well enough, "but from their greenness [they] lost heavily." Indeed, Tyler's division reported 1,500 casualties, many of them "friendly fire" victims. A quartermaster described one deadly mixup: "First there was Kitching's brigade firing at the enemy; then Tyler's men fired into his; up came Birney's division and fired into Tyler's; while the artillery fired at the whole damned lot."

Yet, despite blunders due to their rawness, the foot artillerists had earned their comrades' respect. "After Spotsylvania I never heard a word spoken against the heavy-artillery men," wrote Frank Wilkeson of the 11th New York Battery. They had often fought ineptly, "but they fought confounded plucky," an officer told Charles Page, a New York *Tribune* correspondent.[202]

GRANT WAS DISAPPOINTED when the Confederate Second Corps returned to its entrenchments under cover of night. He had urged Meade to cut off Ewell and destroy his corps, but Meade's efforts were "so feeble" that Ewell escaped. Once again, the Army of the Potomac was too slow to exploit a potential advantage.[203]

The Rebel attack delayed Grant's march south from Spotsylvania. The operation was pushed back to the night of May 20–21.

Northern newspaper reports that Lee was retreating spurred Lyman to write in disgust to his wife Elizabeth: "More absurd statements could not be. Lee is *not* retreating: he is a brave and skillful soldier and he will fight while he has a division or a day's ration left. These Rebels are not half-starved and ready to give up—a more sinewy, tawny, formidable-looking set of men could not be. . . . They know how to handle weapons with terrible effect."[204]

The Rebels were skillful, tenacious fighters, but Spotsylvania had also proven their adeptness at parrying Grant's "hammering" by quickly building breastworks that were nearly attack-proof. Private David Holt of the 16th Mississippi proudly wrote, "We had become expert in the matter of making rifle pits on the skirmish line and throwing up breastworks for the line of battle."

In two weeks, the war in the East had irrevocably changed. During the weeks and months to come, entrenchments would become the dominant feature of Grant's and Lee's chess game across northern Virginia.[205]

CHAPTER 4

The Battle That Never Happened

THE NORTH ANNA

The cold relentless energy with which [Grant] is pursuing Lee is actually sublime. The rebels call him "butcher" and "bull-dog."

—CAPTAIN SAMUEL C. SCHOYER,
139TH PENNSYLVANIA[1]

It's no use killing these fellows; a half-dozen take the place of every one we kill.

—A CONFEDERATE SOLDIER
DESCRIBING THE UNION ARMY[2]

1

Friday, May 20–Saturday, May 21, 1864
North Anna River

LATE MAY 20, Hancock's II Corps, reinforced to 20,000 men by Robert Tyler's heavy artillerymen, left its camps at Anderson's Mill, east of Spotsylvania Court House. Teenage artilleryman Frank Wilkeson wrote that as the army began to move that night, "all around us, the air hummed and vibrated with life." II Corps' infantry brigades passed Wilkeson's battery "at a swinging gait, with their arms at will." The men, he said, "growled and swore, and grumbled and enjoyed life right savagely."[3]

A little after midnight, the corps' leading brigades left the Telegraph Road and turned eastward toward Guiney Station. The tread of infantrymen and the rumble of iron wheel rims on the hard roads—portions of them corduroyed by army pioneers—filled the sultry night air with the unmistakable sounds of large numbers of soldiers on the move. Near Massaponax Church Road, Hancock's infantrymen stepped aside to let the artillery pass; every wagon was packed with sleeping gun crewmen.

Wade Hampton's Confederate cavalrymen were watching and reporting to Lee what they saw. At 4 a.m. on May 21, Lee dispatched Ewell's Second Corps to block the Telegraph Road at Mud Tavern, three miles south of where Hancock had turned toward Guiney Station. By mid-morning, Ewell's Rebels reached Stanard's Mill on the Po River, a mile from Mud Tavern, and barricaded the Telegraph Road.[4]

V Corps did not start south until II Corps had finished passing its camps at mid-morning. By then, Grant and Meade knew that Ewell's corps was moving toward the Telegraph Road, but they were unsure whether the First and Third Corps were behind Ewell; indeed, they could have used Phil Sheridan's Cavalry Corps for reconnaissance and to screen their movements, but he had not yet returned from his Richmond expedition. Lacking good information, Grant and Meade diverted V corps onto the Guiney Station road, behind Hancock's corps, rather than send it down the Telegraph Road and into a certain fight with an enemy force of unknown size.[5]

After II and V Corps had gone, Burnside's IX Corps and Wright's VI Corps withdrew from their positions and followed them, and Lee then ordered his First and Third Corps to follow Ewell to the Telegraph Road. The Army of Northern Virginia was athwart the shorter, more direct route south, while the Army of the Potomac was hoping that its left hook would land between Lee and Richmond.

THE UNION ARMY'S new objective was the North Anna River, fifteen miles south of Spotsylvania Court House, and Hanover Junction, north-central Virginia's railroad hub. Its rail lines connected the Rebel army, Richmond, and their larder, the Shenandoah Valley. If the Yankees got there first, the Confederates, pledged to protect Richmond at all costs, would have to attack the Army of the Potomac on Grant's terms.[6]

Moreover, nested within the grand strategy was the trap to destroy Lee's army. By sending II Corps miles ahead of the rest of the army, Grant hoped to tempt Lee to attack it in open country as it passed through Guiney's Station, Bowling Green, and Milford Station. He was gambling that if Lee attacked it, its sister corps could come to its aid in time. "If the enemy make a general move to meet this [Hancock's maneuver], they will be followed by the other three corps of the army, and attacked, if possible, before time is given to intrench," Grant's order said.

Indeed, if that happened, they would need to move fast, before Lee destroyed Hancock's corps. Speed was not an attribute of any of Grant's infantry corps—save Hancock's, the one being dangled as bait. It was a risky plan.

Besides entailing risk, the movement marked a temporary strategic shift: for the time being, Lee's army was no longer the objective; enticing it to attack Grant's army now was. Halleck, evidently not understanding Grant's gambit, felt compelled to remind him of his surpassing mission. In a telegram pledging more troops, Halleck wrote, "Every man we can collect should be hurled against Lee, wherever he may be. . . . When that army is broken, Richmond will be of very little value to the enemy." The chief of staff evinced little enthusiasm for collateral operations in West Virginia or south of Richmond. "If you succeed in crushing Lee, all will be well; if you fail, we immediately lose whatever we may have gained in West Virginia or around Richmond."[7]

Believing that the army had too much artillery, Grant had sent ninety-two guns—the Army of the Potomac's artillery reserve—to Washington for use in the city's defenses. Their gunners remained with the army, reassigned to corps batteries. "This relieved the roads over which we were to march of more than two hundred six-horse teams, and still left us more artillery than could be advantageously used," Grant wrote.[8]

He made two other changes for efficiency's sake. He moved his supply depot from Belle Plain to Port Royal, and, at long last, incorporated IX Corps into the Army of the Potomac. Burnside would now report to Meade, not Grant, even though Burnside was senior to Meade in rank. The change aimed "to secure the greatest attainable unanimity in co-operative movements." Burnside appeared to welcome it: "I am glad to get the order assigning the corps to the Army of the Potomac, because I think good will result from it."[9]

To the north, seemingly endless lines of ambulances filled with the wounded rumbled toward Fredericksburg day and night over the rutted, corduroyed roads from the battlefield aid stations. From Fredericksburg and Belle Plain, the casualties would be sent to hospitals in Washington. At least 26,000 wounded Yankees completed the slow, agonizing journey north during the first weeks of May. Others died during the torturous journey.

At the steamboat landing at Belle Plain, troops just arriving in the war zone met the stretcher lines of maimed men bound for steamers taking them to Washington—a dose of gritty reality for the newcomers. A mile away from this busy scene, about 7,000 Rebel prisoners were held in a valley hemmed by steep hills. Navy Secretary Gideon Welles, who had come to Belle Plain to see it for himself, wrote, "The prisoners were rough, sturdy-looking men, good and effective soldiers, I should judge."[10]

In Washington, crowds gathered to watch the steamers tie up at the city wharves and unload their highly damaged cargoes. "Long trains of ambulances are in waiting," wrote newspaper correspondent Noah Brooks, "and the suffering heroes are tenderly handled and brought out upon stretchers, though with some of them the lightest touch is torture and pain." He witnessed the melancholy sight of "the long procession of shattered wrecks; the groups of tearful, sympathetic spectators; the rigid shapes of those who are bulletined as 'since dead'; the smoothly flowing river and the solemn hush."[11]

Some of those who died in transit or in Washington were buried on the gentle slopes of Arlington, Robert E. Lee's former plantation home on the Potomac River's south bank. Private William Christman of the 67th Pennsylvania was the first, interred on May 13 in what became known as Section 27. A month later, Arlington National Cemetery was formally established.[12]

In fifteen days, Grant's army had suffered a breathtaking 37,000 casualties, nearly one-third of his 120,000 men—more killed, wounded, and captured than in any campaign of the war. Only Gettysburg's three-day casualty total of 23,000 Union troops exceeded the 18,400 losses at Spotsylvania. The unbroken combat operations, rising to crescendos of savagery, were unprecedented in this war or any other ever fought in North America, and there was no foreseeable end to it.

Although Lee's 23,700 casualties were fewer, they cut deeper. More than 35 percent of the 66,000 troops that had fought in the Wilderness were now dead, recovering from wounds, or in captivity.[13]

"It seems to me I am quite callous to death now, and that I could see my dearest friend die without much feeling," John Perry, the 20th Massachusetts's surgeon, wrote to his wife Martha. "I have witnessed hundreds of men shot dead, have walked and slept among them, and surely I feel it possible to die myself as calmly as any." Of twenty officers who began the campaign with the regiment, just six were still alive, he wrote.[14]

WHEN AN OFFICER and more than 100 men arrived in Washington in one of the caravans of wounded with minor or nonexistent injuries, Army Chief of Staff Henry Halleck railed that the "unquestionably cowardly deserters . . . deserve the death penalty." War Secretary Stanton agreed, recommending that they be tried by a drumhead court and, if convicted, executed immediately.

But deserters were rarely shot; Lincoln often commuted their death sentences. Rough justice was instead meted out. General David Birney placed men with suspicious wounds to their fingers or toes in the first rank during battle, with the men behind them under orders to shoot them if they faltered. Shirking officers were shorn of buttons and shoulder straps, and sent with their hands bound to Grant's headquarters for trial.[15]

Harsh though he was with deserters and stragglers, and impassive though he was in the heat of battle, and inured to its human wreckage, the general-in-chief simply could not abide animal abuse. One day, Grant and his staff came upon a wagon mired in a swamp. The teamster was loudly swearing and striking his horses' faces with the butt end of his whip.

Grant was deeply incensed; he loved horses and abhorred profanity. He galloped toward the teamster, his hand raised in a clenched fist. He cried, "What does this conduct mean, you scoundrel? Stop beating those horses!" The teamster regarded Grant coolly, struck one of the horses again, and replied, "Well, who's drivin' this team anyhow—you or me?"

Aide Horace Porter wrote that it was the only time that he saw Grant lose his temper. Grant shook his fist in the man's face, and shouted, "I'll show you, you infernal villain!" He ordered the man tied to a tree for six hours as punishment.[16]

THE WOUNDED THAT filled Washington's military hospitals to bursting threw cold water on the optimistic belief that soon "Lee's grand army must be captured or utterly dissolved," because his losses, many thought, were higher than Grant's. "Our troops are driving him [the enemy] slowly, as [at] the point of the bayonet," Attorney General Edward Bates had written. But just a few days later, the tide of bandaged, maimed men inundating the capital from the Wilderness and Spotsylvania dashed that expectation. "The public feeling is decidedly blue, everybody forgetting, apparently, that reverses, great and small, must form a part of every campaign," Noah Brooks wrote May 19. "The great public, like a spoiled child, refuses to be comforted, because Richmond is not taken forthwith, and because we do not meet with an unbroken success at every point."[17]

The spirit of pessimism prepared the ground for a hoax—an alleged presidential proclamation announcing the failure of Grant's campaign and the designation of May 26 as a national day "of fasting, humiliation, and prayer." A skeptical New York *Times* editor exposed the piece of trickery; two reporters had made it up. But the false story ran in a pair of anti-Lincoln newspapers, the New York *Herald* and the *Journal of Commerce*. Stanton retaliated by closing both of them.[18]

GRANT'S DETERMINATION TO press on, despite no battlefield victories, heartened his troops and puzzled the Confederates. Captain Charles Francis Adams Jr. wrote to his father, the US ambassador to Great Britain, that the Confederates "outfight us, but we outnumber them," and the Union army "has done the one thing needful before the enemy—it has advanced. The result is wonderful. Hammered and pounded as this Army has been; worked, marched, fought and reduced as it is, it is in better spirits and better fighting trim today than it was in the first day's fight in the Wilderness."

Lee's aide, Walter Taylor, confessed that he did not understand Grant. "He does not pretend to bury his dead, leaves his wounded without proper attendance; and seems entirely reckless as regards the lives of his men." Yet, Taylor evinced grudging respect for his doggedness. "He certainly holds on longer than any of them." Captain Thomas Lineburger of the 28th North Carolina agreed with Taylor's assessment. "Half such a whipping would have sent McClellan, Hooker, Burnside or Meade crossing to the other side of the Rappahannock. It seems that Grant is determined to sacrifice his army or destroy Lee's."[19]

Grant's "unparalleled stubbornness and tenacity," and "constant 'hammering' with his largely superior force had, to a certain extent, a depressing effect upon both officers and men," wrote Confederate General Evander Law. He said he often heard Rebel soldiers say, "It's no use killing these fellows; a half-dozen take the place of every one we kill."[20]

LEE EXERCISED TACTICAL and strategic autonomy over the Army of Northern Virginia, but Jefferson Davis ran military operations practically everywhere else, acting as both commander-in-chief and secretary of war. One reason was that War Secretary James Seddon's health was failing; the other was Davis's supreme confidence in his own military judgment, formed during his years as US War Secretary and while commanding the Mississippi Rifles during the Mexican War.

Consequently, Davis, not Lee, was Grant's counterpart respecting grand strategy in all the war theaters. Davis had directed Longstreet's winter operations in eastern Tennessee, and General Leonidas Polk's movements in

Mississippi early that spring—before sending him to Joseph Johnston's army in Georgia. And now Davis was supervising operations along the James River against Benjamin Butler, while worrying about Lee's safety.

"I have been pained to hear of your exposure of your person in various conflicts," Davis wrote to Lee. "The country could not bear the loss of you, and, my dear friend, though you are prone to forget yourself, you will not, I trust, again forget the public interest dependent on your life." The Richmond *Whig* seconded Davis's concern. "Too great a cause and too many hopes rest on General Lee's shoulders to admit the exposure of his life. Jackson and Stuart have fallen; Longstreet is disabled; Lee cannot be spared."[21]

Lee continued to badger Davis for reinforcements. General William F. "Baldy" Smith's XVIII Corps from the Carolinas, Georgia, and Florida had reinforced Butler. "Cannot we now draw more troops from those departments?" Lee asked.

After Grant's failed attack May 18 on Lee's Second Line at Spotsylvania, Lee wrote: "The forts around Washington & the Northern cities are being stripped of troops. The question is whether we shall fight the battle here or around Richmond," he wrote. "If the troops are obliged to be retained at Richmond I may be forced back." This got Davis's attention; he sent Lee 9,200 men: from Drewry's Bluff came General George Pickett's division and General Robert Hoke's brigade, and from the Shenandoah Valley came General John Breckinridge's division, temporarily at large after defeating Franz Sigel at New Market.[22]

NEVER HAVING CAMPAIGNED in the countryside between Spotsylvania and Richmond, the Army of the Potomac had no reliable maps of the region. "The maps were incorrect, and the guides unwilling or false," wrote Adam Badeau, Grant's military secretary. Theodore Lyman, Meade's aide, said the topographical maps were coarsely executed, sometimes a mile or more off the mark, and printed on "wretched spongy paper" that wore out after a few days in a coat pocket. As his corps marched south, Warren at one point grumped, "The map is so erroneous that it is difficult to tell which way to go, by anything named on it."

Grant's frustration was still evident years later, when he wrote in his *Personal Memoirs*, "We had neither guides nor maps to tell us where the roads were, or where they led to." Engineering officers were given the dangerous assignment of venturing into areas where Rebel scouts and cavalry were active, in order to sketch maps and find guides. "Every house was entered in the search for information," wrote Badeau.

Lyman described the army's remarkable, map-as-they-went process: "Topographers are sent out as far as possible in the front and round the flanks. By taking the directions of different points, and by calculating distances by the pacing of their horses, and in other ways, they make little local maps, and these they bring in in the evening, and during the night they are compiled and thus a map of the neighborhood is made." The master map was photographed and copies sent to the individual commands, where engineers might make corrections if necessary.[23]

2

Saturday, May 21–Sunday, May 22, 1864
Southeast of Spotsylvania Court House

THE NIGHT OF their departure from Spotsylvania, a violent thunderstorm intensified the soldiers' misery from sleep deprivation and constant marching at all hours. Private Herbert Willand of the 5th New Hampshire described the continual operations as "a method of wearing us out on short notice." "We begin to feel used up," wrote surgeon Daniel Holt of the 121st New York. "We seldom march in the road, as that has to be given to the artillery," observed Private Wilbur Fisk of the 2nd Vermont, "but across fields, brooks, ditches and fences, through woods that are almost impenetrable, and through mud holes that are very impenetrable indeed." Colonel Charles Wainwright, V Corps' artillery commander, said it was a "wretched life. . . . I am astonished to find how little sleep I can get along with, when kept up by constant excitement." "I do not think I was ever nearer worn out," wrote Lieutenant Joseph Hoyle of the 55th North Carolina. Union brigade commander Robert McAllister said this was "the hardest campaigning I have ever seen. Before it commenced, I would not have believed that I could have gone through it."[24]

After stealing away in the nighttime from Spotsylvania's muddy trenches, shattered woods, and fields carpeted with rotting bodies, Grant's troops were delighted when daylight Saturday morning revealed that they had entered a place untouched by war. It was a welcome change for men who for weeks had not seen any "signs of peace and scenes of comfort," like what lay before them.

"It was like a garden blooming in the midst of desert places," gushed Private Warren Goss of the 2nd Massachusetts Heavy Artillery. "The rich bottomlands of the river were green with grass and sprouting wheat. Herds of cattle grazed in fenced pastures."[25]

"The magnolias were in full bloom. The cherries were ripe," wrote David Craft, a chaplain with the 141st Pennsylvania.

The corn seemed to be "miles high," wrote Lyman, also observing "fruit trees and rose bushes in flower, the strawberries beginning to ripen, and the apples as big as bullets." War correspondent Sylvanus Cadwallader said the area abounded in large, prosperous farms, "with elegant residences and commodious outbuildings. . . . Fields of waving grain stretched away from the road for miles."[26]

Cadwallader also observed that the area's inhabitants "did not have the starved and destitute appearance of those in parts of Tennessee, Mississippi, Alabama, and Georgia where I had previously campaigned."[27]

At Guinea Station, Grant rested on the porch of the Thomas Chandler plantation home and learned that "Stonewall Jackson of blessed memory" had died in a plantation outbuilding a year earlier, after being accidentally shot by his own men at Chancellorsville and losing his arm. Mrs. Chandler said that "wet applications made to the wound" brought on Jackson's fatal pneumonia. She nearly broke down while relating the story. Grant told Mrs. Chandler that he had been at West Point with Jackson, and they had both fought in the Mexican War. "He was a gallant soldier and a Christian gentleman, and I can understand fully the admiration your people have for him."[28]

Grant's men lifted their caps when their general-in-chief passed them on the road on his "little black Canadian pony, not a great beauty, either," wrote Captain Samuel C. Schoyer of the 139th Pennsylvania. The regiment had lost 312 men in three weeks—two-thirds of the men that it began the campaign with. Grant smiled and returned the quiet greetings. "He looked calm, satisfied and resolute," Schoyer observed. "The cold relentless energy with which he is pursuing Lee is actually sublime. The rebels call him 'butcher' and 'bull-dog.'"[29]

The people were united in their hostility toward the Yankees. As II Corps marched through Bowling Green, Lieutenant Joseph Hodgkins of the 19th Massachusetts thought the town was "about the prettiest place I have seen in Virginia. There are some very fine residences there at the windows of which sat some good looking ladies but as we passed they put on some very sour looks."[30]

The girls "looked scornfully at us as we marched through the pretty town to kill their fathers and brothers," wrote Private Wilkeson, the teenage artillerist. He asked one of them for water from her well. "She calmly looked through me and over me, and never by the slightest sign acknowledged my presence." He filled his canteen and moved on.

Others could not resist vandalizing a well-kept enemy town miraculously untouched by the war. "One splendid residence was completely riddled," wrote one soldier. "Furniture broken, two pianos kicked to pieces, large mirrors trampled under foot . . . everything about the place recklessly destroyed." Cavalrymen rode by with braces of chickens and sacks of meal tied to their saddles. Soldiers looted a village store of all its silver. Orders went out reminding commanders that pillaging was forbidden, although foraging was not. A thin line separated the two.[31]

As they traveled through the rich countryside, Hancock's men briefly regained that sense of invincibility they had carried into the Wilderness— and that had been lost in the tangled woods there and in Spotsylvania's muddy fields and trenches. "We could look back from hill-tops and see the long steel-tipped column stretching for miles behind us," Wilkeson wrote with pride. II Corps followed the Richmond, Fredericksburg, and Potomac Railroad to Milford Station, a mile beyond Bowling Green and dug in for the night.[32]

The heavy artillerymen sent to Hancock's corps as infantry reinforcements had undergone a baptism by fire at Harris Farm on May 19, but they still had much to learn, as the 7th New York Heavy Artillery found out when II Corps stopped for the day. The New York "heavies" were preparing to eat dinner in their newly built breastworks when they heard scattered shots from the nearby woods. They grabbed their muskets and their officers were moving them to the right when bullets struck two men. Reverting to their reaction two days earlier during their first combat at Harris Farm, the New Yorkers broke and ran. But this time, Confederates had not stampeded them; skirmishers from another inexperienced heavy artillery regiment, the 1st Maine, had mistakenly fired on them.[33]

WHILE II AND V corps rested and their two sister corps clogged the road to Guinea Station, all three of Lee's corps united on the Telegraph Road near Stanard's Mill and turned south. If the armies' respective routes were represented by a stringed bow pointing southward, the curved part represented Grant's path, and the taut string, Lee's. Having decided to march to the North Anna River, Lee had the shorter distance to travel.

Lee reached this decision after being informed that Grant was marching toward Bowling Green. Lee had never seriously considered attacking II Corps, although Grant believed he had made it a tempting target by pushing it ahead of the rest of his army. His sole concern was where to position the Army of Northern Virginia to best defend Richmond from attack.

Lee concluded that it was too risky to try to head off Grant in the open country above the North Anna River. If he miscalculated, part of Grant's army "might slip by [and] possibly surprise them in Richmond on the north side, while Beauregard is attending to Butler on the south side." Better to march directly south to the North Anna River, a potentially strong defensive line that would bar Grant's path to Richmond, just twenty-three miles to the south. From the south bank of the North Anna, Lee could defend Hanover Junction, or send troops east to the Pamunkey River if Grant chose to approach Richmond from the northeast.

Consequently, during the night of May 21–22, thousands of Confederate infantrymen, horses, and wagons streamed down the Telegraph Road, just a few miles from where II and V Corps had bivouacked. Incredibly, although Union videttes and skirmishers observed the massive movement during the night, no attempt was made to attack Lee, even though drawing the Confederates into the open was the whole point of the army's rambling march to Bowling Green and Milford Station. Rather than gobble Grant's bait—"he never again had such an opportunity of dealing a heavy blow," Grant grumbled—Lee exposed his own army to flank attack, without consequences.[34]

Early May 22, reports reached Grant suggesting that Lee had again eluded him. The night before, Ewell's Second Corps had gotten as far south as Golansville, nine miles from the North Anna. The Confederates would undoubtedly reach the North Anna before Grant's army.

Later that day, the Army of Northern Virginia crossed the river at Chesterfield Bridge. The three Confederate corps fanned out on the south bank.

A. P. Hill had recovered from his illness and returned to duty. After ably leading the Third Corps in Hill's absence, Jubal Early went back to division command in the Second Corps.[35]

Lee now awaited Grant's next move. To Jefferson Davis, he wrote, "Whatever route he pursues, I am in a position to move against him, and shall endeavor to engage him while in motion." As he had before, Lee proposed joining Beauregard's army to the Army of Northern Virginia and together attacking Grant. "It seems to be our best policy to unite and endeavor to crush it [Grant's army]." Lest Davis worry about the army's latest southward movement, Lee wrote, "The courage of this army has never been better, and I fear no injury to it from any retrograde movement that may be dictated by sound military policy."[36]

LEE'S REBUFF OF the II Corps bait and his speedy march to the North Anna had foiled Grant's second attempt to flank the Southern army. The Army of the Potomac was caught flat-footed; Grant was outmaneuvered and outgeneraled. Consequently, the Army of Northern Virginia once more stood between the Army of the Potomac and Richmond.

Grant and his generals pondered their next move while the Union army rested. Colonel Wainwright, V Corps' artillery commander, was unhappy with Grant for not pressing on. "I fear that Grant has made a botch of this move also," he wrote in his diary on May 22, "for Lee is certainly ahead of us now."

The army, however, enjoyed the rare day of repose, one that had "dawned beautiful and bright," wrote Chaplain Craft. "For once the army lay comparatively still on the Sabbath, and as the forenoon advanced the bands began to play, mostly sacred music."

Country churches were fixtures at virtually every northern Virginia crossroad, and the Union command found them spacious enough to accommodate a crowd of high-ranking officers. On Saturday, Grant and his generals rested outside the Massaponax Church east of Spotsylvania on benches brought outdoors. On Sunday, Meade and his staff stopped at New Bethel Church south of Guinea Station—and found it already occupied. "Burnside and his staff sat within, in the pews, after the manner of a congregation," wrote Theodore Lyman of Meade's staff.[37]

South of Milford Station, Grant and his staff halted for a couple of hours at a plantation house that overlooked the Mattapony River valley. Grant ascended the porch steps, and bowing to a young woman standing in the doorway with her mother-in-law, asked their permission to spend a few hours there. The younger woman assented, while the older one, described as "a simple and narrow person," tartly said, "I do hope you will not let your soldiers ruin our place and carry away our property." Grant said that he would post a guard.

In whispers, the women asked Grant's aide, Horace Porter, who Grant was. They grew excited when he informed them that he was the Union army's general-in-chief.

The young woman told Grant that her husband was a Confederate colonel in General Joseph Johnston's army, and she asked him if he had heard any reports about the fighting in Georgia.

Grant replied, "Sherman is advancing upon Rome, and ought to have reached that place by this time."

The older woman retorted, "General Sherman will never capture that place. I know all about that country, and you have not the army that will ever take it."

Just then, a courier bringing dispatches for Grant from Washington reined up. Among the messages was a telegram from Sherman that Grant read aloud to his staff: Sherman had just captured Rome.

The young woman burst into tears. Her mother-in-law bitterly interjected, "I came from Richmond not long ago, where I lived in a house on the James River which overlooks Belle Isle; and I had the satisfaction of looking down every day on the Yankee prisoners. I saw thousands and thousands of them, and before this campaign is over I want to see the whole Yankee army in Southern prisons."[38]

GRANT AND MEADE debated whether to follow Lee to the North Anna, or to swing farther east and cross the Pamunkey River, formed by the confluence of the North Anna and South Anna. Meade favored the Pamunkey option: the Confederates would be unlikely to oppose that crossing, and Grant could easily shift his supply base from Port Royal to White House Landing—the former Pamunkey plantation of cavalry General W. H. F.

"Rooney" Lee, a son of Robert E. Lee. George McClellan had used White House as a supply depot during the 1862 Peninsular Campaign, and Phil Sheridan's Cavalry Corps was currently operating in the area.

But the Army of Northern Virginia was not on the Pamunkey. Grant had pried Lee from his Spotsylvania entrenchments, and he remained determined to force Lee to fight a climactic battle. Grant ordered the Army of the Potomac to be ready to march at 5 a.m. May 23 to the North Anna River. "At that hour each command will send out cavalry and infantry on all roads to their front leading south, and ascertain, if possible, where the enemy is."

Indeed, Grant did not know for certain where Lee was; he sorely missed Sheridan's cavalry. As a consequence, the four infantry corps were ordered to march south on a broad front, behind their respective reconnaissance units. II Corps, on the left, would travel down the Telegraph Road while the other three corps would operate to the west on whatever roads they could find. The army's abysmal maps showed just two roads for the four corps to march upon but, Grant added hopefully, "no doubt by the use of plantation roads and pressing in guides, others can be found to give one for each corps."[39]

WHILE GRANT WAS moving ever closer to Richmond, Butler and his 33,000-man Army of the James, after initial success between Richmond and Petersburg, was dammed up inside Bermuda Neck. Because of Butler's timidity and his bickering generals—William F. "Baldy" Smith, commander of XVIII Corps, and X Corps commander Quincy Gillmore—the Army of the James had neither disrupted communications between Petersburg and Richmond, nor seriously threatened either city with capture. While Butler had dithered, Jefferson Davis had quickly assembled a composite force of 20,000 men under General P. G. T. Beauregard.

On May 12, Butler and 25,000 of his men left their entrenchments at Bermuda Neck and turned north onto the Richmond turnpike, bound for Drewry's Bluff, the principal Confederate stronghold between Bermuda Hundred and Richmond. Faced with stubborn enemy resistance, the Yankees got as far as Proctor's Creek, about two-thirds of the way, and stopped for the day. On May 13, they crossed the creek; the Rebels were gone. But rifle pits just ahead stopped the advance, and Smith devoted the rest of the day to reconnaissance. The following day, the army found that the rifle pits were empty, and Butler's men dug in along the approaches to Drewry's Bluff. On the 15th, Butler learned that Grant was going to march around Lee's right flank, and he decided to withdraw to Bermuda Hundred without attacking, believing Grant would soon cross the James River.

But before Butler could begin his withdrawal, Beauregard's 18,000 infantrymen and artillery suddenly appeared out of the morning fog on May 16, striking Butler's center and rolling up his left flank. Butler retreated all the way to Bermuda Neck with Beauregard's men in pursuit. The Rebels entrenched less than a mile away, "stoppering" the bottle enclosing Butler's army.

Having neutralized Butler, Beauregard sent Pickett's division and Hoke's brigade to Lee's army north of Richmond under cover of an artillery bombardment of Gillmore's X Corps.

Butler's men hunkered down in their Bermuda Neck defenses. The Army of the James had lost 5,000 men, 15 percent of its effective force, during a misbegotten campaign that had accomplished nothing.[40]

GRANT HAD ENVISIONED the Army of the James swooping down on Richmond, without the aid of the Army of the Potomac. Butler might have done just that, if he had moved quickly upon reaching Bermuda Hundred on May 5. But he had believed that he was supposed to cooperate with Meade and not act independently. The result was failure and disappointment. Butler's standing sank in the Lincoln administration, which had kept him as a field commander for political reasons. Lincoln's secretary, John Hay, described Butler as "perfectly useless & incapable for campaigning."

Not only was Butler's army evidently unable to act offensively, it was not even tying up an equivalent Confederate force. "I fear there is some difficulty with the forces at City Point which prevents their effective use," Grant understatedly wrote to Halleck. Grant asked Halleck to send "a competent officer" to investigate. "The fault may be with the commander, or, it may be with his subordinates."

Halleck immediately dispatched two distinguished generals, Montgomery Meigs and John Barnard, who were respectively, the Union Army's

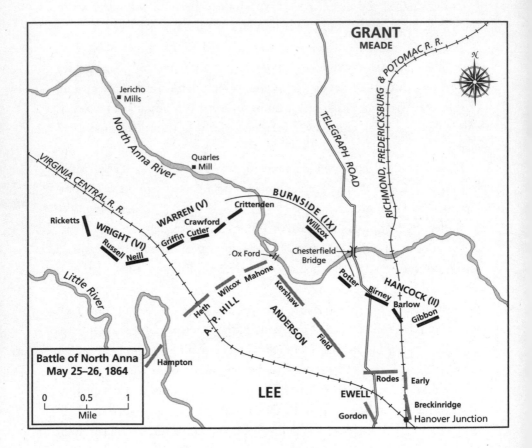

Battle of North Anna
May 25–26, 1864

0   0.5   1
Mile

quartermaster general and its chief engineer. After their three-day inspection visit, the generals recommended two courses of action: either relieving Butler of command, or detaching up to 20,000 of his men and sending them to Grant under Smith's command.

Politics legislated against Butler's removal, so Grant chose to appropriate his troops. Butler's army "is not detaining 10,000 men in Richmond, and is not even keeping the roads south of the city cut," Grant wrote. Send him every man from the Army of the James except a skeleton force to hold City Point, he instructed Halleck. Smith's corps and any other men Butler was not using were to board troop transports; sail down the James and up the Pamunkey to White House Landing; and join Grant's army.[41]

3

Monday, May 23–Thursday, May 26, 1864
North Anna River

II CORPS REACHED the North Anna River to find Chesterfield Bridge guarded by a South Carolina brigade behind fortifications, supported by artillery. Winfield Scott Hancock deployed his men to capture the bridge, as well as the Fredericksburg, Richmond, and Potomac Railroad bridge a half-mile downriver. He saw "a good many troops" on the south bank, but did not think they could stop his corps from crossing the river.

Grant wanted every crossing in the area seized, with II Corps to capture Chesterfield Bridge and the railroad bridge, and its three sister corps to take control of all the crossings upstream for five miles. Warren's V Corps moved toward the ford at Jericho Mills, and IX Corps to Ox Ford between Hancock and Warren—a place dominated by high ground on the south bank. VI Corps went looking for a crossing upstream from Warren. After capturing the Jericho Mills ford, Warren was to establish a bridgehead on the river's south bank. "I would have Warren cross all the men he can to-night, and entrench himself strongly," Grant told Meade.[42]

Neither Grant nor Lee was convinced the other wanted a battle on the North Anna. Grant's staff believed that Lee would make a stand on the South Anna or outside Richmond. Lee hoped that if Grant did cross the North

Anna, it would turn into a debacle like Fredericksburg. But Lee also could not shake the nagging suspicion that Grant was actually planning to cross the Pamunkey downriver—the option that Grant had rejected.

Reports reached Lee that Union troops were poised to cross a few miles upriver from Jericho Mills, and he went there in a carriage—he was suffering from a painful intestinal ailment and could not ride horseback—to study the enemy with a spyglass. Then, he was overheard saying, "Orderly, go back and tell General A.P. Hill to leave his men in camp; this is nothing but a feint, the enemy is preparing to cross below."[43]

If by "below," Lee meant Jericho Mills, Hill did not need to be told. Moving into the woods and fields in front of him on the river's south bank were hundreds, if not thousands, of bluecoats. But Hill was unaware that Warren's entire corps had already crossed the North Anna.

At about 5 p.m., Hill ordered Cadmus Wilcox's division to attack. Henry Heth's division was ready to come to Wilcox's support if needed. Wilcox's men suddenly rose from behind a railroad embankment and struck Warren's right flank, held by Lysander Cutler's division. Cutler's former command, the once vaunted "Iron Brigade," broke and fled to the river, with some of the soldiers splashing across to the north bank.

After this brief success, the Confederate attack lost momentum, enabling Colonel Charles Wainwright to move his artillery brigade into position and begin shelling the Rebels. This slowed them long enough for Warren's other divisions to swarm to Cutler's aid. "I do believe the artillery saved the day," Wainwright proudly wrote.

Wilcox's attack was repulsed before Hill could send him reinforcements. He withdrew to the railroad, after having lost 700 men, many of them made captives. "They were more discouraged than any set of prisoners I ever saw before," wrote Assistant War Secretary Charles Dana. "Lee had deceived them, they said, and they declared that this army would not fight again except behind breastworks."[44]

AS THE FIGHTING wound down at Jericho Mills, two brigades from David Birney's division attacked Chesterfield Bridge, defended by a few hundred South Carolina infantrymen and artillerymen. They overran the redoubts, capturing more than 100 Confederates. The rest fled—some bolting across the bridge through a hailstorm of musket and artillery fire, others attempting to wade the river and drowning in the swift waters.

After dark, as engineers built two pontoon bridges over the river, prefatory to II Corps' crossing the next morning, Confederates burned the Fredericksburg, Potomac, and Richmond Railroad bridge downriver. Then, they briefly recaptured Chesterfield Bridge and tried to burn it, too, as rain fell. Union troops drove them away.[45]

ROBERT E. LEE rose hours before daylight each day after a few hours' sleep to take up his burdens as strategic and tactical commander of the Army of Northern Virginia. Long days in the saddle, hasty meals, and stress had taken their toll on his fifty-seven-year-old body; his hair, iron-gray when the war began, was now silver-white.

Before the campaign began, Lee had confessed to his oldest son, Custis, "I want all the aid I can get now. I feel a marked change in my strength since my attack last spring at Fredericksburg, and am less competent for my duty than ever." In April 1863, Lee was confined to bed by what is believed to have been angina pectorus, heralding the onset of the coronary artery disease that ultimately would claim his life in 1870.[46]

He was ill again, but the complaint this time was a more common one: dysentery. He had crossed the North Anna in a carriage and not on horseback because the symptoms had worsened. In severe pain, frustrated by his incapacity to even leave his tent, Lee's iron self-control gave way to a surprisingly volatile temper, which surfaced only when he was ill.

After Wilcox's failed attack on Warren at Jericho Mills, Lee exploded at A. P. Hill, "Why did you not do as Jackson would have done, thrown your whole force upon those people and driven them back?"[47]

WITH NO ONE to fill his place until he could recover, Lee managed as best he could. The night of May 23, he summoned his top generals to a war council. Hancock's corps had seized Chesterfield Bridge, and Warren's corps was across the river at Jericho Mills. Lee had held the Army of Northern Virginia in readiness to shift downriver to counter Grant if he crossed the Pamunkey. But Grant had followed him to the North Anna and was spoiling for a fight.

General Martin Smith, Lee's chief engineer, was an exceptionally sharp-eyed topographer; it was he who had found the unfinished railroad by which Longstreet's troops had struck Hancock's left flank on May 6. Now, the native New Yorker proposed an ingenious solution to Lee's problem.

He had personally scouted the south bank of the North Anna and had taken particular notice of Old Stage Road, which ran along a steep bluff overlooking the river. The bluff, he believed, might serve as the tip of an un-usual defensive alignment, with the left anchored on the Little River, while the right continued along the North Anna for a half-mile before veering southeast to a swamp northeast of Hanover Junction.

The defensive formation would resemble an inverted "V" whose apex, held by First Corps, would be aimed at Ox Ford and Burnside's IX Corps. Its left leg, occupied by Hill's Third Corps, would block V and VI Corps, and its right leg, manned by Ewell's Second Corps, would bar Hancock's path to the railroad junction. Anchored by the river and the swamp, Lee's line could not be flanked, and the Rebels could obliterate any attack aimed at its tip.[48]

But even better, if Hancock led his army across Chesterfield Bridge, as anticipated, Grant's left wing would be separated by Lee's defenses from Warren and Wright on the right wing. For one wing to reinforce the other, Union troops would have to cross the river twice: from the south bank to the north, and then from the north bank to the south. Conversely, the Con-federates would occupy the interior lines, and could quickly shuttle troops from one side to the other to counter Grant's attacks—or, best of all, to launch a crushing attack of their own.[49]

Of course, Lee approved of Smith's plan. "I seem to have acquired the confidence of Genl Lee to the extent of his being willing to place his troops on the line of my selection and stake the issue of battle," Smith told his wife.[50]

Lee's army labored all that night to complete the defenses, while Lee wrote dispatches. To Jefferson Davis, he said of Grant: "His difficulties will be increased as he advances, and ours diminished, and I think it would be a great disadvantage to us to uncover our railroads to the west, and injurious to open to him more country than we can avoid." Lee had elected to stand and fight and, if possible, to exploit the division of Grant's army on the North Anna.[51]

By early morning May 24, the Army of Northern Virginia occupied the fortifications that Smith had proposed.

AT FIRST, GRANT'S men believed that Lee had withdrawn. Skirmishers from Warren's brigades near Jericho Mills initially encountered sharpshooters and a few pickets, but no organized defenses. At 7:30 a.m., Warren informed Meade, "My skirmish line has gone far out in every direction," without finding the enemy. Thirty minutes later, Meade told Warren that two slaves had reported that the Confederates "left Hanover Junction last night, taking the Richmond road."

Hancock's troops began crossing the Chesterfield Bridge, drawing artillery fire from a Rebel battery on the bluffs overlooking Ox Ford. At 8 a.m., General John Gibbon reported to Hancock, "From all appearances, I have nothing in my front but a few scattering men. I have seen them retiring in squads of five or six." Three hours later, Hancock grumbled to Meade, "The crossing at my permanent bridge is not very safe until the battery in front of General Burnside [at Ox Ford] is silenced." Hancock dispatched Colonel Nelson Miles's brigade upriver to clear the Confederates from the bluffs.

Around midday, Assistant War Secretary Dana wrote, "The general opinion of every prominent officer in the army on the morning of the 24th was that the enemy had fallen back, either to take up a position beyond the South Anna or to go to Richmond." Grant informed Halleck: "The enemy have fallen back from the North Anna; we are in pursuit."

Meade confidently issued orders for Warren to prepare to march to the South Anna River "so as to cross that river early to-morrow morning," and for Hancock at the same time to push through Hanover Junction.

Meade's optimism was premature.[52]

AS HANCOCK'S AND Warren's troops advanced, Rebel sharpshooting became "exceedingly severe and murderous," claiming scores of Union casualties. Then, Hancock encountered "a good deal of picket-firing on my right. . . . I don't know that it indicates anything of importance."[53]

As it turned out, this proved to be of utmost importance. As the afternoon wore on, Rebel pickets, when driven back, uncovered enemy skirmish lines and rifle pits. Rebel prisoners "report Ewell's corps in our front,"

Hancock told Meade at 4 p.m. "Another man, who came in on the right of my lines, belongs to a division of Longstreet's corps." Then, 250 yards ahead, II Corps encountered the Confederate battle line. "That the enemy are in strong force is probable, as we meet them in works all along our front some distance out," Hancock told Meade at 5:10 p.m.

A little over an hour later, he was reporting a Rebel attack on Gibbon along the railroad line. "It looks to me," Hancock wrote, "as if the enemy had a similar line to that on the Po, with the salient resting opposite to Burnside [at Ox Ford], and their right, so far as we are concerned thrown back toward Hanover Junction." This was followed later by Hancock's observation: "The latest information leads me to believe that a large force, if not the whole of Lee's army, is in our front."[54]

With enemy infantry and artillery on the heights above Ox Ford, Burnside had sent Thomas Leonidas Crittenden's division upriver to cross at Quarles Mills, midway between Jericho Mills and the Chesterfield Bridge. He hoped that Crittenden could blast the Confederates out of their commanding positions. Burnside sent Robert Potter's division downriver to join II Corps.

One of Crittenden's brigades, commanded by General James Ledlie, was readying an attack downriver to clear the bluffs and connect with Colonel Miles's brigade, sent upriver by Hancock for the same purpose. Hancock had halted Miles so that his brigade would not run into Ledlie's. He need not have worried; between the two brigades was A. P. Hill's Third Corps, well-entrenched on the high ground General Martin's keen eye had discerned during his topographical survey the previous day.

LEDLIE, A THIRTY-TWO-YEAR-OLD civil engineer from upstate New York, was a political appointee who had previously served in coastal artillery garrisons in Virginia and North Carolina. He joined Burnside's corps outside Spotsylvania Court House in time to participate in the failed attack of May 18.[55]

When Ledlie drank heavily, which happened often, his behavior ran the gamut from foolhardy to cowardly. Late in the day on May 24 near Quarles Mills, Ledlie was feeling bulletproof.

After his brigade had waded the North Anna and a Rebel battery began firing on it, Ledlie dispatched Captain John Anderson of the 57th Massachusetts to Crittenden to request three regiments so that he could attack and capture the battery. Crittenden was unenthusiastic about Ledlie's plan; Crittenden's division was still crossing the river, and he had no regiments to spare. Moreover, his information suggested that the battery was strongly supported, "and if he charges I am afraid it will be a failure," he told Anderson. But he said that if Ledlie "sees a sure thing," to go ahead.

On his way back to Ledlie, Anderson rode across high ground that gave him a good view of the Rebel lines. He observed more than one artillery battery, as well as strong infantry breastworks. Moreover, dust clouds indicated that reinforcements were on the way.

Anderson returned to Ledlie and reported Crittenden's response, "but in the excited state of mind in which he found the commanding officer, it is doubtful if he heard."

"The General was inspired with that artificial courage known through the army as 'Dutch courage,'" he wrote. Some of his staff officers were also under the influence. One of them stood in front of the brigade with a small revolver, "firing wildly toward the rebel battery, about eight hundred yards distant."

Ledlie personally led the attack. After the brigade had advanced a short distance, order was lost, and "it was just a wild tumultuous rush where the more reckless were far to the front and the cautious ones scattered back, but still coming on." Some of the Rebels stood on the breastworks, taunting them to "come on to Richmond."

"We had almost reached the silent batteries, when suddenly every gun flashed out a shower of grape and canister which shook the very ground and swept everything in front," wrote Anderson. Then, Confederate infantry counterattacked and closed in on Ledlie's flanks. The attack "became a confused and demoralized flight." The brigade lost more than 450 men. "Nothing whatever was accomplished, except a needless slaughter," Anderson wrote in disgust.[56]

As an exclamation point to the brigade's desolating defeat, a powerful thunderstorm drenched Ledlie's men as they began building defensive works with fallen timber. Lightning crashed into nearby trees. Theodore Lyman was crossing the North Anna on a pontoon bridge with Meade at Jericho Mills when the storm burst upon them. "The flashes seemed verily to hiss," he wrote. Ledlie, who ought to have been cashiered for squandering his men, was unaccountably promoted to division command.[57]

DOWNRIVER, THE STORM interrupted a two-brigade Rebel attack on II Corps' left flank between the Chesterfield and railroad bridges. When the storm ended, the Confederate attack resumed, and the Union line held.[58]

Grant and his generals now understood that Lee's entire army was in front of them. Grant suspended Burnside's transfer of his supply train to the south bank, "the situation of the enemy appearing so different from what I expected." He halted Hancock's advance and ordered him to dig in where he was. At the end of May 24, Dana reported to War Secretary Edwin Stanton that the assumption that Lee had withdrawn "proves to have been a mistake" for the "enemy show such strength on their lines that it appears very probable that Lee's whole army is here. His entrenchments are in the form of the Letter V, having the points of angle opposite the Ox Ford." Grant will attack, Dana said, "if a promising chance offers . . . otherwise, he will maneuver without attacking."[59]

Indeed it was difficult to know just what to do. Early May 25, Warren and Wright probed the Confederate left to ascertain its configuration, and found cleared fields of fire and heavily fortified breastworks stretching southwest to the Little River. Grant and Meade were beginning to see the problem as an obdurate one, with neither wing able to reinforce the other without crossing the North Anna not once, but twice. "The position of the two armies here is certainly a very queer one," remarked Charles Wainwright, V Corps' artillery commander.[60]

LEE'S ARMY WAS in an excellent position to smash up Grant's forces on the south bank and drive them over the North Anna. Indeed, Lee had been waiting for just such an occasion to go back on the offensive. With his army wedged between Hancock and Warren, Lee might attack either of them in relative isolation, while using his shorter interior lines to shuttle men from one side of the "V" to the other.

The Confederates failure to attack was as puzzling to Grant and Meade as the trap that Lee had laid for them; they concluded that they had so weakened Lee's army that it was now incapable of offensive action.

"Lee's army is really whipped. The prisoners we now take show it, and the action of his army shows it unmistakably," Grant wrote to Halleck on May 26. Adam Badeau, Grant's military secretary, said, "He [Lee] had now one of those opportunities that occur but rarely in war, but which, in the grasp of a master, make or mar the fortunes of armies and decide the result of campaigns." Badeau ascribed Lee's failure to act to his army's fighting spirit having been "stamped out at the Wilderness." Dana's telegram to Stanton echoed the Union headquarters thinking. "Rebels have lost all confidence, and are already morally defeated," Dana wrote. "This army has learned to believe that it is sure of victory. Even our officers have ceased to regard Lee as an invincible military genius."[61]

This was hyperbole; officers and newspaper correspondents were mightily impressed by Lee's "V" on the North Anna. "The game of war seldom presents a more effectual checkmate than was here given by Lee," wrote William Swinton of the New York *Times*. Francis Walker of Hancock's staff believed that the Southern lines were so ingeniously placed that "it seemed impossible to produce any serious impression upon them"; it "would have involved a useless bloody repulse."[62]

LEE DID NOT seize the shining opportunity that fate and Martin Smith's inspired defensive alignment had handed him because severe diarrhea prevented him from leaving his cot. He had no Jackson, Longstreet, or Stuart to whom to delegate authority; there was Ewell and Hill, whom Lee no longer completely trusted, and Richard Anderson, new to corps command. When Grant and Meade finally recognized their peril and ordered their men to dig in, every shovelful of dirt further foreclosed the Confederates' brief moment to strike the Yankees in the open. It was small consolation to know that the "V" had stymied Grant.

As he lay on his cot and read reports from the field, Lee raged against his impotence. "We must strike them! We must never let them pass us again! We must strike them!" To his doctor, he said, "If I can get one more pull at him [Grant], I will defeat him." But Lee could not go to the front, and without him, it was apparent that his army could not attack. "It was there rendered more manifest than ever, that he was the head and front, the very life and soul of his army," wrote General Jubal Early.

Pain, sleep deprivation, and the realization that he was missing his main chance dissolved Lee's famous self-control. Everything vexed him, and he lashed out at his aides, who could be seen leaving his tent practically in tears. After emerging flustered from Lee's tent following "a violent scene," Charles Venable burst out in exasperation, "I have just told the old man that he is not fit to command this army, and that he had better send for Beauregard!"[63]

GRANT'S MAY 26 telegram to Halleck described his alternative to assaulting Lee's "V": to withdraw from the North Anna's south bank to its north bank, and to then swing southeast in a third wide flanking movement downriver near Hanovertown. It was more "elbowing," the Rebels' nickname for Grant's maneuvering—and, in fact, the very movement Meade had proposed earlier. Grant instructed Halleck to move the army's supply depot to White House Landing.

As Grant later wrote, "We could do nothing where we were unless Lee would assume the offensive. I determined, therefore, to draw out of our present position and make one more effort to get between him and Richmond. I had no expectation now, however, of succeeding in this." But he believed that the maneuver would pin Lee outside Richmond so that the Army of the Potomac could reach the James River "high up," near the Confederate capital.

The plan aroused skepticism and grumbling. Colonel Wainwright, Warren's artillery chief, angrily wrote, "Can it be that this is the sum of our lieutenant-general's abilities? Has he no other resource in tactics? . . . Officers and men are getting tired of it and would like a little variety on night marches and indiscriminate attacks on earth works in the daytime."[64]

Grant conceded that Lee's position on the North Anna was virtually unassailable. "To make a direct attack from either wing would cause a slaughter of our men that even success would not justify," he wrote. Moreover, it would be futile to attempt to turn Lee's right or left flank, anchored as they were, respectively, in a swamp, and on the Little River.

It was a draw, and Grant had made the right decision to not force a major battle under such unpromising conditions. As a kind of consolation prize, the army would destroy as much of the Virginia Central and the Fredericksburg, Potomac, and Richmond railroads as possible before it moved on, he told Halleck. "I want to leave a gap in the roads north of Richmond so big that to get a single track they will have to import rails from elsewhere."[65]

GRANT BEGAN THE preparations during the night of May 25–26, quietly shifting artillery and men that were already north of the river from his far right to his left. During the coming night, the entire army would be in motion.

Fortunately for the Army of the Potomac, Phil Sheridan's cavalry corps had returned after a sixteen-day absence. Grant was pleased to see one of his favorite generals—and amused when he saw some of Sheridan's officers wearing naval uniforms from the Union fleet on the James River. "Hallooo, Sheridan, have you captured the navy?" Grant asked by way of greeting.

With a humorous gleam in his eye, Grant addressed the officers around him: "Now, Sheridan evidently thinks he has been clear down to the James River, and has been breaking up railroads, and even getting a peep at Richmond; but probably this is all imagination, or else he has been reading something of the kind in the newspapers. I don't suppose he seriously thinks he made such a march as that in two weeks." Sheridan replied in the same spirit, "Well, after what General Grant says, I do begin to feel doubtful as to whether I have been absent at all from the Army of the Potomac."

Sheridan's men would lead Grant's looping left hook, riding downriver to seize the Pamunkey River crossings and then setting up a screen to shield the army from Lee's men. Behind Sheridan would come General David Russell's VI Corps division and the corps' artillery, which would capture Hanovertown across the river. The rest of the army would follow Russell and Sheridan. If the maneuver succeeded, the Army of the Potomac would be just fifteen miles from Richmond.

In a driving rainstorm on May 26, James Wilson's cavalry division feinted toward the Little River on the Confederate left, while V and VI Corps withdrew across the North Anna. At nightfall, they began the downriver march, with Hancock and Burnside falling in behind them. Union bands played into the night to mask the noise made by thousands of troops, horses, and wagons.[66]

In attempting such a complicated maneuver on short notice, Grant was demanding a great deal from his army, and flirting with calamity. Withdrawing from positions opposite the enemy was risky, even at nighttime. Grant worried that the Confederates would strike his army while it was pulling back.

Had Grant known of Lee's indisposition, he might have been less concerned. For that reason and because the Army of the Potomac was becoming better at maneuvering, its withdrawal across the North Anna proceeded smoothly and did not provoke an attack.[67]

CAVALRY SCOUTS HAD reported Grant's preparations to Lee on his sickbed. He initially suspected that Grant might march southwest, rather than southeast: Wilson's diversion near the Little River and the preponderance of troops on the Union right suggested it. "From present indications he seems to contemplate a movement on our left flank," Lee told War Secretary James Seddon.

But this time, Lee's intuition failed him. At daybreak May 27, the Yankee entrenchments south of the North Anna were empty, and cavalry reported Union troops crossing the Pamunkey at Hanovertown, signaling that Grant was moving southeast. Then, Fitz Lee's cavalrymen spotted Union troopers south of the Pamunkey at Haw's Shop; Fitz Lee promised to "check any demonstration the enemy might make."

Lee ordered Ewell's corps to immediately march south on the Richmond, Fredericksburg, and Potomac Railroad to Ashland, west of Hanovertown. Anderson, John Breckinridge, and Hill would follow Ewell. Lee would again pivot toward the southeast to shield Richmond from the Yankees.[68]

LEE DID NOT realize that his army, and not Richmond, was Grant's real object. As a Union soldier once put it, "It is the rat we are after, not so much the rat hole." The distinction probably didn't matter; Lee could do nothing but continue to interpose his army between Grant and the Confederate capital. Yet, in so doing, Lee was abetting Grant in his aim of grinding down the Rebel army by attrition. The Army of Northern Virginia had begun the campaign with just over 66,000 men. Casualties had slashed Lee's numbers to 41,000 after Spotsylvania, and the North Anna had claimed another 1,500. The welcome arrival of 9,900 reinforcements sent by Davis had pushed Lee's numbers back up to 49,000 men.[69]

Veterans in both armies missed their dead comrades and felt the strain of almost daily fighting. "Our ranks melt away like snow under an April sun," wrote Union brigade commander Robert McAllister in a letter to his wife.

Constant fighting and maneuvering were sapping both sides. Major Alfred Kelly of the 21st Virginia told his brother that he had never experienced a more trying twenty-one days. "For the first time I find myself in the rear, not sick but completely worn down." Lee again requested more reinforcements. "All the forts and posts have been stripped of their garrisons" in the North, he told Davis. "This makes it necessary for us to do likewise . . . to meet the present emergency."

As it had at the campaign's outset, the Army of the Potomac enjoyed a nearly two-to-one manpower advantage over the Army of Northern Virginia. After the Bloody Angle, it had reported 56,000 effectives—not counting thousands of stragglers—and then it had lost another 2,600 men on the North Anna. But the 24,500 reinforcements promised by Halleck were arriving steadily and with Sheridan's return the army's numbers had grown to 90,000 men.

Numerical superiority notwithstanding, General John Gibbon said Union officers and men were beginning to exhibit "decided evidences of the wear and tear of this hard and continuous work." Whenever the men stopped marching, they instantly dropped to the ground and fell asleep, wrote Gibbon. Captain Benjamin Justice of the Confederate Third Corps observed the same phenomenon in the Rebel ranks: "Twenty-one days & nights of marching, fighting, watching, & lying in the trenches begins to tell on them, in the loss of flesh, & sunken eyes, & falling asleep anywhere just as soon as they become still." Union artilleryman Frank Wilkeson wrote, "How we longed to get away from the North Anna." The army's fighting men, he said, "began to grow discouraged" there. "Here I first heard savage protests against . . . launching good troops against intrenched [sic] works which the generals had not inspected."

Surgeon Daniel Holt of the 121st New York wrote, "It is fight and run. Run and fight, move to the left *all the while*." It was impossible to imagine "that *so much* can be endured by mortal man." Even more would soon be required.[70]

CHAPTER 5

"Not War But Murder"

Cold Harbor

It seemed more like a volcanic blast than a battle. . . . The men went down in rows just as they marched in the ranks.
            —Captain Asa Bartlett, 12th New Hampshire[1]

The infantry and our Napoleon guns tore them to pieces.
            —Confederate artillerist William Dames[2]

I have always regretted that the last assault at Cold Harbor was ever made.

                    —General Ulysses Grant[3]

1

Friday, May 27–Tuesday, May 31, 1864
Northeast of Richmond

PHIL SHERIDAN AND two cavalry divisions rode to Dabney Ferry, the Pamunkey River crossing opposite the once thriving port of Hanovertown, now largely abandoned. Behind them marched General David Russell's VI Corps infantry division—and miles to its rear, thousands of bluecoats jammed the roads north of the North Anna. At the ferry landing, engineers began laying down pontoon bridges to be floored with planks so that men, horses, and wagons could cross.

The fierce-looking cavalry chief was in high spirits. His Cavalry Corps had beaten Jeb Stuart's cavalry at Yellow Tavern and penetrated Richmond's outer defenses before fighting its way out of a tight spot at Meadow Bridge on the Chickahominy River. Even better, the general-in-chief was pleased with Sheridan's work.

Riding with Sheridan were Alfred Torbert, one of his division commanders, and George Armstrong Custer, Sheridan's favorite brigadier, whose aggressiveness matched Sheridan's, although verging sometimes on recklessness. Custer was a phenomenon, having risen to general rank at twenty-three. In appearance, he personified the popular image of the cavalry officer: reddish-blond ringlets, handlebar moustache, bright red necktie, black velvet jacket, gold braid and stars, and broad-brimmed hat. In a show of fealty to Custer, the Wolverine Brigade made its commander's red neckwear the brigade's signature apparel.[4]

Impatient as always, Custer decided to swim the Pamunkey on horseback. He and his mount plunged in. The current, stronger than it looked, upended Custer and swept him downriver a short distance before he was able to reach shore, soaked to the skin. Highly amused by the spectacle, Sheridan inquired whether he had enjoyed his bath. Custer good-naturedly replied, "I always take a bath in the morning when convenient and have paid a quarter for many not as good as this."[5]

Once across the river, Sheridan's cavalrymen rode another five miles toward Haw's Shop, driving off Rebel cavalry thrown out to the east by Lee to observe Grant's flanking movement. The Cavalry Corps, acting as the

Army of the Potomac's shield, was efficiently performing its job on this day. About noon, Russell's infantrymen, having marched thirty miles, crossed the Pamunkey and bivouacked in the fields around Hanovertown. The spearhead of Grant's army was south of the Pamunkey.[6]

It was a superlative feat. Grant had just performed one of the most difficult maneuvers in warfare: disengagement from within "musket-range of a powerful enemy," crossing one river, and marching forty hours on unfamiliar roads before crossing another. The movement neutralized the Army of Northern Virginia's V-shaped defenses on the North Anna and forced Lee to move to new positions closer to Richmond.[7]

THE MARCH SHOULD have been satisfying to Meade, who four days earlier, when the army was traveling down the Telegraph Road, had proposed to Grant that it not follow Lee to the North Anna, but march southeast and cross the Pamunkey. Grant had rejected that advice, but was now tardily implementing Meade's plan.

While this should have been gratifying to Meade, it was not. Three weeks into the campaign, Grant had more or less elbowed Meade out of his role as commander. It was because of his dissatisfaction with Meade's management of the army in the Wilderness, during the march to Spotsylvania Court House, and during the early battles there. Sloppy staff work had spoiled the attacks of May 10 at Laurel Hill and the Salient. It was true that Grant was both the better tactician and strategist, but his command style was loose—the manner of a Western commander, not one from the East. Grant issued orders and left the details to subordinates, who were often not up the job. Meade's role remained murky. The Army of the Potomac had two commanders, but sometimes it seemed that neither was in charge.[8]

At first, Meade had accepted the situation philosophically, although he was pleased when, during a visit to the front on May 18, Senators John Sherman of Ohio and William Sprague of Rhode Island "wished me to know that in Washington it was well understood these were my battles." He deflected the compliment and credited Grant, who had gradually taken control. "It would be injurious to the army to have two heads," he told them. He was amused by a description about the army's division of authority that he read in a magazine: "The Army of the Potomac, directed by Grant, commanded by Meade, and led by Hancock, Sedgwick and Warren."

But his attitude toward Grant curdled on the North Anna. In a letter to his wife, he said that she expected too much of Grant. "I don't think he is a very magnanimous man, but I believe he is above any littleness, and whatever injustice is done me, and it is idle to deny that my position is a very unjust one, I believe is not intentional on his part, but arises from the force of circumstances, and from that weakness inherent in human nature which compels a man to look to his own interests."[9]

Meade began to believe that he was being cheated of the credit he deserved, and he became sensitive to perceived slights. At army headquarters on the North Anna, Assistant War Secretary Charles Dana had read a cipher dispatch aloud from General William Sherman to Grant, in which Sherman reported that his Army of the West had fought and could now afford to maneuver. "If [Grant's] inspiration could make the Army of the Potomac do its share," Sherman added, "success would crown our efforts." Meade's "grey eyes grew like a rattlesnake's," wrote his aide, Lieutenant Colonel Theodore Lyman. And then, "in a voice like cutting an iron bar with a handsaw," Meade burst out, "'Sir! I consider that dispatch an insult to the army I command and to me personally. The Army of the Potomac does not require General Grant's inspiration or anybody else's inspiration to make it fight." Meade brooded the rest of the day, grumbling that the Western army was "an armed rabble."[10]

In the days ahead, as Meade increasingly sensed that his importance was diminishing in the eyes of the Lincoln administration and the public, his suspicion grew into something approaching paranoia.

BECAUSE LEE HELD the interior lines, he had a shorter distance to travel than Grant. His destination was the headwaters of Totopotomoy Creek, northwest of Atlee's Station, from where he believed he could counteract Grant's movements toward Richmond. Grant's proximity to Richmond, however, made Lee uneasy: he was just fifteen miles away.[11]

Lee was slowly recovering from his bout of dysentery, and he rode in a carriage and not on horseback. Ewell was now also prostrated by dysentery and traveling in an ambulance. Lee temporarily relieved him from command, placing Jubal Early at the head of the Second Corps. Early had led the Third Corps during Hill's absence, but had returned to his Second Corps division when Hill recovered and resumed his duties.

Lee's approval of Early's performance had coincided with his growing disenchantment with Ewell. The once fiery, aggressive combat leader had become erratic and overly excitable; at the Bloody Angle, Lee had threatened to relieve him on the spot. Lee was not unhappy to replace Ewell with Early. When Ewell attempted to return to the Second Corps a few days later, Lee sent him on a leave of absence. Later, after Ewell fully recovered, he was placed in charge of the Department of Richmond, and Early remained Second Corps' commander.[12]

ON MAY 28, Grant, Meade, and Winfield Scott Hancock, II Corps' commander, stood under a tree beside the Pamunkey River, watching the army cross on the pontoon bridges. "Grant looked tired," wrote gunner Frank Wilkeson. "He was sallow. He held a dead cigar firmly between his teeth. His face was as expressionless as a pine board." Hancock spoke animatedly, while Meade "thoughtfully stroked his own face."

As the exhausted troops strode by, they stared at the generals. Some of them looked back at them. No one cheered.[13]

For all their weariness, the troops could not help but notice that they were again traveling through a countryside that was "never before trodden by either army." "The sun was in its glory. Peach and apple blossoms filled the air with their perfumes . . . the green grass and tree-covered hills surrounded us," wrote Captain Robert Carter of the 22nd Massachusetts.

The pristine landscape also appealed to the soldiers' stomachs. Rich in livestock and poultry, it "could not be resisted. . . . Everything disappeared before the knife and gun, until the whole immediate country was swept clean," observed Carter.[14]

HAVING LEFT THE North Anna by different routes, shielded by their respective cavalries, Grant and Lee awakened on May 28 urgently needing to know one another's position. As their bloody game of wits continued in its fourth week, their thinking had grown eerily similar, and on this Saturday they did exactly the same thing.

Union General Irvin Gregg's cavalry division was sent probing westward from Hanovertown to find the Confederate army. Lee sent Wade Hampton and Fitz Lee with five cavalry brigades from Atlee's Station eastward to find the Yankees. The rival forces, with the Rebels outnumbering the Union troopers 4,500 to 3,500, were riding from opposite directions toward Haw's Shop, named for its large blacksmith shop, now a scorched ruin.

During Grant's slugging offensive across northern Virginia, new cavalry tactics had rapidly evolved. Cavalrymen now frequently fought dismounted and from behind breastworks—rather like dragoons—and less frequently on horseback with swords and pistols. And so it was today. After pushing through Haw's Shop and traveling about a mile west, Gregg's riders found Hampton's Confederates waiting for them behind breastworks.

Hampton, a South Carolina planter reputed to be the richest man in the South, was regarded as the likely heir to Jeb Stuart. He was an able, cool-headed commander, and Stuart's antithesis in his modest demeanor and attire. With him today was a brigade of green South Carolina troops armed with long-range Enfield rifle-muskets.

Gregg's men dismounted, dug in, and then tried unsuccessfully to dislodge the Confederates. The enemies, just a few hundred yards apart in places, waged a vicious infantry-style battle for the next several hours, with Gregg sometimes pressed back by intensive shellfire and musketry, other times threatening Hampton's flanks.

With most of the Army of the Potomac now across the Pamunkey, Sheridan was able to send Gregg reinforcements. About 4 p.m., the 1,000 veterans of Custer's Wolverine Brigade, wearing their trademark red ties, reached the battlefield. Major James Kidd of the 6th Michigan Cavalry said the brigade arrived in mid-battle and beheld "a fearful and awe-inspiring spectacle." Gregg's men were pleased to see Custer's men dismount and mass behind their line.

Custer, who remained mounted, rode along his line, waving his hat above his head and calling for three cheers as the brigade band struck up "Yankee Doodle." The Wolverines attacked. Directly in front of them lay

BLOODY SPRING

the South Carolina brigade, in its very first engagement. Although inexperienced, the South Carolinians fought tenaciously and proved the "most stubborn foe" the Michigan regiments had ever faced, according to Kidd. "The sound of their bullets sweeping the undergrowth was like that of hot flames crackling through dry timber."

Custer's attack broke the Confederate line, and Hampton and Fitz Lee were forced to withdraw toward Atlee's Station. But they had found out what they had come for—information from Yankee prisoners about the location of Grant's infantry corps.

It was "a decidedly severe" battle, wrote Sheridan—the largest cavalry battle since Brandy Station. His troopers now held the Haw's Shop crossroad, important because from there, Grant might advance to Cold Harbor, while also protecting the new Union supply depot at White House Landing, downriver on the Pamunkey. But Grant and Meade still did not know Lee's whereabouts.[15]

The artillerist Wilkeson, camped near Haw's Shop that night, was looking for fresh water when he stumbled upon several bodies from that day's cavalry battle. After being wounded, they had evidently crawled into the woods to die. Wilkeson struck a match to get a better look—and instantly regretted it, being "greatly shocked to see large black beetles eating the corpses. I looked at no more dead bodies that night."[16]

Theodore Lyman of Meade's staff encountered more gruesome evidence from the battle when he entered Salem Church at Haw's Shop the next morning, a Sunday. "The church was small, rather neatly painted within, but the pulpit and pews were stained with blood. It had been a hospital for the cavalry."[17]

THE ENDLESS CARAVANS of wounded men pouring into Washington aroused "intense anxiety" over the fate of the Army of the Potomac. "The immense slaughter of our brave men chills and sickens us all," wrote Navy Secretary Gideon Welles. "The hospitals are crowded with the thousands of mutilated and dying heroes who have poured out their blood for the Union cause. Lee has returned to the vicinity of Richmond, overpowered by numbers, beaten but hardly defeated."[18]

Welles had accurately divined the morale of Lee's army. "Although we have fallen back on Richmond, yet we have not been whipped back," wrote Lieutenant Joseph Hoyle of the 55th North Carolina to his wife Sarah. "On the other hand, we have whipped the enemy whenever he has attacked us. So the Yankees have got here not by driving us back but by moving around our flank. . . . Our soldiers are in hopeful spirits. It seems Grant is now mustering all his strength for a final struggle, and we hope this will end the war."[19]

The Yankees were weary, but remained confident in victory. Robert Tilney of V Corps admired the finesse displayed by Grant in extricating the army from the North Anna, swinging around the South Anna, and landing "twelve miles nearer Richmond, without a fight or the loss of a single life." Contrary to Lieutenant Hoyle's assertion that the Rebels had beaten Grant's men whenever they attacked, Tilney said the army had "not suffered a defeat; every movement has been successful, and brought us nearer to our goal. Grant has proven a match for Lee and, if prisoners are to be credited, the latter is at a loss to know how to keep himself before Grant." With such diametrically opposed perspectives, it was no wonder that the enemies remained eager to destroy one another after twenty-five days of fighting.[20]

"WE HAVE CROSSED the Pamunkey, and are now within eighteen miles of Richmond," George Meade wrote to his wife on May 29. "Lee has fallen back from the North Anna, and is somewhere between us and Richmond. We shall move forward to-day to feel him."[21]

The Army of the Potomac spent the late morning organizing a four-mile-long line facing west, its right on the Pamunkey River and its left on Totopotomoy Creek. Afterward, Grant and Meade sent infantry divisions in three directions to locate the Army of Northern Virginia.

It was an odd decision to use infantry for reconnaissance with Sheridan's Cavalry Corps available. Sheridan's troops would have been nimbler and able to cover more ground faster. But Sheridan had told Grant that his men needed rest after their fight at Haw's Shop. Grant granted Sheridan's request.

While the army's mounted troops relaxed behind the lines, divisions commanded by Charles Griffin of V Corps, Francis Barlow of II Corps, and David Russell of VI Corps, each with artillery, fanned out on roads to the southwest, west, and northwest. Their corps commanders were ordered to rush support to them if they encountered large enemy forces and, if necessary, to summon Burnside's IX Corps, massed in ready reserve behind the battle line.[22]

TOTOPOTOMOY CREEK FLOWS sluggishly through the flat country between Richmond and Hanovertown and is shallow-banked like the Chickahominy River. When it rained heavily, the creek overflowed its banks, flooding the timbered bottomland around it and transforming it into a nearly impassable swamp.[23]

Lee's three corps were dug in along the creek east of Atlee's in strong defensive positions on high ground, buffered by the swampy land and areas that they had scrupulously cleared to create killing zones. Lee knew Grant's approximate location, and he expected him to march west from Haw's Shop toward Atlee's Station. But if Grant did not, the Confederates were positioned to react quickly and block any of the crossroads leading to Richmond.

As reports reached him of Grant's probing movements, Lee was content to wait and see what happened. "I do not propose to move the troops to-day unless it becomes necessary." Lee told General John Breckinridge to let his men rest, but to be ready to move fast.[24]

Grant was equally cautious. When, a few miles west of Haw's Shop, Barlow and Griffin confirmed the presence of Rebel infantry in strong positions, they were told to stop. Supporting troops moved up and they all dug in at the farthest point of the advance. Firing flared up and down the lines into the night, but did not erupt into a pitched battle.[25]

BLOCKED AT TOTOPOTOMOY Creek, the Army of the Potomac began sidling again to the south on May 30, moving toward Cold Harbor. It was a crossroad named for a hostel, now abandoned, that did not offer hot food. Cold Harbor would soon connote something else entirely.

When Warren's V Corps, marching southeast on Shady Grove Road, crossed Totopotomoy Creek, Jubal Early saw an opportunity to go on the offensive. Lee had expected Grant to initiate another movement to the south, toward the Chickahominy River. Early's Second Corps, on the extreme right of Lee's line, was in a prime position to strike the Union troops while they were in motion and vulnerable. Early proposed that his corps march east toward Bethesda Church, then swing north toward Shady Grove Road in the hope of cutting off part of V Corps. Lee approved.

General Robert Rodes's division of Second Corps encountered Union cavalry probing southward toward the church and the Yankee troopers quickly withdrew. Behind Rodes was Early's old division, now led by General Stephen Ramseur, just a day shy of his twenty-seventh birthday. One of Ramseur's brigades, commanded by Colonel Edward Willis, pushed ahead to the north. It passed through some woods, emerging into a large field. Union artillery was massed on the other side, along Shady Grove Road, with infantry brigades busy throwing up breastworks.

Lieutenant Colonel C. B. Christian noticed that his 49th Virginia was not displaying its colors. This was not particularly surprising, because the regiment had lost nine color bearers since the beginning of the campaign.

Christian approached a boy named Orendorf. "Can you carry the colors?" Christian asked.

Orendorf replied that he would, adding bitterly, "They killed my brother the other day; now, damn them, let them kill me, too."

When Willis's brigade was halfway across the field, the Union artillery opened up, instantly transforming the Rebel battle lines into windrows of bleeding men. No orders were given to withdraw, so the Confederates pressed their attack, and the slaughter continued. Orendorf was blown to pieces by cannon fire just twenty feet from the Union line. The Rebels withdrew after suffering more than 500 casualties.[26]

That night, Meade and Hancock rode through the camp of the 141st Pennsylvania. Rather than cheer the two generals, the men shouted, "Hard tack! Hard tack!" Supply wagons had not kept up with the army, and the men were hungry.[27]

Meade wrote to his wife that the army was sixteen miles from Richmond, "working our way along slowly but surely. I expect we shall be a long while getting in, but I trust through the blessing of God we will at last succeed, and . . . that they will be sensible enough to give it up."[28]

ONCE MORE, THE roads were jammed with dusty fighting men. As the armies shifted south, they picked the countryside clean. Amazingly, Grant, who had lost about one-third of his infantrymen since crossing the Rapidan, was still able to field 100,000 troops or more, thanks to the tens of thousands of replacements that continued to arrive daily. Lee had about 53,000 men in his ranks after the arrival of Breckinridge's division and units from Richmond and the Carolinas.

And then, disturbing news from Bermuda Hundred reached Lee's headquarters: troop transports were spotted sailing down the James River with at least 7,000 men from Benjamin Butler's "corked" army. There were more than that, actually—12,500 or more, belonging to General William F. "Baldy" Smith's XVIII Corps. Their destination, Lee learned, was White House Landing, the ruined home of his son Rooney. Smith's men began debarking during the afternoon of May 30.[29]

This was extremely troubling to Lee. Smith's corps had only to march 15 miles directly west from White House in order to occupy Cold Harbor without any opposition. Yet, Lee didn't dare withdraw even one corps from the Totopotomoy Creek defenses and move it to Cold Harbor with Grant's army menacing his entire line. He desperately needed reinforcements.

GENERAL PIERRE G. T. Beauregard's Creole pride had taken a beating over the past two years. His career in the Confederate army had begun auspiciously with his reduction of Fort Sumter and his important role in the victory at First Manassas. When General Albert Sidney Johnston was killed at Shiloh in April 1862, Beauregard became commander of the Army of the Tennessee, and it appeared that he would soon command all of the Confederate armies in the West. But when he withdrew his army from Corinth, Mississippi, without a fight, Jefferson Davis reassigned him to Charleston to oversee the defense of the South Carolina and Georgia coasts, a rebuke to his aspirations of becoming a grand strategist. Since then, relations between Davis and Beauregard had been frosty. However, Butler's appearance at Bermuda Hundred had compelled Davis to summon Beauregard and his men to Virginia. Beauregard was a player again, and he was making the most of it.[30]

Lee's exasperation with Beauregard's stubborn refusal to send any of his 12,000 men to reinforce Lee's army had grown steadily since May 20, when Beauregard had proposed to Davis that Lee send *him* 15,000 troops. Naturally, Davis balked, but the pushy Louisianan had persisted, recommending that Lee fall back, clear to the Chickahominy River, where they would unite their armies and attack Grant's flank before finishing off Butler's army. Davis left it up to Lee. "I cannot do better than to leave your judgment to reach its own conclusions."

Lee rejected Beauregard's plan, but on May 23 he told Davis, "I should be very glad to have the aid of General Beauregard" in striking at Grant, and two days later, he tried again. None of Lee's efforts availed in prying troops from Beauregard, who was unwilling to weaken his separate command.[31]

On May 28 Lee told Davis that with Grant moving inexorably closer to Richmond, he would soon be near enough "for General Beauregard to unite with me if practicable." Beauregard, perhaps thinking that he and Lee would command together, rode to Atlee's Station to meet with Lee.

Lee wanted Beauregard's troops, but not necessarily Beauregard. "In conference with Genl Beauregard he states that he has only twelve thousand Infantry and can spare none," Lee wrote to Davis that night, tersely adding. "If Genl Grant advances tomorrow I will engage him with my present force."

In a letter to Davis the next morning, Lee asked whether troops from Richmond's defenses might be sent to him. "Even if they be few in numbers, they will add something to our strength," he wrote, but warned, "If this army is unable to resist Grant, the troops under Genl Beauregard and in the city will be unable to defend it."[32]

XVIII CORPS' ARRIVAL at White House gave Lee's efforts to obtain reinforcements new urgency. He fired off a telegram to Beauregard again asking him to send men to Lee. Beauregard again balked. He told Lee the decision was not his to make, but the War Department's. "If you cannot determine what troops you can spare, the Department cannot," Lee snapped in response.

He then sent a telegram to Davis relating what Beauregard had told him. "The result of this delay will be disaster," Lee told the Confederacy's president. "Butler's troops (Smith's corps) will be with Grant tomorrow. Hoke's division, at least, should be with me by light tomorrow."

Lee was not an alarmist, and he never used the word "disaster." When Davis read Lee's telegram, he instantly knew that this was a genuine emergency. Beauregard was ordered to have General Robert Hoke ready his 6,800-man division to move at once. With Hoke's troops, Lee's force would number 60,000. To Lee, Davis wrote, "Every effort will be made by use of rail road to place it with you early to-morrow."

Beauregard had earlier told Hoke to be ready to move at a moment's notice, and he gave him the order to join Lee just minutes before he was ordered to do so. Somewhat tardily, Beauregard also conceded that 16,000 Union troops had left Bermuda Hundred for White House, and if General Gillmore's X Corps also went, he could send Lee more units besides Hoke's.[33]

OLD COLD HARBOR—Cold Harbor's formal name, distinguishing it from New Cold Harbor a mile and a half to the southwest—was an obscure crossroad of historical and strategic importance. At nearby Gaines's Mill on June 27, 1862, Lee's army had crushed General Fitz-John Porter's small Union force in the third of the so-called Seven Days battles. Relentless Rebel attacks drove Pope across the Chickahominy River, saving Richmond and persuading George McClellan to abandon his Peninsular campaign.

Old Cold Harbor was strategically important because five roads intersected there: one from the north; one connecting it with White House Landing to the east; two that traveled southeast, crossing the Chickahominy River; and one continuing west toward Richmond. There were "roads radiating from it in all directions," wrote Major James Kidd.[34]

Believing that Smith's XVIII Corps would march directly to Old Cold Harbor from White House Landing and that Grant's army was shifting in that direction, Lee dispatched his nephew's two cavalry brigades and an infantry brigade from Hoke's division to the crossroad on May 31.

Lee had accurately divined Grant's intention to seize Old Cold Harbor. Hoping to reach the crossroad first, Grant had ordered Sheridan to ride there.

But when Sheridan arrived with General Alfred Torbert's cavalry division, he saw that Fitz Lee's cavalrymen had gotten there first and thrown up fence-rail breastworks. Sheridan sent a courier pounding off to summon General David Gregg's cavalry division to the crossroad.[35]

Torbert simultaneously attacked Fitz Lee's left and front, with George Custer leading a saber charge. The Rebel troopers repulsed the attack, but then abandoned their position after receiving a report—erroneous, it turned out—that Union infantry was approaching.

Although Henry Davies's brigade from Gregg's cavalry division had now arrived, giving him 5,500 men, Sheridan was unhappy with his situation: Confederate infantry units were close by, while his army's foot soldiers were nine miles distant. "My isolated position therefore made me a little uneasy. I felt convinced that the enemy would attempt to regain the place," Sheridan wrote. Late in the day, he learned that the rest of Hoke's division was coming to do just that.

Sheridan informed Meade that he planned to withdraw during the night. Just after he sent the message, orders arrived from Meade directing Sheridan to hold Old Cold Harbor "at every hazard." Sheridan's men returned to the crossroad and reversed Fitz Lee's breastworks so that they faced westward.

At daybreak June 1, the Union cavalrymen were crouched behind the breastworks with boxes of ammunition close at hand behind them, but without any reserves. Beyond their skirmish line, they could hear the Confederates giving commands prefatory to an attack, but the situation was even worse than Sheridan knew.[36]

Now CONVINCED THAT Grant was moving southward, Lee improvised a plan to march to the crossroad with an infantry corps and drive out the Union cavalry. Then, pivoting to the north, his infantrymen could roll up Grant's left flank—just as Longstreet had nearly done May 6 on the Orange Plank Road.

June 1 was the second anniversary of Lee's appointment as commander of the Army of Northern Virginia. It was fitting that Lee was going on the attack on his anniversary day, and also appropriate that he chose the First Corps, Longstreet's own, to carry out the attack jointly with Hoke's infantrymen.

With George Pickett's division back in its ranks, the First Corps was at full strength once again, with 15,000 men. Lee ordered Richard Anderson to withdraw First Corps from the Totopotomoy Creek line and ready it for an attack at dawn on the Union cavalry at Cold Harbor.[37]

Grant, too, had withdrawn an infantry corps from his line—Horatio Wright's VI Corps—and sent it to the crossroad. The race to Cold Harbor resembled the strenuous night marches to Spotsylvania Court House on May 8, a race won by Anderson's corps.

ANDERSON GOT THERE first again, and at dawn, Joseph Kershaw's division attacked. Unfortunately for the Rebels, Colonel Lawrence Keitt, a former South Carolina congressman, commanded the lead brigade. He had never been in combat, and neither had the 20th South Carolina, the regiment spearheading the brigade's assault.

Sheridan's veterans, crouched behind their breastworks, armed with Spencer repeating carbines, and supported by horse artillery, waited until the Confederates had crossed half of the 200 yards of open ground in front of their breastworks. Then, they shredded them with their "magazine rifles" and twelve guns.

Keitt, charging at the head of the brigade in the old style of 1861, made "a fine target for the sharpshooters," and was killed. The South Carolinians broke and ran, spreading confusion through the rest of the brigade. A second attack was launched, with the same result. Hoke's division played no role.

Edward Porter Alexander, the First Corps' artillery chief, wrote that the First Corps fully intended to destroy Sheridan, then wheel left and hit Grant's flank and rear. "The reason we did not destroy Sheridan was solely & entirely because he had magazine guns," he said.

The Spencers alone had not won the battle; strong fieldworks that Sheridan's men had perfected overnight were just as important a factor. In repelling attacking enemy infantry from behind breastworks, the Union cavalry had achieved something that was unprecedented in this war. Sheridan and his troopers would reap additional benefits from their experience in the months ahead.

It was almost anticlimactic when VI Corps arrived at Cold Harbor later in the morning and relieved Sheridan's men, although Major Kidd wrote,

"Never were reinforcements more cordially welcomed." It was the beginning of a close working relationship between Sheridan's Cavalry Corps and VI Corps.

The arrival of VI Corps meant that Lee's army would neither be able to seize the crossroad nor to roll up Grant's left flank. Lee and Grant hustled their armies into positions between Old Cold Harbor and New Cold Harbor and began furiously entrenching.[38]

BALDY SMITH's XVIII Corps was supposed to have reached the Cold Harbor crossroad that morning, but it did not. The 14,000-man corps had arrived at White House Landing late May 31. There, Smith received orders—erroneous ones, as it turned out—from Grant's headquarters to march northwest to New Castle Ferry, several miles up the Pamunkey River. Smith set out immediately without waiting for his supplies. Smith's orders said that at New Castle, XVIII Corps would join a battle line between V and VI Corps.

But when Smith reached New Castle early June 1, there was no sign of the two corps, and he asked Grant for clarification. An aide galloped up with the answer: headquarters had fouled up Smith's orders; he was supposed to have been sent due west from White House to Cold Harbor, not New Castle. The weary Yankees turned southward and began the six-mile trek to the new destination. When they went through Haw's Shop, they passed dead horses lining the road from Sheridan's fight with Hampton. The carcasses had lain in the heat and rain for four days, and the smell was revolting. Smith's infantrymen quickened their pace and reached Cold Harbor about 3 p.m., hours after the battle had ended, having marched ten extra miles. XVIII Corps dug in on VI Corps' right.[39]

The forty-year-old Smith, described as short and stout, with "the air of a German officer—one of those uneasy, cross-grained ones," was a known troublemaker. After the disaster at Fredericksburg, where he commanded VI Corps, Smith and General William B. Franklin wrote a letter to Lincoln criticizing the army commander at that time, Ambrose Burnside. For that, Smith was relieved of command and reassigned to obscure posts in the West. But he reemerged during the Rebel siege of Chattanooga when he opened the so-called "Cracker Line," bringing supplies to the hungry

Union army—and winning Grant's unstinting praise. When Grant was promoted to general-in-chief, he brought Smith to the East.

It was Smith's criticism of Butler that had led to the inspection of Butler's army by Generals Meigs and Barnard. In a letter to James Wilson on Grant's staff, Smith had complained that the Army of the James was demoralized. When shown Smith's letter by Wilson, Grant asked Chief of Staff Henry Halleck to investigate. As a result of the inquiry, Grant had brought Smith's corps, along with several X Corps regiments, to Cold Harbor.[40]

2

Wednesday, June 1–Thursday, June 2, 1864
Near Cold Harbor

IT HAD BEEN the bloodiest May in American history, each day costing the Union $4 million and 1,000 casualties in Virginia alone. Nonetheless, the Army of the Potomac's manpower, because of generous reinforcements, remained near what it had been at the beginning of the campaign. And the army's frequent maneuvering had produced an unexpected collateral benefit: besides keeping the Rebels off balance, the army's movements helped to protect the Yankees from "malarial season" outbreaks—against which they had no immunity.[41]

As the Union army shifted closer to Richmond, the Richmond *Examiner* wondered where Grant was at the moment, describing him as "an Artful Dodger." But it then predicted with surprising accuracy where he was going. "Old Church [Road] is on a direct line of march from Hanovertown to Cold Harbour. If he comes there with his army, perhaps he still designs to win or lose all in another tremendous battle."[42]

Grant was in fact discussing with his top generals whether to try once more to defeat Lee north of the James River before maneuvering to the James's south bank. In electing to attack, Grant reasoned that because he had broken the enemy's lines at Chattanooga and Spotsylvania, where conditions were no better, he could do it again at Cold Harbor. "The results to be obtained now would be so great in case of success that it seemed wise to make the attempt," wrote Horace Porter, who participated in the discussions. Furthermore, Grant feared that if the army crossed the James without fighting another major battle, there would be a political backlash from Northerners already discouraged by the war's cost and length.[43]

The San Francisco *Bulletin* did not doubt the outcome, with the Army of the Potomac having evolved into the "Grand Army, poised to deliver mightier blows than ever before, knowing that there will be blows to take as well as blows to give."[44]

In the Northern cities, crowds gathered outside newspaper and telegraph offices for daily, even hourly, bulletins. "The important struggle between the armies of Grant and Lee occupies the minds of all classes of our people to the exclusion almost, of business or the pursuit of pleasure," reported the Newark (New Jersey) *Daily Advertiser.*[45]

VILIFIED IN THE South, exalted in the North, Grant remained unchanged. He continued to dress plainly, to eat sparingly, and to speak only when necessary. He never swore. Meade wrote to his wife that when the army stopped for the night, Grant habitually made a big fire, laid down on a board with a bag for a pillow, and promptly fell asleep. His health was invariably good, although he was prone to "sick headaches"—migraines—which he treated with chloroform. F. M. Pixley of the San Francisco *Bulletin* wrote that Grant "padlocks his mouth, while his countenance in battle or repose . . . indicates nothing—that is gives no expression of his feelings and no evidence of his intentions. . . . There is no glitter or parade about him. To me he seems but an earnest business man."[46]

His mild demeanor puzzled a Mrs. Brockenbrough, "a conceited, curious, shallow middle-aged woman itching to 'tackle' a Northerner," whom Grant encountered on his way to Cold Harbor. When she had finished lecturing Grant, he replied so calmly that "she looked plainly taken aback, as she looked for a volley of gasconade."[47]

He remained a picky eater. His aide, Horace Porter, wrote that staff officers took turns catering the headquarters mess, and they found that Grant was "the most difficult person to cater for in the whole army." He "ate less than any man in the army; sometimes the amount of food taken did not seem enough to keep a bird alive, and his meals were frugal enough to satisfy the tastes of the most avowed anchorite."[48]

Porter observed that constant exposure to gunfire upset the troops' nervous systems—with rare exceptions. "The men would start at the slightest sound, and dodge at the flight of a bird or the sight of a pebble tossed past them." Porter said that he knew just two men "who could remain absolutely immovable under a heavy fire, without even the twitching of a muscle. One was a bugler in the cavalry, and the other was General Grant."[49]

INURED TO HARDSHIP though they were, Lee's men were also feeling the effects of a month of constant fighting, marching, digging—and semi-starvation. When they reached the Totopotomoy area, some units had received no rations in two days, although they were supposed to receive a pint of corn meal and one-fourth of a pound of bacon each day. "We were pretty badly off," wrote Private John Casler of the 33rd Virginia. When they did get rations, "the corn bread would get so hard and moldy that when we broke it, it looked like it had cobwebs in it." The troops often shared their slim rations with homeless Southern civilians who had been cleaned out by foraging Yankees before their homes were burned.

The Confederates wondered when the bloody endurance contest would end, and whether they would survive it. In Richmond, government officials wondered, too. "This is the time to try the nerves of the President and his counselors!" John B. Jones, a War Department clerk, wrote in his diary.[50]

Lee had done what he could to ready the Army of Northern Virginia for the next onslaught. He had brought up thousands of reinforcements from Beauregard's army. He directed his corps commanders to rake up the stragglers and scour the field hospitals in order to bring every available man into the lines by June 1. "We had absolute faith in Lee's ability to meet and repel any assault that might be made, and to devise some means of destroying Grant," wrote Sergeant Major George Eggleston of Lamkin's Virginia Battery.[51]

Lee had nearly recovered from the dysentery that had laid him low on the North Anna. He was able to ride again and strong enough to live under canvas. He told his wife Mary to stop sending him medicinal blackberry wine, adding with characteristic fatalism, "We are all in the hands of our Merciful God, whom I know will order all things for our good, but we do not know what that is or what He may determine."[52]

LEE MAY NOT have known God's plan for the Army of Northern Virginia, but as his troops dug trenches in the Virginia clay just ten miles from

Richmond, he remained convinced that a purely defensive strategy would assure the Confederacy's defeat.

In this—his eagerness to take the offensive and destroy Grant's army—Lee was truly Grant's doppelganger. "Do everything for the grand object, the destruction of the enemy," he told Richard Anderson a week earlier.

Outside of Cold Harbor, Lee wrote to A. P. Hill, "The time has arrived, in my opinion, when something more is necessary than adhering to lines and defensive positions. We shall be obliged to go out and prevent the enemy from selecting such positions as he chooses. If he is allowed to continue that course we shall at last be obliged to take refuge behind the works of Richmond and stand a siege, which would be but a work of time. You must be prepared to fight him in the field, to prevent him from taking positions such as he desires."[53]

But even as Lee wrote those words, the time when his army might act offensively was coming to an end.

THE TWO ARMIES gravitated to Cold Harbor throughout June 1—Grant, aiming to launch a massive attack early the next morning; Lee, to interpose his army between Grant and Richmond and possibly strike Grant in the open.

That day, Warren's skirmishers spotted a heavy Confederate column—Pickett's and Field's divisions of First Corps—moving rapidly to the Union left behind Early's Second Corps, which was opposite V Corps. Early's gunners kept Warren's skirmishers at arm's length, and Warren was too slow in moving his artillery within range to begin a counter fire. By the time the artillery was ready to fire, the tail of the column was disappearing to Warren's left.

Next, Horatio Wright's VI Corps was ordered to attack the same Rebel column, but the Confederates were gone before Wright could act. "Grant was bitterly disappointed at the double mishap," wrote Adam Badeau, his military secretary. The Army of the Potomac had again displayed its inability to move quickly.[54]

Both VI and XVIII Corps now occupied the place where Sheridan's cavalrymen had repelled two attacks by the Confederate First Corps the previous day. Meade proposed that the infantry corps push closer to the

Rebel lines so they would be in better positions for Grant's planned attack on June 2.

At 5 p.m., four divisions from the two Union corps—about 20,000 troops—lunged toward the Confederate entrenchments with "shouts and cheers" across an open field two-thirds of a mile wide, fringed by a strip of pine woods. As a red sun began to sink in the west, "the shot and shell of the artillery shrieked and howled like spirits of evil," wrote surgeon George Stevens of the 77th New York. VI Corps struck a fifty-yard gap in the Rebel lines between Hoke's and Kershaw's divisions, capturing 500 prisoners.[55]

A battle on the grand scale it was not, but it was a battle nonetheless, and hard-fought. Moreover, it was the first time in combat for the 2nd Connecticut Heavy Artillery, which until recently had guarded forts in Washington. Commanded by Colonel Elisha Kellogg, it was now part of General Emory Upton's VI Corps brigade—famed for its penetration of the Salient at Spotsylvania on May 10. The Connecticut artillerymen hadn't been there, but they never forgot the June 1 attack.

The Union troops advanced to within twenty yards of the Rebel breastworks when General Thomas Clingman shouted to his North Carolina brigade, "Aim low and aim well!" And then, "a sheet of flame, sudden as lightning, red as blood, and so near that it seemed to singe the men's faces, burst along the rebel breastwork," wrote Lieutenant Theodore Vaill of the 2nd Connecticut. The initial volley into the "thick, dark mass" knocked down the front ranks like tenpins. Then, enfilading fire from the left struck the foot artillerymen. Clingman's men poured in volley after volley. "Men staggered in every direction, some of them falling upon the very top of the rebel parapet, where they were completely riddled with bullets," wrote Vaill. Colonel Kellogg was killed.

Upton rode up shouting, "Lie down!"—excellent advice for a regiment that had never been in combat before. Confederate brigades swarmed into the gap between Hoke's and Kershaw's divisions, along a swampy piece of ground following a shallow ravine that would become known as "Bloody Run." From behind a tree in the front line, the tightly wound Upton fired muskets as fast as his men could load and hand them to him. To a major who said he could not hold if there was another Rebel attack, Upton sent this message: "He *must* hold. If they come there, catch them on your bayonets, and pitch them over your heads!"[56]

The Rebels closed the breach with a "horseshoe connection," but Wright's and Smith's troops clung to parts of the Rebel first line of rifle pits. As night fell, the two corps commanders requested reinforcements, warning that Lee was sending more troops to the area.

When one of Smith's aides told Meade that XVIII Corps had left White House with little ammunition and was now in dire need of it. Meade roared, "Then, why in Hell did he come at all for?"

The late-day attack had cost Wright and Smith 2,200 men, and the Rebels 1,800—so that Union troops might occupy positions a few hundred yards closer to the Confederate line for the next morning's attack.[57]

REINFORCEMENTS WERE COMING. Grant's favorite shock troops, Hancock's II Corps, were ordered to march from the extreme right of the Union line to the far left in order to spearhead the next morning's attack. After withdrawing his corps to the Bethesda Church area, Hancock was to march through the night down the line behind Burnside's and Warren's positions, all the way to VI Corps' left. Although the distance was ten miles, Meade believed II Corps would be in position to attack by 6 a.m.

That night, Meade told his wife: "We are pegging away here and gradually getting nearer and nearer to Richmond." The Confederates, he said, entrenched in strong positions, forcing the Union army to move to its left, "after trying to find some weak point to attack. . . . We shall have to do it once more before we get them into their defenses at Richmond, and then will begin the tedious process of a quasi-siege . . . "[58]

HEAVY SKIRMISHING AND attacks delayed II Corps' departure until 9 p.m. After a long day of fighting, Hancock's tired men began marching toward the army's far left flank. The day's heat did not dissipate, but remained trapped beneath the canopy of trees. Twenty thousand men, horses, and the wheels of the artillery caissons stirred up the ankle-deep dust on the road, and it hung suspended in the still air in suffocating clouds, making it difficult even to breathe. Before long, all the men were covered in white powder. It was "almost beyond the limits of endurance," wrote a member of Hancock's staff.[59]

Even worse, II Corps' guide, one of Meade's staff officers, led the corps along a "short cut through a wood road," that gradually narrowed until the guns became wedged between the trees. Regiments became confused, and the woods rang with shouts and oaths. The column had to backtrack and find the right road. It took hours.[60]

The corps' leading brigades, "in an exhausted condition" after nine hours of fumbling through the hot woods, reached their new position between 6 a.m. and 7 a.m. Meade postponed the attack until 5 p.m. that day. "Such examinations and arrangements as are necessary will be made immediately," he said. In the afternoon, the attack was delayed again—until 4:30 a.m. on Friday, June 3. "Unless the enemy attack us, the time will be devoted to rest," read the postponement order.[61]

WATCHING THE REINFORCEMENT of the Union left by VI and XVIII Corps with mounting concern, Lee ordered John Breckinridge's division to march during the night from the Confederate left to its right, six miles away—mirroring II Corps' movement. Like the guide on II Corps' overnight march, the Confederate guide had neither a decent map nor a clear notion of how to get where he was going.

When the division had not arrived by mid-morning of June 2 and Lee observed the Union II Corps filing into positions opposite his right, he went looking for Breckinridge. He found the former US vice president and his men at Mechanicsville, six miles from the battle lines. Unfamiliar with the area's farm roads, the guide that Lee had chosen to lead them, Major H. B. McClellan, had stuck to the main roads to be safe, thereby doubling the length of the march. Lee hurried the exhausted division into the line, and also ordered William Mahone's and Cadmus Wilcox's Third Corps divisions to move to the Confederate right in response to the Union troop buildup there.

Lieutenant J. F. J. Caldwell of the 1st South Carolina had fought near Cold Harbor two years earlier, at Gaines's Mill. "We passed the spot where we had first tasted the sweets and the bitterness of battle, and the very graves where our dead lay," he wrote. "The war was repeating itself with singular accuracy." Captain George Mills of the 16th North Carolina, another Gaines's Mill veteran, wrote, "In passing down to the right I walked over the place where I saw a number of Rutherford [North Carolina] boys buried in '62."

Indeed, the place was familiar to thousands of men in both armies. Eerily, "the very works that still remained were used again by the two armies, but the position of the troops and the object of the fortifications were exactly reversed," wrote Adam Badeau. In 1862, Lee had attacked. This time, he would be on the defensive.

AFTER PLACING BRECKINRIDGE'S division on the Rebel right, Lee summoned Major McClellan to his tent. Lee rarely reprimanded subordinates for mistakes, but he sometimes let them know when they failed. Fearing the worst, McClellan reported to Lee. He found Lee seated on a campstool in front of his tent, with a map spread out on his knees.

Without a word, with his index finger Lee traced a road on the map and then quietly said, "Major, this is the road to Cold Harbor."

"Yes, General," McClellan replied. "I know it now."

Nothing more was said, but Lee's "quiet reproof sunk deeper and cut more keenly than words of violent vituperation would have done," McClellan wrote.[62]

As Lee shuffled the three infantry divisions to his right, he sent three divisions on his left—two from Early's Second Corps, plus Heth's division of First Corps—into action on the north side of the seven-mile battle line, which now curved from Shady Grove Road to the Chickahominy River. Lee wanted to discourage Grant from shifting more divisions and to push back Grant's right, held by Burnside and Warren. "It was a quick bold move, &, had there been more troops to give it force, it might have produced important results," wrote Edward Porter Alexander, the First Corps' artillery commander. Fighting raged around Bethesda Church, where the armies had battled three days earlier. The rebels seized Union forward trenches and pressed Warren and Burnside hard from the north and west. Some Federal units were nearly surrounded. But the Confederates were unable to break through.[63]

Because of the condition of the roads, Grant did not learn for hours about the second Battle of Bethesda Church. When he found out about it, he was displeased with his two corps commanders for not counterattacking. "I was so annoyed at this that I directed Meade to instruct his corps commanders that they should seize all such opportunities when they occurred, and not wait for orders, all of our manoeuvers being for the very purpose of getting the enemy out of his cover." The incident confirmed the impression held by Grant and his staff that the Army of the Potomac's corps command-ers—Hancock and Sheridan excepted—moved too slowly and too often appeared "content with preventing disasters or repelling assault."[64]

Lee remembered that Turkey Hill on his right had been a good place for artillery during his 1862 campaign, because it overlooked the Chickahominy River bottomlands. Grant's troops, however, had gotten there first this time.

But during the afternoon of June 2, Lee sent two infantry divisions to capture Turkey Hill; they drove off Nelson Miles's Union brigade, and Confederate guns were brought up.[65]

HAD GRANT ATTACKED on June 2, when the Rebels had not yet fortified their positions, he might have been able to shatter and roll up the thin enemy lines. But the Army of the Potomac was incapable of mobilizing and acting quickly. And so Lee's army dug all day June 2.

Theodore Lyman had observed the Confederates long enough to admire their proficiency in building fortifications and to apprehend their system. During the first day, he wrote, they usually built good rifle pits, "the sec-ond, a regular infantry parapet with artillery in position; and the third a parapet with abatis in front and entrenched batteries behind. Sometimes they put this three days' work into the first twenty-four hours."

The delay gave the Rebels an extra day to complete a series of cun-ning defenses that sprawled across varied terrain: flat, hilly, bare, wooded, swampy, dry. When they finished, a series of interlocking trenches covered all of the likely attack routes, overlooking cleared, overlapping fields of fire, defended by abatis.[66]

General Evander Law's Alabama brigade had reinforced the right side of the Rebel line on June 2, occupying breastworks that angled back sharply on the right and ran along a slope. Behind it was swampy ground; in front of it was a hill. With the woods before him full of Yankees, Law had to wait until dark to begin a new battle line. That night, he and two staff officers went out with hatchets and armloads of stakes and marked the new line. It was behind the marshy ground and gave the defenders "a clear sweep across it with our fire from the slope on the other side." Law formed his troops along the staked line, "and before morning the works were finished."[67]

THE UNION COMMANDERS had only a general idea of the Rebel lines' location, and no idea of where there might be weak spots. Virtually no reconnaissance was attempted—and none by Grant, Meade, or their staff officers. Reconnaissance was left to the corps commanders. "The corps commanders were to select the points in their respective fronts where they would make their assaults," Grant wrote. Little scouting was done, though.

Later, after Badeau had an opportunity to examine the Confederate defenses, he would write with admiration: "Protected thus by swamps on one side and ravines on the other, and with a sunken road in front, the position was quite as formidable as any assumed by the rebels during the entire campaign. . . . Everywhere the enemy was absolutely covered, and the assailants were exposed to the full force of the rebel fire."[68]

This might not have been apparent as darkness fell on June 2, but the soldiers that would make the attack in the morning were aware that many of them would soon lose their lives. The soldiers' stoical preparations for their possible deaths were not unique to the coming battle, but Porter, Grant's aide, who passed along the front on foot that evening, had never witnessed anything like it before.

"I noticed that many of the soldiers had taken off their coats, and seemed to be engaged in sewing up rents in them." However, "upon closer examination it was found that the men were calmly writing their names and home addresses on slips of paper, and pinning them on the back of their coats, so that their dead bodies might be recognized upon the field, and their fate made known to their families at home. . . . Such courage is more than heroic—it is sublime."[69]

Early that night, a drenching rain began falling.

3

Friday, June 3, 1864
Cold Harbor

RAIN FELL INTERMITTENTLY all night, tapering to a sullen drizzle by the time a dull gray light appeared in the eastern sky. Ground fog obscured the no man's land between the armies. On both sides of the line, the soldiers were awake, alert, and tense with anticipation.

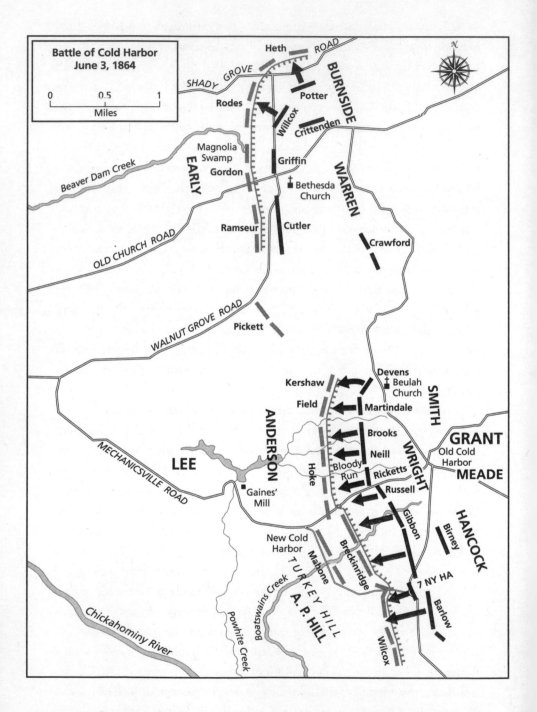

Battle of Cold Harbor
June 3, 1864

0   0.5   1
Miles

Heth
SHADY GROVE ROAD
BURNSIDE
Potter
Rodes
Willcox
Crittenden
WARREN

Magnolia
Swamp
EARLY
Gordon
Griffin
† Bethesda
Church

Beaver Dam Creek

OLD CHURCH ROAD
Ramseur
Cutler
Crawford

WALNUT GROVE ROAD
Pickett

Devens
† Beulah
Church
SMITH
Kershaw
Field
Martindale
MECHANICSVILLE ROAD
ANDERSON
Brooks
WRIGHT
GRANT
LEE
Neill
Old Cold
Harbor
Hoke
Bloody
Run
Ricketts
MEADE
Gaines'
Mill
Russell
Gibbon
Birney
HANCOCK
New Cold
Harbor
Breckinridge
Boatswains Creek
Mahone
TURKEY HILL
A. P. HILL
7 NY HA
Barlow
Chickahominy River
Powhite Creek
Willcox

At Army of the Potomac headquarters, which had been moved to a place behind the army's left to be closer to the action, Grant and Meade waited for the signal gun.

Grant was planning an all-out assault on the right side of the Confederate front. A turning movement would not work with Lee's two flanks strongly secured by swamps—on Lee's right, those near the Chickahominy River, and on his left, the soggy woodlands at the headwaters of Totopotomoy Creek. "The front was the assailable part," wrote his chief of staff, General Andrew Humphreys, "though it had not been reported that it was practicable to carry it by assault."

"An attack on the enemy's right promised the better results," observed Horace Porter, Grant's aide. Grant wanted to attempt it before beginning another sidle southward. If the attack succeeded, the Army of the Potomac might also inflict "severe loss upon Lee when falling back over the Chickahominy."[70]

Grant had pointed out to his generals on the command-center map what he wanted done: on the left, II, VI, and XVIII Corps would attack Lee's right, in the hope of crushing it and then cutting off the Rebels from Richmond; on Grant's right, V and IX Corps would pin the Rebels opposite them so they could not reinforce Lee's right, and attack the center if their sister corps broke through.

The plans all appeared to be reasonable enough except that, astonishingly, no one had bothered to carefully scout the Confederate positions; Grant, Meade, their staffs, and the corps commanders had all been delinquent. "No opportunity had been afforded to make an adequate reconnaissance," General Francis Walker, Hancock's chief of staff, later conceded.

Fifty-thousand bluecoats from three infantry corps were poised to go into action against Rebel positions that had been cleverly concealed in the woods, hills, and swamps. Seduced by the potential "momentous consequences" of a quick victory, Grant had chosen to forgo the careful preparations that might have identified a weakness in the Confederate lines that could be exploited. Instead, he was blindly hoping to break through somewhere.[71]

During the night, Private Frank Wilkeson, the teenage artilleryman, and his unit set up their guns behind a hill opposite II Corps' attack objective.

Nearby, the 7th New York Heavy Artillery, one of the huge regiments of foot artillerists that had joined Hancock's corps, was preparing for its first major combat. It would be in the forefront of the lead assault brigade. "They were sad of heart," Wilkeson said of the New Yorkers. "They dreaded the work. The whole army seemed to be greatly depressed."[72]

AT 4:30 A.M.—twenty-two days nearly to the minute since the Bloody Angle attack—the signal cannon boomed from the 10th Massachusetts Battery. II Corps surged toward Lee's right, led by the doom-ridden 7th New York Heavy Artillery, with 600 yards of pasture to cross. The armies furiously exchanged artillery fire, rattling windows in Richmond, seven miles away.

"The vibrations . . . could be felt in the houses. It could be heard distinctly in all parts of the city," wrote John Jones, a Confederate War Department clerk. Rousted from bed, people poured into the streets. The city braced for a wave of wounded soldiers.[73]

The New Yorkers, in the vanguard of Colonel John Brooke's brigade of General Francis Barlow's division, quick-timed across the open ground, shouting "Huzzah! Huzzah!" as bullets zipped past them and shells exploded. The well-entrenched defenders on Lee's right, their flank protected by swamps, came from an assortment of veteran Rebel divisions—William Mahone's Third Corps division, John Breckinridge's division from the Shenandoah Valley, and Robert Hoke's from Bermuda Hundred.

Brooke's foot artillerists ducked into a swale below the crest of Watt's Hill. Above them lay Echols Brigade of Breckinridge's division—the 22nd and 23rd Virginia Regiments and 26th Virginia Battalion—whose commander, General John Echols, was ill. The temporary commander was Colonel George S. Patton, whose grandson would become a household name in the next century.

Red-haired Corporal Terrence Bagley leaped to his feet and sprinted to the Rebel works. At close range, he shot the 26th Virginia Battalion's color bearer, bayoneted an officer, snatched the colors, and ran back to his comrades, amid a fusillade of musketry, miraculously escaping injury.

Inspired by Bagley, the 7th charged up the slope, cheering. The Virginians fired a last volley into the New Yorkers and then came out of their breastworks to fight. In an instant, 2,000 men were in a rough-and-tumble brawl, shooting, bayoneting, and bludgeoning one another. The Rebels, outnumbered three to one, were forced back to their second line. The New Yorkers captured 300 men and four guns, which they turned against the enemy and loaded, only to then discover that the Rebel gunners had taken the friction primers.

It was a promising start. But as the 7th prepared to attack the second Rebel line, the reinforcements that were supposed to come to their support did not appear. Colonel John Brooke had been wounded the instant that he ordered the second Union line to attack, and his successor, Colonel James Beaver, inexplicably did not follow through.

The 7th New York was marooned in the Rebel first line without support.

Echols' Brigade, the 2nd Maryland, and a brigade of Floridians led by General Joseph Finnegan that had been victorious at the Battle of Olustee, Florida, three months earlier, swarmed to the counterattack. "The thrilling battle-cry of the Confederate infantry floated to us," wrote Wilkeson, puzzled that Union support troops "did not go forward and make good the victory." The Rebels scorched the foot artillerists with musketry and artillery fire from three sides. With nowhere to go and no supports, they bolted downhill, scores of them shot down as they ran. The triumphant Rebels shouted and swung their hats.

The New Yorkers, however, were not finished; they re-formed and charged twice more, getting within thirty yards of the hillcrest before digging in. In a little more than twenty minutes, the regiment lost 422 men, 145 of them killed. During the war, only three regiments lost more men in a single engagement. Later, the Richmond *Sentinel* was moved to make the rare gesture of praising the 7th's gallantry, "in spite of the loss of many of their men, who fell like autumn leaves, until the ground was almost blue and red with their uniforms and their blood."[74]

The 7th New York's assault was the attack's high water mark, along with the advances of Nelson Miles's brigade and the Irish Brigade on the 7th's left, also stopped thirty yards from the Confederate breastworks.

To the right of the 7th, John Gibbon's four brigades split into two columns to avoid a swamp. The two brigades on the right, led by General Robert Tyler and Colonel H. Boyd McKeen, made a "desperate charge" into "a terrible fire of grape and canister from the enemy batteries while the musketry rolled terribly." The gunfire "broke our ranks," wrote Lieutenant Joseph Hodgkins of the 19th Massachusetts, "and we were obliged to halt under the brow of the hill, where we passed up rails from a fence near by and piled them up, and with dippers and plates threw up the dirt making a good line of works." McKeen was killed during the attack, and Tyler was badly wounded.

Colonel Peter Porter, commander of the 8th New York Heavy Artillery, was wounded in the neck as he gave his last order, "Dress upon the colors!" He was then shot six more times before falling dead. His men were new to major combat; they wore bright blue uniforms and advanced in a handsome line, carrying their knapsacks. "The lead and iron filled the air as the snow flakes in an angry driving storm," wrote Captain James Maginnis. Private Nelson Armstrong said "the army seemed to melt away like a frost in July." They were "cut down like mown grass," wrote Chaplain Alanson Haines. "Their destruction seemed like the host of Sennacherib [whose Assyrian army was destroyed before Jerusalem in Biblical times], so complete and so sudden. It was the most sickening sight of this arena of horrors."

Colonel Frank Haskell of the 36th Wisconsin took command of Porter's unit, and Hancock ordered him to get the men moving. Haskell leaped to his feet and waved his sword, shouting, "Forward, boys!" and was dead an instant later. The survivors resumed digging. "We did not go much farther as our men were falling like leaves and we could not stand the fire from the Rebs," wrote Private Josiah Murphey of the 20th Massachusetts.

On the other side of the swamp, the ground was better and Colonel Thomas Smythe's brigade reached the Rebel works, but he was unable to capture them without support. None came. "The assault was a complete failure," wrote Gibbon, who lost 1,100 men—500 in the 8th New York alone, surpassing the 7th New York's losses for the most casualties by any regiment that day. To Hancock, Gibbon wrote, "I regard any further assault on the enemy's works as inadvisable."

Barlow's division sustained similar losses. "Scarcely twenty-two minutes after the signal had been given, the repulse of the corps was complete," wrote General Francis Walker, who lamented the corps' heavy casualties during the past month—"the very flower of the corps . . . men who never could be replaced."[75]

AT 6 A.M., Hancock wrote to Meade that his First and Second Divisions had advanced to positions close to the Rebel front line, "but seem unable to carry it." Remembering the lesson of the Bloody Angle, Hancock said piling in more troops would make no difference, and he intended to hold General David Birney's Third Division in reserve. "I shall await your orders, but express the opinion that if the first dash in an assault fails, other attempts are not apt to succeed later."

Meade fired back: "You will make the attack and support it well, so that in the event of being successful, the advantage gained can be held." Then, twenty-five minutes later, after receiving reports about the failures of VI and XVIII Corps' attacks, Meade evidently had second thoughts. He wrote to Grant: "I should be glad to have your views as to the continuance of these attacks, if unsuccessful." Grant immediately responded, "The moment it becomes certain that an assault cannot succeed, suspend the offensive, but when one does succeed push it vigorously."[76]

THE ORDER TO attack that morning had pleased no one at VI Corps, which had bled on the same ground two days earlier and understood the deadly peril of the swampy ravine at Bloody Run. When Lewis Grant, commander of the Vermont Brigade, learned about the attack plan, "the order came like a death warrant. . . . I felt as I never felt at any other time." So strongly did Grant believe that he would not survive that he left his belongings with men in the rear with instructions on where to send them.

When VI Corps met the same ferocious gunfire that had greeted Gibbon's men on their left, the troops halted and commenced digging. Lewis Grant withdrew his regiments and left a skirmish line in their place. Colonel Emory Upton's brigade did not attack at all. "Another assault was ordered, but, being deemed impracticable along our front, was not made," Upton wrote.[77]

TWO DIVISIONS FROM XVIII Corps charged along a ravine—and right into the open jaws of a diabolical V-shaped system of interlocking breastworks created by Kershaw's division of the Confederate First Corps. John Martindale's two brigades ran into a buzz saw. A "dreadful storm of lead and iron . . . met the charging column," wrote Captain Asa Bartlett of the 12th New Hampshire, which spearheaded one of the brigades. "It seemed more like a volcanic blast than a battle, and was about as destructive. The men went down in rows just as they marched in the ranks."

Confederate General Evander Law watched with satisfaction as the XVIII Corps brigades quick-timed into the marshy salient that his Alabamans had abandoned during the night after Law straightened his line. The 4th Alabama, with bayonets and bare hands, had overnight built a five-foot parapet with a wide, shallow ditch and firing step inside and a four-foot ditch outside. Law's men overlooked their old salient—now an efficient killing ground.

The Yankees attacked with a loud cheer. "Line followed line until the space enclosed by the old salient became a mass of writhing humanity, upon which our artillery and musketry played with cruel effect," Law wrote. Rebel artillerist William Dames said the batteries fired double canister into the head of the column, transforming it into "a formless crowd, that still stood stubbornly there, but could not get one step farther. And then, for three or four minutes, at short pistol range," Dames wrote, "the infantry and our Napoleon guns tore them to pieces. . . . The mass was simply melting away under the fury of our fire." Colonel P. D. Bowles said the Confederate artillery mowed them down "by the dozen, while heads, arms, legs, and muskets were seen flying high in the air."

Georgia troops loaded for the firing Alabamans. "We really mowed them down," Private William Griffin wrote to his wife. Law went into the trenches to find his men reveling in their bloody work. They were "in fine spirits, laughing and talking as they fired." Colonel William Oates, commander of the 15th Alabama, said the Yankees were hit by "the most destructive fire I ever saw" from the front and both flanks. "I could see the dust fog out of a man's clothing in two or three places at once where as many balls would strike him at the same moment. In two minutes not a man of them was standing."

The New Hampshire troops bent forward into the gunfire "as if trying . . . to breast a tempest" and tumbled down like "rows of blocks or bricks pushed over by striking against each other," wrote Sergeant John Piper. Sergeant Jacob Tuttle saw so many men go down that he mistakenly thought that an order to lie down had been given "and dropped myself among the dead," until he saw his living comrades still advancing.

Law had never seen a slaughter like what he witnessed this morning, not at Marye's Hill at Fredericksburg nor at the railroad cut at Second Manassas. "It was not war; it was murder," he wrote. Lieutenant Colonel Moxley Sorrel of the First Corps staff wrote, "The sight in our front was sickening, heart rending to the stoutest soldier." Only a handful of Law's Alabamans became casualties, Law one of them—wounded in the hand by a stray bullet.[78]

BARTLETT'S NEW HAMPSHIRE regiment was "literally cut to pieces or torn into fragments," but Martindale's other regiments did not give up; they tried three times to reach the Confederate breastworks. The hurricane of bullets and shells assailing them from three sides finally compelled them to dig in. Just one regiment, the 25th Massachusetts, made the last attack. Adjutant R. T. Coles of the 4th Alabama said the New Englanders' raw courage "excited the admiration" of the Alabamans. "It appeared to be downright murder to kill men in the performance of an act so courageous." But the Alabamans did anyway. "When the smoke from our rifles cleared away, not a man was standing, except one, and he was shot down as he ran away."

After another of "Baldy" Smith's brigades, commanded by Gilman Marston and part of General William Brooks's division, was mauled by a Confederate crossfire in the open "V," Smith had seen enough; he suspended the attack. "My troops are very much cut up, and I have no hopes of being able to carry the works in my front unless a movement of the Sixth Corps on my left may relieve at least one of my flanks from this galling fire," Smith wrote to Meade.

The fighting had slackened by 7:30 a.m., but Meade ordered Smith to continue his assault "without reference to General Wright's," and he also tried to prod Smith and Wright into renewing their attacks. To Hancock, Meade wrote at 8:45 a.m. that Wright believed that a second assault might succeed, if II and XVIII Corps supported it. "No effort should be spared,"

Meade said, but he then hedged, adding, "unless you consider it hopeless." Hancock sent Birney's reserve division to Wright, but did not send his two other divisions into another attack.

Elsewhere, Meade's order to renew the attacks elicited the same reaction: field commanders ignored it. "An assault under such conditions I looked on as involving a wanton waste of life," replied Smith. No one attacked, although the soldiers sometimes fired furiously from cover.[79]

BURNSIDE'S IX CORPS and Warren's V Corps were also supposed to attack at 4:30 a.m., but they did not. Two and a half hours later, at 7 a.m., they finally began their advance—after the assaults by II, VI, and XVIII Corps were spent and the Union left flank was becoming quiet. IX and V Corps advanced a few hundred yards and dug in without capturing any Rebel breastworks.

Grant rode along the lines about 11 a.m., consulting with his generals. What he learned was not encouraging. At 12:30 p.m., he wrote to Meade, "The opinion of the Corps commanders not being sanguine of success in case an assault is ordered, you may direct a suspension of farther advance for the present. Hold our most advanced positions, and strengthen them."[80]

Theodore Lyman thought he saw a bright side in the army's colossal failure. The troops, he wrote, demonstrated "staunchness" by not retreating when "the fire was too hot for them to advance and the works too strong . . . but lay down where some small ridge offered a little cover, and there staid [sic]."[81]

GRANT'S REPORT TO General Halleck was terse and understated. "We assaulted at 4:30 a.m. this morning, driving the enemy within his entrenchments at all points, but without gaining any decisive advantage. . . . Our loss was not severe, nor do I suppose the enemy to have lost heavily."

Grant later conceded that it was a mistake to continue the attacks after the first one failed. "I have always regretted that the last assault at Cold Harbor was ever made," he wrote in his *Memoirs*. "I might say the same thing of the assault of the 22nd of May 1863 at Vicksburg. At Cold Harbor no advantage whatever was gained to compensate for the heavy loss we sustained. Indeed, the advantages, other than those of relative losses, were on the Confederate side."[82]

Fighting flared and receded throughout the day, and as darkness fell, the Confederates launched limited counterattacks on Gibbon's and Barlow's lines, only to suffer the same fate that had befallen II Corps that morning.

BLUE, CRUMPLED FORMS covered the ground where the attacks were made. Union losses for the day came to 5,600, according to Grant's chief of staff, Andrew Humphreys, but modern historians have placed the casualty total closer to 5,000. While sobering enough, it fell short of the single-day losses at the Wilderness and Spotsylvania Court House on May 5, 6, and 12.

But the losses were shocking because most of the casualties occurred in just an hour, and because of the battle's one-sidedness: the Rebels' losses amounted to just several hundred.[83]

Half of the Union casualties had occurred in Hancock's II Corps, which had committed seven of its twelve brigades to the fight, compared with three brigades from XVIII Corps and just one from VI Corps. It was a "terrible slaughter," wrote Hancock. "The old corps had received a blow from which it can scarcely recover. . . . Altogether this has been one of the most disastrous days the Army of the Potomac has ever seen, and the old Second Corps has especially suffered."

Private Robert Gomaer of the 8th New York Heavy Artillery wrote, "Dead and wounded lie from the pits we left to the rebel works, but at the works they were almost heaped up in places." Gibbon's division had begun the campaign with 6,799 men, and its losses now totaled 4,700. "The quality of the loss was what made it almost disastrous," Gibbon wrote, "for the very best officers, and the very bravest men were those who fell."[84]

Yet, the soldiers that were still in the lines remained full of fight. After Gibbon's men repelled a Confederate counterattack late in the day, the men shouted, "Bring on some more Johnnies, there aren't enough of you!"

Days after the June 3 attacks, burial details found a bloodstained diary among the personal effects collected from the Union dead on the battlefield. The diary's final entry read, "June 3. Cold Harbor. I was killed."[85]

LEE WAS ABSENT from the battlefield, after having supervised the placement of his defenses with his usual engineer's thoroughness. Still recovering from his illness, Lee tired quickly, and so he kept close to his headquarters near Gaines's Mill, less than a mile from the fighting. Listening to the roar of artillery and musketry, he tried to imagine what was happening. If the Yankees breached the line, Lee would have to weaken another area in order to scrape up reinforcements. He had no reserves.

He breathed easier as the minutes passed without any sign that his wiry veterans were in retreat. Shells sent up geysers of mud in the field where he had located his headquarters, and wounded soldiers appeared, headed for the rear, but their numbers were small. Lee dispatched couriers and staff officers to the front to bring him reports of the fighting.

They were all favorable. A. P. Hill led the courier sent to him to a field where Union dead lay in heaps. "Tell General Lee it is the same all along my front."[86]

"The dead and dying lay in front of the Confederate lines in triangles," wrote Charles Venable, Lee's aide, "of which the apexes were the bravest men who came nearest to the breastworks under the withering, deadly fire." He characterized the victory as "perhaps the easiest ever granted to Confederate arms by the folly of Federal commanders."[87]

About 11 a.m., Confederate Postmaster General John Reagan and two judges from Richmond arrived at Lee's headquarters. They nervously inquired about the artillery fire, which to them seemed dangerously close. Lee replied that there was more gunfire than usual, but "that does not do much harm here." He waved his hand toward the lines, where, according to Reagan, the musketry sounded like a sheet being ripped. "It is that that kills men," said Lee.

Lee asked Reagan to have potatoes and onions sent to the army when he returned to Richmond. "Some of the men now have scurvy," Lee said. Reagan promised to send the vegetables.

Later, Jefferson Davis, who had spent the morning in Richmond celebrating his fifty-sixth birthday with his family, rode out to army headquarters, where the mood was jubilant.[88]

In a brief report to War Secretary James Seddon, Lee said that every Union attack that day had been repulsed. "Our loss today has been small, and our success, under the blessing of God, all that we could expect."[89]

WHEN ASKED BY Meade for his opinion on renewing the assault, "Baldy" Smith, the XVIII Corps commander, replied, "I can only say, that what I failed to do to-day—namely, to carry the enemy's works on the front by columns of assault . . . I would hardly dare to recommend as practicable to-morrow with my diminished force."[90]

The Union attack was haphazardly planned and executed by the Army of the Potomac leadership. Little reconnaissance was conducted. The attack's postponement from June 2 was a gift to the Confederates, enabling them to establish unassailable defenses. The attack was dispersed along a seven-mile front, rather than concentrated at one or two points. Fewer than half of the brigades in the three corps that attacked Lee's right even went into action.

Had Grant and Meade concentrated on Lee's right and attacked June 1 or 2, they might have driven him from his lines. One also wonders what might have happened if Grant had not sent away half of his artillery—if he had been able to train every gun on the Confederate breastworks and perhaps blast a path through them.

Meade, the operational commander, had not unduly exerted himself to ensure the attack's success. With unseemly smugness, he viewed its failure as vindication of his views on the futility of attacking entrenched enemy troops. To his wife, Meade could not help but crow, "I think Grant has had his eyes opened, and is willing to admit now that Virginia and Lee's army is not Tennessee and [Braxton] Bragg's army."[91]

Northern newspaper accounts of the battle ranged from sober and factual to hyperbolic. Among the latter was the New York *Daily News*, which reported: "Since Wednesday morning we have lost at least ten thousand men, and but few of that number were captured. The wounds are horrible and ghastly." William Swinton of the New York *Times* wrote, "Judged by the severity of the encounter and the heavy losses we have experienced, the engagement which opened at gray dawn this morning, and spent its fury in little over an hour, should take its place among the battles of the war; but, viewed in its relations to the whole campaign, it is, perhaps, hardly more than a grand reconnaissance." "The attack was brave and our loss was severe, but the result was indecisive. Generally our line was advanced materially," reported the New York *Tribune*. The Savannah (Georgia) *Republican's* report concluded: "A gracious God has given the Confederate arms another victory—a victory that is almost bloodless to them, but fearfully fatal to their enemies."[92]

Assistant War Secretary Dana observed that the Battle of Cold Harbor has been "exaggerated into one of the bloodiest disasters in history. . . . It was nothing of the kind. The outlook warranted the effort. The breaking of Lee's lines meant his destruction and the collapse of the rebellion." The British historian and general J. F. C. Fuller believed that the battle's importance has been "grossly exaggerated." "It was not a great battle, or a decisive battle, or a very costly battle," he wrote in 1932.[93]

Indeed, on this war's crimson scale, Cold Harbor was not in the upper range. Daily slaughter on the battlefields of Virginia and Georgia had become almost commonplace. General William Sherman wrote to his wife Ellen that he had begun to view "the death and mangling of a couple thousand men as a small affair, a kind of morning dash—and it may be well that we become so hardened."[94]

4

Saturday, June 4–Saturday, June 11, 1864
Cold Harbor

AT TWILIGHT ON June 3, the mortal enemies uneasily occupied positions that were just thirty yards apart in places. Theodore Lyman told his wife, "I think nothing can give a greater idea of deathless tenacity of purpose, than the picture of those two hosts, after a bloody and near continuous struggle of thirty days, thus lying down to sleep with their hands almost on each other's throats!"[95]

Indeed, a week would pass before anything changed, for strategic reasons important to Grant. "To aid the expedition under General [David] Hunter it is necessary that we should detain all the army now with Lee until the former gets well on his way to Lynchburg," Grant said.[96]

For soldiers of both armies it meant living like burrowing animals. They broiled in the June heat while crouched in a welter of stitched-together trenches and bomb shelters that reminded Surgeon George T. Stevens of VI Corps "of the colonies of prairie dogs with their burrows and mounds." For many, the misery experienced during the days following Cold Harbor exceeded anything they had previously endured.

"The heat is intolerable, and the roads are covered with dust six or eight inches deep, which every gust of wind sweeps up, covering everything with a dirty, white coating," wrote surgeon John Perry of the 20th Massachusetts.

The dust got into everything—clothes, coffee, and food. "It fills our hair and mingles with the sweat on our faces," wrote Private Wilbur Fisk of the 2nd Vermont.[97]

The Confederates made lean-to shelters by jabbing their muskets in the ground, bayonets first, and inserting the corners of a blanket under the musket hammers. Four men could crowd into the shade made by one blanket.[98]

The squalid conditions eerily adumbrated the static trench warfare that would grip Europe fifty years hence. Artillery fire erupted periodically, and sharpshooters "put a bullet wherever you show a head." There were trench raids. The open field between the armies was "a strip of land across which no man dares to pass," Private Fisk observed. "An attacking party from either side would be mown down like grass."[99]

The Yankees who dug in where their attacks stopped were brought—at great peril, under fire—proper entrenching tools to deepen their trenches at night. The ditches did not follow straight lines, but zigzagged, in order to thwart flanking fire, and were linked by communications trenches. Deep passageways, covered with leaves and boughs, were excavated from the rear to the fighting trenches. Farther back, the ground was honeycombed with one-man rifle pits. As the days passed, the trenches acquired embellishments: shell-proofs, firing steps, loopholes, even carved shelves for cartridges.

Anyone who dared to rise out of the trenches, day or night, even to relieve himself, instantly drew the sharpshooters' fire. "The air was filled with whistling bullets," wrote Union engineer Wesley Brainerd, "yet not a man could be seen, nothing but a dull line of fresh yellowish earth. During the daytime, puffs of white smoke might be seen rising above the dirt and, at night, "bright flashes of fire."[100]

Siege approaches were begun by engineering troops assigned to each corps. Brainerd wrote, "We had now no idea but that we were to approach Richmond from this point." Only II Corps, whose lines were closest to the Rebels, made any progress. The innovative Barlow took matters further, assigning men to dig a mine that approached the enemy line—the first in the Army of the Potomac's history. The mine advanced forty feet before it was abandoned.[101]

"Constant fighting is going on, killing without any battle," a Union man observed. Brief assaults were attempted and repulsed. Soldiers drew lots to decide who would hazard the trip to replenish empty canteens; often, the runner was shot down before he got water and a replacement had to be sent, sprinting back with full canteens as musket fire spattered around him. The day and night gunfire by skirmishers and sharpshooters made Yankees and Rebels jittery and irritable. Edward Porter Alexander, the Confederate artillery commander, wrote to his wife that he wished Grant would "do something, for I am very tired of stooping & crawling through the trenches every day in the hot sun, with Minie balls shaving the parapet above & soldiers crowding the ground beneath."[102]

Soldiers in both armies grew to hate the incessant sharpshooting. Confederate Major Robert Stiles said a sharpshooter seemed "little better than a human tiger lying in wait for blood," training his weapon on a particular spot until the target "darkens the hole, crash goes a bullet through his brain." Snipers' and skirmishers' bullets chipped and gouged cannons, and when someone set a tin cup on the breastworks, "in less than a minute they put three holes through it."[103]

Private Fisk, whose battery was under fire almost constantly from skirmishers and sharpshooters, made a study of the various sounds made by the bullets: sometimes a "sharp 'clit,' like striking a cabbage leaf with a whip lash"; other times, "a sort of screech, like stepping on a cat's tail"; others whistled "on a much higher key," or made a sound like "a huge bumble bee."[104]

A corporal in the 15th New Jersey was digging a grave when he asked the colonel to send a man to help lay the dead soldier in the ground. At that instant, "he drew himself up, and instantly a musket ball struck him in the face, and he fell, dying." The grave was widened to accommodate two.[105]

One day, Alexander sprinted across a gap in the parapets and dove into a hole. He found himself sharing it with two dead soldiers, recently killed by gunshot wounds to the head, and a living one, crouched in a corner. "By Gosh!" the survivor exclaimed. "You have to be mighty careful how you shows a head around here."[106]

MEADE POLLED HIS corps commanders about whether they believed a new assault stood a good chance of success. Without exception, they said no. A letter that Barlow wrote to Hancock on this subject found its way into the hands of Meade and Grant, and they decided to make no more attacks at Cold Harbor. "I do not think it expedient to assault again at present. The men feel just at present a great horror and dread of attacking earth-works again," Barlow had written. "I think the men are so wearied and worn out by the harassing labors of the past week that they are wanting in the spirit and dash necessary for successful assaults." Soon after reading Barlow's letter, Grant decided that the army would again sidle to the southeast—once he was certain that Hunter's Shenandoah Valley army had marched beyond Lee's reach.[107]

In the meantime, the heat and constant gunfire exacted their toll. "I am almost give out. I wonder at my holding up as well as I do," Colonel William Speer of the 28th North Carolina told his parents. "This is 32 days we have been fighting & I have been under fire every day in the time, except about four days. I have never seen anything like this in my life, but I will not grumble, if my life will only be spared."[108]

All around the armies were the shallow graves of soldiers killed two years earlier at the Battle of Gaines's Mill. At night, some soldiers noticed a strange phenomenon, probably caused by phosphorus gases escaping from the still decomposing corpses. "At night these old graves would shine with a phosphorescent light most spooky and weird, while on the surface of the ground, above the ghastly glimmering dead, lay thousands of dead that could not be buried," wrote Private David Holt of the 16th Mississippi.[109]

Perhaps the worst of the miseries of trench life, as the days passed, was the stench of those unburied dead, accompanied by the fading cries of the wounded, fewer by the hour, stranded in no man's land. "Under the rays of the hot June sun, the bodies of the fast-decomposing dead sent over into our trenches a most sickening and nauseating stench," wrote Adjutant R. T. Coles of the 4th Alabama, "while the helpless and fly-infested wounded were left to die a most horrible death." Surgeon Daniel Holt of the 121st New York wrote that the smell of putrefying bodies "flavors your food." Colonel William C. Oates of the 15th Alabama noted that the dead from Smith's XVIII Corps covered more than five acres "about as thickly as they could be laid." Fortunately for the Rebels, he wrote, breezes carried the odor away from them and toward the Union lines.[110]

Captain A. C. Brown of the 4th New York Heavy Artillery noted that while nighttime was cooler, it was not peaceful; both armies' artillery periodically sent shells into the enemy lines. But Brown derived enjoyment from witnessing what he described as "a beautiful sight . . . the lines of fire in the darkness caused by the burning fuses of the shells when coming toward us."[111]

WOUNDED MEN WERE dying hourly on the battlefield. The situation was especially bad in front of the 7th New York Heavy Artillery—the regiment that had suffered some of the highest losses on June 3, and that also was less than thirty yards away from the Rebel line. In the dead zone lay the regiment's wounded and dead comrades.

They might as well have been miles away, for all the good their proximity did. The Rebels shot the wounded where they lay and fired on anyone who tried to rescue them. "This caused some bitter feelings toward the rebels, to permit their troops to fire on our stretcher bearers, when our object and our mission was so plainly to be seen," a soldier wrote. The New Yorkers could only watch in horror as dehydration and lack of medical treatment carried off their wounded comrades, and as the sun and insects obliterated the features of the dead.[112]

Early June 7, Private Daniel McCullock of the 7th crawled the last yards from no man's land to an advance trench and fell in. His Yankee comrades were stunned by his sudden appearance. McCullock said he had found shelter on June 3 in a shallow trench with two other wounded men. Each night they dragged themselves closer to the Union lines, hiding during the daytime from the Rebel sharpshooters. His companions had died. After spending a day with their corpses in a rifle pit, McCullock made it to the lines. That night, he, too, died from the effects of his ordeal.[113]

GRANT DID NOT attempt to retrieve his wounded until June 5, two days after the battle. In a letter to Lee, Grant proposed that "when no battle is raging, either party be authorized to send to any point between the picket and skirmish line, unarmed men bearing litters, to pick up their dead or wounded without being fired upon by the other party."

Professing concern that "such an arrangement will lead to misunderstanding and difficulty," Lee rejected Grant's plan. Instead, he said, whenever Grant wished to remove dead or wounded men, he should send a flag of truce to the Confederate command. "It will always afford me pleasure to comply with such a request, as far as circumstances will permit."[114]

Grant very much wished to avoid sending a flag of truce seeking Lee's permission to retrieve his casualties, with its implied acknowledgment that he had lost the battle and that the Southerners controlled the battlefield.

Rather than send a flag of truce, on June 6 Grant announced to Lee that he would send out parties between noon and 3 p.m. to collect the dead and wounded.

Lee would have none of it. "I . . . regret to find that I didn't make myself understood in my communication of yesterday," Lee wrote, adding that he could not give his consent until he received Grant's request for a truce. For Lee, collecting the wounded was of no consequence; the Rebels had none stranded between the lines.

With great reluctance, Grant gave in and sent his request to Lee under a truce flag. "The knowledge that wounded men are now suffering from want of attention . . . compels me to ask a suspension of hostilities," Grant wrote.

Lee replied late June 6 that Grant's request arrived so late that it could not be complied with until nighttime. He agreed to a truce between 8 and 10 that night. "During the interval, all military movement will be suspended," he said.

But Grant did not receive Lee's message until midnight, he told Lee at 10:30 a.m. on June 7, and he missed the period for gathering up his wounded. Lee responded with a proposal that the truce take place that night, between 6 and 8 p.m. Grant acceded and also volunteered to return six Rebels captured while attempting to retrieve an officer's body.[115]

AT 8 P.M. on June 7—four and a half days after the battle—the truce went into effect. "Hundreds and thousands of both parties swarmed over the neutral ground, conversing in the most kind and friendly manner," wrote David Holt, the Mississippi private. Enemy officers shared bottles of alcohol. Thousands of troops emerged from behind their breastworks to shake out their dusty blankets and enjoy freedom of movement for an hour or two.[116]

As the enemies mingled and conversed, there was temporary amity, but sometimes discord. "The Rebels were anxious to know who would be the next President," wrote Theodore Lyman, who helped arrange the truce. "'Wall,' said one of our men, 'I am in favor of Old Abe.' 'He's a damned Abolitionist!' promptly exclaimed a grey-back. Upon which our man hit his adversary between the eyes, and a general fisticuff ensued, only stopped by the officers rushing in."[117]

Of the thousands of wounded men left on the field after the June 3 battle, all but two had succumbed to either sharpshooters, exposure to the hostile elements, or lack of water, food, and medical care. One of the miracle survivors, his leg fractured by enemy fire, subsisted on grass that he pulled up with his hands, and the dew that collected on it. Pride and callousness in both armies' high commands had caused the unnecessary tragedy.[118]

By this time, the dead were "black as coal," putrid, and crawling with beetles. Their bodies fell to pieces when any attempt was made to move them. Some were rolled into shallow graves where they fell; others were laid side-by-side in trenches with a cloth placed over their faces before dirt was thrown on them.[119]

REBELS AND YANKEES entrenched a stone's throw from one another were soon shouting questions back and forth. On June 8, Lieutenant Joseph Hodgkins of the 19th Massachusetts, whose regiment was fifty yards away from the enemy trenches, reported that the Rebels "agreed not to fire this morning, if we would not."

It was a quiet day on the battle lines. The 15th New Jersey and the Georgia troops across from them exchanged newspapers, shaking hands and "parting with good wishes for each other's welfare." The spatters of gunfire that briefly occurred were aimed high or low and did no harm.

On June 9, the enemies swapped knives, tobacco, and coffee, and talked politics. But then, Rebel officers stopped the fraternization and ordered the Confederates to open fire. The Rebels called out, "Get into your holes, Yanks, we are going to fire," and fired over their heads until they were able to take cover. The hostilities resumed, but casualties fell off sharply.[120]

The Confederates had developed a grudging respect for Grant's relentlessness, even if they did not entirely understand it. "Grant is the most obstinate fighter we have ever met," wrote Major Eugene Blackford of the

5th Alabama. "He has resolved to lose every man rather than retreat, which he knows is equivalent to our independence." General Evander Law said the Rebels had expected Grant to be "bold and aggressive," but were unprepared for "the unparalleled stubbornness and tenacity with which he persisted in his attacks under the fearful losses which his army sustained at the Wilderness and at Spotsylvania."[121]

"Brave men have been killed and maimed most fearfully," wrote Navy Secretary Gideon Welles after Cold Harbor, "*but Grant persists* [emphasis added]."[122]

GEORGE MEADE, WHO was prone to brooding even in good times, was feeling slighted and unhappy again. The Northern press and the Lincoln administration were overlooking his contributions, he believed, and Grant was getting all of the credit. In a letter to his wife, Meade remarked on an editorial extolling "the wonderful genius of Grant. Now, to tell the truth, the letter has greatly disappointed me, and since this campaign I really begin to think I am something of a general."

His mood darkened even more when the Philadelphia *Inquirer* published an article alleging that Meade had advocated withdrawal across the Rapidan River on May 6, after the second day of battle in the Wilderness. Furious, Meade summoned the reporter, Edward Crapsey, and demanded an explanation for his "base and wicked lie." Crapsey said it had been "the talk of the camp," but could not otherwise back up the story.

Meade decided to make an example of Crapsey. He issued a proclamation denouncing his "falsehood" and ordered Crapsey paraded through the camps. The reporter was lashed to a broken-down mule, facing its tail, and was forced to wear a placard bearing the inscription, "Libeler of the Press." With a drum corps playing the "Rogue's March," Crapsey was expelled from the army. Meade told his wife that Grant had agreed to the punishment, even though he knew Crapsey and his family from Illinois and regarded them favorably.[123]

The army instinctively distrusted the press, jealously guarding its plans from prying reporters. Early in the campaign, Grant had given a staff officer verbal instructions for the night and then had read them verbatim

three days later in a Richmond newspaper, which reprinted a report from a
Northern publication. Not long afterward, William Swinton, an English-
man who wrote for the New York *Times*, was caught eavesdropping outside
Grant's tent and driven off. Weeks later, at Cold Harbor, Burnside ordered
Swinton shot for eavesdropping. Grant commuted Swinton's death sentence
to expulsion from the army.[124]

But by publicly humiliating Crapsey, Meade had gone too far, in the opinion of the other newspaper correspondents, and he paid a price for it. The
reporters reached an "expressed understanding to ignore General Meade in
every possible way and manner," wrote Sylvanus Cadwallader. "From that
time till the next spring, Gen. Meade was quite as much unknown, by any
correspondence from the army, as any dead hero of antiquity."[125]

Meade's disgruntlement became aggrievement when he discovered that
in letters written by Stanton about the campaign's progress, "my name was
never alluded to." Suspecting that Grant was trumpeting his own accomplishments in reports to Stanton without mentioning Meade's role, Meade
was poised to confront Grant. But he then learned that Assistant War Secretary Dana, and not Grant, was the author of the reports.

Meade broached the subject with Grant and, to his relief, Grant agreed
with him that the reports were unfair to Meade. "He told me he had never
sent a dispatch [sic] to Mr. Stanton since crossing the Rapidan, the few
despatches [he] had sent being directed to General Halleck," Meade told
his wife. "I was glad to hear this, because it removed from my mind a prej-
udice I had imbibed"—that Grant was stealing credit from him. This crisis
had passed, but Meade would always believe that he received inadequate
recognition.[126]

NO OTHER UNION corps was as battered as Grant's best fighting unit, II
Corps. Its losses through Cold Harbor, where its casualties totaled 2,500,
now added up to 15,710, roughly two-thirds of its original complement.
Among the dead and wounded were 27 general and field officers. In the
22nd Massachusetts, Walter Carter was able to count just twenty familiar
faces out of the "many score" with whom he had crossed the Rapidan. "It is
so sad," he wrote. Worse, several II Corps regiments demobilized after Cold
Harbor when their three-year men completed their service.

Hancock's corps had been heavily reinforced, but the replacements' quality was noticeably lower. Many were slum-dwellers and criminals who had been recruited and given sizeable bounties—and who were ready to desert at the first opportunity. The veterans were contemptuous of the new soldiers. "Lee's veterans drown them?" one of them said to Private Frank Wilkeson. "Yes, they could push them into the James River with pine poles, and as they sank would howl for mercy in 27 languages."[127]

The veterans had had their confidence in their leaders "severely shaken" by the hopeless Cold Harbor attacks into which II Corps had sent more brigades than any other corps. A regimental commander returning to the lines after one of the failed attacks said that he "would not take his regiment into another such charge, if Jesus Christ himself should order it."

At Cold Harbor, wrote Lieutenant Colonel Charles Morgan, II Corps "received a mortal blow, and never again was the same body of men." Engineer George D. Bowers wrote, "There was no demoralization visible but a settled commotion which showed itself plainly in the faces of every Officer and every man."[128]

WOUNDED MEN CONTINUED to pour into Washington. "I was glad to get home out of the city," Elizabeth Lee wrote to her husband, Admiral Samuel Phillips Lee. "The lines of ambulances & the moans of their poor suffering men were too much for our nerves." A little later, Mrs. Lee reported that the hospitals "cannot accommodate any more—they will take the churches again and urge the Citizens to open their houses to those too ill to go further."[129]

Steamers kept constantly in service transporting the wounded to hospitals became cesspools of contagion and infection. After inspecting some of the vessels, Charles Dana concluded that the steamers USS *Connecticut* and *State of Maine* "are not clean enough to transport wounded. On *State of Maine* I saw one bed which had become saturated from its former occupants and was now putrid, containing maggots. On the *Connecticut* I also saw beef, cut up for the wounded, so fat and gristly that even the well could not eat it."[130]

Reinforcements continued to flow to Grant's army. On June 7, Henry Halleck told Grant that since the campaign began, he had sent him 48,265 replacement troops, but that he was now near the end of the manpower on hand. "I shall send you a few regiments more, when all the resources will be exhausted till another draft is made."[131]

GRANT WAS DISAPPOINTED by his army's failure at Cold Harbor, but it did not affect his belief in ultimate victory. "Success was only a matter of time," he told his military secretary, Adam Badeau, the day after the attack. A few days later, in a letter to Congressman Elihu B. Washburne, Grant wrote, "Everything is progressing favorably but slowly. All the fight, except defensive and behind breast works, is taken out of Lee's army. Unless my next move brings on a battle, the balance of the campaign will settle down to a siege."[132]

During the lull, Grant wrote letters home. He sent his wife Julia a lock of his hair, which she had requested. He told her, "War will get to be so common with me if this thing continues much longer that I will not be able to sleep after a while unless there is an occasional gun shot near me during the night." To his eight-year-old daughter, Nelly, he promised a buggy so that she and her brother Jess "can ride about the country during vacation."[133]

GRANT'S ARMY REMAINED in its Cold Harbor entrenchments, pinning Lee's men in front of Richmond while General Hunter advanced southward through the Shenandoah Valley. Hunter routed a small Rebel force at Piedmont and captured 1,000 men. Confederate General W. E. "Grumble" Jones was killed during the battle while trying to rally his men. On June 6, Hunter's men seized Staunton, which stood at the crossroads of the Shenandoah Valley and roads leading east to Richmond. Two days later, Hunter was joined by two divisions from West Virginia, those of Generals George Crook and William Averell, increasing the army's strength to 20,000 men.[134]

When Grant learned that Hunter had reached Staunton, he ordered Phil Sheridan to ride at dawn June 7 with two cavalry divisions to rendezvous with Hunter at Charlottesville. Sheridan's 5,500 cavalrymen and four horse-artillery batteries were to destroy the Virginia Central Railroad "from about Beaver Dam for some 25 or 30 miles west," and wreck the James River canal. The railroad and the canal were the conduits for food, clothing, and weapons to Lee and Richmond from the Shenandoah Valley and Lynchburg. "It is desirable that every rail on the road destroyed should be so bent or twisted as to make it impossible to repair the road without supplying new rails," Grant said. James Wilson's cavalry division would remain with Grant for the campaign's last act.[135]

FOR WEEKS, GRANT had anticipated crossing the James River and uniting with Benjamin Butler's Army of the James. Besides destroying Lee's army, Grant had also wanted to sever the supply lines to Richmond from the west and south. While Sheridan and Hunter tore up the railroad and canal west of Richmond, Meade and Butler's men would cut the railroad lines entering Petersburg from the south and southwest, and thence continue to Richmond.

Halleck, however, disliked Grant's plan; he believed the Army of the Potomac should approach Richmond from Cold Harbor in slow, methodical stages—much as Halleck had done in Corinth, Mississippi, in 1862. (Halleck's approach, in fact, was so glacial that the Confederates were gone when Union troops reached the city.)

But Richmond's defenses were formidable, and Grant knew that a prolonged siege would sap public support and might cost Lincoln reelection in November. "Without a greater sacrifice of human life than I am willing to make all cannot be accomplished that I had designed outside of the city," he wrote. The enemy was now operating "purely on the defensive, behind breast works, or feebly on the offensive immediately in front of him." Movement was now the army's best strategy, said Grant. "Our Army is not only confidant [sic] of protecting itself, without intrenchments, but that it can beat and drive the enemy whenever and wherever he can be found without this protection."

He pointed out that by maneuvering south of the James, he could intercept supplies bound for Richmond, except those coming down the James River canal from the west. "If Hunter succeeds in reaching Lynchburg that will be lost to him [Lee] also," Grant wrote.[136]

RICHMOND WAS ALREADY in a bad way. "During the week all are shabby," John Jones, the War Department clerk, wrote in his diary. "The wonder is that we are not naked, after wearing the same garments three or four years." Food shortages had become routine because the rail lines were frequently cut by Union troops. "No provisions have come in, especially for the army," Jones wrote at the end of May. Speculators had bid up prices to astronomical levels: flour was selling for up to $400 a barrel and corn meal, $125.[137]

But during the days after the Cold Harbor attack, Lee's army received a rations shipment that included not only bacon and cornbread, but coffee, sugar, molasses, peas, cabbage, and onions. Confederate surgeon Thomas Wood, working at a field hospital in a Hanover County apple orchard, told his wife that the army's proximity to Richmond meant that soldiers were getting "a-plenty of everything," sometimes even wheat, or "a ration of baker's bread." Wishing to help hungry civilians in Richmond, some Confederate units set aside one day's ration from their weekly allotment for the city's poor. General Clement Evans's Georgia Brigade of the Second Corps contributed 1,000 pounds of bacon, 2,000 pounds of flour, and coffee and sugar. The Richmond *Examiner* praised the soldiers' generosity, adding, "We trust that their generous contribution will awaken throughout the country a hearty response."[138]

The hiatus from want would not last.

5

Saturday, June 11–Monday, June 13, 1864
Trevilian Station

ON JUNE 7, as Sheridan and his cavalrymen were leaving for Charlottesville on their destroying mission, Lee was sending General John Breckinridge's division back to the Shenandoah Valley. Lee and Jefferson Davis knew that Breckinridge's 2,100 men were too few to stop Hunter's army and so, after deliberation, they decided to dispatch Early's Second Corps as well. The combined force, plus the Confederate troops already in the Valley, would give the Rebels 15,000 men to Hunter's 20,000. But it drew Lee's army down to 40,000 troops or less, which concerned Lee and Davis. However, General Braxton Bragg assured Davis that Grant's army was unlikely to attack again at Cold Harbor. "Grant has been so much crippled by his constant repulses . . . that I apprehend but little damage from him now," he wrote.[139]

Lee certainly hoped so, having sent away two fighting divisions. But he believed that Early could drive Hunter from the Shenandoah Valley—and then be positioned to "strike a decisive blow." Lee foresaw Early marching down the valley into Maryland and threatening Washington and Baltimore. Looking over the vast chessboard compassing all of Virginia and Maryland, Lee the grand strategist saw this as benefiting him in one of two ways. It would compel Grant either to weaken his army in order to deal with Early, or to launch a desperate attack on Lee in the hope of forcing Lee to recall Early.[140]

Learning that Sheridan had crossed the Pamunkey River on June 8 with two cavalry divisions, horse artillery, ambulances, wagons, and cattle, Lee sent the cavalry divisions of Fitz Lee and Wade Hampton up the Virginia Central Railroad to shadow the Union troopers, "keeping the enemy on their right, and shape their course according to this." It went without saying that if the opportunity presented itself, Hampton and Fitz Lee should bar Sheridan's way to Charlottesville and force him to fight.[141]

The departure of the Confederate cavalry pleased Grant, who had hoped to lure Hampton and Lee away from Cold Harbor so that he might execute his next maneuver without their interference. He later wrote that this "freed us from the annoyance by the cavalry of the enemy for more than two-weeks." Grant's orders to Sheridan never stipulated that this was an object of Sheridan's ride toward Charlottesville, but Sheridan claimed that it was. "The diversion of the enemy's cavalry from the south side of the Chickahominy was [the raid's] main purpose," he later wrote.[142]

As a diversion, Sheridan's expedition succeeded brilliantly. But little else went right.

At Trevilian Station, a whistle stop on the Virginia Central Railroad fifty miles northwest of Richmond, Sheridan's two divisions collided with Hampton's and Lee's troopers, their adversaries at Haw's Shop and Cold Harbor.

Hampton's division blocked Sheridan's way and forced him to fight. Fitz Lee joined in, and at the end of a pitched battle lasting all day June 11, Sheridan's troopers occupied Trevilian Station.

When the Yankees resumed their march westward the next day, they discovered that Hampton's and Lee's cavalrymen had dug entrenchments in the Union troopers' path. Repeated attacks failed to break the Rebel lines.

And then, from Rebel prisoners Sheridan learned that the situation in Charlottesville was not what he had expected: Confederate General John Breckinridge's infantry division, and not Hunter, occupied the city; Hunter had not gone to Charlottesville, but was marching directly to Lynchburg.

Not relishing the prospect of taking on Hampton, Lee, and Breckinridge with a dwindling ammunition supply and 500 wounded, Sheridan turned back, after first tearing up a few miles of rails between Trevilian Station and Louisa Court House.[143]

Southern newspapers pronounced Trevilian Station a Confederate victory, but Sheridan's expedition had efficiently deprived the Army of Northern Virginia of its "eyes" when it would need them most.

LEE WAS CERTAIN that Grant would move again, but where? Grant had several viable options, Lee believed, but he was unsure which of them Grant would pursue. Grant might try to slip around the Confederates and push toward Richmond; he could march to McClellan's old battleground on the Peninsula between the Chickahominy and James Rivers and besiege the capital; he could return Smith's XVIII Corps to Butler and then attack Richmond and Petersburg simultaneously; or he could cross the James and invest Petersburg. Having sent away nearly one-fourth of his army to deal with Hunter and Sheridan, Lee could only watch and wait.[144]

P. G. T. Beauregard, his men acting as the "cork" in Butler's bottled-up army at Bermuda Hundred, discerned Grant's intentions with eerie prescience. "Should Grant have left Lee's front," he warned Braxton Bragg on June 7, "he doubtless intends operating against Richmond, along James River [sic], probably on the southern side. Petersburg, nearly defenseless, would be captured before it could be reinforced." He recommended that Ransom's and Hoke's divisions be returned to him. Petersburg's capitulation, he said, would be Richmond's death knell.[145]

GRANT'S PLAN TO steal a march on Lee was daringly audacious: to quietly withdraw more than 100,000 men from a ten-mile front—in some places thirty yards from the enemy—march forty miles over dust-choked roads to the James River, and cross it on pontoon bridges, ferries, and anything else that floated.

Because crossing the James had always been part of Grant's campaign strategy, the army had been stockpiling bridging material since mid-April. The plan reprised Grant's 1863 crossing of the Mississippi River below Vicksburg in which he outflanked John Pemberton's army.[146]

The logistics were trickier than at Vicksburg. There were more troops involved, and two rivers to cross. The engineers were busy. Entrenchments were dug beyond Grant's left flank to protect the place where the army would cross the sluggish Chickahominy River, whose brown waters were broken by tall cypresses. The river was low-banked and swampy, and corduroying was necessary around the bridge approaches and three pontoon bridges. Then, pontoon boats and their hardware had to be shipped to Wilcox's Landing, the designated crossing on the James River. Also sent there were ferries, schooners, and tugboats, as well as gunboats to protect the convoy.[147]

After nightfall on Sunday, June 12, regimental bands played every song in their repertoires and pickets opened fire sporadically to conceal the noise of the Army of the Potomac's withdrawal from the Cold Harbor lines—a slickly synchronized movement that culminated nearly a week of planning. Corn stalks had been spread on the ground to muffle the sound of hooves. Gun crews wrapped their wheel rims in straw. The Yankees crept out of their trenches on their hands and knees and left Cold Harbor.[148]

James Wilson's cavalry division went first, wading the Chickahominy at Long Bridge, where the bridges had been destroyed. When the cavalry secured the south bank, pontoon boats were brought up, and V Corps went over. Warren's men and Wilson's troopers then turned west, marching to Riddell's Shop in a feint toward Richmond.

They seized every crossroad between the Chickahominy and James rivers to prevent the Confederates from observing the army's movement. II Corps followed V Corps over the river at Long Bridge, while VI and IX Corps marched to Jones's Bridge five miles downriver. The three corps headed directly for the James, shielded by Warren's and Wilson's screen.

Meanwhile, Smith's XVIII infantrymen marched down the Pamunkey River to White House and boarded transports to return to Butler's army at Bermuda Hundred.[149]

GRANT WAS GONE, Lee's skirmishers reported after finding the Union trenches empty early June 13—the fortieth day of Grant's campaign. "At daybreak this morning it was discovered that the army of Genl Grant had left our front," Lee reported to War Secretary James Seddon. "The army was moved to conform to the route taken by him."

Lee sent the First and Third Corps—Early's Second Corps was on its way to the Shenandoah Valley—across the Chickahominy to block the roads to Richmond. The few Confederate cavalrymen that remained with the army after Hampton's and Fitz Lee's departure probed toward Riddell's Shop. Union cavalry drove them off.

Lee did not know where Grant's army was.

Early June 14, Lee sent the Third Corps to strike the Yankees on Long Bridge Road. They were not there.[150]

"A new element had entered into this move—the element of uncertainty," wrote Major Robert Stiles, a First Corps artilleryman. "Even Marse Robert, who knew everything knowable, did not appear to know what his old enemy proposed to do or where he would be most likely to find him."

Just as he did at the Rapidan River forty days earlier, so now, too, did Lee wait for Grant to act.[151]

CHAPTER 6

Race to Stalemate

THE JAMES RIVER

But, oh! That they had attacked at once. Petersburg would have gone like a rotten branch.

—LIEUTENANT COLONEL THEODORE LYMAN[1]

I begin to see it. You will succeed. God bless you all.

—ABRAHAM LINCOLN[2]

1

Wednesday, June 15–Saturday, June 18, 1864
Near Wilcox's Landing, Virginia

HANDS CLASPED BEHIND his back, Grant stood on the north bank of the James River on Wednesday morning, June 15, observing the grand spectacle unfolding before him—the Union army's passage over the sparkling waters of the James on possibly the longest pontoon bridge in military history. Seemingly endless columns of troops, wagons, and artillery from Ambrose Burnside's IX Corps filed over the 2,100-feet-long, 13-feet-wide span, the rifle and cannon barrels glittering in the sunlight.

Steamboats and transports plied the waters upriver from the bridge, carrying Winfield Scott Hancock's II Corps to the south bank "with the regularity of weavers' shuttles," observed Horace Porter. "Drums were beating the march, bands were playing stirring quicksteps, the distant booming of cannon on Warren's front showed that he and the enemy were still exchanging compliments."

The sounds mingled with the cheers of soldiers and sailors and the rumbling of caissons and wagons. The scene, "conceived and combined by a single man, for a single purpose—gave significance and moral grandeur to the scene," wrote Adam Badeau, Grant's military historian.[3]

Lieutenant Colonel Charles Francis Adams Jr. of the 5th Massachusetts Cavalry penned a more sobering description in a letter to his father, the US ambassador to England. "The men look dirty and tired; they toil along in loose, swaying columns. . . . Their clothes are torn, dusty and shabby." Along the way, Adams encountered his old friend, General Francis Barlow. Climbing a cherry tree, they snacked on cherries and chatted.[4]

After corduroying the swampy areas around the bridge approaches, Army engineers had assembled the span in just seven hours, finishing at 2 a.m. The crossing began immediately, with James Wilson's cavalry division going first. The bridge consisted of ninety-two pontoons, secured to three large schooners anchored upstream. It was "a great wonder," wrote Theodore Lyman, Meade's aide. Here, at Wilcox's Landing, the river ran fast and strong and was eighty-five feet deep. A tidal river, the James rose and fell four feet twice daily. Edward Porter Alexander, the Confederate First

Corps' artillery chief, pronounced it "the greatest bridge of boats since the time of Xerxes." By 10 a.m., II Corps was on the James's south bank.[5]

While waiting to cross, some soldiers looted the late President John Tyler's home, Sherwood Forest, just two miles away. "The house was stripped of almost everything," wrote George Stevens, a surgeon with the 77th New York. "The large library had lost many of its choicest volumes, while the remainder, with heaps of letters, lay thrown in wild confusion about the floor."[6]

"I WILL HAVE Petersburg secured if possible before they [Lee's troops] get there in much force," Grant telegraphed General Henry Halleck in Washington. "Our movement from Cold Harbor to the James River has been made with great celerity, and so far, without loss or accident."

Throughout the withdrawal from the Cold Harbor lines, Grant was unusually tense, unable to shake the fear that Lee would strike the Union army when it was vulnerable. But the complicated maneuver proceeded smoothly; Grant was even able to relax and take a nap on a board in a cool spot out of the choking dust. "Everything went perfectly from the start," wrote Assistant War Secretary Charles Dana. "All day on the 14th everything went like a miracle."

Badeau wrote that V Corps' screen across the Peninsula "completely masked the operations of the Army of the Potomac," contributing greatly to what he characterized as "one of the finest achievements in logistics during the war."[7]

GRANT WAS DISAPPOINTED that he had not been able to attack Lee's army outside its fortifications. But he had withdrawn from Cold Harbor without a single casualty and planned to beat Lee to Petersburg and cut the supply lines to the Confederate army and capital. On June 15, he wrote to his wife Julia, "We have been engaged in one of the most perilous movements ever executed by a large army, that of withdrawing from the front of an enemy and moving past his flank, crossing two rivers. . . . So far it has been eminently successful and I hope will prove so to the end."

In the North, however, it appeared to many observers that Grant was moving *away* from Richmond, not toward it. New York City diarist George

Templeton Strong wrote that he could "see no bright spot anywhere." A visitor to Philadelphia noted a marked change from 1863: "No signs of any enthusiasm, no flags; most of the best men gloomy and despairing." The maneuver, which Halleck had opposed, also caused uneasiness in the Lincoln administration.

Badeau understatedly observed, "The strategic importance of the new position and of the railways [converging on Petersburg] was not apparent to the unmilitary mind." Indeed, Petersburg, a city of 18,000 residents twenty-two miles south of Richmond, was where three railroads and a dozen highways converged; its fall would hasten Richmond's capitulation. Many in Washington, however, failed to recognize the city's importance and believed that Grant's movement left the Union capital vulnerable to attack, although Grant had repeatedly argued that he could best defend Washington by keeping Lee occupied.

But Lincoln wholeheartedly endorsed Grant's decision to cross the James. "I begin to see it," he wrote on June 15. "You will succeed. God bless you all." The previous day, the president had expressed impatience with those who expected Grant to capture Richmond and end the war that fall. "As God is my judge, I shall be satisfied if we are over with the fight in Virginia within a year," Lincoln told newspaper correspondent Noah Brooks. "I hope we shall be 'happily disappointed,' as the saying is; but I am afraid not—I am afraid not."[8]

While Union engineers were assembling the pontoon bridge, XVIII Corps commander William F. "Baldy" Smith and 16,000 troops left Bermuda Hundred and crossed the Appomattox River prefatory to assaulting Petersburg. It was the Army of the James's second march on the city in a week. Grant wanted to attack quickly—with Smith's troops and his favorite strike force, Hancock's II Corps—while Lee's army was still north of the James River.

The Army of the James's previous offensive against Petersburg, on June 9, had been a fiasco. General Quincy Gillmore approached the city's outskirts with 4,000 troops from X Corps, lost his nerve, and withdrew to Bermuda Hundred without attacking. It was a singularly pathetic performance even by the Army of the James's standards, and Gillmore was relieved of his command.[9]

GRANT'S FLANKING MANEUVER had put Lee in a quandary. The screen thrown out by Wilson's cavalry division and Warren's V Corps was so effective in concealing the Union army's movement from Cold Harbor that Lee, for the first time during the campaign, was ignorant of its whereabouts. Grant might march up the Peninsula and menace Richmond from the east, as George McClellan had attempted in 1862, or he might cross the James River and try to seize Petersburg. Lee strongly suspected the latter, but if he acted on that presumption and was wrong, Richmond's eastern approaches would be exposed to attack. Lee could not take that chance.

Moreover, he had just 35,000 troops. Jubal Early's Second Corps and John Breckinridge's division were on their way to the Shenandoah Valley, and two cavalry divisions were shadowing Sheridan west of Richmond.

Eager to strike Grant while he was away from his breastworks, Lee drew up a plan to attack Wilson's cavalry division and Warren's V Corps outside Richmond on June 14. But before the dawn assault could begin, the Yankees "disappeared before us during the night," and Lee's cavalry could not find them. Two days after Grant's withdrawal from Cold Harbor, Lee still did not know where he was.

From Petersburg, Beauregard reported that "Baldy" Smith's corps had rejoined Butler, but he had no news of Grant's army. Lee sent Robert Hoke's 6,000-man division to Beauregard and ordered Robert Ransom to ready his 1,800-man brigade to march to Petersburg.

Lee continued to withhold his remaining two army corps until he was certain that Grant was over the James. The Confederates, as befuddled as blind hunting dogs, continued to grope for their adversary in the Peninsula's woods and swamps. Confederate artillery Major Robert Stiles characterized the search for Grant as "a slow, stupid affair."

Edward Porter Alexander later concluded that Grant's brilliant movement away from Cold Harbor and the ensuing Rebel inertia was the war's final turning point. "Thus the last, and perhaps the best, chances of Confederate success were not lost in the repulse at Gettysburg, nor in any combat of arms. They were lost during three days of lying in camp, believing that Grant was hemmed in by the broad part of the James below City Point, and had nowhere to go but to attack us."[10]

GRANT NOW HAD a supreme opportunity to seize Petersburg, sever Richmond's southern lifelines, and ring down the curtain on the Confederacy.

The general given the all-important task of overwhelming the undermanned Petersburg defenses was "Baldy" Smith. Unfortunately, Smith had grown jaded and overcautious because of XVIII Corps' severe losses during the June 3 Cold Harbor attacks.

Hancock's II Corps, ferried to the James's south bank during the predawn hours of June 15, was supposed to join Smith in a dawn attack of 35,000 Union troops against Beauregard's 2,200 men. As Grant had informed Butler on June 14, Hancock, upon reaching Windmill Point on the James's south bank, would "march in the morning directly for Petersburg," after receiving 60,000 rations sent from City Point, Grant's new headquarters at the confluence of the Appomattox and James Rivers. But at 10:30 a.m., the rations had not arrived; it turned out that the river at Windmill Point was too shallow for the supplies to be landed. Hancock and his men left for Petersburg without having received any rations for a day and a half.

Everything had proceeded according to Grant's plan since June 12, but now things began to unravel. Because of a communications breakdown, neither Smith nor Hancock were aware that they were to cooperate in an attack. Hancock was on the road to Petersburg when he received a note from Smith asking him to join him. "This seems to be the first information that General Hancock had received of the fact that he was to go to Petersburg, or that anything particular was expected of him," Grant wrote.[11]

While II Corps was awaiting rations at Windmill Point, Smith's corps reached the northeast side of Petersburg. The XVIII Corps troops could see Petersburg's spires two miles away. Across a broad valley lay a jagged line of rifle pits connecting a series of fortified redans. "Everything now depended on the speedy capture of Petersburg," wrote Badeau.

Smith, however, was taking no risks after the blind attack at Cold Harbor that had cost his corps so many men; for seven hours, "when every moment was of supreme importance," he painstakingly reconnoitered the lightly defended Confederate line, sometimes crawling on his hands and knees. One of Smith's frustrated aides remarked that Smith "seemed to think the whole art of war consisted in making reconnaissances, and that time was not an element that entered into it."[12]

After hours of peering at the Rebel lines from every angle and arranging and rearranging his troops, at 7 p.m. Smith threw half of his corps into a skirmish line and attacked. Led by two black regiments, the 5th and 22nd US Colored Troops, the Yankees swarmed over the Confederates' outer entrenchments, capturing fifteen guns and 260 prisoners. It was the first successful assault by black units in the East.[13]

Then, II Corps' two lead divisions arrived, after yet another delay, this one caused by the corps marching miles off course because of an inaccurate map. Hancock pronounced his men ready for action, wherever Smith wished to send them, even though they had not yet eaten. While Hancock was senior to Smith, he did not assume command of the two corps, probably because of his presumption that Smith was more familiar with the battleground, and also because his year-old thigh wound was causing him intensive pain. (Hancock would soon hand over command of II Corps to General David Birney. A week later, his wound discharged "a big piece of bone," and he rapidly recovered and returned to duty.)[14]

Grant and Meade had insisted that Petersburg be captured in one swift movement if possible; Butler urged Smith to press on and complete the job. "I grieve for the delays," he wrote. "Time is the essence of this movement. . . . Now push and get the Appomattox between you and Lee. Nothing has passed down the railroad to harm you yet." Butler knew that Smith was positioned to block the railroad to Petersburg as well as the approaches to the Appomattox River.

But Smith believed that he had accomplished enough for one day, and he worried that the Rebels might have already reinforced Petersburg. "I must have the Army of the Potomac re-enforcements immediately," he told Butler. Instead of launching an all-out assault with his and Hancock's corps, Smith merely requested that Hancock's troops relieve his men in the captured entrenchments.

Petersburg was more than ready to fall, but Smith did not continue the attack that night. "It is impossible for me to go farther to-night," he wrote to Butler at midnight, "but, unless I misapprehend the topography, I hold the key to Petersburg." But rather than fit the key into the lock, Smith went to the rear to receive treatment for a recurrence of his malaria.

Smith's failure to press the assault was one of the worst decisions of the war. The men of II Corps knew it, too. "The most blood-curdling blasphemy I ever listened to I heard that night, uttered by men who knew they were to be sacrificed on the morrow," wrote artillerist Frank Wilkeson. "The rage of the intelligent enlisted men was devilish."

Theodore Lyman wrote in an anguish of frustration, "But, oh! That they had attacked at once. Petersburg would have gone like a rotten branch."[15]

MEADE ASSUMED TACTICAL command of the army at Petersburg, while Grant devoted his time at City Point to his broader duties as general-in-chief. He was pleased with the army's maneuver over the James. "I think it is pretty well to get across a great river, and come up here and attack Lee in his rear before he is ready for us," he said with a smile to Meade's aide, Lyman, when he delivered a report to Grant's tent. Lyman had found Grant sitting on the edge of his cot in his shirt and drawers, ready for bed.[16]

Beauregard's inability to verify that he faced Grant's men, and Lee's unwillingness to commit the rest of his army to Petersburg until Beauregard did, prolonged the opportunity for Meade to seize Petersburg. Denied reinforcements from Lee's two corps, Beauregard removed General Bushrod Johnson's division early June 16 from the Bermuda Hundred bottleneck and brought it to Petersburg. Johnson's division, along with Hoke's division and Ransom's brigade, gave Beauregard 15,000 men—a much stronger force than the 2,200 troops that he initially had, but still overmatched by more than three-to-one by the Yankees from II, IX, and XVIII Corps massing before him.

Meade launched an attack late June 16, but it was so poorly coordinated—XVIII Corps did not even participate—that it only pushed back part of Beauregard's line without breaking it, although capturing two guns and 400 prisoners. Meade wrote in frustration: "The attacks have not been made with the rigor & force which characterized our fighting in the Wilderness."

Two hours before the attack, Lieutenant Fred Mather of the 7th New York Heavy Artillery heard train whistles in Petersburg, and then observed

fresh enemy troops—probably Bushrod Johnson's—jogging into two redans opposite his regiment. Through binoculars, he watched "the incoming
tide of Gray Backs." When Lieutenant Colonel John Hastings, the regiment's commander, told Mather that they were to attack at 6 p.m., Mather
replied, "Colonel, it looks like another Cold Harbor to charge now. We
could have walked over, an hour ago."

The 7th New York had lost 422 men at Cold Harbor; this time, it lost
425, advancing to within fifty yards of the Rebel line while being riddled
by ferocious enemy fire from three sides.[17]

Meade ordered another attack the next morning, June 17, but only IX
Corps advanced on time; II Corps was two hours late, while V Corps, just
arrived, and XVIII Corps did not attack at all. With his thin gray line,
Beauregard was able to fend off the Yankees. Skirmishing and sniping continued for the rest of the day.[18]

2

Petersburg

AFTER TWO DAYS of Union attacks, Lee's all-important question of
whether the Army of the Potomac had joined Butler's army outside Petersburg yet remained unanswered on Friday, June 17. Either Beauregard truly
did not know or, as some historians have suggested, he wanted Lee's troops
in Petersburg, but not Lee; the proud Creole was sensitive to the fact that
Lee would supersede him upon his arrival.

It was one of the most trying times of the spring campaign for Lee. At
one point, Lee uncharacteristically exploded in a "furious passion," wrote
General Eppa Hunton. "He was mad because he could not find out what
Grant was doing."

Until he was certain that Grant's army was south of the James, Lee would
not withdraw his army from east of Richmond and turn over the capital's
defense to local troops. Yet, at the same time, he could not allow Petersburg
to fall if he could help it. After having sent Hoke's and Ransom's 7,800 men
to Beauregard, Lee straddled the James with about 22,000 Confederate
troops on each side.

The tone of his messages to Beauregard grew sharper: "Has Grant been seen crossing the James River?" he asked late June 16. At noon on the 17th—four days after Grant's disappearance from Cold Harbor—he replied to yet another of Beauregard's requests for troops: "Until I can get more definite information on Grant's movements I do not think it prudent to draw more troops to this [south] side of the river." A few hours later, Lee ordered his son Rooney to push out from Malvern Hill with his cavalry division "to ascertain what has become of Grant's army."[19]

WHEN BEAUREGARD WITHDREW Bushrod Johnson's 6,000-man division from its Bermuda Hundred lines to aid in Petersburg's defense, he asked Lee to send troops to occupy Johnson's former lines. Until Lee's troops arrived, Butler possessed a glittering opportunity to seize the Petersburg Pike and the Richmond and Petersburg Railroad and sever road and rail traffic between Richmond and Petersburg.

Early June 16, more than 4,000 of Butler's troops entered Johnson's empty entrenchments and then proceeded to capture the pike and railroad, where they tore up three miles of tracks. If Butler could hold on, Lee would not be able to send more reinforcements to Beauregard, and Petersburg would not be able to resist Meade's attacks for much longer.[20]

But when Lee learned that Beauregard had withdrawn Johnson's division, he sent Pickett's division, personally led by First Corps' commander, Richard Anderson, to Bermuda Hundred. Lee accompanied the task force as far as Drewry's Bluff.

After crossing the James, Lee knelt in the dust by the side of the road and joined a minister in praying "that God would give him wisdom and grace in the new stage of the campaign."[21]

Pickett's men failed to move Butler's troops, so Lee sent a second division from First Corps—Charles Field's. Together, they dislodged Butler's troops, occupied Johnson's trenches, and reopened the roads to Petersburg. The attack was "a very pretty thing," wrote Charles Venable of Lee's staff.

Grant ordered VI Corps to counterattack and to recapture the railroad, but Horatio Wright's men did not go into action. Confederate soldiers continued streaming down the railroad and the pike to Petersburg.[22]

STILL AWAITING SOLID information about Grant's whereabouts, Lee continued to hold A. P. Hill's Third Corps north of the James. Joseph Kershaw's division of the First Corps was poised to cross a pontoon bridge over the James whenever Lee received confirmation that Grant was on the south bank.

At last, late in the afternoon of June 17, the suspense ended: Beauregard informed Lee that he had captured troops from Hancock's II Corps. "It crossed day before yesterday & last night from Harrison's Landing—Could we not have more reinforcements here?" wrote Beauregard.

Further confirmation came that night from Rooney Lee, whose cavalry division had reached Wilcox's Landing, where it had seen the Union pontoon bridge. "Grant's entire army is across the river," he told his father.

Lee ordered Kershaw and Hill to march immediately to Petersburg. Hours before daybreak on June 18, the Third Corps was striding down the reopened Petersburg Pike.

Captain D. Augustus Dickert of the 3rd South Carolina wrote that Kershaw's brigadiers set a fast pace. "It was evident that our troops somewhere were in imminent peril. The march started as a forced one, but before daylight it had gotten almost to a run." Captain Henry Clay Albright of the 26th North Carolina described it as "the hardest day's march we had during [this] campaign. I think I never was so tired in all my life." Third Corps reached Petersburg around sunrise.

The citizens ran to their doors when they heard the approach of martial music, and watched the Third Corps pass through the streets. A woman wrote in her diary after seeing local men from the 12th Virginia march by, "Oh! So worn with travel and fighting, so dusty and ragged, their faces so thin and *drawn* by privation that we scarcely knew them. It made one's heart ache to look at them. . . . It was a sad homecoming, and even now they were hurrying on to the front to save their homes from the enemy."

Beauregard had withdrawn to a shorter, more easily defended line closer to the city, and Lee's troops began filing into the new entrenchments opposite the Union army.[23]

EARLY JUNE 18, Colonel Robert McAllister formed his brigade's lead regiment, the 11th New Jersey, into two lines. The bluecoats advanced in the morning daylight across open ground toward the Rebel breastworks, expecting to be met by thunderous volleys of musketry and cannon fire. Instead, they found the works lightly occupied and the trenches piled deep with dead and dying men from the furious attacks and counterattacks of the past three days. "If there was ever a place on earth that looked like the infernal regions, this was the place," a soldier of the 34th Virginia had observed the night before, when the Rebels had withdrawn from the works.

So tantalizingly close to victory, Meade and Grant could not resist trying once more to smash through the Confederate lines. The Army of the Potomac lay just a mile from the Confederacy's keystone city. The stakes had never been higher: Petersburg's capture would open the door to Richmond and assure the collapse of the Southern cause.

Meade's men pushed past the abandoned enemy positions. Three-fourths of a mile in front of McAllister's brigade, another line of works became visible, the entrenchments that Beauregard's men had dug overnight—and that Field's and Kershaw's First Corps divisions were at that moment occupying. The works facing McAllister's men bristled with infantrymen, mortars, and artillery, all arranged in a "curved-line death trap." To reach the enemy lines, the Yankees would have to cross 100 to 300 yards of cleared ground while ascending a hill.

Not liking the situation, McAllister halted his brigade and requested support. Instead, McAllister and his men were ordered to advance alone.

Then, the Rebel defenders opened fire. "I could compare it to a great hail storm cutting down the grain and grass," McAllister wrote. "Our ranks melted away and we could not advance further." He ordered his troops to lie down and plant their regimental flags, "that they would wave in the breeze before us." He was permitted to withdraw his brigade.

But Meade wanted the assaults to continue, believing that his 80,000 troops would surely crack the Rebel lines. The 1st Maine Heavy Artillery was sent into action at the same place where McAllister's men had failed, this time with other units in support.

The supports made no difference. Veterans exhorted the Maine foot artillerists to "lie down, you damn fools, you can't take them forts!" But they grittily advanced over 350 yards of fire-swept ground, sustaining "monstrous losses"—in under five minutes, 638 of the 1st Maine's 955 men were killed or wounded, the heaviest loss by any regiment during the war.[24]

The 4th New York Heavy Artillery advanced, believing "we were going to almost certain death," wrote Captain A. C. Brown. The Confederates were ready for the New Yorkers. "I shall never forget the hurricane of shot and shell which struck us as we emerged from the belt of trees," wrote Brown, likening the enemy fire to "the terrific hissing of some gigantic furnace." When Brown discovered that his regiment was on its own, he ordered it to lie down in a cornfield.[25]

All day long, Meade shoved divisions, brigades, and regiments piecemeal into the killing zones prepared by the Confederates. John Gibbon's II Corps division attacked at noon and was met by a "perfectly murderous fire of musketry, canister and spherical case," but managed to take some prisoners. David Birney, placed in temporary command of II Corps when Hancock went on the disabled list, attacked with nine brigades at 4. V and IX Corps tried their luck later. They gained little and left the field "thickly covered with . . . dead and wounded."[26]

Meade's aide Theodore Lyman wrote that staff officers had trouble all day moving V and IX Corps' divisions forward together, "or, indeed, of getting them forward at all." The men were clearly worn out. "Forty-five days of death, danger, and toil are no preparation for a rush!" Lyman wrote. "The men moved up without spirit, received a withering fire, and fell back behind the first crest."[27]

The fragmented assaults only provoked Meade's wrath—although the blame was his—and caused him to rage at his corps commanders when they requested a delay so that they could better coordinate their efforts. To Birney, Meade said, "I have sent a positive order to Generals Burnside and Warren to attack at all hazards with their whole force. I find it useless to appoint an hour to effect co-operation, and I am therefore compelled to give you the same order."[28]

The attacks disgusted Walter Carter, who watched his 22nd Massachusetts lose 400 men that day. "It is one great fault in this campaign," he wrote. "We always move by brigades or skirmish lines; no heavy charges by massed column; you see the result."[29]

Fortunately for Beauregard, the Union attacks repeatedly targeted the Rebel's most formidable defensive points, and not where the Rebels were vulnerable. Because of fatigue or lack of imagination, Meade and his staff evidently never considered a flank attack. If Meade had dispatched a corps around Beauregard's right flank south and west of the city, "I would have been compelled to evacuate Petersburg without much resistance," Beauregard later conceded. "But they persisted in attacking on my front, where I was strongest."[30]

Indeed, as late as 6:30 p.m., thirteen hours after the attacks began, Meade continued to believe that one might yet succeed, although the approaches to the Confederate breastworks were already carpeted with fallen bluecoats. "I have yet hopes that a successful assault may be made," he told Grant.

But Grant told Meade to desist. "I think after the present assault, unless a decided advantage presents itself, our men should have rest, protecting themselves as well as possible. If this assault does not carry we will try to gain advantages without assaulting fortifications." This attack, too, failed, and Meade informed Grant that he had suspended operations. "I feel satisfied that all that men could do under the circumstances was done," he said.

At supper that evening, Meade was clearly disappointed, although he made a show of being cheerful. "I had hoped all alone to have entered Petersburg this day," without sharing credit with Grant, he confided to Lyman.[31]

GRANT'S INFANTRYMEN KNEW it was useless to assault enemy fortifications. In one II Corps brigade, the men shouted, "Played out!" and refused orders to advance. Horace Porter noticed the changed attitude. The troops did not go into action with "the same vigor that they had displayed in the Wilderness campaign," he wrote. The army was exhausted, Porter concluded, and had lost too many of its best men during the past six weeks. "All of us see the frail threads that our lives hang upon more vividly day by day," wrote Walter Carter. "A bullet may cut it at any moment."

Charles Francis Adams Jr. told his father that the army was "fought out, so dispirited and hopeless. . . . Grant has pushed his Army to the extreme limit of human endurance. It cannot and it will not bear much more."[32]

SIX DAYS AFTER stealing away from Cold Harbor, the Army of the Potomac again faced Lee's army, once more entrenched behind formidable breastworks. It had conducted its vast maneuver so flawlessly that, incredibly, Lee had lost track of Grant's 100,000 men for four days. The army had crossed the James River on a pontoon bridge that was an engineering marvel, and had massed before Petersburg.

And then, at the climax of Grant's campaign, just when the Union army should have easily brushed aside Petersburg's handful of defenders, the offensive faltered—due to the Army of the Potomac's inherent slowness, lack of coordination, and mediocre leadership, Grant and Hancock excepted. "I believed then, and still believe, that Petersburg could have been easily captured at that time," Grant wrote in his *Memoirs*, his disappointment still evident two decades later.

In the four days after crossing the James, the fumbling Union attacks against the Rebel fortifications had cost Grant 11,000 casualties, nearly as many as his army suffered during its twelve days at Cold Harbor.

The Army of the Potomac's spectacular breakdown was a gift to the Confederacy—one might say an answer to Lee's roadside prayer beside the James.[33]

IN AN IMPORTANT respect, however, the failure was Grant's. At the climactic moment, he ceded tactical command to Meade, Butler, and Smith, and went to City Point, ostensibly to direct all of the Union armies. For the first time during the campaign, Meade alone commanded the Army of the Potomac, and Smith and Butler were suddenly making decisions that literally determined the course of the war. None of them was up to the job.

"We find the enemy, as usual, in a very strong position, defended by earthworks," Meade told his wife, as though this had been expected, "and it looks very much as if we will have to go through a siege of Petersburg before entering on the siege of Richmond, and that Grant's words of keeping at it all summer will prove to be quite prophetic."[34]

Just as prophetic would prove to be Lee's candid words to Jubal Early at Cold Harbor before Early departed for the Shenandoah Valley. Lee had grimly told him, "We must destroy this army of Grant's before he gets to the James River. If he gets there, it will become a siege, and then it will be a mere question of time."[35]

The Beginning of the End

Hold on with a bulldog grip, and chew and choke as much as possible.

—Abraham Lincoln to Ulysses Grant[1]

THE NORTH REELED from the Overland Campaign's breathtaking human toll: 66,000 Union soldiers killed, wounded, or captured between May 5 and June 18. Nothing like Grant's "butcher bill" had been experienced in this or any other war on the North American continent. It equaled two-thirds of the North's casualties during the previous three years.[2]

The losses might have been palatable if the Army of the Potomac had produced a tangible result—the destruction of Lee's army, or the capture of Richmond or Petersburg. But Lee's army was intact, although battered and diminished by its own losses, which surpassed 35,000. And the Rebel fortifications at Petersburg appeared more daunting than ever.[3]

Many judged the campaign a failure. "Who shall revive the withered hopes that bloomed at the beginning of General Grant's campaign?" asked the New York *World*. "This war, as now conducted, is a failure without hope of other issue than the success of the rebellion." The London *Times* reported that in America the campaign had wrought "sad reflections caused by the slaughter of half an army, the doubtful issue of the operations against Richmond."[4]

In Washington, many in government were dismayed that the army's march "in blood and agony from the Rapidan to the James" had ended in stalemate outside Petersburg. Navy Secretary Gideon Welles bitterly wrote,

"The waste of war is terrible; the waste from imbecility and mismanagement is more terrible and more trying than from the ravages of the soldiers. It is impossible for the country to bear up under these monstrous errors and wrongs." Lieutenant Colonel Charles Francis Adams Jr. of the 5th Massachusetts Cavalry, the grandson of John Quincy Adams, wrote to his ambassador father in London, "At present there is one thing to be said of this campaign and its probable future. In it the rebellion will feel the entire strength of the Government exerted to the utmost."[5]

Grant and Lincoln were not discouraged. "You people up North now must be of good cheer," Grant told his friend, J. Russell Jones. "Recollect that we have the bulk of the Rebel Army in two grand Armies [the other being Joseph Johnston's army in Georgia] both besieged and both conscious that they cannot stand a single battle outside their fortifications with the Armies confronting them." Grant noted that the Confederacy had no more men to send to their armies, whereas the Union could replace its losses. "If the rebellion is not perfectly and thoroughly crushed it will be the fault and through the weakness of the people North," Grant wrote.[6]

Knowing that Petersburg's capture would doom Richmond and, thus, the Confederacy, Grant explained his plan to besiege the "Cockade City" in a dispatch to General Henry Halleck. When Halleck showed Grant's letter to Lincoln, the president was so gratified that he read it to his aides, and then responded to Grant, "I have seen your dispatch expressing your unwillingness to break your hold where you are. Neither am I willing. Hold on with a bulldog grip, and chew and choke as much as possible."[7]

In a speech before the Great Central Sanitary Fair in Philadelphia on June 16, just when the campaign's long casualty lists were causing many to despair, Lincoln defended the conduct of the war. "We accepted this war for an object, a worthy object, and the war will end when that object is attained," Lincoln said. "Under God, I hope it never will until that time." The president invoked Grant's pledge of "going through on this line if it takes all summer," to make a vow of his own: "I say we are going through on this line if it takes three years more."[8]

DESPITE GRANT'S OPTIMISTIC words, his army was numbed by losses and exhaustion. Outside Petersburg, Lieutenant Colonel Cyrus Comstock of Grant's staff jotted in his diary, "Troops do not fight as well as when we started. Best officers and best men gone—losses enormous." Meade wrote to his wife that the army had been "very quiet" for two days and was "exhausted with forty-nine days of continued marching and fighting, and absolutely requires rest to prevent its *morale* being impaired." Some men had been pushed beyond their tolerances. "I tell you many a man has gone crazy since this campaign begun [sic] from the terrible pressure on mind & body," Captain Oliver Wendell Holmes Jr. wrote to his parents.

One of them was Lieutenant Samuel Gilbreth, in charge of a company of sharpshooters attached to the 20th Massachusetts at Petersburg. Gilbreth accepted a Rebel sharpshooter's challenge to "single combat," and he and his adversary stood on their respective earthworks and fired. The Rebel fell. Brushing off entreaties to step down, Gilbreth accepted several more challenges, killing every contender.

That night, Gilbreth, giddy with his string of kills, boasted to his comrades that he had "a charmed life; said nothing would kill him," wrote the regimental surgeon, John Perry. His comrades tried to dissuade him from resuming the murderous duels the next morning, but he would not listen. "The man seemed crazed with the faith in his charmed life," wrote Perry. The next morning, June 19, Gilbreth stood on the earthworks and issued a fresh challenge. As he and his opponent took aim, a Confederate in another part of the enemy line shot Gilbreth through the mouth. As he died, he said to Perry, "I hit him anyway, doctor."[9]

GILBRETH WAS JUST one of the hundreds of casualties that reduced the 20th Massachusetts's roster from 535 to 162 during May and June. "We have had no single battle since the Wilderness in which we have lost very largely, but there has been an almost daily loss," wrote Lieutenant Henry Patten, who became the regiment's commander.[10]

II Corps' casualties were greater than those of any other corps in the Army of the Potomac. The Union army's most famous corps had stormed Bloody Lane at Antietam, suffered severe losses at Fredericksburg, and flung back Pickett's charge at Gettysburg. During Grant's campaign, Winfield Scott Hancock's troops had nearly broken A. P. Hill's corps on the Orange Plank Road on May 6. II Corps broke through at the Bloody Angle on May

12. At Cold Harbor, it was the only corps that captured Rebel breastworks. In the battles outside Petersburg, II Corps continued to lose heavily. By late June, its losses surpassed 16,000.

Half of the corps' casualties were in John Gibbon's division—in aggregate, more men than the division began the campaign with. Seventy-two percent of the troops that Gibbon led across the Rapidan had fallen—along with many of their replacements, whose inexperience made them casualty-prone. Gibbon's division accounted for 12 percent of the Army of the Potomac's total casualties. "The troops, which at the commencement of the campaign were equal to any undertaking, became toward the end of it unfit for almost any," Gibbon observed. In late June, even with its replacements, II Corps' roster listed just 17,201 men.[11]

GRANT'S CAMPAIGN HAD tested the Army of Northern Virginia to its utmost, and less than half of the 65,000-man Confederate force that marched into the Wilderness survived to enter Petersburg in June. Lee's decision to send Jubal Early's Second Corps and John Breckinridge's small division to the Shenandoah Valley pared the army to 35,000 men, even with thousands of reinforcements. Combined with Beauregard's men and assorted other units from Richmond and Petersburg, Lee's army in June mustered 50,000 troops.

They were tired and dirty, thin and hungry. Meade wrote that when he promised good treatment to a Confederate prisoner, the man replied, "Oh, sir, you cannot treat us worse than we are treated on the other side."

Yet, the Rebels' fighting spirit remained high. The warm reception they received in Petersburg was a tonic to them. "Ladies, old and young, met us at their front gates with hearty welcome, cool water, and delicious viands," wrote artillery Major Robert Stiles. "There is nothing more inspiring to a soldier than to pass through the streets of a city he is helping to defend, and to be greeted as a deliverer by its women and children."[12]

Charles Venable of Lee's staff said that at Petersburg, the army's rations improved, and so did its confidence. But he observed "a somber tinge to the soldier within our thinned ranks which expressed itself in the homely phrase, 'what is the use of killing these Yankees? It is like killing mosquitoes—two come for every one you kill.'"[13]

Now handcuffed to Petersburg, the Confederate Army's mission was reduced to two narrow objects: to protect communications between Petersburg and Richmond, and to retain control of Weldon and Southside rail lines entering the city from the south. "If this cannot be done, I see no way of averting the terrible disaster that will ensue," Lee wrote.[14]

Not since the May 5–6 battles in the Wilderness had Lee's army attacked Grant, and Lee knew that it would be foolish to assault Grant's entrenchments at Petersburg except in the last ditch. While Lee yearned to go on the offensive, at which he excelled, he also realized that failure would doom the Confederacy. When Beauregard proposed on June 18 that they throw every man into a desperate attack on the Union rear and flank, Lee rejected the plan as too risky.[15]

Lee, however, hoped that his gambit of sending Early's and Breckinridge's veterans to crush Union General David Hunter's army in southwest Virginia would provide an opening for him at Petersburg. Like a good chess player, Lee was looking several moves ahead. Once Hunter was removed from the picture, Early could march down the Shenandoah Valley, cross the Potomac, and menace Washington. Grant would be compelled to rush troops from Petersburg to the capital's defense, possibly enabling Lee to attack Grant. While Lee's plan would work to perfection, it would not appreciably change the situation outside Petersburg; even after Grant sent troops to Washington to help drive away Early, the Union force remaining at Petersburg would be too powerful to attack.

MEANWHILE, THE ARMY of the Potomac continued to bungle its operations outside Petersburg in late June and July. II and VI corps were improbably routed by Confederate General William Mahone's division on June 22–23 as they set out to cut supply routes into Petersburg, and the detonation of a mine on July 30 at what became known as the Crater began promisingly, but ended tragically. These embarrassments did nothing to buoy flagging spirits in the North.

But they were temporary setbacks. Lee was in a box, the Army of Northern Virginia would never again fight in northern Virginia, and the Confederacy was scraping the bottom of the barrel for manpower and supplies. Petersburg would finally fall on April 2, 1865, after Phil Sheridan's victory at Five Forks, and Lee would surrender a week later at Appomattox Court House.[16]

Captain D. Augustus Dickert of the 3rd South Carolina wrote that there was "scarcely an able-bodied man in the South—nay, not one who could be of service—who was not either in the trenches, in the ranks of the soldiers, or working in some manner for service. All from sixteen to fifty were now in actual service, while all between fourteen and sixteen and from fifty to sixty were guarding forts, railroads, or Federal prisoners."[17]

As Lee had feared, the campaign had become a siege, and it would be a mere matter of time.

GRANT WROTE THAT the battles of the Wilderness, Spotsylvania, North Anna, and Cold Harbor, "bloody and terrible as they were on our side," had "so crippled [the enemy] as to make him wary ever after of taking the offensive."[18]

This is a serviceable definition for "war of attrition." Grant had envisioned a campaign of maneuver, hoping to pry Lee from his breastworks and to then defeat his army in open combat. Too cagey to risk his army on one roll of the dice, though, Lee forced Grant to instead wage what Grant described as a "hammering" campaign, one that unfairly typecast him as a heartless butcher. In reality it was closer in spirit to what others have called a "strategy of exhaustion," its goal being not only to destroy the enemy's army but also to devastate all of his war-making resources—from railroads to cattle to fields of corn.

In the process, Grant forever changed the course of the war. He steadily forced Lee back toward Richmond, until the Army of the Potomac could see the city's church steeples, while tearing down Lee's army. Lee had failed to turn Grant's flank, break his line, or carry an important Union position. Significantly, Lee did not mount an offensive after the May 6 attack on the Orange Plank Road; his army now fought from behind breastworks.

The South's last hope was that Abraham Lincoln would be defeated in the November election. Indeed, Early's march in July to the outskirts of Washington spread panic and caused many to condemn Lincoln's and Grant's strategy.

Grant alone would not save Lincoln, but he would "hold a leg," in Lincoln's parlance, so that someone else could skin. While Grant pinned Lee to Petersburg, Sherman and Sheridan would "skin" in Georgia and the Shenandoah Valley, assuring Lincoln's reelection and, ultimately, Union victory.

NOTES

PROLOGUE

1. United States War Department, *The War of the Rebellion: A Compilation of the Official Records of the Union and Confederate Armies.* 4 series, 128 volumes. Vol. 33, 1283. Washington: United States Government Printing Office, 1880–1901. Available online through the Cornell Library website at http://ebooks.library.cornell.edu/m /moawar/waro.html. (Henceforth "O.R."; series 1 unless otherwise indicated.)

2. Freeman, *Lee's Lieutenants*, 660.

3. Laine and Penny, *Law's Brigade*, 232–235; Law, "From the Wilderness," 119; Foote, *Red River to Appomattox*, 142–144; O.R., vol. 33, 1244–1245, 1268, 1283–1284.

4. O.R., vol. 33, 1332; McCabe, *Letterbook*, 112.

5. Fuller, *Generalship*, 222; Freeman, *Lee's Lieutenants*, 660.

6. Foote, *Red River to Appomattox*, 5.

7. Grant, *Memoirs*, 283–284; 301.

1. SPRING 1864

1. J. E. Smith, *Grant*, 300.

2. Meade, *Life and Letters*, 191.

3. L. M. Starr, *Bohemian Brigade*, 272–273.

4. Kimmel, *Lincoln's Washington*, 137; McFeely, *Grant*, 153.

5. L. M. Starr, *Bohemian Brigade*, 288.

6. J. E. Smith, *Grant*, 300; Foote, *Fredericksburg to Meridian*, 218; Foote, *Red River to Appomattox*, 5.

7. Nicolay, *Lincoln's Secretary*, 194–195; Brooks, *Lincoln Observed*, 104.

8. Goodwin, *Team of Rivals*, 560; *Congressional Globe*, 38th Congress, 1st Session, 430; Nicolay, *Lincoln's Secretary*, 195–197; Grant, *Papers*, vol. 10, 195.

9. Porter, *Campaigning with Grant* (unabridged), 63–64; Grant, *Memoirs*, 272–273.

10. Grant, *Memoirs*, 34: Porter, *Campaigning with Grant* (unabridged), 213–214.

11. J. E. Smith, *Grant*, 301.

12. Nicolay, *Lincoln's Secretary*, 181.

13. Gray, *Hidden Civil War*, 15–23, 70, 168, 161; *Congressional Globe*, 38th Congress, 1st Session, 1499–1503.

14. Donald, *Lincoln*, 491.

15. Brands, *Man Who Saved*, 280–281; McPherson, *Tried by War*, 211.

16. Donald, *Lincoln*, 491.

17. Longacre, *Grant*, 7–8, 17.

18. Wheelan, *Invading Mexico*, 190, 192–193, 377–378.

19. McFeely, *Grant*, 48–55, 58–65; Marszalek, *Sherman*, 172; Longacre, *Grant*, 1–3.

20. Brands, *Man Who Saved*, 102, 121; McFeely, *Grant*, 65–66, 73, 76; Warner, *Generals in Blue*, 184.

21. Catton, *Never Call Retreat*, 299.

22. Dana, *Recollections*, 1–2, 20–22, 61.

23. J. H. Wilson, *Life of Rawlins*, 53, 60–61, 128–129.

24. Carpenter, *Six Months*, 247.

25. Badeau, *Military History*, 14–15; O.R., vol. 32, part III, 49; Warner, *Generals in Blue*, 315–317; Lincoln, *Collected Works*, vol. 6, 327–328; Rhea, *Wilderness*, 36; Hennessey, "I Dread," 66–67; Schurz, *Reminiscences*, 20–21; Grant, *Memoirs*, 581; Williams, *Lincoln and His Generals*, 301–303.

26. Hennessey, "I Dread," 82–83.

27. Badeau, *Military History*, 16.

28. Dana, *Recollections*, 189; McFeely, *Grant*, 158; Lyman, *Notebooks*, 126; Meade, *Life and Letters*, 180, 189, 191.

29. Badeau, *Military History*, 16–17; Carpenter, *Six Months*, 57.

30. Stoddard, *White House*, 220–222.

31. O.R., vol. 10, 187.

32. Marszalek, *Sherman*, 178–180; J. E. Smith, *Grant*, 200–201; Grant, *Papers*, vol. 10, 187–188fn.

33. Marszalek, *Sherman*, 253–254; Badeau, *Military* 28, 23–24; Foote, *Red River to Appomattox*, 13.

34. O.R., vol. 34, part I, 8–9; Hattaway and James, *How the North Won*, 489; Donald, *Lincoln*, 334; Grant, *Memoirs*, 373; Badeau, *Military History*, 100.

35. O.R., vol. 33, 394–395; McPherson, *Tried by War*, 210–211; Hattaway and James, *How the North Won*, 512–515; Gordon, *Reminiscences*, 236–237.

36. O.R., vol. 32, part II, 411–413.

37. Hay, *Inside Lincoln's White House*, 193–194; Atkinson, *Grant's Campaigns*, 28.

38. S. B. Oates, *Malice toward None*, 212, 385; O.R., vol. 33, 887–888; Grant, *Papers*, vol. 10, 240; Catton, *Grant Takes Command*, 139.

39. O.R., vol. 34, part I, 8–11; McPherson, *Tried by War*, 209; Grant, *Memoirs*, 366fn; Atkinson, *Grant's Campaigns*, 24; Fuller, *Generalship*, 216.

40. Grant, *Papers*, vol. 10, 274–275, 370, 252; Grant, *Memoirs*, 368–369fn; Porter, *Campaigning with Grant* (abridged), 43.

41. Butler, *Autobiography*, 592–595; O.R., Series II, vol. 7, 615, 62–63.

42. Rhea, *Wilderness*, 31; Wilkeson, *Inside Out*, 21–22; O.R., vol. 36, part I, 276–278; Hennessey, "I Dread," 72–80.

43. Curtis, *24th MI*, 217–218; Badeau, *Military History*, 40–41.

44. Fite, *Conditions in the North*, 1, 5, 24, 27, 43–44, 67, 85–87, 105, 213, 263, 232; Catton, *Glory Road*, 235–241; M. R. Wilson, *Business of Civil War*, 1–2; Gallman, *Northerners*, 104, 108; Carruth, *What Happened When*, 411.

45. Badeau, *Military History*, 41; J. E. Smith, *Grant*, 307, 309–310; J. H. Wilson, *Life of Rawlins*, 426–427; Catton, *Never Call Retreat*, 298; Grant, *Memoirs*, 372; Grant, *Papers*, vol. 10, 357, 362–363.

46. Catton, *Mr. Lincoln*, 23, 39.

47. Flower, *Stanton*, 247; Reardon, "Hard Road," 175.

48. Long and Long, *Day by Day*, 479; Flower, *Stanton*, 240–244, 247.

49. Gray, *Hidden Civil War*, 156–157; Wilkeson, *Inside Out*, 2–16.

50. Miller, *Harvard*, 350; Kreiser, *Defeating Lee*, 30–31; Wilkeson, *Inside Out*, 194–195.

51. S. B. Oates, *Malice toward None*, 211–212.

52. Brooks, *Lincoln Observed*, 107; S. B. Oates, *Malice toward None*, 385; Grant, *Memoirs*, 370 [Forrest quote]; Flower, *Stanton*, 235–236; Bates, *Diary*, 365; Long and Long, *Day by Day*, 484; Welles, *Diary*, 17.

53. Warner, *Generals in Blue*, 57–58; Trudeau, *Bloody Roads*, 18; Grant, *Papers*, vol. 10, 343.

54. J. B. Jones, *Rebel War Clerk*, vol. 2, 156, 184–185, 154, 192; Wheelan, *Libby Prison*, 8–11, 16, 134; E. Thomas, *Confederate State*, 119–120; Brands, *Man Who Won*, 294; Massey, *Ersatz*, 26.

55. J. B. Jones, *Rebel War Clerk*, vol. 2, 188; Massey, *Ersatz*, 3–5, 15, 28; Gallman, *Northerners*, 99–100; Aley, "Good Scavengers," 92–93.

56. E. Thomas, *Confederate Nation*, 260–265, 199; Power, *Lee's Miserables*, 3; Massey, *Ersatz*, 25–27; O.R., Series IV, vol. 3, 354.

57. J. W. Jones, *Christ in Camp*, 56, 58, 330, 352; David Holt, *Mississippi Rebel*, 231; Dowdey, *Lee's Last Campaign*, 229; Gordon, *Reminiscences*, 236; Gallagher, "Our Hearts," 39–40, 55–57.

58. Richmond *Whig*, May 2, 1864; Goodwin, *Team of Rivals*, 617–618; W. C. Davis, *Jefferson Davis*, 551–553.

59. J. Davis, *Papers*, vol. 10, 378–387.

60. Laine and Penny, *Law's Brigade*, 231; Alexander, *Fighting*, 345–346; Dowdey, *Lee's Last Campaign*, 10, 138–140.

61. McCabe, *Letterbook*, 104; Venable, "Wilderness to Petersburg," 240; Alexander, *Fighting*, 111; Thomas, *Lee*, 321; Gordon, *Reminiscences*, 235.

62. E. M. Thomas, *Robert E. Lee*, 17–18; J. E. Smith, *Grant*, 340–342.

63. Nichols, *Soldier's Story*, 140–141; Taylor, *Lee's Adjutant*, 139 [letter to Bettie Sanders]; Alexander, *Fighting*, 345; Porter, *Campaigning with Grant* (abridged), 44.

64. R. E. Lee, *Wartime Papers*, 666–667.

65. Dame, *Rapidan to Richmond*, 20; Howard, "Notes and Recollections," 86–87; Venable, "Lee in the Wilderness," 243; O.R., vol. 33, 1275; Law, "Wilderness to Cold Harbor," 119; J. B. Jones, *Rebel War Clerk*, vol. 2, 194; Scott, *Into the Wilderness*, 24–25; Gordon, *Reminiscences*, 235; Gallagher, "Our Hearts," 57.

66. R. E. Lee, *Wartime Papers*, 719–720; Dowdey, *Lee's Last Campaign*, 39–40; O.R., vol. 33, 1299–1301, 1332; Alexander, *Fighting*, 348; Taylor, *Four Years*, 124–125.

67. Reardon, "Hard Road," 172–173; Gallagher, "Our Hearts," 58; Bradwell, *Southern Cross*, 150; Stiles, *Marse Robert*, 241.

2. TWO BLOODY ROADS—THE WILDERNESS

1. Melville, *Selected Poems*, 135.

2. Clark, *NC Regiments*, vol. 3, 75.

3. O.R., vol. 36, part II, 331–334; Warner, *Generals in Blue*, 566–567, 187–188; Schaff, *Wilderness*, 81; Grant, *Memoirs*, 397; Foote, *Red River to Appomattox*, 146; Pyne, *Ride to War*, 183; Freeman, *Lee: Biography*, vol. 3, 149.

4. Haines, *15th NJ*, 140–141; Schaff, *Wilderness*, 83–84; Page and Gilmore, *War Correspondent*, 47–48.

5. Grant, *Memoirs*, 391–392, 401; Haines, *15th NJ*, 134.

6. Carter, *Four Brothers*, 389–390; Gerrish, *Army Life*, 157; Haines, *15th NJ*, 141; Scott, *Into the Wilderness*, 17–18; Wilkeson, *Inside Out*, 39–40; Welch, *Boy General*, 93.

7. Badeau, *Military History*, 77–79, 90, 99; Porter, *Campaigning with Grant* (abridged), 39–40; J. E. Smith, *Grant*, 303.

8. Lincoln, *Collected Works*, vol. 7, 324.

9. Grant, *Papers*, vol. 10, 380.

10. Ibid., 394.

11. Badeau, *Military History*, 99; J. E. Smith, *Grant*, 334; Porter, *Campaigning with Grant* (abridged), 41.

12. Grant, *Memoirs*, 369–370; Hattaway and James, *How the North Won*, 527; Grant, *Papers*, vol. 10, 371.

13. Grant, *Papers*, vol. 10, 397; Porter, *Campaigning with Grant* (abridged), 41–42; O.R., vol. 36, part II, 372.

14. Rhea, *Wilderness*, 55; Warner, *Generals in Blue*, 240–242; Humphreys, *Virginia Campaign*, 20; Marshall-Cornwall, *Grant as Commander*, 147.

15. Walker, *General Hancock*, 159–161.

16. O.R., vol. 36, part I, 18.

17. O.R., vol. 38, part IV, 25; vol. 36, part I, 23–24; vol. 33, 1009; Porter, *Campaigning with Grant* (abridged), 43; Longacre, *Amateurs*, 67; Badeau, *Military History*, 100.

18. O.R., vol. 36, part II, 378.

19. Schaff, *Wilderness*, 109.

20. O.R., vol. 36, part II, 371–372; Coles, *Huntsville to Appomattox*, 158–159; Scott, *Into the Wilderness*, 187; Taylor, *Four Years with General Lee*, 124–125; A. C. Young, *Lee's Army*, 232.

21. Alexander, *Fighting*, 348–349.

22. Ibid., 351.

23. Foote, *Red River to Appomattox*, 150–151; O.R., vol. 36, part I, 1054; Longstreet, *Manassas to Appomattox*, 556–557; Scott, *Into the Wilderness*, 25–26.

24. Dame, *Rapidan to Richmond*, 71–72.

25. Freeman, *Lee's Dispatches*, 169–173.

26. O.R., vol. 36, part II, 948.

27. Alexander, *Fighting*, 350.

28. A. Long, *Robert E. Lee*, 327; Venable, "Lee in the Wilderness," 240–241.

29. Foote, *Red River to Appomattox*, 273.

30. McAllister, *Letters*, 415; Craft, *141st PA*, 176; Freeman, *Lee: Biography*, vol. 3, 149; Wilkeson, *Inside Out*, 47, 49–51; Schaff, *Wilderness*, 119–120.

31. LaRocca, *124th NY*, 214; Craft, *141st PA*, 176.

32. Catton, *Glory Road*, 202; Welch, *Boy General*, 13–29, 39, 53–59, 70–78, 84–90; Lyman, *Meade's Headquarters*, 107; T. Buell, *Warrior Generals*, 87–88, 108–109; Schurz, *Reminiscences*, 7–8; Miller, *Harvard*, 327; Warner, *Generals in Blue*, 171–172.

33. Kreiser, *Defeating Lee*, ix–x, 159–160, 162–163; Walker, *General Hancock*, 155; Hess, *Trench Warfare*, 135; Conyngham, *Irish Brigade*, x; Catton, *Mr. Lincoln*, 167; Miller, *Harvard*, 315, 32–35, 319–320.

34. Warner, *Generals in Blue*, 202–204; Walker, *General Hancock*, 33, 143–144, 148; Grant, *Memoirs*, 582; Schurz, *Reminiscences*, 14; Foote, *Fredericksburg to Meridian*, 199, 483–484, 545, 561.

35. Wilkeson, *Inside Out*, 47–48; Hess, *Trench Warfare*, 20; Scott, *Into the Wilderness*, 31; Swinton, *Campaigns*, 428–429fns; Dowdey, *Lee's Last Campaign*, 52–53.

36. Abbott, *Fallen Leaves*, 241; Perry, *Letters from a Surgeon*, 166.

37. Grant, *Memoirs*, 391; Foote, *Red River to Appomattox*, 5; Porter, *Campaigning with Grant* (abridged), 38.

38. O.R., vol. 36, part II, 371.

39. Ibid., I, 1028.

40. *History 121st PA*, 76.

41. Schaff, *Wilderness*, 97, 126–127; Pullen, *20th ME*, 181–184; Hennessey, "I Dread," 89–90; Lyman, *Meade's Headquarters*, 26.

42. Foote, *Fredericksburg to Meridian*, 503, 792–794.

43. O.R., vol. 36, part II, 403.

44. Ibid., 404; Swinton, *Campaigns*, 421fn.

45. O.R., vol. 36, part II, 418–419.

46. Ibid., 403.

47. Schaff, *Wilderness*, 201; Hay, *Inside Lincoln's White House*, 64.

48. Hay, *Inside Lincoln's White House*, 63.

49. Humphreys, *Virginia Campaign*, 56.

50. Badeau, *Military History*, 104–105; Porter, *Campaigning with Grant* (abridged), 36–37; Scott, *Into the Wilderness*, 41.

51. Foote, *Fort Sumter to Perryville*, 420; Stiles, *Marse Robert*, 244; Dowdey, *Lee's Last Campaign*, 17–20; A. C. Buell, *Cannoneer*, 221; McKim, *Recollections*, 134.

52. Stiles, *Marse Robert*, 245.

53. C. Brown, *Brown's Civil War*, 247.

54. Ibid., 248.

55. *History 121st PA*, 76.

56. J. E. Smith, *Grant*, 321.

57. C. Brown, *Brown's Civil War*, 247–248.

58. Prentice, "Opening Hours," 117.

59. Humphreys, *Virginia Campaign*, 55–56; Shepard, *Out of the Wilderness*, 5–8; Prentice, "Opening Hours," 118.

60. Chamberlin, *150th PA*, 214; Porter, *Campaigning with Grant* (abridged), 67.

61. *History 121st PA*, 77.

62. Clark, *NC Regiments*, vol. 1, 150–151.

63. T. Buell, *Warrior Generals*, 5, 66–67, 119, 219; Wheeler, *Fields of Fury*, 109.

64. Gordon, *Reminiscences*, 238–239.

65. Gordon, *Reminiscences*, 238–241; Bradwell, *Southern Cross*, 151–152; Nichols, *Soldier's Story*, 141.

66. A. L. Long, *Memoirs of Robert E. Lee*, 333.

67. Prentice, "Opening Hours," 114–115.

68. A. C. Buell, *Cannoneer*, 159–160; Rhea, *Wilderness*, 162–163.

69. Lyman, *Notebooks*, 134; Foote, *Red River to Appomattox*, 161.

70. G. T. Stevens, *Sixth Corps*, 305–307; O.R., vol. 36, part I, 665–666; Hyde, *Greek Cross*, 184–185; Humphreys, *Virginia Campaign*, 35; Dowdey, *Lee's Last Campaign*, 99.

71. Wheeler, *Fields of Fury*, 100–101.

72. Warner, *Generals in Gray*, 288; Howard, "Notes and Recollections," 99.

73. O.R., vol. 36, part II, 406–407.

74. Warner, *Generals in Blue*, 170–171; O.R., vol. 36, part I, 676; H. Stevens, "Sixth Corps in the Wilderness," 189–191; Scott, *Into the Wilderness*, 45–47; Beaudry, *5th NY Cavalry*, 122; Catton, *Grant Takes Command*, 141; Kreiser, *Defeating Lee*, 166.

75. Taylor, *Four Years*, 126.

76. Royall, *Some Reminiscences*, 28.

77. Warner, *Generals in Gray*, 133; Catton, *Glory Road*, 314; Scott, *Into the Wilderness*, 50–51.

78. Royall, *Some Reminiscences*, 28.

79. Freeman, *Lee: Biography*, vol. 3, 278–279.

80. LaRocca, *124th NY*, 220; Humphreys, *Virginia Campaign*, 32; Miller, *Harvard*, 331; O.R., vol. 36, part II, 410.

81. Fisk, *Hard Marching*, 215–216.

82. Perry, *Letters from a Surgeon*, 38.

83. O.R., vol. 36, part I, 677; part II, 414–415; Humphreys, *Virginia Campaign*, 32–34.

84. Badeau, *Military History*, 113; Hess, *Trench Warfare*, 39–40.

85. Caldwell, *South Carolinians*, 131; Albright *Papers, Diary*.

86. Clark, *NC Regiments*, vol. 1, 596.

87. Ibid., vol. 3, 75.

88. Robertson, *A.P. Hill*, 258.

89. Weygant, *124th NY*, 288; LaRocca, *124th NY*, 220–221.

90. Hancock, *Reminiscences*, 99–103; Lyman, *Notebooks*, 135.

91. Weygant, *124th NY*, 287–288.

92. Scott, *Into the Wilderness*, 78–79.

93. Lyman, *Meade's Headquarters*, 92–93; Grant, *Memoirs*, 403; Porter, *Campaigning with Grant* (abridged), 48.

94. Wilcox, "Lee and Grant," 492–493; Catton, *Grant Takes Command*, 192; Clark, *NC Regiments*, vol. 2, 665.

95. O.R., vol. 36, part II, 441; Heth, *Memoirs*, 183; Scott, *Into the Wilderness*, 88–89.

96. Freeman, *Lee: Biography*, vol. 3, 278–279; Dowdey, *Lee's Last Campaign*, 135.

97. Schaff, *Wilderness*, 209–210; Catton, *Grant Takes Command*, 193.

98. Wilkeson, *Inside Out*, 67, 201–202.

99. O.R., vol. 36, part I, 615; Robertson, *A.P. Hill*, 257–259; Griffith, *Battle Tactics*, 160; Alexander, *Fighting*, 357.

100. Graham, "26th MS," 169 (archive.org/stream/confederateveter15conf/confederateveter15conf_djvu.txt); Royall, 29–30.

101. Humphreys, *Virginia Campaign*, 34.

102. Trudeau, *Bloody Roads*, 73.

103. Dawes, *6th WI*, 261.

104. Humphreys, *Virginia Campaign*, 34; Carter, *Four Brothers*, 391.

105. J. H. Wilson, *Life of Rawlins*, 380–384.

106. O.R., vol. 36, part II, 428.

107. O.R., vol. 36, part II, 876–877; vol. 36, part II, 428; Humphreys, *Virginia Campaign*, 36; Marshall-Cornwall, *Grant as Commander*, 154; Rhea, *Wilderness*, 261.

108. Grant, *Memoirs*, 404; O.R., vol. 36, part II, 404–406, 412, 425; Atkinson, *Grant's Campaigns*, 162–164.

109. Badeau, *Military History*, vol. 1, 113–115; Porter, *Campaigning with Grant*, (abridged), 49; J. E. Smith, *Grant*, 324.

110. O.R., vol. 36, part II, 952; Scott, *Into the Wilderness*, 107.

111. O.R., vol. 36, part II, 951.

112. Robertson, *A.P. Hill*, 260–261; Warren, *Generals in Gray*, 135; Dowdey, *Lee's Last Campaign*, 20–24; Clark, *NC Regiments*, vol. 2, 665; Krick, "Lee to the Rear," 161; Dame, *Rapidan to Richmond*, 82.

113. Heth, *Memoirs*, 184; Patterson, *Blue to Gray*, 78.

114. Royall, *Some Reminiscences*, 31.

115. Lee, *Wartime Papers*, 721; Dowdey, *Lee's Last, Campaign*, 133; Scott, *Into the Wilderness*, 109.

116. Mills, *16th NC*, 47; Royall, *Some Reminiscences*, 31–32; Clark, *NC Regiments*, vol. 1, 676; vol. 2, 665.

117. O.R., vol. 36, part II, 439; Wilkeson, *Inside Out*, 70.

118. Lyman, *Notebooks*, 136–138.

119. Robertson, *A.P. Hill*, 266; Freeman, *Lee: Biography*, vol. 3, 286.

120. Royall, *Some Reminiscences*, 31–32; Clark, *NC Regiments*, vol. 1, 548; Freeman, *Lee: Biography*, vol. 3, 287; Dowdey, *Lee's Last Campaign*, 149–150; O.R., vol. 36, part I, 677; Scott, *Into the Wilderness*, 116–117; Robertson, *A.P. Hill*, 265–266; Venable, "Wilderness to Petersburg," 525.

121. Warner, *Generals in Gray*, 192–193.

122. Longstreet, *Manassas to Appomattox*, 557–558; Alexander, *Fighting*, 350; Freeman, *Lee: Biography*, vol. 3, 283; Laine and Penny, *Law's Brigade*, 234.

123. Longstreet, *Manassas to Appomattox*, 559–560; Alexander, *Fighting*, 350; Dowdey, *Lee's Last Campaign*, 135; Dickert, *Kershaw's Brigade*, 344–345.

124. Rhea, *Wilderness*, 298; Krick, "Lee to the Rear," 164–165; Law, "Wilderness to Cold Harbor," 124.

125. Dame, *Rapidan to Richmond*, 84–85.

126. Wheeler, *Fields of Fury*, 124; Royall, *Some Reminiscences*, 33.

127. Venable, "Wilderness to Cold Harbor," 525–526; Krick, "Lee to the Rear," 177; Campbell, *Lone Star*, 106–108; Taylor, *Four Years*, 128.

128. Coles, *Huntsville to Appomattox*, 160.

129. Royall, *Some Reminiscences*, 32; Sorrel, *Recollections*, 40.

130. Clark, *NC Regiments*, vol. 4, 191–192; vol. 1, 548; Caldwell, *South Carolinians*, 134; Melville, *Selected Poems*, 135.

131. A. C. Young, *Lee's Army*, 48; David Holt, *Mississippi Rebel*, 343; Laine and Penny, *Law's Brigade*, 238–241; Law, "Wilderness to Cold Harbor," 125; Polley, *Hood's Texas Brigade*, 232–233; O.R., vol. 36, part I, 611 [Cutler report]; Coles, *Huntsville to Appomattox*, 161–163.

132. Wilkeson, *Inside Out*, 72.

133. Fisk, *Hard Marching*, 216–217.

134. Lyman, *Notebooks*, 138; Fisk, *Hard Marching*, 217.

135. O.R., vol. 36, part I, 677–680.

136. Lyman, *Meade's Headquarters,* 103; Grant, *Memoirs*, 405; Swinton, *Army of the Potomac*, 431–433; Dowdey, *Lee's Last Campaign*, 155.

137. O.R., vol. 36, part II, 440.

138. Lavery and Jordan, *John Gibbon*, 104–105; Grant, *Memoirs*, 405.

139. Walker, *General Hancock*, 170–171.

140. Gallagher, *Ramseur*, 103; Dowdey, *Lee's Last Campaign*, 158; Freeman, *Lee: Biography*, vol. 3, 289.

141. Lyman, *Notebooks*, 137; Freeman, *Lee: Biography*, vol. 3, 290–293; Freeman, *Lee's Lieutenants*, 666; Sorrell, *Recollections*, 242–243; Weygant, *124th NY*, 293–294;

Warner, *Generals in Gray*, 286–287; Longstreet, *Manassas to Appomattox*, 568; Freeman, *Lee: Biography*, vol. 2, 293–294.

142. Work, *Political Generals*, 14; Wert, *Brotherhood*, 248–249; Warner, *Generals in Blue*, 532–533; Sorrell, *Recollections*, 243; Dickert, *Kershaw's Brigade*, 352; Hay, *Lincoln and the Civil War*, 182.

143. Miller, *Harvard*, 338–340.

144. Longstreet, *Manassas to Appomattox*, 563–567; Rhea, *Wilderness*, 369; Alexander, *Fighting*, 365; Taylor, *General Lee*, 236–237; Sorrel, *Recollections*, 243–244; Stiles, *Marse Robert*, 246–247.

145. Dawson, *Confederate Service*, 116.

146. Scott, *Into the Wilderness*, 160; Alexander, *Fighting*, 360–362; Taylor, *General Lee*, 236; Field, "1864 and 1865," 545.

147. Longstreet, *Manassas to Appomattox*, 565.

148. Grant, *Papers*, vol. 10, 398fns, 402fns; Lyman, *Notebooks*, 135–136; O.R., vol. 36, part II, 461.

149. Lyman, *Notebooks*, 136; Walker, *General Hancock*, 178.

150. Porter, *Campaigning with Grant* (abridged), 56; Porter, *Campaigning with Grant* (unabridged), 215; Scott, *Into the Wilderness*, 177–178.

151. Scott, *Into the Wilderness*, 161–163; Lyman, *Meade's Headquarters*, 96fn1 [from Lyman's journal]; 96–97.

152. O.R., vol. 36, part II, 444–445.

153. Freeman, *Lee: Biography*, vol. 3, 294; Weygant, *124th NY*, 295–296.

154. Miller, *Harvard*, 344; McAllister, *Letters*, 415–416; J. D. Smith, *19th ME*, 138.

155. Badeau, *Military History*, 124; Grant, *Memoirs*, 407; Wilkeson, *Inside Out*, 73.

156. O.R., vol. 36, part I, 514 [Dow]; Badeau, *Military History*, 124; Goss, *Private*, 277; Weygant, *124th NY*, 298; Gibbon, *Personal Recollections*, 215–216; Miller, *Harvard*, 345–346.

157. Alexander, *Fighting*, 363; Walker, *General Hancock*, 179–180.

158. Woodbury, *Burnside*, 374; Hopkins, *7th RI*, 167.

159. A. Buell, *Cannoneer*, 168.

160. Hess, *Trench Warfare*, 35.

161. Early, *Autobiographical Sketch*, 348; Gordon, *Reminiscences*, 243–245, 255–256.

162. O.R., vol. 36, part I, 1071; Early, *Autobiographical Sketch*, 348–349.

163. Gordon, *Reminiscences*, 258–260; Rhea, *Wilderness*, 411–414.

164. Gordon, *Reminiscences*, 249.

165. Nichols, *Soldier's Story*, 148; Daniel Holt, *Surgeon's Civil War*, 183; Page and Gilmore, *War Correspondent*, 57.

166. Gordon, *Reminiscences*, 249, Page and Gilmore, *War Correspondent*, 57; Morrow, *77th NY*, 112–113.

167. Page and Gilmore, *War Correspondent*, 58; Catton, *Grant Takes Command*, 215; Porter, *Campaigning with Grant* (abridged), 65–68.

168. Cilella, *121st NY*, 289–291; Hess, *Trench Warfare*, 38; Freeman, *Lee: Biography*, vol. 3, 298; Gordon, *Reminiscences*, 251.

169. Robertson, *A.P. Hill*, 267; Perry, *Letters from a Surgeon*, 166–170; Porter, *Campaigning with Grant* (abridged), 67; Miller, *Harvard*, 346; O.R., vol. 36, part I, 218.

170. O.R., vol. 36, part I, 2.

171. J. H. Wilson, *Life of Rawlins*, 215–217; Porter, *Campaigning with Grant* (abridged), 65.

172. Lyman, *Notebooks*, 141.

173. Sandburg, *Abraham Lincoln: The War Years*, vol. 3, 45.

174. Cadwallader, *Three Years*, 180–182.

175. O.R., vol. 36, part II, 430.

176. Carpenter, *Six Months*, 30; S. B. Oates, *Malice toward None*, 386; Bates, 245; Sandburg, vol. 3, 43; Welles, *Diary*, 25.

177. Dana, *Recollections*, 188–189; Wheeler, *Fields of Fury*, 146–147.

178. Wing, *Lincoln Kissed Me*, 34–39; L. M. Starr, *Bohemian Brigade*, 298, 301.

179. Lyman, *Meade's Headquarters*, 101–102.

180. Schaff, *Wilderness*, 327–328.

181. Badeau, *Military History*, 100, 123.

182. Ibid., 126.

183. Rhea, *Wilderness*, 435–436, 440; A. C. Young, *Lee's Army*, 235; Trudeau, *Bloody Roads*, 119; www.nps.gov/anti/historyculture/casualties.htm.

184. Fisk, *Hard Marching*, 219; Polley, *Soldier's Letters*, 233.

185. Casler, *Stonewall Brigade*, 207–208.

186. Hotchkiss, *Map of the Valley*, 201; Polley, *Hood's Brigade*, 233–234; Casler, *Stonewall Brigade*, 208; Rhea, *Spotsylvania*, 17 [from Capt. Seymour, 116–118]; Carter, *Four Brothers*, 392.

187. S. B. Oates, *Woman of Valor*, 104; Catton, *Mr. Lincoln*, 188–189; Welch, *Boy General*, 121–122; G. T. Stevens, *Sixth Corps*, 314, 317; Wilkeson, *Inside Out*, 149–150; Perry, *Letters from a Surgeon*, 174.

188. Pullen, *20th ME*, 195–196; G. T. Stevens, *Sixth Corps*, 339–342.

189. O.R., vol. 36, part II, 482–483; Pullen, *20th ME*, 196–197; G. T. Stevens, *Sixth Corps*, 342.

190. S. B. Oates, *Clara Barton*, 233–234.

191. Ibid., 9–10, 68–75, 91, 237; Schlaifer and Freeman, *Heart's Work*, 130–132; Welch, *Boy General*, 126.

192. Wilkeson, *Inside Out*, 88–89; Hess, *Trench Warfare*, 40–41; Swinton, *Army of the Potomac*, 428; Lyman, *Notebooks*, 189; Weygant, *124th NY*, 294; Alexander, *Fighting*, 354.

193. Schaff, *Wilderness*, 326.

194. O.R., vol. 36, part I, 18–19; Fuller, *Generalship*, 238.

195. O.R., vol. 36, part II, 513.

196. Scott, *Into the Wilderness*, 139–141; O.R., vol. 36, part I, 816–817, 833–834; Atkinson, *Grant's Campaigns*, 203; Sheridan, *Memoirs*, vol. 1, 362–362; Kidd, *Custer*, 278.

197. Sheridan, *Memoirs*, vol. 1, 364; Longacre, *Fitz Lee*, 146; Rhea, *Spotsylvania*, 35.

198. O.R., vol. 36, part II, 515–516.

199. Porter, *Campaigning with Grant* (abridged), 70; Muffly, *148th PA*, 846; Grant, *Memoirs*, 412; Grant, *Papers*, vol. 10, 411; O.R., vol. 36, part II, 481.

200. Grant, *Memoirs*, 415–416; O.R., vol. 36, part I, 1041; part II, 969; Humphreys, *Virginia Campaign*, 71; Freeman, *Lee: Biography*, vol. 3, 302–303; Trudeau, *Bloody Roads*, 125.

201. Royall, *Some Reminiscences*, 35; Dowdey, *Lee's Last Campaign*, 181–182.

202. Freeman, *Lee: Biography*, vol. 3, 303; Royall, *Some Reminiscences*, 35; Robertson, *A.P. Hill*, 268; O.R., vol. 36, part II, 968.

203. Freeman, *Lee: Biography*, vol. 3, 301; O.R., vol. 36, part II, 967.

204. Williams, *Lincoln and His Generals*, 309–310; McPherson, *Tried by War*, 216–217.

205. Badeau, *Military History*, 134; Porter, *Campaigning with Grant* (abridged) 78–79; Grant, *Memoirs*, 411; Wilkeson, *Inside Out*, 78–80; Foote, *Red River to Appomattox*, 191.

206. Johnson and Buel, *Battles and Leaders*, vol. 4, 248.

207. Rhea, *Spotsylvania*, 29; Freeman, *Lee's Lieutenants*, 673; A. C. Young, *Lee's Army*, 48; Catton, *Grant Takes Command*, 207.

208. Clark, *NC Regiments*, vol. 2, 263; Caldwell, *South Carolinians*, 135–136.

209. O.R., vol. 36, part I, 1028.

210. Longacre, *Fitz Lee*, 2–4, 61, 144.

211. Cilella, *121st NY*, 293.

212. O.R., vol. 36, part II, 551–552.

213. Ibid., 553.

214. Sheridan, *Memoirs*, vol. 1, 365–367; Badeau, *Military History*, 139–141; Humphreys, *Virginia Campaign*, 70.

215. Catton, *Stillness*, 94–95.

216. Wainwright, *Personal Journals*, 356.

217. Cook and Beale, *12th MA*, 129.

218. Wise, *Long Arm of Lee*, 795; Longacre, *Fitz Lee*, 147; Foote, *Red River to Appomattox*, 194–196.

219. O.R., vol. 36, part II, 554.

220. Ibid., vol. 36, part I, 878.

221. Dickert, *Kershaw's Brigade*, 357; Foote, *Red River to Appomattox*, 196.

222. Dickert, *Kershaw's Brigade*, 357–358; Thomason, *Jeb Stuart*, 489.

223. O.R., vol. 36, part II, 539; Foote, *Red River to Appomattox*, 199–200; Powell, *Fifth Army Corps*, 632–634; Catton, *Grant Takes Command*, 213.

224. Dame, *Rapidan to Richmond*, 130; Foote, *Red River to Appomattox*, 200.

225. O.R., vol. 36, part II, 54.

226. Dame, *Rapidan to Richmond*, 113–118.

227. O.R., vol. 36, part II, 540.

228. Rhea, *Spotsylvania*, 59; Cannan, *Spotsylvania*, 54; Wainwright, *Personal Journals*, 359.

229. O.R., vol. 36, part II, 540–541.

230. Ibid., 541.

231. Ibid.; Lyman, *Notebooks*, 145; Lyman, *Meade's Headquarters*, 105.

232. Lyman, *Meade's Headquarters*, 105.

233. Freeman, *Lee: Biography*, vol. 3, 304; O.R., vol. 51, part II, 902.

234. O.R., vol. 51, part II, 902; vol. 36, part II, 974; Freeman, *Lee: Biography*, vol. 3, 305.

235. O.R., vol. 36, part II, 974.

236. Foote, *Red River to Appomattox*, 202; Trudeau, *Bloody Roads*, 132; Wise, *Long Arm of Lee*, 777; Carter, *Four Brothers*, 394; Powell, 636fn1; Humphreys, *Virginia Campaign*, 65–66; Grant, *Memoirs*, 413–414.

3. THE RED HOUR—SPOTSYLVANIA COURT HOUSE

1. O.R., vol. 36, part II, 627.
2. Long and Long, *Day by Day*, 499–500.
3. Heth, *Memoirs*, 187.
4. Porter, *Campaigning with Grant* (abridged), 98.
5. Freeman, *Lee's Dispatches*, 176–177.
6. Heth, *Memoirs*, 182.
7. O.R., vol. 36, part I, 3.
8. Badeau, *Military History*, 146.
9. Venable, "Lee in the Wilderness," 242.
10. Warner, *Generals in Gray*, 180; E. M. Thomas, *Robert E. Lee*, 225; Catton, *Grant Takes Command*, 219–220; Hess, *Trench Warfare*, 205.
11. Humphreys, *Virginia Campaign*, 117.
12. Hess, *Trench Warfare*, xv, 19; Foote, *Red River to Appomattox*, 204.
13. Humphreys, *Virginia Campaign*, 75.
14. Hess, *Trench Warfare*, 48.
15. Marshall-Cornwall, *Grant as Commander*, 156–157.
16. Seymour, *Memoirs*, 120; Freeman, *Lee: Biography*, vol. 3 311–313.
17. Porter, *Campaigning with Grant* (abridged), 75–76.
18. O.R., vol. 36, part II, 552; Kidd, *Custer*, 288.
19. Wheelan, *Terrible Swift Sword*, 73; Rhea, *Spotsylvania*, 100; Kidd, *Custer*, 287; Sheridan, *Memoirs*, vol. 1, 370–371.
20. O.R., vol. 36, part I, 15–16.
21. Longacre, *Amateurs*, 67–68.
22. Ibid., xi–xii, 27.
23. Warner, *Generals in Blue*, 60–61.
24. Badeau, *Military History*, 246–247.
25. Butler, *Autobiography*, vol. 2, 642–643; Longacre, *Amateurs*, 73–74.
26. Longacre, *Amateurs*, 40–43; O.R., vol. 51, part II, 935; vol. 36, part II, 989; J. B. Jones, *Rebel War Clerk*, vol. 2, 204.
27. Longacre, *Amateurs*, 5, 74–81; O.R., vol. 36, part I, 20; Grant, *Memoirs*, 376–377; Badeau, *Military History*, 251–252; Foote, *Red River to Appomattox*, 253–259.
28. Rhea, *Spotsylvania*, 92.
29. McMahon, "Cold Harbor," 175.
30. H. W. Thomas, *Doles-Cook*, 76.
31. Porter, *Campaigning with Grant* (abridged), 80; Lyman, *Meade's Headquarters*, 107; Daniel Holt, *Surgeon's Civil War*, 185; Welles, *Diary*, 27–28.
32. Warner, *Generals in Blue*, 408.
33. O.R., vol. 36, part II, 561.
34. Ibid., 567–568; Grant, *Memoirs*, 416–417; Muffly, *148th PA*, 852.
35. O.R., vol. 36, part I, 331.
36. Ibid., 66.
37. Lyman, *Meade's Headquarters*, 107; Lyman, *Notebooks*, 147; Walker, *Second Corps*, 451–455; Walker, *General Hancock*, 188–190; Muffly, *148th PA*, 854–855; O.R., vol. 36, part I, 331–333 [Hancock's report]; Welch, *Boy General*, 107–108.
38. Welch, *Boy General*, 109.
39. Alexander, *Memoirs*, 514.

40. Humphreys, *Virginia Campaign*, 82.

41. O.R., vol. 36, part II, 606–607.

42. Ibid., part I, 356; part II, 609–610.

43. Ibid., part I, 3.

44. Ibid., part II, 11, 614–615.

45. Ibid., part II, 600.

46. Gibbon, *Personal Recollections,* 218–219; Warner, *Generals in Blue*, 171–172; Wert, *Brotherhood*, 100–101.

47. Gibbon, *Personal Recollections*, 219.

48. Coles, *Huntsville to Appomattox*, 168–169.

49. Laine and Penny, *Law's Brigade*, 260; Law, "Wilderness to Cold Harbor," 129.

50. J. D. Smith, *19th ME*, 150; Rhea, *Spotsylvania*, 146; Dame, *Rapidan to Richmond*, 158.

51. Miller, *Harvard*, 354.

52. Coles, *Huntsville to Appomattox*, 168–169; Laine and Penny, *Law's Brigade*, 260.

53. Dame, *Rapidan to Richmond*, 158–159.

54. Smith, *19th ME*, 150.

55. Lyman, *Notebooks*, 170; Grant, *Memoirs*, 418–419.

56. Griffith, *Battle Tactics*, 152; Warner, *Generals in Blue*, 519–520.

57. Cilella, *121st NY*, 295–297; Hess, *Trench Warfare*, 55–56.

58. McAllister, *Letters*, 417.

59. O.R., vol. 36, part I, 667–668; Zeller, *2nd VT*, 189; Badeau, *Military History*, 163.

60. Clark, *NC Regiments*, vol. 3, 48–49.

61. O.R., vol. 36, part I, 667–668; Zeller, *2nd VT*, 189; Lyman, *Notebooks*, 150–151.

62. Taylor, *General Lee*, 240; Clark, *NC Regiments*, vol. 3, 48; Hess, *Trench Warfare*, 56–57.

63. Badeau, *Military History*, 164–165; Zeller, *2nd VT*, 190.

64. O.R., vol. 36, part I, 668, 66–67; Walker, *General Hancock*, 193; Humphreys, *Virginia Campaign*, 89; Lyman, *Meade's Headquarters*, 110; Wainwright, *Personal Journals*, 363–364; Grant, *Memoirs*, 418.

65. Coffin, *Redeeming*, 111–112.

66. Daniel Holt, *Surgeon's Civil War*, 186.

67. Weygant, *124th NY*, 310.

68. Law, "Wilderness to Cold Harbor," 130; W. C. Oates, *Union and Confederacy*, 355–356; Coles, *Huntsville to Appomattox*, 169; A. C. Young, *Lee's Army*, 48; LaRocca, *124th NY*, 242–243; O.R., vol. 36, part I, 334 [Hancock], 66–67; Lyman, *Notebooks*, 151.

69. Stiles, *Marse Robert*, 255–256.

70. Hess, *Trench Warfare*, 47, 62–63; Taylor, *Four Years*, 130; Freeman, *Lee: Biography*, vol. 3, 431–432, 312–313.

71. Freeman, *Lee: Biography*, vol. 3, 314; O.R., vol. 36, part II, 982–983.

72. Freeman, *Lee's Dispatches*, 176; Venable, *Papers*, Folder 7.

73. H. W. Thomas, *Doles-Cook*, 479.

74. Longacre, *Custer*, 49; E. Thomas, *Bold Dragon*, 13–25, 54–58, 111–116, 196, 245–246; Foote, *Red River to Appomattox*, 228; Wheelan, *Terrible Swift Sword*, 65; S. Z. Starr, *Union Cavalry*, 32–33; McPherson, *Tried by War*, 191; Freeman, *Lee: Biography*, vol. 3, 366fn.

75. Kidd, *Custer*, 295; S. Z. Starr, *Union Cavalry*, 99; B. Davis, *Jeb Stuart*, 386.

76. Coffey, *Sheridan's Lieutenants*, 12; B. Davis, *Jeb Stuart*, 388; Sheridan, *Memoirs*, vol. 1, 374–375.

77. Urwin, *Custer Victorious*, 136; Sheridan, *Memoirs*, I, 375; S. Z. Starr, *Union Cavalry*, 100.

78. B. Davis, *Jeb Stuart*, 389.

79. Foote, *Red River to Appomattox*, 227.

80. B. Davis, *Jeb Stuart*, 390; E. Thomas, *Bold Dragon*, 289.

81. O.R., vol. 51, part II, 911.

82. Hergesheimer, *Sheridan*, 182; O.R., vol. 51, part II, 912, 916; Kidd, *Custer*, 291.

83. O.R., vol. 36, part I, 790; B. Davis, *Jeb Stuart*, 394.

84. Longacre, *Amateurs*, 83–85.

85. B. Davis, *Jeb Stuart*, 392–393.

86. O.R., vol. 36, part I, 790; S. Z. Starr, *Union Cavalry*, 101–102; Wheelan, *Terrible Swift Sword*, 77; B. Davis, *Jeb Stuart*, 397–399.

87. S. Z. Starr, *Union Cavalry*, 102–103; Kidd, *Custer*, 295.

88. Wheelan, *Terrible Swift Sword*, 78; Thomason, *Jeb Stuart*, 499; B. Davis, *Jeb Stuart*, 408–409. (Huff died weeks later, after being wounded at Haw's Shop.); O.R., vol. 36, part I, 319, 790–791; Sheridan, *Memoirs*, vol. 1, 376–379.

89. Sheridan, *Memoirs*, vol. 1, 387.

90. Ibid., 379–382; Foote, *Red River to Appomattox*, 233.

91. Wheelan, *Terrible Swift Sword*, 80; Urwin, *Custer Victorious*, 146–147; Kidd, *Custer*, 310–312; O.R., vol. 36, part I, 776–778, 791; Sheridan, *Memoirs*, vol. 1, 392.

92. B. Davis, *Jeb Stuart*, 411–417; Richmond *Whig*, May 17, 1864.

93. Freeman, *Lee: Biography*, vol. 3, 327; Lee, *Wartime Papers*, 736.

94. Porter, *Campaigning with Grant* (abridged), 86–87.

95. O.R., vol. 36, part II, 627–628; Grant, *Papers*, vol. 10, 422; Badeau, *Military History*, 169.

96. Porter, *Campaigning with Grant* (abridged), 87–88; Welles, *Diary*, 33; Rice, *Abraham Lincoln*, 337.

97. Rice, *Abraham Lincoln*, 337–338; S. B. Oates, *Malice toward None*, 380; Donald, *Lincoln*, 513.

98. Hay, *Lincoln and the Civil War*, 196; D. H. Bates, *Lincoln in the Telegraph Office*, 7–9, 38, 40–42.

99. Brooks, *Mr. Lincoln's Washington*, 148–149.

100. McGuire, "Southern Refugee," 193, 191.

101. Hay, *Lincoln and the Civil War*, 195; Carpenter, *Six Months*, 283.

102. Grant, *Papers*, vol. 10, 426.

103. Meade, *Life and Letters*, 197.

104. Dana, *Recollections*, 189–190.

105. Lyman, *Meade's Headquarters*, 110.

106. Alexander, *Fighting*, 373; Fowler, *Memorials*, 182; O.R., vol. 36, part I, 629.

107. Lyman, *Meade's Headquarters*, 110; Badeau, *Military History*, 193.

108. Craft, *141st PA*, 192; Hodgkins, *Civil War Diary*, 85; Weygant, *124th NY*, 312–313.

109. O.R., vol. 36, part I, 335; Barlow, *Fear*, 191–192; Walker, *General Hancock*, 195–196; Welch, *Boy General*, 110–114; Muffly, *148th PA*, 256–257; Black, "Bloody Angle," 423–424.

110. Muffly, *148th PA*, 856–857; Welch, *Boy General*, 114.

111. O.R., vol. 36, part I, 1044 [Pendleton's report]; Alexander, *Fighting*, 374–376; Freeman, *Lee: Biography*, vol. 3, 315–316; Heth, *Memoirs*, 186–187; Robertson, *A.P. Hill*, 270.

112. Kreiser, *Defeating Lee*, 154; Warner, *Generals in Blue*, 203; Lyman, *Notebooks*, 182; Muffly, *148th PA*, 861–862.

113. Walker, *General Hancock*, 180–181.

114. O.R., vol. 36, part I, 335; Muffly, *148th PA*, 256–257; Welch, *Boy General*, 115.

115. Miller, *Harvard*, 357–358; Grant, *Memoirs*, 421–422; LaRocca, *124th NY*, 249.

116. Black, "Bloody Angle," 425–426; Fuller, *Generalship*, 250; Muffly, *148th PA*, 856; Hess, *Trench Warfare*, 65–67; Mulholland, *116th PA*, 209.

117. O.R., vol. 36, part I, 1044, 1080; Seymour, *Memoirs*, 123–124.

118. Chapla, *50th VA*, 91–93; Dowdey, *Lee's Last Campaign*, 201–202; Bradwell, *Southern Cross*, 166–167.

119. National Park Service site, www.nps.gov/frsp/bloody.htm; Alexander, *Fighting*, 376; Hodgkins, *19th ME*, 85; Chapla, *50th VA*, 93; Clark, *NC Regiments*, I, 152–153; Mulholland, *116th PA*, 210.

120. Wert, *Brotherhood*, 300, 302; Houghton, *17th ME*, 177; Robertson, *Stonewall Brigade*, 224–225.

121. Foote, *Red River to Appomattox*, 216; Warner, *Generals in Gray*, 158–159; O.R., vol. 36, part I, 1080.

122. O.R., vol., 36, part I, 335 [Hancock report].

123. Black, "Bloody Angle," 428–429; Lyman, *Notebooks*, 153–154; Wainwright, *Personal Journals*, 37. (When Johnson died in 1873, he left Hancock a jewel-hilted sword that Johnson had received from the state of Virginia. Hancock, *Reminiscences*, 105.)

124. Clark, *NC Regiments*, vol. 3, 502; O.R., vol. 36, part II, 657; Welch, *Boy General*, 117–118; O.R., vol. 36, part II, 658.

125. Canaan, *Spotsylvania*, 128; Clark, *NC Regiments*, vol. 1, 289, 642; O.R., vol. 36, part II, 1044.

126. Porter, *Campaigning with Grant* (abridged), 93; O.R., vol. 36, part II, 656–657.

127. Porter, *Campaigning with Grant* (abridged), 94.

128. Freeman, *Lee: Biography*, vol. 3, 317–318.

129. Bradwell, *Southern Cross*, 168; Gordon, *Reminiscences*, 278–280; Seymour, *Memoirs*, 125.

130. Miller, *Harvard*, 360–362; Nichols, *Soldier's Story*, 151.

131. Freeman, *Lee: Biography*, vol. 3, 319; Seymour, *Memoirs*, 125; Rhea, *Spotsylvania*, 256; Gordon, *Reminiscences*, 280–281; Nichols, *Soldier's Story*, 152–156; Gallagher, *Ramseur*, 108–110.

132. Foote, *Red River to Appomattox*, 219; O.R., vol. 36, part II, 656.

133. David Holt, *Mississippi Rebel*, 252–253.

134. Ibid., 255–259; Freeman, *Lee: Biography*, vol. 3, 320–321; *Southern Historical Society Papers*, vol. 8, 105–107; Krick, "Insurmountable Barrier," 90.

135. Freeman, *Lee: Biography*, vol. 3, 321; Caldwell, *South Carolinians*, 141; Rhea, *Spotsylvania*, 259.

136. Caldwell, *South Carolinians*, 132–133.

137. Stiles, *Marse Robert*, 261.

138. Clark, *NC Regiments*, vol. 2, 384.

139. O.R., vol. 36, part II, 663, 671; Grant, *Papers*, vol. 10, 433; Jordan, *General Warren*, 151–152; Grant, *Memoirs*, 422–423; Badeau, *Military History*, 183–184.

140. Atkinson, *Grant's Campaigns*, 297, 303.

141. Krick, "Insurmountable Barrier," 90; Muffly, *148th PA*, 859–860.

142. Galloway, *95th PA*, 170–172.

143. Miller, *Harvard*, 362; Hodgkins, *19th ME*, 86.

144. Krick, "Insurmountable Barrier," 101; Black, "Bloody Angle," 431; Battle, *Forget-Me-Nots*, 116–117; Gordon, *Reminiscences*, 284–285; NPS site: www.nps.gov /frsp/bloody.htm; Galloway, *95th PA*, 172; McAllister, *Letters*, 419.

145. Badeau, *Military History*, 179–180.

146. O.R., vol. 36, part II, 679.

147. Barlow, "Capture of the Salient," 255; Hess, *Trench Warfare*, 8–79; Porter, Campaigning with Grant (abridged), 98–99; Walker, *General Hancock*, 200–201; Galloway, *95th PA*, 173–174. (After Lee surrendered at Appomattox Court House, Nelson Miles's II Corps division stopped at Spotsylvania Court House on its way to Washington. The red oak was gone. A black servant, however, whispered to Miles that it was locked in the hotel's smokehouse. The proprietor refused to supply a key, so the lock was broken with an ax. Upon reaching Washington, Miles presented the stump to War Secretary Stanton. For years, it stood at the entrance to the War Department, and it was displayed at the 1893 Chicago World's Fair in Chicago. Later, it was moved to the Smithsonian Institution's Museum of American History. Black, "Bloody Angle," 433–434.)

148. Black, "Bloody Angle," 432, 428.

149. Ibid., 430; O.R., vol. 36, part II, 710.

150. Lyman, *Notebooks*, 156.

151. O.R., vol. 36, part II, 675.

152. Power, *Lee's Miserables*, 32.

153. David Holt, *Mississippi Rebel*, 261; Hess, *Trench Warfare*, 79–80.

154. David Holt, *Mississippi Rebel*, 260.

155. Freeman, *Lee: Biography*, vol. 3, 325–326; Battle, *Forget-Me-Nots*, 116–117; David Holt, *Mississippi Rebel*, 261–263.

156. Power, *Lee's Miserables*, 38.

157. Venable, "Wilderness to Petersburg," 533; Speer, *Cemetery Hill*, 132–133.

158. O.R., vol. 36, part I, 68.

159. Fuller, *Generalship*, 256; Marshall-Cornwall, *Grant as Commander*, 160.

160. Badeau, *Military History*, 183.

161. Hess, *Trench Warfare*, 82; O.R., vol. 36, part II, 702–703; Dana, *Recollections*, 197–198.

162. Clark, *NC Regiments*, vol. 3, 53; Trudeau, *Bloody Roads*, 187; Miller, *Harvard*, 363; Carter, *Four Brothers*, 396; Hess, *Trench Warfare*, 83; Swinton, *Army of the Potomac*, 454; Porter, *Campaigning with Grant* (abridged), 99.

163. Dana, *Recollections*, 197.

164. Black, "Bloody Angle," 432–433.

165. Wheeler, *Fields of Fury*, 221; Nichols, *Soldier's Story*, 158–159; Haines, *15th NJ*, 182–183; Fisk, *Hard Marching*, 221.

166. Cilella, *121st NY*, 308–309; Daniel Holt, *Surgeon's Civil War*, 190; Galloway, *95th PA*, 174; Rhea, *Spotsylvania*, 311.

167. Gordon, *Reminiscences*, 285; Humphreys, *Virginia Campaign*, 100.

168. Alexander, *Fighting*, 380.

169. O.R., vol. 36, part I, 71; Welch, *Boy General*, 125; Cilella, *121st NY*, 302, 309; O.R., vol. 36, part I, 72; Dana, *Recollections*, 199; Humphreys, *Virginia Campaign*, 109; A. C. Young, *Lee's Army*, 232, 221–222, 236, 245; Apperson, *Hospital Steward*, 545; Kreiser, *Defeating Lee*, 178; Rhea, *Spotsylvania*, 311–312.

170. Daniel Holt, *Surgeon's Civil War*, 188.

171. Holmes, *Touched with Fire*, 122.

172. Carter, *Four Brothers*, 397; Caldwell, *South Carolinians*, 150–151.

173. O.R., vol. 36, part I, 4; Grant, *Papers*, vol. 10, 443–444.

174. Grant, *Memoirs*, 424.

175. Porter, *Campaigning with Grant* (abridged), 102–103.

176. Meade, *Life and Letters*, 195.

177. Freeman, *Lee: Biography*, vol. 3, 326–328, 331–332.

178. Long and Long, *Day by Day*, 499–500; McGuire, "Southern Refugee," 195.

179. O.R., vol. 36, part II, 720–722, 728–729.

180. Swinton, *Army of the Potomac*, 455.

181. Humphreys, *Virginia Campaign*, 106–108; O.R., vol. 36, part I, 5; Badeau, *Military History*, 197.

182. Wainwright, *Personal Journals*, 372; Freeman, *Lee: Biography*, vol. 3, 329; O.R., vol. 36, part I, 70 [Dana Report]; Casler, *Stonewall Brigade*, 217–218.

183. McAllister, *Letters*, 422–423.

184. Worsham, *Jackson's Foot Cavalry*, 216.

185. Freeman, *Lee: Biography*, vol. 3, 331.

186. O.R., vol. 36, part II, 844.

187. Jackman, *121st NY*, 250; O.R., vol. 36, part I, 361; Stewart, *Camp, March*, 384.

188. O.R., vol. 36, part I, 1987; Jackman, *121st NY*, 249; Cutshaw, "Spotsylvania Court House," 211; Miller, *Harvard*, 368–369.

189. Rhodes, *All for Union*, 146; O.R., vol. 36, part I, 73 [Dana], 337 [Hancock], 1054; Houston, *32nd ME*, 156–157; Seymour, *Memoirs*, 128; Lyman, *Notebooks*, 162–163.

190. O.R., vol. 36, part I, 1087; Cutshaw, "Spotsylvania Court House," 210.

191. Hess, *Trench Warfare*, 89; Porter, *Campaigning with Grant* (abridged), 106–107.

192. Freeman, *Lee: Biography*, vol. 3, 334–335; Lyman, *Notebooks*, 163; Porter, *Campaigning with Grant* (abridged), 108; O.R., vol. 36, part II, 840–841; I, 20; J. E. Smith, *Grant*, 308.

193. O.R., vol. 36, part I, 73.

194. Grant, *Memoirs*, 428; O.R., vol. 36, part II, 865.

195. O.R., vol. 36, part II, 1015; Freeman, *Lee's Dispatches*, 183–185.

196. Rhea, *North Anna*, 170–171; Taylor, *General Lee*, 243–244; Grant, *Papers*, vol. 10, 430, 457–459; Warner, *Generals in Blue*, 515–516.

197. A. C. Brown, *Line Officer*, 48–51.

198. Porter, *Campaigning with Grant* (abridged), 110–111.

199. Porter, *Campaigning with Grant* (abridged), 112; Keating, *Carnival of Blood*, 32.

200. Keating, *Carnival of Blood*, 46–50.

201. Roe and Nutt, *Heavy Artillery*, 153–156; Badeau, *Military History*, 207–208; Gallagher, *Ramseur*, 114; O.R., vol. 36, part I, 1083 [Ramseur's report], 1072 [Ewell's report]; Grant, *Papers*, vol. 10, 468fn; Keating, *Carnival of Blood*, 57–58.

202. Lyman, *Notebooks*, 164; Wainwright, *Personal Journals*, 379; Wilkeson, *Inside Out*, 86; Page and Gilmore, *War Correspondent*, 72.

203. Grant, *Memoirs*, 427.

204. Lyman, *Meade's Headquarters*, 100.

205. David Holt, *Mississippi Rebel*, 266.

4. THE BATTLE THAT NEVER HAPPENED—THE NORTH ANNA

1. Schoyer, *Road to Cold Harbor*, 92.

2. Law, "Wilderness to Cold Harbor," 143–144.

3. Wilkeson, *Inside Out*, 100–101.

4. Hess, *Trench Warfare*, 121–122; Keating, *Carnival of Blood*, 63–64; Cowles, *Official Military Atlas*, Plate 81, 203, Map 2.

5. Dowdey, *Lee's Last Campaign*, 251–252.

6. Badeau, *Military History*, 217.

7. Grant, *Memoirs*, 428; Fuller, *Generalship*, 219; Grant, *Papers*, vol. 10, 478fn.

8. Humphreys, *Virginia Campaign*, 110; Grant, *Memoirs*, 427–428.

9. Wainwright, *Personal Journals*, 380; O.R., vol. 36, part III, 77, 169; Porter, *Campaigning with Grant* (unabridged), 145.

10. Welles, *Diary*, 31–32.

11. Brooks, *Mr. Lincoln's Washington*, 323.

12. www.arlingtoncemetery.mil/History.

13. Humphreys, *Virginia Campaign*, 116–117; A. C. Young, *Lee's Army*, 235–236.

14. Perry, *Letters from a Surgeon*, 185, 176.

15. Grant, *Papers*, vol. 10, 428, 500–503; Krieser, *Defeating Lee*, 182.

16. Porter, *Campaigning with Grant* (unabridged), 164–165.

17. E. Bates, *Diary*, 366–367; Brooks, *Lincoln Observed*, 109.

18. Trudeau, *Bloody Roads*, 194.

19. Ford, *Adams Letters*, vol. 2, 131; Taylor, *Four Years*, 132–133; Hess, *Trench Warfare*, 98.

20. Law, "Wilderness to Cold Harbor," 143–144.

21. W. C. Davis, *Jefferson Davis*, 555–556; O.R., vol. 51, part II, 933; Power, *Lee's Miserables*, 45–46 [Richmond *Whig*, 17 May].

22. R. E. Lee, *Wartime Papers*, 728, 733; Freeman, *Lee: Biography*, vol. 3, 339–340; A. C. Young, *Lee's Army*, 233.

23. Badeau, *Military History*, 223; Lyman, "Uselessness of the Maps," 79–80; O.R., vol. 36, part III, 117; Grant, *Memoirs*, 429; Lyman, *Meade's Headquarters*, 136–137.

24. Kreiser, *Defeating Lee*, 181; Daniel Holt, *Surgeon's Civil War*, 193; Fisk, *Hard Marching*, 223; Wainwright, *Personal Journals*, 380; Hoyle, *"Deliver Us,"* 178; McAllister, *Letters*, 426.

25. Goss, *Private*, 301–302.

26. Craft, *141st PA*, 207; Cadwallader, *Three Years*, 204; Lyman, *Notebooks*, 167.

27. Cadwallader, *Three Years*, 204.

28. www.nps.gov/frsp/js.htm; Porter, *Campaigning with Grant* (unabridged), 135.

29. Schoyer, *Road to Cold Harbor*, 92.

30. Hodgkins, *19th ME*, 88.

31. Keating, *Carnival of Blood*, 63–64; O.R., vol. 36, part III, 96.

32. Wilkeson, *Inside Out*, 104–105.

33. Keating, *Carnival of Blood*, 68–69.

34. Freeman, *Lee: Biography*, vol. 3, 341; Pendleton, *Memoirs*, 335; Grant, *Memoirs*, 429–430.

35. O.R., vol. 36, part III, 813–814; Rhea, *North Anna*, 250; Freeman, *Lee: Biography*, vol. 3, 343.

36. R. E. Lee, *Wartime Letters*, 747–748.

37. Craft, *141st PA*, 207; Wainwright, *Personal Journals*, 383; Lyman, *Notebooks*, 169.

38. Lyman, *Notebooks*, 169–170; Porter, *Campaigning with Grant* (unabridged), 136–139.

39. Rhea, *North Anna*, 259; O.R., vol. 36, part III, 81–82.

40. Longacre, *Amateurs*, 87–100, 104–107.

41. Ibid., 63–64, 111–113; Hay, *Lincoln and the Civil War*, 197; O.R., vol. 36, part III, 43, 77, 183; Grant, *Papers*, vol. 10, 475, 477.

42. O.R., vol. 36, part III, 119.

43. Dana, *Recollections*, 203; Neese, *Horse Artillery*, 275.

44. Carter, *Four Brothers*, 408–409; Foote, *Red River to Appomattox*, 267–268; Wainwright, *Personal Journals*, 384–386; Dana, *Recollections*, 202–203.

45. Craft, *141st PA*, 204–205; Wilkeson, *Inside Out*, 110–115; Dickert, *Kershaw's Brigade*, 360; Miller, *Harvard*, 372; Keating, *Carnival of Blood*, 72–73.

46. R. E. Lee, *Wartime Papers*, 695–696; E. M. Thomas, *Robert E. Lee*, 278–279.

47. Freeman, *Lee: Biography*, vol. 3, 357.

48. Hess, *Trench Warfare*, 128–129.

49. Freeman, *Lee: Biography*, vol. 3, 356–360.

50. Hess, *Trench Warfare*, 129.

51. Freeman, *Lee's Dispatches*, 194–197.

52. O.R., vol. 36, part III, 157–159, 149, 145, 151–152; Dana, *Recollections*, 203.

53. Wilkeson, *Inside Out*, 120–121; O.R., vol. 36, part III, 151.

54. O.R., vol. 36, part III, 152–153, 155.

55. Warner, *Generals in Blue*, 277.

56. Anderson, *57th MA*, 99–102; O.R., vol. 36, part I, 79.

57. Anderson, *57th MA*, 102; Lyman, *Notebooks*, 173; Warner, *Generals in Blue*, 277.

58. Miller, *Harvard*, 373.

59. O.R., vol. 36, part III, 168, 155–156; part I, 78.

60. Wainwright, *Personal Journals*, 387.

61. O.R., vol. 36, part I, 9, 79; Badeau, *Military History*, 233, 235.

62. Swinton, *Army of the Potomac*, 477; Walker, *Second Corps*, 496.

63. Venable, "Lee in the Wilderness," 244; Taylor, *Four Years*, 134; Freeman, *Lee: Biography*, vol. 3, 359.

64. McAllister, *Letters*, 441; Grant, *Memoirs*, 433; Wainwright, *Personal Journals*, 388.

65. O.R., vol. 36, part I, 8–9.

66. Wheelan, *Terrible Swift Sword*, 81; Porter, *Campaigning with Grant* (abridged), 116; O.R., vol. 36, part I, 8–9; part III, 183.

67. Atkinson, *Grant's Campaigns*, 395–398.

68. Rhea, *Cold Harbor*, 31; Venable, *Papers*, File 7; O.R., vol. 36, part III, 834; vol. 51, part II, 962; Freeman, *Lee: Biography*, vol. 3, 361.

69. Rhea, *Cold Harbor*, 91; A. C. Young, *Lee's Army*, 238.

70. McAllister, *Letters*, 427; Lee, *Wartime Papers*, 750; Power, *Lee's Miserables*, 51; Gibbon, *Personal Recollections*, 225; Wilkeson, *Inside Out*, 121–123; Daniel Holt, *Surgeon's Civil War*, 194.

5. "NOT WAR BUT MURDER"—COLD HARBOR

1. Bartlett, *12th NH*, 202.

2. Dame, *Rapidan to Richmond*, 203.

3. Grant, *Memoirs*, 444.

4. Dowdey, *Lee's Last Campaign*, 268; Wheelan, *Terrible Swift Sword*, 76.

5. Rhea, *Cold Harbor*, 42 [Deloss Burton, *Civil War Times* 22 (1983), 26–27].

6. Miller, *Harvard*, 374–376.

7. Badeau, *Military History*, 266–267.

8. Matter, "Federal High Command," 31, 40–46.

9. Meade, *Life and Letters*, 197–198.

10. Lyman, *Notebooks*, 172–173.

11. Freeman, *Lee: Biography*, vol. 3, 363–364.

12. Freeman, *Lee: Biography*, vol. 3, 367–368, 394; Seymour, *Memoirs*, 131; R. E. Lee, *Wartime Papers*, 776.

13. Wilkeson, *Inside Out*, 124.

14. Carter, *Four Brothers*, 410.

15. Kidd, *Custer*, 323–327; Wheelan, *Terrible Swift Sword*, 82–83; S. Z. Starr, *Union Cavalry*, 117–118; Sheridan, *Memoirs*, vol. 1, 399–403; Foote, *Red River to Appomattox*, 277; Badeau, *Military History*, 269–270; Dowdey, *Lee's Last Campaign*, 272–274.

16. Wilkeson, *Inside Out*, 125–126.

17. Lyman, *Notebooks*, 180–181.

18. Welles, *Diary*, 44.

19. Hoyle, "*Deliver Us*," 180.

20. Tilney, *Fifth Corps*, 79–80.

21. Meade, *Life and Letters*, 199.

22. O.R., vol. 36, part III, 293–294.

23. Walker, *General Hancock*, 213.

24. Freeman, *Lee: Biography*, vol. 3, 366–367; O.R., vol. 36, part III, 848.

25. J. E. Smith, *Grant*, 360–361; Grant, *Memoirs*, 437.

26. Freeman, *Lee: Biography*, vol. 3, 369–371; *Southern History Society Papers*, 33, 59; Gallagher, *Ramseur*, 115–116; A. C. Young, *Lee's Army*, 279–285.

27. Craft, *141st PA*, 207–208.

28. Meade, *Life and Letters*, 199.

29. J. E. Smith, *Grant*, 361; O.R., vol. 51, part II, 971–972; R. E. Lee, *Wartime Papers*, 758; Grant, *Memoirs*, 439; Longacre, *Amateurs*, 114.

30. Warner, *Generals in Gray*, 22–23.

31. J. Davis, *Papers*, vol. 10, 425–426.

32. R. E. Lee, *Wartime Papers*, 754, 756–757.

33. Ibid., 758–759; Venable, "Lee in the Wilderness," 244; J. Davis, *Papers*, vol. 10, 441; Dowdey, *Lee's Last Campaign*, 282; A. C. Young, *Lee's Army*, 247; Venable, *Papers*, Folder 7.

34. Humphreys, *Virginia Campaign*, 171; Hess, *Trench Warfare*, 144; Kidd, *Custer*, 331.

35. Sheridan, *Memoirs*, vol. 1, 405–406.

36. Ibid., 406–408.

37. Freeman, *Lee: Biography*, vol. 3, 375.

38. Sheridan, *Memoirs*, vol. 1, 408–410; Wheelan, *Terrible Swift Sword*, 83; Freeman, *Lee: Biography*, vol. 3, 375, 377–378; Dickert, *Kershaw's Brigade*, 370; Alexander, *Fighting*, 399; Badeau, *Military History*, 275–276; Kidd, *Custer*, 332–334; Lyman, *Notebooks*, 184; Fuller, *Generalship*, 275–276.

39. Humphreys, *Virginia Campaign*, 172–173; Longacre, *Amateurs*, 115–117; Foote, *Red River to Appomattox*, 281–285; Badeau, *Military History*, 278–279.

40. Lyman, *Notebooks*, 187; Warner, *Generals in Blue*, 462–463; Longacre, *Amateurs*, 111–113.

41. Porter, *Campaigning with Grant* (abridged), 123.

42. Richmond *Examiner*, May 30, 1864, in GenealogyBank.com.

43. Porter, *Campaigning with Grant* (unabridged), 172.

44. San Francisco *Bulletin*, June 2, 1864, in GenealogyBank.com.

45. Newark *Daily Advertiser*, May 24, 1864, in GenealogyBank.com.

46. Lyman, *Meade's Headquarters*, 156; Stoughton [MA] *Sentinel*, June 18, 1864, in GenealogyBank.com; Lyman, *Notebooks*, 178; McFeely, *Grant*, 159.

47. Lyman, *Notebooks*, 179.

48. Porter, *Campaigning with Grant* (abridged), 149–150.

49. Ibid., 113.

50. Dowdey, *Lee's Last Campaign*, 276; Casler, *Stonewall Brigade*, 220–221; Freeman, *Lee: Biography*, vol. 3, 384–385; J. B. Jones, *Rebel War Clerk*, vol. 2, 209.

51. R. E. Lee, *Wartime Papers*, 759; Eggleston, "Cold Harbor," 231.

52. R. E. Lee, *Wartime Papers*, 765.

53. O.R., vol. 36, part III, 828; R. E. Lee, *Wartime Papers*, 759–760.

54. O.R., vol. 36, part III, 447–448; Badeau, *Military History*, 276–278.

55. G. T. Stevens, *Sixth Corps*, 347.

56. Rhea, *Cold Harbor*, 242; Clark, *NC Regiments*, vol. 5, 201–203; Vaill, *2nd CT*, 63–66.

57. Alexander, *Fighting*, 400–401; Hess, *Trench Warfare*, 147–149; Miller, *Harvard*, 377; Lyman, *Notebooks*, 185; Foote, *Red River to Appomattox*, 286.

58. O.R., vol. 36, part III, 440; Meade, *Life and Letters*, 200.

59. G. T. Stevens, *Sixth Corps*, 347; Walker, *General Hancock*, 218–219.

60. O.R., vol. 36, part III, 441; Walker, *General Hancock*, 218–219; Lavery and Jordan, *Iron Brigade*, 111.

61. O.R., vol. 36, part III, 482–483.

62. Caldwell, *South Carolinian*, 157–158; Mills, *16th NC*, 54; Badeau, *Military History*, 385; Freeman, *Lee: Biography*, vol. 3, 382–383.

63. R. E. Lee, *Wartime Papers*, 762; Alexander, *Fighting*, 402–404; Rhea, *Cold Harbor*, 301–305.

64. Grant, *Memoirs*, 440; Badeau, *Military History*, 281–282.

65. Foote, *Red River to Appomattox*, 287–288.

66. Ibid., 287–288; Catton, *Grant Takes Command*, 261–262; Lyman, *Meade's Headquarters*, 100.

67. Law, "Wilderness to Cold Harbor," 139–141.

68. Grant, *Memoirs*, 441; Badeau, *Military History*, 287, 290.

69. Porter, *Campaigning with Grant* (abridged), 125.

70. Humphreys, *Virginia Campaign*, 181; Porter, *Campaigning with Grant* (abridged), 124.

71. Badeau, *Military History*, 304–305; Walker, *General Hancock*, 219.

72. Wilkeson, *Inside Out*, 128.

73. J. B. Jones, *Rebel War Clerk*, vol. 2, 224–225; Alexander, *Memoirs*, 540.

74. Keating, *Carnival of Blood*, 117–132, 178 (Corporal Bagley later was awarded the Medal of Honor for his feat.); Wilkeson, *Inside Out*, 132; Foote, *Red River to Appomattox*, 291.

75. Haines, *15th NJ*, 208; Gibbon, *Personal Recollections*, 232–233; Welch, *Boy General*, 138–141; Hodgkins, *19th ME*, 91; Dunn, *8th NY Artillery*, vol. 2, 310, 313, 324; Miller, *Harvard*, 379–382; Rhea, *Cold Harbor*, 361; O.R., vol. 36, part III, 534; Walker, *General Hancock*, 222.

76. O.R., vol. 36, part III, 252–253.

77. Zeller, *2nd VT*, 181; O.R., vol. 36, part I, 671.

78. Bartlett, *12th NH*, 202; Law, "Wilderness to Cold Harbor," 141–142; Wheeler, *Fields of Fury*, 259; Laine and Penny, *Law's Brigade*, 272; Dame, *Rapidan to Richmond*, 203–204; Coles, *Huntsville to Appomattox*, 173; W. C. Oates, *Union and Confederacy*, 366–367; O.R., vol. 36, part I, 1059; Dunn, *8th NY Artillery*, vol. 2, 348; Foote, *Red River to Appomattox*, 293.

79. Bartlett, *12th NH*, 202–203; Coles, *Huntsville to Appomattox*, 174–175; Rhea, *Cold Harbor*, 351–353; O.R., vol. 36, part I, 1003–1004; Walker, *General Hancock*, 223–224; W. F. Smith, "Eighteenth Corps," 227; Foote, *Red River to Appomattox*, 292.

80. O.R., vol. 36, part III, 526.

81. Lyman, *Meade's Headquarters*, 144, 147.

82. O.R., vol. 36, part I, 11, 367; Grant, *Memoirs*, 444–445.

83. Humphreys, *Virginia Campaign*, 184–185, 191; Rhea, *Cold Harbor*, 359–362.

84. Hess, *Trench Warfare*, 163; O.R., vol. 36, part I, 366–367; Dunn, *8th NY Artillery*, vol. 2, 317; Gibbon, *Personal Recollections*, 227.

85. Lyman, *Notebooks*, 190; Trudeau, *Bloody Roads*, 297.

86. Freeman, *Lee: Biography*, vol. 3, 287–288; Robertson, *A.P. Hill*, 285.

87. Venable, "Lee in the Wilderness," 245; Venable, "Wilderness to Petersburg," 537.

88. Freeman, *Lee: Biography*, vol. 3, 389–390; Foote, *Red River to Appomattox*, 293.

89. R. E. Lee, *Wartime Papers*, 764.

90. W. F. Smith, "Eighteenth Corps," 227–228.

91. Meade, *Life and Letters*, 201.

92. New York *Daily News*, June 13, 1864; National *Intelligencer*, June 14, 1864; Cleveland *Plain Dealer*, June 7, 1864; Augusta (Georgia) *Daily Constitutionalist*, June 12, 1864 (all from GenealogyBank.com).

93. Dana, *Recollections*, 209; Fuller, *Grant and Lee*, 221; Fuller, *Generalship*, 277.

94. Sherman, *Home Letters*, 299.

95. Lyman, *Notebooks*, 190.

96. O.R., vol. 36, part III, 526.

97. G. T. Stevens, *Sixth Corps*, 354; Perry, *Letters from a Surgeon*, 189; Fisk, *Hard Marching*, 225–226.

98. Alexander, *Memoirs*, 543.

99. Holmes, *Touched with Fire*, 139; Fisk, *Hard Marching*, 225.

100. Miller, *Harvard*, 382–384; Hess, *Trench Warfare*, 188–189.

101. Hess, *Trench Warfare*, 170–176; O.R., vol. 36, part III, 646.

102. Welles, *Diary*, 53; Wilkeson, *Inside Out*, 137–138; Power, *Lee's Miserables*, 72.

103. Stiles, *Marse Robert*, 290; Hess, *Trench Warfare*, 189.

104. Fisk, *Hard Marching*, 226.

105. Haines, *15th NJ*, 210.

106. Alexander, *Fighting*, 411–412.

107. Hess, *Trench Warfare*, 175–176; O.R., vol. 36, part III, 646–647.

108. Speer, *Portals to Hell*, 137–138.

109. David Holt, *Mississippi Rebel*, 276.

110. Coles, *Huntsville to Appomattox*, 177; Cilella, *121st NY*, 15; W. C. Oates, *Union and Confederacy*, 367.

111. A. C. Brown, *Line Officer*, 71.

112. Keating, *Carnival of Blood*, 139.

113. Ibid., 160–161.

114. Grant, *Papers*, vol. 11, 17.

115. Ibid., 223–227.

116. David Holt, *Mississippi Rebel*, 201–202.

117. Lyman, *Meade's Headquarters*, 154.

118. Gibbon, *Personal Recollections*, 233–234; Kreiser, *Defeating Lee*, 189.

119. Wilkeson, *Inside Out*, 139; Miller, *Harvard*, 384.

120. Hodgkins, *19th ME*, 93; Haines, *15th NJ*, 213–214; A. C. Brown, *Line Officer*, 78.

121. Tapert, *Brothers' War*, 198; Hess, *Trench Warfare*, 200.

122. Welles, *Diary*, 46.

123. Meade, *Life and Letters*, 202–203; Lyman, *Notebooks*, 196; Cadwallader, *Three Years*, 206–207.

124. Grant, *Memoirs*, 373–374; Cadwallader, *Three Years*, 210–213.

125. Cadwallader, *Three Years*, 209.

126. Meade, *Life and Letters*, 203, 205.

127. Walker, *General Hancock*, 228–229; Carter, *Four Brothers*, 427; Wilkeson, *Inside Out*, 185, 194.

128. Walker, *General Hancock*, 228–229; Kreiser, *Defeating Lee*, 188–189; Hess, *Trench Warfare*, 163.

129. E. B. Lee, *Wartime Washington*, 386.

130. O.R., vol. 36, part I, 92.

131. O.R., vol. 36, part III, 665.

132. Badeau, *Military History*, 318; Grant, *Papers*, vol. 11, 32.

133. Grant, *Papers*, vol. 11, 16, 30.

134. Freeman, *Lee: Biography*, vol. 3, 392–394; Warner, *Generals in Gray*, 166–167; Wheelan, *Terrible Swift Sword*, 84.

135. Grant, *Papers*, vol. 11, 21; Wheelan, *Terrible Swift Sword*, 84.

136. Grant, *Papers*, vol. 11, 19–20.

137. J. B. Jones, *Rebel War Clerk*, vol. 2, 235, 217.

138. Apperson, *Hospital Steward*, 552; Wood, *Confederate Surgeon*, 145–146; Power, *Lee's Miserables*, 73–74.

139. O.R., vol. 38, part IV, 762.

140. O.R., vol. 37, part I, 346; vol. 40, part II, 667.

141. R. E. Lee, *Wartime Papers*, 769–771.

142. Grant, *Memoirs*, 378–379; Sheridan, *Memoirs*, vol. 1, 416.

143. Sheridan, *Memoirs*, vol. 1, 423–425; Foote, *Red River to Appomattox*, 309–310; Wheelan, *Terrible Swift Sword*, 84–88.

144. Freeman, *Lee: Biography*, vol. 3, 400.

145. O.R., vol. 36, part III, 878–879.

146. Dana, *Recollections*, 212; J. E. Smith, *Grant*, 360.

147. Catton, *Grant Takes Command*, 280–281; Lyman, *Notebooks*, 201.

148. Badeau, *Military History*, part 2, 346, 348; O.R., vol. 36, part I, 92–93; Keating, *Carnival of Blood*, 167–168.

149. Badeau, *Military History*, 348; Walker, *General Hancock*, 230–231; Alexander, *Fighting*, 419–420; Porter, *Campaigning with Grant* (abridged), 133.

150. Freeman, *Lee: Biography*, vol. 3, 402–403.

151. Stiles, *Marse Robert*, 308.

6. RACE TO STALEMATE—THE JAMES RIVER

1. Lyman, *Meade's Headquarters*, 160–162.

2. Lincoln, *Collected Works*, vol. 7, 393.

3. Porter, *Campaigning with Grant* (abridged), 137; Badeau, *Military History*, 356–357.

4. Ford, *Adams Letters*, vol. 2, 140, 149–150.

5. Lyman, *Notebooks*, 204–205; Alexander, *Fighting*, 420.

6. Wheeler, *Fields of Fury*, 265.

7. Grant, *Papers*, vol. 11, 45; Brands, *Man Who Saved*, 309; Lyman, *Notebooks*, 201; Dana, *Recollections*, 218–219; Badeau, *Military History*, 348–349, 375.

8. McPherson, *Tried by War*, 232; Dana, *Recollections*, 214–215; Grant, *Papers*, vol. 11, 55; Badeau, *Military History*, 352–353, 380–381; Robertson, *A.P. Hill*, 282; Lincoln, *Collected Works*, vol. 7, 393; Brooks, *Lincoln Observed*, 149.

9. Longacre, *Amateurs*, 130–135; Catton, *Grant Takes Command*, 283.

10. J. W. Jones, *Christ in Camp*, 47; R. E. Lee, *Wartime Papers*, 777–778, 781; Stiles, *Marse Robert*, 308; Alexander, *Memoirs*, 547.

11. Grant, *Papers*, vol. 11, 45–46; Grant, *Memoirs*, 455; Keating, *Carnival of Blood*, 174, 178.

12. Badeau, *Military History*, 357–359; Howe, *Petersburg Campaign*, 28; Longacre, *Amateurs*, 80.

13. Badeau, *Military History*, 359; Longacre, *Amateurs*, 147.

14. Walker, *General Hancock*, 233–234; Keating, *Carnival of Blood*, 178; Grant, *Papers*, vol. 11, 50–51; Badeau, *Military History*, 359–361; Meade, *Life and Letters*, 208–209.

15. O.R., vol. 40, part II, 83; Longacre, *Amateurs*, 152; Badeau, *Military History*, 360–362; Wilkeson, *Inside Out*, 162; Lyman, *Meade's Headquarters*, 160–162; Grant, *Memoirs*, 457; Longacre, *Grant*, 239.

16. McFeely, *Grant*, 175; Lyman, *Notebooks*, 208.

17. Beauregard, "Four Days," 540–542; Badeau, *Military History*, 64–66; Grant, *Papers*, vol. 11, 62–63; Howe, *Petersburg Campaign*, 48; Keating, *Carnival of Blood*, 181–191.

18. Beauregard, "Four Days," 541.

19. Howe, *Petersburg Campaign*, 58, 52; R. E. Lee, *Wartime Papers*, 785–789.

20. Longacre, *Amateurs*, 156.

21. Freeman, *Lee: Biography*, vol. 3, 410–411; J. W. Jones, *Christ in Camp*, 51.

22. Freeman, *Lee: Biography*, vol. 3, 411–414; Longacre, *Amateurs*, 157; Badeau, *Military History*, 366–368; Grant, *Papers*, vol. 11, 59; Venable, "Lee in the Wilderness," 245.

23. R. E. Lee, *Wartime Papers*, 787–789; Macrae, *Americans at Home*, 159; Freeman, *Lee: Biography*, vol. 3, 420–424; O.R., vol. 51, part II, 1020; Venable, *Papers*, Folder 10; Dickert, *Kershaw's Brigade*, 380; Albright, *Papers, Diary*.

24. Venable, "Lee in the Wilderness," 245; Carter, *Four Brothers*, 433–434; Howe, *Petersburg Campaign*, 102, 107–108; McAllister, *Letters*, 443–444; Kreiser, *Defeating Lee*, 199; Walker, *General Hancock*, 241.

25. A. C. Brown, *Line Officer*, 108.

26. Badeau, *Military History*, 268–269; Carter, *Four Brothers*, 441; Gibbon, *Personal Recollections*, 245.

27. Lyman, *Notebooks*, 213.

28. O.R., vol. 40, part II, 167.

29. Carter, *Four Brothers*, 440.

30. Beauregard, "Beauregard to Wilcox," 121.

31. Grant, *Papers*, vol. 11, 79–80; Lyman, *Notebooks*, 214–215.

32. Kreiser, *Defeating Lee*, 199; Porter, *Campaigning with Grant* (abridged), 146–147; Carter, *Four Brothers*, 439; Ford, *Adams Letters*, vol. 2, 150.

33. Longacre, *Grant*, 239; O.R., vol. 36, part I, 188, 166–180; Grant, *Memoirs*, 454.

34. Meade, *Life and Letters*, 205–206.

35. Marshall-Cornwall, *Grant as Commander*, 184–186.

EPILOGUE: THE BEGINNING OF THE END

1. Porter, *Campaigning with Grant* (abridged), 195.

2. O.R., vol. 36, part I, 188; Badeau, *Military History*, 331–332; McPherson, *Tried by War*, 231.

3. A. C. Young, *Lee's Army*, 242–243; Howe, *Petersburg Campaign*, 136; Alexander, Memoirs, 559.

4. McPherson, *Tried by War*, 231; London *Times*, June 29, 1864, in www.genealogy bank.com.

5. Welles, *Diary*, 73; Ford, *Adams Letters*, vol. 2, 140–142.

6. Grant, *Papers*, vol. 11, 176.

7. Porter, *Campaigning with Grant* (abridged), 195.

8. Lincoln, *Collected Works*, vol. 7, 395.

9. Meade, *Life and Letters*, 206; Holmes, *Touched with Fire*, 149–150; Comstock, *Diary*, 276; Perry, *Letters from a Surgeon*, 190–193; Miller, *Harvard*, 90.

10. Miller, *Harvard*, 385.

11. Gibbon, *Personal Recollections*, 227–228; Catton, *Stillness*, 212–214; Kreiser, *Defeating Lee*, 203; Miller, *Harvard*, 385.

12. Meade, *Life and Letters*, 241; Stiles, *Marse Robert*, 309.

13. Venable, "Wilderness to Petersburg," 537.

14. O.R., vol. 40, part II, 690.

15. Foote, *Red River to Appomattox*, 441.

16. Robertson, *A.P. Hill*, 285–287.

17. Dickert, *Kershaw's Brigade*, 385.

18. O.R., vol. 36, part I, 23.

BIBLIOGRAPHY

Abbott, Major Henry Livermore. *Fallen Leaves: The Civil War Letters of Major Henry Livermore Abbot,* edited by Robert Garth Scott. Kent, OH: The Kent State University Press, 1991.

Albright, Henry Clay. *Papers, Diary.* State Archives of North Carolina, Raleigh.

Alexander, General Edward Porter. *Fighting for the Confederacy: The Personal Recollections of General Edward Porter Alexander,* edited by Gary W. Gallagher. Chapel Hill: The University of North Carolina Press, 1989.

————. *Military Memoirs of a Confederate: A Critical Narrative.* New York: Charles Scribner's Sons, 1907.

Aley, Ginette. "'We Are All Good Scavengers Now.' The Crisis in Virginia Agriculture during the Civil War." In *Virginia at War 1864,* edited by William C. Davis and James I. Robertson Jr., 81–98. Lexington: University Press of Kentucky, 2009.

Allen, Private Matthew Wood. *Personal Journals of Matthew Wood Allen, Private, Grimes Battery—Portsmouth Light Artillery. July 1, 1862 through June 23, 1865.* Transcribed by Walter Lee Shepherd, 1999. Virginia Historical Society, Richmond.

Anderson, John. *The Fifty-Seventh Regiment of Massachusetts Volunteers in the War.* Boston: E.B. Stillings & Co., 1896.

Apperson, John. *The Civil War of John Samuel Apperson, Hospital Steward in the Stonewall Brigade, 1861–1865,* edited by John Herbert Roper. Macon, Georgia: Mercer University Press, 2001.

Arlington National Cemetery website: www.arlingtoncemetery.mil/History

Atkinson, Lieutenant C. F. *Grant's Campaigns of 1864 and 1865: The Wilderness and Cold Harbor (May 3–June 3, 1864).* London: Hugh Reese, Ltd., 1908.

Badeau, Adam. *Military History of Ulysses S. Grant, from April 1861 to April 1865,* Volume 2. New York: D. Appleton and Company, 1882.

Baltz, Louis J., III. *The Battle of Cold Harbor, May 27–June 13, 1864.* Lynchburg, Virginia: H.E. Howard, 1994.

Barlow, Francis G. "The Capture of the Salient, May 12, 1864," in *Papers of the Military Historical Society of Massachusetts,* Volume 4: *The Wilderness Campaign, May–June 1864,* 245–262. Boston: Military Historical Society of Massachusetts, 1905.

————. *Fear Was Not in Him: The Civil War Letters of Major General Francis C. Barlow, U.S.A.,* edited by Christian G. Samito. New York: Fordham University, 2004.

Bartlett, Asa W. *History of the Twelfth Regiment, New Hampshire Volunteers, in the War of the Rebellion*. Concord, New Hampshire: Ira C. Evans, Printer, 1897.

Bates, David Homer. *Lincoln in the Telegraph Office: Recollections of the United States Military Telegraph Corps during the Civil War*. New York: The Century Co., 1907.

Bates, Edward. *The Diary of Edward Bates, 1859–1866*, Volume 4, edited by Howard K. Beale. Washington: United States Government Printing Office, 1933.

Battle, Laura Elizabeth Lee. *Forget-Me-Nots of the Civil War*. St. Louis: A.R. Fleming Printing Co., 1909.

Beaudry, Louis Napoleon. *Historic Records of the Fifth New York Cavalry, First Ira Harris Guard*. Albany, New York: S.R. Gray, 1865.

Beauregard, General P. G. T. "Four Days of Battle at Petersburg," in *Battles and Leaders of the Civil* War, Volume 4, edited by Robert Underwood Johnson and Clarence Clough Buel, 540–544. New York: The Century Co., 1888.

———. "Letter of General G. T. Beauregard to General C.M. Wilcox," in *Papers of the Military Historical Society of Massachusetts*, Volume 5, 119–123.

Bidwell, General Daniel Davidson. *History of the Forty-Ninth New York Volunteers*, edited by Frederick David Bidwell. Albany, New York: J.B. Lyon Company, 1916.

Black, Brevet Major John D. "Reminiscences of the Bloody Angle," in *Military Order of the Loyal Legion of the United States*, Series 4, Volume 29, 420–436. Wilmington, North Carolina: Broadfoot Publishing Co., 1991.

Bradwell, Isaac Gordon. *Under the Southern Cross: Soldier Life With Gordon Bradwell and the Army of Northern Virginia*, edited by Pharris Deloach Johnson. Macon, Georgia: Mercer University Press, 1999.

Brands, H. W. *The Man Who Saved the Union: Ulysses Grant in War and Peace*. New York: Doubleday, 2012.

Brewster, Charles Harvey. *When This Cruel War Is Over: The Civil War Letters of Charles Harvey Brewster*, edited by David W. Blight. Amherst: University of Massachusetts Press, 1992.

Brooks, Noah. *Lincoln Observed: Civil War Dispatches of Noah Brooks*, edited by Michael Burlingame. Baltimore, Maryland: The Johns Hopkins University Press, 1998.

———. *Mr. Lincoln's Washington. Selections from the Writings of Noah Brooks, Civil War Correspondent*. South Brunswick, New Jersey: T. Yoseloff, 1967.

Brown, Captain Augustus C. *The Diary of a Line Officer*. E-book, University of North Carolina, originally published 1906.

Brown, Campbell. *Campbell Brown's Civil War: With Ewell and the Army of Northern Virginia*. Baton Rouge: Louisiana State University Press, 2001.

Buell, Augustus C. *The Cannoneer: Recollections of Service in the Army of the Potomac*. Washington: The National Tribune, 1890.

Buell, Thomas B. *The Warrior Generals: Combat Leadership in the Civil War*. New York: Crown Publishers, Inc., 1997.

Burne, Alfred H. *Lee, Grant and Sherman: A Study in Leadership in the 1864–1865 Campaign*. Lawrence: University of Kansas Press, 2000.

Butler, Major General Benjamin F. *Autobiography and Personal Reminiscences of Major-General Benjamin F. Butler*, 2 volumes. Boston: A.M. Thayer, 1892.

Cadwallader, Sylvanus. *Three Years With Grant*, edited by Benjamin P. Thomas. Lincoln: University of Nebraska Press, 1996.

Caldwell, J. F. J. *The History of a Brigade of South Carolinians*. Philadelphia: King & Baird, Printers, 1866.

Campbell, Robert. *Lone Star Confederate: A Gallant and Good Soldier of the Fifth Texas Infantry*, edited by George Skoch and Mark Perkins. College Station: Texas A&M University Press, 2003.

Cannan, John. *The Spotsylvania Campaign: May 7–21, 1864*. Conshohocken, Pennsylvania: Combined Publishing, 1997.

Carmichael, Peter S. "Escaping the Shadow of Gettysburg: Richard S. Ewell and Ambrose Powell Hill at the Wilderness," in *The Wilderness Campaign*, edited by Gary W. Gallagher, 136–159. Chapel Hill: The University of North Carolina Press, 1997.

———. "We Respect a *Good* Soldier, No Matter What Flag He Fought Under: The 15th New Jersey Remembers Spotsylvania," in *The Spotsylvania Campaign*, edited by Gary W. Gallagher, 202–222. Chapel Hill: The University of North Carolina Press, 1998.

Carpenter, F. B. *Six Months at the White House with Abraham Lincoln. The Story of a Picture*. New York: Hurd and Houghton, 1866.

Carruth, Gorton. *What Happened When: A Chronology of Life and Events in America*. New York: Signet, 1991.

Carter, Captain Robert Goldthwaite. *Four Brothers in Blue*. Austin: University of Texas Press, 1978.

Casler, John O. *Four Years in the Stonewall Brigade*. Girard, Kansas: Appeal Publishing Company, 1906.

Catton, Bruce. *The Army of the Potomac: A Stillness at Appomattox*. Garden City, New York: Doubleday, 1953.

———. *The Army of the Potomac: Glory Road*. Garden City, New York: Doubleday, 1952.

———. *The Army of the Potomac: Mr. Lincoln's Army*. New York: Doubleday, 1962. First published in 1951.

———. *Grant Takes Command*. Boston: Little, Brown and Company, 1968.

———. *Never Call Retreat*. Garden City, New York: Doubleday, 1965.

———. *Reflections on the Civil War*, edited by John Leeley. New York: Berkley Books, 1982.

Chamberlin, Lieutenant Colonel Thomas. *History of the One Hundred and Fiftieth Regiment, Pennsylvania Volunteers*. Philadelphia: F. McManus, Jr. & Co., 1905.

Chapia, John D. *The Fiftieth Virginia Regiment*. Lynchburg, Virginia: H.E. Howard, Inc., 1997.

Chesnut, Mary Boykin. *A Diary from Dixie, as Written by Mary Boykin Chesnut*, Isabella D. Martin and Myrta Lockett Avary, eds. New York: D. Appleton and Company, 1905.

Cilella, Salvatore G., Jr. *Upton's Regulars: The 121st New York Infantry in the Civil War*. Lawrence: University Press of Kansas, 2009.

Clark, Walter, ed. *Histories of the Several Regiments and Battalions From North Carolina in the Great War, 1861–1865*. 5 volumes. Raleigh, North Carolina: E.M. Uzzell, 1901.

Clifton, J. B. *Diary*. State of North Carolina Archives, Raleigh.

Coffey, David. *Sheridan's Lieutenants: Phil Sheridan, His Generals, and the Final Years of the Civil War*. Lantham, Maryland: Rowman and Littlefield, Publishers, Inc., 2005.

Coffin, Charles Carleton. *Redeeming the Republic. The Third Period of the War of the Rebellion in the Year 1864*. New York: Harper & Brothers, Franklin Square, 1890.

Coles, R. T. *From Huntsville to Appomattox: R.T. Coles's History of the 4th Regiment, Alabama Volunteer Infantry, C.S.A., Army of Northern Virginia*, edited by Jeffrey D. Stocker. Knoxville: University of Tennessee Press, 1996.

Colfax, Schuyler. In *Reminiscences of Abraham Lincoln by Distinguished Men of His Time*, edited by Allen Thorndike Rice, 331–349. New York: North American Review, Volume 19, 1888.

Comstock, Cyrus B. *The Diary of Cyrus B. Comstock*. Dayton, Ohio: Morningside, 1997.

Confederate Southern Memorial Association, ed. *Confederate Veteran* magazine. Nashville, Tennessee: S.A. Cunningham, 1893.

Connelly, Thomas L. *The Marble Man: Robert E. Lee and His Image in American Society*. New York: Alfred A. Knopf, 1977.

Conyngham, David Power. *The Irish Brigade and Its Campaigns*, edited by Lawrence Frederick Kohl. New York: Fordham University Press, 1994.

Cook, Lieutenant Colonel Benjamin F., and James Beale. *History of the Twelfth Massachusetts Volunteers (Webster Regiment)*. Boston: Twelfth (Webster) Regiment Association, 1882.

Cowles, Captain Calvin, Major George B. Davis, Leslie J. Perry, Joseph W. Kirkley, eds. *The Official Military Atlas of the Civil War*. Washington: United States Government Printing Office, 1891–1895. Barnes & Noble edition, 2003.

Craft, David. *History of the One Hundred Forty-first Regiment, Pennsylvania Volunteers, 1862–1865*. Towanda, Pennsylvania: Reporter-Journal Printing Co., 1885.

Curtis, Owen Blair. *History of the Twenty-fourth Michigan of the Iron Brigade*. Detroit: Winn & Hammond, 1891.

Cutshaw, William E. "Spotsylvania Court House on May 18, 1864. Address of Colonel William E. Cutshaw, before Lee Camp, Richmond, Virginia, January 20, 1905," in *Southern History Society Papers*, Volume 39, 195–212. Richmond, Virginia: William Ellis Jones's Sons, 1914.

Dame, William Meade. *From the Rapidan to Richmond and the Spottsylvania Campaign*. Baltimore: Green-Lucas Company, 1920.

Dana, Charles A. *Recollections of the Civil War*. Lincoln: University of Nebraska Press, 1996.

Davis, Burke. *Jeb Stuart: The Last Cavalier*. New York: Rinehart & Company Inc., 1957.

Davis, Jefferson. *The Papers of Jefferson Davis*, edited by Haskell M. Monroe Jr. and James T. McIntosh. Baton Rouge: Louisiana State University Press, 1971–2012.

Davis, William C. *Jefferson Davis: The Man and His Hour*. New York: HarperCollins Publishers, 1991.

Davis, William C., and James I. Robertson Jr., eds. *Virginia at War 1864*. Lexington: University Press of Kentucky, 2009.

Dawes, Rufus Robinson. *Service with the Sixth Wisconsin Volunteers*. Marietta, Ohio: E.R. Alderman & Sons, 1890.

Dawson, Francis W. *Reminiscences of Confederate Service, 1861–1865*. Baton Rouge: Louisiana State University Press, 1980.

DeForest, John William. *A Volunteer's Adventures: A Union Captain's Record of the Civil War,* edited by James H. Croushore. New Haven, Connecticut: Yale University Press, 1946.

Dickert, D. Augustus. *History of Kershaw's Brigade*. Newberry, South Carolina: Elbert H. Aull Company, 1899.

Dixon, Harry St. John. *Papers*. Chapel Hill: Southern History Collection, University of North Carolina.

Donald, David Herbert. *Lincoln*. New York: Simon & Schuster, 1995.

Dowdey, Clifford. *Lee's Last Campaign: The Story of Lee and His Men against Grant—1864*. New York: Skyhorse Publishing, 2011.

Dunn, Wilbur Russell. *Full Measure of Devotion: The Eighth New York Volunteer Heavy Artillery*. 2 volumes. Kearney, Nebraska: Morris Publishing, 1997.

Early, Lieutenant General Jubal Anderson. *Autobiographical Sketch and Narrative of the War Between the States*. Philadelphia and London: J. B. Lippincott Company, 1912.

Eggleston, Sergeant Major George. "Notes on Cold Harbor," in *Battles and Leaders of the Civil War*, Volume 4, edited by Robert Underwood Johnson and Clarence Clough Buel, 230–236. New York: The Century Co., 1888.

Egnal, Marc. *Clash of Extremes: The Economic Origins of the Civil War*. New York: Hill and Wang, 2009.

Field, Major General Charles. "Campaign of 1864 and 1865," in *Southern History Society Papers*, Volume 15, 542–562. Richmond, Virginia: William Ellis Jones's Sons, 1914.

Fisk, Wilbur. *Hard Marching Every Day. The Civil War Letters of Private Wilbur Fisk, 1861–1865*, edited by Emil and Ruth Rosenblatt. Lawrence: University Press of Kansas, 1983.

Fite, Emerson David. *Social and Industrial Conditions in the North during the Civil War*. New York: The MacMillan Company, 1910.

Flower, Frank Abial. *Edward McMasters Stanton: The Autocrat of Rebellion, Emancipation, and Reconstruction*. Akron, Ohio: The Saalfield Publishing Company, 1905.

Foote, Shelby. *The Civil War: A Narrative*. Volume 1: *Fort Sumter to Perryville*. New York: Vintage Books, 1986. First published 1958.

———. *The Civil War: A Narrative*. Volume 2: *Fredericksburg to Meridian*. New York: Vintage Books, 1986. First published 1963.

———. *The Civil War: A Narrative*. Volume 3: *Red River to Appomattox*. New York: Vintage Books, 1986. First published 1974.

Ford, Worthington Chauncey. *A Cycle of Adams Letters, 1861–1865*. 2 volumes. Boston, New York: Houghton Mifflin, 1920.

Fowler, Reverend P. H., ed. *Memorials of William Fowler*. New York: A.D.F. Randolph & Co., 1875.

Freeman, Douglas Southall, ed. *Lee's Dispatches. Unpublished Letters of General Robert E. Lee, C.S.A., to Jefferson Davis and the War Department of the Confederate States of America, 1862–1865*. New York, London: C.P. Putnam's Sons, 1915.

———. *Lee's Lieutenants: A Study in Command*. Abridged. New York: Simon & Schuster, 2001.

———. *R.E. Lee: A Biography*, Volume 3. New York, London: Charles Scribner's Sons, 1935.

Fuller, J. F. C. *The Generalship of Ulysses S. Grant*. New York: Dodd, Mead and Company, 1929.

———. *Grant and Lee: A Study in Personality and Generalship*. Bloomington: Indiana University Press, 1957.

Gallagher, Gary W. "I Have to Make the Best of What I Have: Robert E. Lee at Spotsylvania," in *The Spotsylvania Campaign*, edited by Gary W. Gallagher, 5–28. Chapel Hill: The University of North Carolina Press, 1998.

————. "Our Hearts Are Full of Hope: The Army of Northern Virginia in the Spring of 1864," in *The Wilderness Campaign*, edited by Gary W. Gallagher, 36–65. Chapel Hill: The University of North Carolina Press, 1997.

————, ed. *The Spotsylvania Campaign*. Chapel Hill: The University of North Carolina Press, 1998.

————. *Stephen Dodson Ramseur: Lee's Gallant General*. Chapel Hill: The University of North Carolina Press, 1985.

————, ed. *The Wilderness Campaign*. Chapel Hill: The University of North Carolina Press, 1997.

Gallman, J. Matthew. *Northerners at War: Reflections on the Civil War Home Front*. Kent, Ohio: The Kent State University Press, 2010.

Galloway, G. Norton. *The Ninety-fifth Pennsylvania Volunteers ("Gosline's Pennsylvania Zouaves") in the Sixth Corps*. Philadelphia, PA: Collins, Printer, 1884.

Genealogybank.com. Northern, Southern newspapers from 1864.

Gerrish, Theodore. *Army Life: A Private's Reminiscences of the Civil War*. Portland, Maine: Hoyt, Fogg & Donham, 1882.

Gibbon, General John. *Personal Recollections of the Civil War*. New York: G.P. Putnam's Sons, 1928.

Goodwin, Doris Kearns. *Team of Rivals: The Political Genius of Abraham Lincoln*. New York: Simon & Schuster, 2005.

Gordon, General John B. *Reminiscences of the Civil War*. Baton Rouge: Louisiana State University Press, 1993. First published 1903.

Goss, Warren Lee. *Recollections of a Private: A Story of the Army of the Potomac*. New York: T.Y. Crowell & Co., 1890.

Graham, W. M. "Twenty-Sixth Mississippi Regiment," in *Confederate Veteran*, Volume 15, edited by Confederate Southern Memorial Association, 169. 1893.

Grant, Ulysses S. *The Papers of Ulysses S. Grant*, Volumes 10 and 11, edited by John Y. Simon. Carbondale: Southern Illinois University Press, 1982, 1984.

————. *Personal Memoirs of U.S. Grant*, edited by E. B. Long. New York: Da Capo Press, 1982.

Gray, Wood. *The Hidden Civil War: The Story of the Copperheads*. New York: The Viking Press, 1942.

Griffith, Paddy. *Battle Tactics of the Civil War*. New Haven, Connecticut: Yale University Press, 2001.

Grimsley, Mark. *And Keep Moving On: The Virginia Campaign, May–June 1864*. Lincoln: University of Nebraska Press, 2002.

Haines, Alanson A. *History of the Fifteenth Regiment New Jersey Volunteers*. New York: Jenkins & Thomas, Printers, 1883.

Hancock, Almira Russell. *Reminiscences of Winfield Scott Hancock by His Wife*. New York: Charles L. Webster & Company, 1887.

Harper, Samuel Finley. *Papers*. State of North Carolina Archives, Raleigh.

Hattaway, Herman, and Archer Jones. *How the North Won: A Military History of the Civil War*. Urbana: University of Illinois Press, 1983.

Hay, John. *Inside Lincoln's White House: The Complete Civil War Diary of John Hay*, edited by Michael Burlingame and John Ettlinger. Carbondale: Southern Illinois University Press, 1997.

————. *Lincoln and the Civil War, in the Diaries and Letters of John Hay*, edited by Tyler Dennett. New York: Da Capo Press, 1988. First published 1939.

Hennessey, John J. "I Dread the Spring: The Army of the Potomac Prepares for the Overland Campaign," in *The Wilderness Campaign*, edited by Gary W. Gallagher, 66–105. Chapel Hill: The University of North Carolina Press, 1997.

Hergesheimer, Joseph. *Sheridan: A Military Narrative*. Boston, New York: Houghton Mifflin Co., 1931.

Hess, Earl J. *Trench Warfare under Grant and Lee: Field Fortifications in the Overland Campaign*. Chapel Hill: The University of North Carolina Press, 2007.

Hesseltine, William Best. *Civil War Prisons: A Study in War Psychology*. Columbus: Ohio State University Press, 1930.

Heth, General Henry. *The Memoirs of Henry Heth*, edited by James L. Morrison Jr. Westport, Connecticut: Greenwood Press, 1974.

History of the 121st Regiment of Pennsylvania Volunteers. "An Account from the Ranks," edited by the US Army. Philadelphia: Press of the Catholic Standard and Times, 1906.

Hodgkins, Lieutenant J. E. *The Civil War Diary of Lieutenant J.E. Hodgkins, 19th Maine, from August 11, 1862, to June 3, 1865*, edited by Kennth C. Turrino. Camden, Maine: Picton Press, 1994.

Holmes, Oliver Wendell, Jr. *Touched with Fire: Civil War Letters and Diary of Oliver Wendell Holmes, Jr., 1861–1864*, edited by De Wolfe Howe. Cambridge, Massachusetts: Harvard University Press, 1946.

Holt, Dr. Daniel M. *A Surgeon's Civil War: The Letters and Diary of Daniel M. Holt, M.D.*, edited by James M. Greiner, Janet L. Coryell, and James R. Smither. Kent, Ohio: The Kent State University Press, 1994.

Holt, David. *A Mississippi Rebel in the Army of Northern Virginia*, edited by Thomas D. Cockrell and Michael B. Ballard. Baton Rouge: Louisiana State University Press, 1995.

Hopkins, William Palmer. *The Seventh Regiment of Rhode Island Volunteers in the Civil War, 1862–1865*. Providence, Rhode Island: The Providence Press, 1903.

Hotchkiss, Jedediah. *Make Me a Map of the Valley: The Civil War Journal of Stonewall Jackson's Topographer*, edited by Archie P. McDonald. Dallas: Southern Methodist University Press, 1973.

Houghton, Edwin B. *The Campaigns of the Seventeenth Maine*. Portland, Maine: Short & Loring, 1866.

Houston, Henry Clarence. *The Thirty-Second Maine Regiment of Infantry Volunteers: An Historical Sketch*. Portland, Maine: Southworth Brothers, 1903.

Howard, Lieutenant McHenry. "Notes and Recollections of Opening of the Campaign of 1864," in *Papers of the Military Historical Society of Massachusetts*, Volume 5, 81–116.

Howe, Thomas J. *The Petersburg Campaign: Wasted Valor, June 15–18, 1864*. Lynchburg, Virginia: H.E. Howard, 1988.

Hoyle, Joseph J. *"Deliver Us from this Cruel War": The Civil War Letters of Lieutenant Joseph J. Hoyle, 55th North Carolina Infantry*, edited by Jeffrey M. Girvan. Jefferson, North Carolina: McFarland & Company, Inc., 2010.

Humphreys, General Andrew A. *The Virginia Campaign of 1864 and 1865*. New York: Da Capo Press, 1995.

Hyde, Thomas Worcester. *Following the Greek Cross: or Memories of the Sixth Army Corps*. Boston, New York: Houghton, Mifflin and Company, 1894.

Jackman, Lynn. *History of the Sixth New Hampshire Regiment in the War for the Union*. Concord, New Hampshire: Republican Press Association, 1891.

Johnson, Robert Underwood, and Clarence Clough Buel, eds. *Battles and Leaders of the Civil War.* 4 volumes. New York: Century Co., 1884–1888.

Jones, J. B. *A Rebel War Clerk's Diary at the Confederate States Capital.* 2 volumes. New York: Old Hickory Bookshop, 1935.

Jones, John William. *Christ in the Camp: Or, Religion in Lee's Army.* Richmond, Virginia: B.F. Johnson & Co., 1888.

———. *Personal Reminiscences of General Robert E. Lee.* New York: D. Appleton and Co., 1874.

Jordan, David. *Happiness Is Not My Companion: The Life of General G.K. Warren.* Bloomington: Indian University Press, 2001.

Keating, Robert. *Carnival of Blood: The Civil War Ordeal of the Seventh New York Heavy Artillery.* Baltimore: Butternut & Blue, 1998.

Kidd, J. H. *Riding With Custer: Recollections of a Cavalryman in the Civil War.* Lincoln: University of Nebraska Press, 1997.

Kimmel, Stanley. *Mr. Lincoln's Washington.* New York: Coward-McCann, Inc., 1957.

Kreiser, Lawrence A., Jr. *Defeating Lee: A History of the Second Corps, Army of the Potomac.* Bloomington: Indiana University Press, 2011.

Krick, Robert K. "An Insurmountable Barrier between the Army and Ruin: The Confederate Experience at Spotsylvania's Bloody Angle," in *The Spotsylvania Campaign,* edited by Gary W. Gallagher, 80–126. Chapel Hill: The University of North Carolina Press, 1998.

———. "Lee to the Rear, the Texans Cried," in *The Wilderness Campaign,* edited by Gary W. Gallagher, 166–200. Chapel Hill: The University of North Carolina Press, 1997.

———. "Like a Duck on a June Bug: James Longstreet's Flank Attack, May 6, 1864," in *The Wilderness Campaign,* edited by Gary W. Gallagher, 236–264. Chapel Hill: The University of North Carolina Press, 1997.

Laine, J. Gary, and Morris M. Penny. *Law's Alabama Brigade in the War between the Union and the Confederacy.* Shippensburg, Pennsylvania: White Main Publishing Company, 1996.

LaRocca, Charles J. *The 124th New York State Volunteers in the Civil War.* Jefferson, North Carolina: McFarland & Company, Inc., Publishers, 2012.

Lavery, Dennis S., and Mark H. Jordan. *Iron Brigade General: John Gibbon, a Rebel in Blue.* Westport, Connecticut: Greenwood Press, 1993.

Law, E. M. "From the Wilderness to Cold Harbor," in *Battles and Leaders of the Civil War,* Volume 4, edited by Robert Underwood Johnson and Clarence Clough Buel, 118–144. New York: The Century Company, 1888.

Lee, Elizabeth Blair. *Wartime Washington: The Civil War Letters of Elizabeth Blair Lee,* edited by Virginia Jeans Laas. Urbana: University of Illinois Press, 1991.

Lee, Laura Elizabeth. *Forget-Me-Nots of the Civil War: A Romance, Containing Reminiscences and Original Letters of Two Confederate Soldiers.* St. Louis: A.R. Fleming Printing Company, 1909.

Lee, Robert E. *The Wartime Papers of Robert E. Lee,* edited by Clifford Dowdey and Louis H. Manarin. New York: Bramhall House, 1961.

Lincoln, Abraham. *Collected Works of Abraham Lincoln,* 8 volumes, edited by Roy P. Basler. New Brunswick, New Jersey: Rutgers University Press, 1953.

Livermore, Colonel Thomas L. "The Failure to Take Petersburg," in *Papers of the Military Historical Society of Massachusetts,* Volume 5, 33–74. Boston: Military Historical Society of Massachusetts, 1906.

Long, A. L. *Memoirs of Robert E. Lee, His Military and Personal History*, edited by Marcus J. Wright. Secaucus, New Jersey: The Blue and Grey Press, 1983.

Long, E. B., and Barbara Long. *The Civil War Day by Day: An Almanac, 1861–1865*. Garden City, New York: Doubleday & Company, Inc., 1971.

Longacre, Edward G. *Army of Amateurs: General Benjamin F. Butler and the Army of the James, 1863–1865*. Mechanicsburg, Pennsylvania: Stackpole Books, 1997.

———. *Custer and His Wolverines. The Michigan Cavalry Brigade, 1861–1865*. Conshocken, Pennsylvania: Combined Publishing, 1997.

———. *General Ulysses S. Grant, the Soldier and the Man*. Cambridge, Massachusetts: Da Capo Press, 2007.

———. *Fitz Lee: A Military Biography of Major General Fitzhugh Lee, C.S.A.* Cambridge, Massachusetts: Da Capo Press, 2005.

Longstreet, James. *From Manassas to Appomattox: Memoirs of the Civil War in America*. Philadelphia: J.B. Lippincott Company, 1908.

Lyman, Theodore. *Meade's Army: The Private Notebooks of Lt. Col. Theodore Lyman*, edited by David W. Lowe. Kent, Ohio: The Kent State University Press, 2007.

———. *Meade's Headquarters, 1863–1865: Letters of Colonel Theodore Lyman from the Wilderness to Appomattox*, edited by George R. Agassiz. Boston: The Atlantic Monthly Press, 1922.

———. "Uselessness of the Maps Furnished to Staff of the Army of the Potomac Previous to the Campaign of May 1864," in *Papers of the Military Historical Society of Massachusetts*, Volume 4, 79–80.

Macrae, David. *The Americans at Home*. Glasgow: J.S. Marr & Sons, 1875.

Marshall-Cornwall, General Sir James. *Grant as Military Commander*. New York: Van Nostrand Reinhold Company, 1970.

Marszalek, John F. *Sherman: A Soldier's Passion for Order*. New York: The Free Press, 1993.

Massey, Mary Elizabeth. *Ersatz in the Confederacy: Shortages and Substitutes on the Southern Homefront*. Columbia: University of South Carolina Press, 1993.

Matter, William D. "The Federal High Command at Spotsylvania," in *The Spotsylvania Campaign*, edited by Gary W. Gallagher, 29–60. Chapel Hill: The University of North Carolina Press, 1998.

———. *If It Takes All Summer. The Battle of Spotsylvania*. Chapel Hill: The University of North Carolina Press, 1988.

McAllister, Robert. *The Civil War Letters of General Robert McAllister*, edited by James I. Robertson Jr. Baton Rouge: Louisiana State University Press, 1995.

McCabe, W. Gordon, ed. *Letterbook 7 June 1863–12 October 1864, Army of Northern Virginia, C.S.A. Lee Headquarters Papers*, Folder 3. Virginia Historical Society, Richmond.

McClure, Alexander Kelly, ed. *Annals of the War Written by Leading Participants North and South*. Philadelphia: The Times Publishing Company, 1879.

McFeely, William S. *Grant: A Biography*. New York and London: W. W. Norton and Company, 1982.

McGuire, Judith Brockenbrough. "Diary of a Southern Refugee during the War, June 1863–July 1864," edited by James I. Robertson Jr., in *Virginia at War, 1864*, edited by Robertson and William C. Davis, 159–224. Lexington: University of Kentucky Press, 2009.

McKim, Randolph H. *A Soldier's Recollections: Leaves from the Diary of a Young Confederate*. New York: Longmans, Green, and Co., 1911.

McMahon, Martin. "Cold Harbor," in *Battles and Leaders of the Civil War*, Volume 4, edited by Robert Underwood Johnson and Clarence Clough Buel, 213–220. New York: The Century Company, 1888.

———. "The Death of General John Sedgwick," in *Battles and Leaders of the Civil War*, Volume 4, edited by Robert Underwood Johnson and Clarence Clough Buel, 175. New York: The Century Company, 1888.

McPherson, James M. *Tried by War: Abraham Lincoln as Commander in Chief.* New York: Penguin Press, 2008.

Meade, George. *The Life and Letters of George Gordon Meade, Major-General United States Army,* Volume 2. New York: Charles Scribner's Sons, 1913.

Melville, Herman. *Selected Poems of Herman Melville: A Reader's Edition,* edited by Robert Penn Warren. Jaffrey, New Hampshire: Nonpareil, 2004.

Michie, Peter S. *The Life and Letters of Emory Upton.* New York: Arno Press, 1979.

Military Order of the Loyal Legion of the United States. 70 volumes. Wilmington, North Carolina: Broadfoot Publishing Co., 1991–1997.

Miller, Richard F. *Harvard's Civil War: A History of the Twentieth Massachusetts Volunteer Infantry.* Hanover, New Hampshire: University Press of New England, 2005.

Mills, Captain George H. *History of the 16th North Carolina Regiment in the Civil War.* Hamilton, New York: Edmonston Pub., 1992.

Morrow, Robert F., Jr. *77th New York Volunteers: "Sojering" in the VI Corps.* Shippensburg, Pennsylvania: White Mane Books, 2004.

Muffly, Joseph Wendel, ed. *The Story of Our Regiment: A History of the 148th Pennsylvania Volunteers, "Written by the Comrades."* Des Moines, Iowa: The Kenyon Printing & Mfg. Co., 1904.

Mulholland, St. Clair A. *The Story of the 116th Regiment Pennsylvania Volunteers in the War of the Rebellion.* New York: Fordham University Press, 1996.

National Park Service websites: www.nps.gov/anti/historyculture/casualties.htm; www.nps.gov/frsp/bloody.htm; www.nps.gov/frsp/js.htm

Neese, George Michael. *Three Years in the Confederate Horse Artillery.* New York: The Neale Publishing Co., 1911.

Nichols, George W. *A Soldier's Story of his Regiment (61st Georgia) and Incidentally of the Lawton-Gordon-Evans Brigade Army of Northern Virginia.* Tuscaloosa: University of Alabama Press, 2011.

Nicolay, Helen. *Lincoln's Secretary: A Biography of John G. Nicolay.* Westport, Connecticut: Greenwood Press, 1971.

Oates, Stephen B. *A Woman of Valor: Clara Barton and the Civil War.* New York: The Free Press, 1994.

———. *With Malice toward None: A Life of Abraham Lincoln.* New York: Harper Collins Publishers, 1994.

Oates, Colonel William C. *The War between the Union and the Confederacy and Its Lost Opportunities with a History of the 15th Alabama Regiment and the Forty-Eight Battles in Which It Was Engaged.* Dayton, Ohio: Press of Morningside Bookshop, 1985.

Page, Charles A., and James Roberts Gilmore. *Letters of a War Correspondent.* Boston: L.C. Page and Company, 1899.

Papers of the Military Historical Society of Massachusetts. Multiple volumes. Boston: Military Historical Society of Massachusetts, 1906.

Parsons, George W. *Put the Vermonters Ahead: The First Vermont Brigade in the Civil War*. Shippensburg, Pennsylvania: The White Mane Publishing Company, Inc., 1996.

Patterson, Gerald A. *From Blue to Gray: The Life of Confederate General Cadmus M. Wilcox*. Mechanicsburg, Pennsylvania: Stackpole Books, 2001.

Peck, R. H. *Reminiscences of a Confederate Soldier of Co. C., 2nd Virginia Cavalry*. Fincastle, Virginia: private publication, 1913.

Pendleton, William Nelson. *Memoirs of William Nelson Pendleton, D.D.: Rector of Latimer Parish*, edited by Susan Pendleton Lee. Philadelphia: J.B. Lippincott, 1893.

Perry, Martha Derby. *Letters from a Surgeon of the Civil War*. Boston: Little, Brown, and Company, 1906.

Polley, Joseph Benjamin. *Hood's Texas Brigade: Its Marches, Its Battles, Its Achievements*. Dayton, Ohio: Press of Morningside Bookshop, 1988.

———. *A Soldier's Letters to Charming Nellie*. New York: The Neale Publishing Company, 1908.

Porter, Horace. *Campaigning with Grant*. Abridged. New York: Bantam Books, 1991.

———. *Campaigning with Grant*. Unabridged. New York: The Century Co., 1907.

Powell, William Henry. *The Fifth Army Corps (Army of the Potomac). A Record of Operations during the Civil War in the United States of America, 1861–1865*. New York and London: G.P. Putnam's Sons. 1896.

Power, J. Tracy. *Lee's Miserables: Life in the Army of Northern Virginia from the Wilderness to Appomattox*. Chapel Hill: The University of North Carolina Press, 1998.

Prentice, Sartell. "The Opening Hours in the Wilderness in 1864," in *Military Order of the Loyal Legion of the United States, State of Illinois*, Volume 2, 99–119. Wilmington, North Carolina: Broadfoot Publishing Company, 1992.

Pullen, John J. *The Twentieth Maine: A Volunteer Regiment in the Civil War*. Philadelphia: J.B. Lippincott Company, 1957.

Pyne, Henry R. *Ride to War: The History of the First New Jersey Cavalry*, edited by Earl Schenck Miers. New Brunswick, New Jersey: Rutgers University Press, 1961.

Rafuse, Ethan S. *George Gordon Meade and the War in the East*. Abilene, Texas: McWhiney Foundation Press, 2003.

Ray, William R. *Four Years with the Iron Brigade: The Civil War Journals of William R. Ray, Co. F, Seventh Wisconsin Infantry*, edited by Lance Herdegen and Sherry Murphy. New York: Da Capo Press, 2002.

Reardon, Carol. "A Hard Road to Travel: The Impact of Continuous Operations on the Army of the Potomac and the Army of Northern Virginia in May 1864," in *The Spotsylvania Campaign*, edited by Gary W. Gallagher, 170–202. Chapel Hill: The University of North Carolina Press, 1998.

Rhea, Gordon C. *Cold Harbor: Grant and Lee, May 26–June 3, 1864*. Baton Rouge: Louisiana State University Press, 2002.

———. *The Battles for Spotsylvania Court House and the Road to Yellow Tavern, May 7–12, 1864*. Baton Rouge: Louisiana State University Press, 1997.

———. *The Battle of the Wilderness: May 5–6, 1864*. Baton Rouge: Louisiana State University Press, 1994.

———. *To the North Anna River: Grant and Lee, May 13–25, 1864*. Baton Rouge: Louisiana State University Press, 2000.

Rhodes, Elisha Hunt. *All for the Union: The Civil War Diary and Letters of Elisha Hunt Rhodes*. New York: Vintage Books, 1992.

Rice, Allen Thorndike, ed. *Reminiscences of Abraham Lincoln by Distinguished Men of His Time*. New York: North American Review, 1888.

Richmond *Daily Enquirer*. Library of Virginia.

Richmond *Dispatch*. Library of Virginia.

Richmond *Whig*. Library of Virginia.

Riggs, David F. *7th Virginia Infantry*. Lynchburg, Virginia: H.E. Howard, Inc., 1982.

Ritchie, David F. *Four Years in the First New York Light Artillery. The Papers of David F. Ritchie*, edited by Norman L. Ritchie. Hamilton, New York: Edmonston Publishing, Inc., 1997.

Robertson, James I., Jr. *General A.P. Hill: The Story of a Confederate Warrior*. New York: Random House, 1987.

———. *The Stonewall Brigade*. Baton Rouge: Louisiana State University Press, 1963.

Robertson, William G. *The Petersburg Campaign: The Battle of Old Men and Young Boys, June 9, 1864*. Lynchburg, Virginia: H.E. Howard, 1989.

Roe, Alfred, and Charles Nutt. *History of the First Regiment of Heavy Artillery, Massachusetts Volunteers*. Boston: The Regimental Association, 1917.

Royall, William Lawrence. *Some Reminiscences*. New York: The Neal Publishing Company, 1909.

Sandburg, Carl. *Abraham Lincoln: The War Years*, Volume 3. New York: Harcourt, Brace & World, 1939.

Schaff, Morris. *The Battle of the Wilderness*. New York, Boston: Houghton Mifflin Co., 1910.

Schlaifer, Charles, and Lucy Freeman. *Heart's Work: Civil War Heroine and Champion of the Mentally Ill, Dorothea Lynde Dix*. New York: Paragon House, 1991.

Schoyer, Samuel C. *The Road to Cold Harbor Field Diary, January 1–June 12, 1864, of Samuel C. Schoyer*, edited by William T. Schoyer. Apollo, Pennsylvania: Closson Press, 1986.

Schurz, Carl. *The Reminiscences of Carl Schurz, 1863–1869*, Volume 3. Garden City, New York: Doubleday, Page & Company, 1917.

Scott, Robert Garth. *Into the Wilderness with the Army of the Potomac*. Bloomington, Indiana: Indiana University Press, 1992.

Seymour, William J. *The Civil War Memoirs of Captain William J. Seymour. Reminiscences of a Louisiana Tiger*. Baton Rouge: Louisiana State University Press, 1991.

Shepard, Corporal Norton C. *Out of the Wilderness: The Civil War Memoir of Cpl. Norton C. Shepard, 146th New York Volunteer Infantry*, edited by Raymond W. Smith. Hamilton, New York: Edmonston Publishing Inc., 1998.

Sheridan, General Philip. *Personal Memoirs of P. H. Sheridan*. 2 volumes. New York: Charles L. Webster & Company, 1888.

Sherman, William Tecumseh. *Home Letters of General Sherman*, edited by M.A. De-Wolfe Howe. New York: Charles Scribner's Sons, 1909.

Siegel, Charles G. *No Backward Step: A Guide to Grant's Campaign in Virginia*. Shippensburg, Pennsylvania: Burd Street Press, 2000.

Smith, Jean Edward. *Grant*. New York: Simon & Schuster, 2006.

Smith, John Day. *The History of the Nineteenth Regiment of Maine Volunteer Infantry*. Minneapolis: The Great Western Printing Col, 1909.

Smith, General William Farrar. "The Eighteenth Corps at Cold Harbor," in *Battles and Leaders of the Civil War*, Volume 4, edited by Robert Underwood Johnson and Clarence Clough Buel, 221–230. New York: The Century Company, 1888.

Sorrel, Gilbert Moxley. *Recollections of a Confederate Staff Officer.* New York: The Neale Publishing Company, 1905.

Southern Historical Society Papers. 52 volumes. Richmond Virginia: Southern Historical Society, 1876–1959.

Speer, Colonel Henry Asbury. *Voices from Cemetery Hill: The Civil War Diary, Reports, and Letters of Colonel William Henry Asbury Speer (1861–1864),* edited by Allen Paul Speer. Johnson City, Tennessee: The Overmountain Press, 1997.

Speer, Lonnie R. *Portals to Hell: Military Prisons of the Civil War.* Mechanicsburg, Pennsylvania: Stackpole Books, 1997.

———. *War of Vengeance: Acts of Retaliation against Civil War POWs.* Mechanicsburg, Pennsylvania: Stackpole Books, 2002.

Starr, Louis M. *Bohemian Brigade: Civil War Newsmen in Action.* Madison: University of Wisconsin Press, 1987.

Starr, Stephen Z. *The Union Cavalry in the Civil War.* Volume 2: *The War in the East from Gettysburg to Appomattox, 1863–1865.* Baton Rouge: Louisiana State University Press, 1979.

Stevens, George Thomas. *Three Years in the Sixth Corps.* Albany, New York: S.R. Gray, Publisher, 1866.

Stevens, Hazard. "The Sixth Corps in the Wilderness," in *Papers of the Military Historical Society of Massachusetts,* Volume 4, 177–203, 1905.

Stewart, Alexander Morrison. *Camp, March and Battle-Field: Three Years and a Half with the Army of the Potomac.* Philadelphia: Jason B. Rodgers, 1865.

Stiles, Robert. *Four Years under Marse Robert.* New York: The Neale Publishing Company, 1904.

Stoddard, William O. *Inside the White House in War Times.* New York: Charles L. Webster & Col., 1890.

Surdam, David George. *Northern Naval Superiority and the Economies of the Civil War.* Thesis. Chicago: University of Chicago, 1994.

Swinton, William. *Campaigns of the Army of the Potomac.* New York: Charles Scribner's Sons, 1882.

Tapert, Annette, ed. *The Brothers' War: Civil War Letters to their Loved Ones from the Blue and Gray.* New York: Times Books, 1988.

Taylor, Walter H. *Four Years with General Lee.* Bloomington: Indiana University Press, 1996.

———. *General Lee: His Campaigns in Virginia, 1861–1865.* Brooklyn, New York: Press of Brauxworth & Col, 1906.

———. *Lee's Adjutant: The Wartime Letters of Colonel Walter Herron Taylor, 1862–1865.* Columbia: University of South Carolina Press, 1995.

Thomas, Emory. *Bold Dragon: The Life of Jeb Stuart.* New York: Harper & Row, Publishers, 1986.

———. *The Confederate Nation, 1861–1865.* New York: Harper & Row, Publishers, 1979.

———. *The Confederate State of Richmond: A Biography of the Capital.* Austin: University of Texas Press, 1971.

———. *Robert E. Lee: A Biography.* New York and London: W. W. Norton & Company, 1995.

Thomas, Henry Walter. *History of the Doles-Cook Brigade, Army of Northern Virginia, C.S.A.* Atlanta: The Franklin Printing and Publishing Company, 1903.

Thomason, John W., Jr. *Jeb Stuart*. Lincoln: University of Nebraska Press, 1994.

Tilney, Robert. *My Life in the Army: Three Years and a Half with the Fifth Corps, Army of the Potomac, 1862–1865*. Philadelphia: Ferris & Leach, 1912.

Trudeau, Noah Andre. *Bloody Roads South: The Wilderness to Cold Harbor, May–June 1864*. Boston: Little, Brown and Company, 1989.

United States Congress. *Congressional Globe*. Washington: Blair & Rives, 1834–1873.

———. *Report of the Joint Committee on the Conduct of the War*. Second Session, Thirty-Eighth Congress, December 1864–March 1865. 3 volumes. Washington: United States Government Printing Office, 1865.

United States War Department. *Annual Reports of the Secretary of War*. Washington: United States Government Printing Office, 1868–1886.

———. *The War of the Rebellion: A Compilation of the Official Records of the Union and Confederate Armies*. 128 Volumes. Washington: United States Government Printing Office, 1880–1901. Available online through the Cornell Library website at digital.library.cornell.edu:80/m/moawar/waro.html.

Urwin, Gregory J. W. *Custer Victorious: The Civil War Battles of General George Armstrong Custer*. Rutherford, New Jersey: Fairleigh Dickinson University Press, 1983.

Vail, Theodore F. *History of the Second Connecticut Volunteer Heavy Artillery*. Winsted, Connecticut: Winsted Printing Co., 1868.

Venable, Colonel Charles S. "The Campaign from the Wilderness to Petersburg," in *Southern Historical Society Papers*, Volume 14, 522–542. Richmond, Virginia: Southern Historical Society, 1886.

———. "General Lee in the Wilderness Campaign," in *Battles and Leaders of the Civil War*, Volume 4, edited by Robert Underwood Johnson and Clarence Clough Buel, 240–245. New York: The Century Co., 1888.

———. *Papers*. Southern Historical Collection, University of North Carolina–Chapel Hill.

Wainwright, Charles S. *A Diary of Battle: The Personal Journals of Colonel Charles S. Wainwright, 1861–1865*, edited by Allan Nevins. New York: Da Capo Press, 1998.

Walker, General Francis A. *General Hancock*. New York: D. Appleton and Company, 1894.

———. *History of the Second Army Corps in the Army of the Potomac*. New York: Charles Scribner's Sons, 1891.

Warner, Ezra J. *Generals in Blue: Lives of the Union Commanders*. Baton Rouge: Louisiana State University Press, 2006.

———. *Generals in Gray: Lives of the Confederate Commanders*. Baton Rouge: Louisiana State University Press, 2000.

Welch, Richard F. *The Boy General: The Life and Careers of Francis Channing Barlow*. Rutherford, New Jersey: Fairleigh Dickinson University Press, 2003.

Welles, Gideon. *Diary of Gideon Welles, Secretary of the Navy under Lincoln and Johnson*, Volume 2. Boston, New York: Houghton Mifflin Company, 1911.

Wert, Jeffrey D. *A Brotherhood of Valor: The Common Soldiers of the Stonewall Brigade, C.S.A., and the Iron Brigade, U.S.A.* New York: Simon & Schuster, 1999.

Weygant, Charles H. *History of the One Hundred and Twenty-fourth Regiment, N.Y.S.V.* Newburgh, New York: Journal Printing House, 1877.

Wheelan, Joseph. *Invading Mexico: America's Continental Dream and the Mexican War, 1846–1848*. New York: Carroll & Graf, 2007.

———. *Libby Prison Breakout: The Daring Escape from the Notorious Civil War Prison*. New York: PublicAffairs, 2010.

————. *Terrible Swift Sword: The Life of General Philip A. Sheridan*. Cambridge, Massachusetts: Da Capo Press, 2012.

Wheeler, Richard. *On Fields of Fury: From the Wilderness to the Crater: An Eyewitness History*. New York: HarperCollins Publishers, 1991.

Wilcox, General C. M. "Lee and Grant in the Wilderness," in *The Annals of the War Written by Leading Participants North and South*, edited by Alexander Kelly McClure, 484–501. Philadelphia: The Times Publishing Company, 1879.

Wilkeson, Frank. *Turned Inside Out: Recollections of a Private Soldier in the Army of the Potomac*. Lincoln: University of Nebraska Press, 1997.

Wilkinson, Warren. *Mother, May You Never See the Sights I Have Seen: The Fifty-Seventh Massachusetts Veteran Volunteers in the Army of the Potomac, 1864–1865*. New York: Harper & Row, 1990.

Williams, T. Harry. *Lincoln and His Generals*. New York: Alfred A. Knopf, 1952.

Wilson, James Harrison. *The Life of John A. Rawlins, Lawyer, Assistant Adjutant-General, Chief of Staff, Major General of Volunteers, and Secretary of War*. New York: The Neale Publishing Company, 1916.

Wilson, Mark R. *The Business of Civil War: Military Mobilization and the State, 1861–1865*. Baltimore: The Johns Hopkins University Press, 2006.

Wing, Henry E. *When Lincoln Kissed Me: The Story of the Wilderness Campaign*. New York, Cincinnati: The Abingdon Press, 1914.

Wise, Jennings Cropper. *The Long Arm of Lee, or the History of the Artillery of the Army of Northern Virginia*, Volume 2. Lynchburg, Virginia: J.P. Bell and Company, Inc., 1915.

Wood, Thomas. *Doctor to the Front. The Recollections of Confederate Surgeon Thomas Fanning Wood, 1861–1865*, edited by Donald B. Koonce. Knoxville: University of Tennessee Press, 2000.

Woodbury, Augustus. *Major General Ambrose E. Burnside and the Ninth Army Corps*. Providence, Rhode Island: S.S. Rider & Brother, 1867.

Work, David. *Lincoln's Political Generals*. Urbana: University of Illinois Press, 2009.

Worsham, John. *One of Jackson's Foot Cavalry*. New York: The Neale Publishing Company, 1912.

Young, Alfred C., III. *Lee's Army during the Overland Campaign: A Numerical Study*. Baton Rouge: Louisiana State University Press, 2013.

Young, James C. *Marse Robert: Knight of the Confederacy*. New York: Rae D. Henkle Co., Inc., 1929.

Zeller, Paul G. *The Second Vermont Infantry Regiment, 1861–1865*. Jefferson, North Carolina: McFarland & Co., 2002.

INDEX